CLEANING UP

The Story Behind the
Biggest Legal Bonanza of Our Time

DAVID LEBEDOFF

THE FREE PRESS

New York   London   Toronto   Sydney   Singapore

ЈР

THE FREE PRESS
A Division of Simon & Schuster Inc.
1230 Avenue of the Americas
New York, NY 10020

Designed by Carla Bolte

Manufactured in the United States of America

10   9   8   7   6   5   4   3   2

Library of Congress Cataloging-in-Publication Data

Lebedoff, David.
    Cleaning up : the story behind the biggest legal bonanza
of our time / David Lebedoff
        p.   cm.
    1. Exxon Corporation—Trials, litigation, etc.   2. Exxon Shipping
Company—Trials, litigation, etc.   3. Hazelwood, Joseph Jeffrey,
1946—Trials, litigation, etc.   4. Exxon Valdez (Ship)   5. Oil
spills—Law and legislation—Alaska.   6. Oil spills—Alaska—Prince
William Sound.   7. Liability for oil pollution damages—Alaska—
Prince William Sound Region.   I. Title.
KF228.E98L43   1997
346.798—dc21   97–28385
                                                                          CIP

ISBN 0–684–83706–4

The verses on pages 100 and 319 of this volume are reprinted by permission of The Putnam Publishing Group from *The Spell of the Yukon* by
Robert Service. Copyright © 1907, 1916 by Dodd Mead and Company, Inc.

For Caroline, Jon, and Nick

Contents

Note to the Reader

This story was reconstructed, not recalled. I was not a participant in the events as they occured, nor even much of a witness, only marginally aware of the drama unfolding in far-off Alaska until its spectacular climax made the great adventure impossible to ignore.

As I set to work, I followed at first a paper trail, soon a steep mountain path, of documentation, the endless written record of everything that had happened from the spill to the verdict—reports, agreements, court orders, depositions, memos, exhibits, decisions, each source suggesting others to be found. Every word of the trial itself exists of course in written transcripts, nearly eight thousand pages in all. Helpful as this script was, I am even more indebted to the actors. Many of those who were part of the production, from the stars to the walk-ons, shared their memories with me, willingly, generously, and, of necessity, patiently. Recollections were sometimes hazy and not all sources were consistent, but the more people I listened to the clearer became the story that every single one of them wanted to be told.

In gaining access to the cast I was very fortunate. My wife had been a partner at Faegre & Benson—not recently enough, alas, to share in the putative treasure—and largely through that association I knew casually a number of the players in the drama, and others in the firm. They were without exception willing to share with me stories and documents that are essential to this narrative. They did not do so through any expectation that I was a partisan of their cause: I explained at the outset that I had no preconceptions as to who was right and who was wrong. It remained my goal to construct an account in which the reader would become the thirteenth juror, choosing what to believe or reject.

Not all my sources where so close to home. I went to Alaska and spoke to many of the participants there; I am particularly grateful to Dave Oesting of Anchorage, whose powers of recall are awesome, to Sarah Armstrong from Clam Gulch, and to the three fine lawyers of the Robinson firm in Soldatna, as well as their gifted investigator, Joe Malatesta.

I am deeply appreciative of having had the opportunity to meet with Captain Joseph Hazelwood in New York, and I thank his attorneys, Mike Chalos and Tom Russo, for permitting me to do so, and for their own accounts of what had transpired.

From thousands of pages of testimony, as well of course as from trial briefs and the public interviews of its executives, it is possible to know and to share with the reader the point of view of the Exxon Corporation. I regret very much that I could not meet or speak directly with Exxon officials or their attorneys. The reason given for their declining such association was the pending appeal.

Though Judge Holland cannot discuss the matter with anyone until after the matter is fully resolved, I am grateful to him: by the manner of his adherence to judicial duty, he is one of the great heroes of this case—his only rivals being the jurors.

Another personal hero is my wise and patient editor at The Free Press, Bruce Nichols, who misses nothing and sometimes prevails, and is the editor that every writer yearns for. I'm grateful also to Norah Vincent, the associate editor, for maintaining the highest standards in the most tactful way, and to Celia Knight, my copy supervisor, for the laser beam of her integrity.

I wish to thank heartfeltly my siblings, Jonathan Lebedoff, Judy Lebedoff, and Lisa Peilen; my sister-in-law Sally Lebedoff; and my friends Tom and Victoria Johnson, William Pohlad, Harry Walsh, Beth Dooley, Amy Klobuchar, and Martha Yunker, all of whom read the evolving drafts of this work and whose insights and suggestions strengthened my efforts. Their encouragement was a gift that cannot be repaid.

I am above all grateful to my wife, Randy, for everything.

David Lebedoff
Summer 1997

1

On the Rocks

Joe Hazelwood couldn't help smiling. His ship was in port and he was ready to go ashore. They had docked late the night before. The paperwork was done, at least for the time being, and all the hurried tasks attendant on arrival seemed now to be under control. They could go into Valdez and relax.

There were three of them: Jerzy Glowaki, a Polish refugee whom they called George and who was the chief engineer of the oil tanker *Exxon Valdez;* Joel Roberson, the radio officer of the ship; and Joe Hazelwood, the captain. They were standing on the pier, their first time on land since refueling in San Francisco. That's the way it was. You loaded the tanker in Valdez, Alaska, where the pipeline ends—loaded it with fifty-three million gallons of North Slope crude—then took that down to Long Beach, California, discharged the oil, returned, with a stop in San Francisco to change crews, refuel, discharge more oil, do maintenance work, and head back up to Valdez for another fifty-three million gallons, only to begin the loop again, and repeat it, over and over, for sixty days. Then you got sixty days off; that is, the *captain* got sixty days off. The tanker kept on making its two-week loop, with another captain on the bridge. And when *his* sixty days were done, then Joe Hazelwood was back, filling up the *Exxon Valdez* at Valdez and returning it empty every two weeks later.

1

They were waiting for a ride into town. It would take all day to fill the tanker and they probably wouldn't be leaving until after nine that evening. This was a welcome break. Valdez certainly wasn't San Francisco; if truth be told, it was a far cry even from Long Beach. But it was close at hand and they had time to kill.

If you looked at the three waiting sailors you knew right away which one was the captain. It wasn't the pea jacket or the pilot's cap or the attaché case. It was the way he held himself, the quiet way he spoke to the others, and the way they listened. He *looked* like a captain. Except for his eyes, of course. A captain's eyes were supposed to be stern and wary, hawklike. But his were friendly and guileless. And he spoke like the well-read man he was, not like some crusty nautical legend. (His favorite book, which he often reread, was Saint-Exupéry's *Night Flight*.) Other than that, he was a central-casting captain: tall, six feet, impressively fit (the *Exxon Valdez* actually had a gym, and he used it), dark beard neatly trimmed, a direct, good-humored gaze—the opaque eyes just for a split second ironic, and the palpable confidence not merely of command but from knowing that no one could do his job any better than he could himself.

Their ride pulled up. Captain Ed Bradley was a pilot for another shipping company. He had things to do in town, too, and was happy to give the others a lift. But first they had to check out. The tanker was docked in the Alyeska Pipeline Marine Terminal, where one-quarter of the nation's oil was loaded into vessels and security is tight. You couldn't get in or out without the gate check. Bradley drove to the shack by the gate and each of them signed his name and the time. It was ten fifty-nine in the morning, March 23,1989.

The town of Valdez was right across the bay, at the end of an inlet of Prince William Sound. The sky was overcast and the road slippery; they drove carefully along Dayville Road, which hugged the curving shore. Even here, at its narrow commercial corner, the splendors of the sound were awesome, the mountains high above the town, the icy water smooth and still thanks to the vast natural barriers to wind and tide. Thus protected, those waters were filled with living things, great whales, humpbacks and orcas, sea otters, uncountable schools of salmon and herring, and, hovering above, the millions of birds who fed on the fish and who nested amidst the foliage of small islands where no human had ever been.

They drove between the end of a land and the start of a sea that seemed limitless, neither yet fully explored. The car was just a dot in that vastness, a slowly moving bug. Nothing that man could build could count for anything here. And yet, looking back at the port, there was, for merely a moment, one challenge to the scope of this place—the vessel they had just left; for on its deck, at this widening distance, the crew members, too, seemed like ants, dwarfed by the astonishing size of the tanker, which was longer than three football fields and sinking lower in the water from the steady ingestion of three hundred forty million pounds of what is called black gold. And as they drove away, even this sea monster shrank and receded into the vast unchanging background of the mountains and the bay.

It didn't take long to reach Valdez. Or to make their way through it. The town of fewer than four thousand is laid out in a grid. It was cold and the broad streets were almost deserted. And something else: there were no old buildings. Everything was relatively new.

There was a reason for this, and the anniversary of that reason was at hand. It was the anniversary of the destruction of Valdez. There were signs of it: they passed a church where the board was already up for the next day's service of commemoration. Tomorrow was Good Friday. Twenty-five years earlier, on Good Friday of 1964, very near to the center of old Valdez, the largest earthquake ever recorded in North America had brutally struck. It registered 9.2 on the Richter Scale. It lasted four full minutes, and people thought the world was ending. Much of South Central Alaska was torn and shaken. Only the Bible has language that applies: the earth was cut asunder and broken. A vast section of the state dropped ten full feet. Large parts of Anchorage were destroyed. More than one hundred people were killed. But nowhere was the devastation more total than in Valdez, so near the epicenter. A huge tsunami swept over the waterfront, killing thirty-two people. The land beneath the dock site sank thirty-five feet. The town was completely destroyed. It was later rebuilt on another site, and the old gold-rush village, named in 1790 in honor of Admiral Antonio Valdez, the commander of the Spanish navy, was now a company town supplying mariners and pipeline workers. But many of its residents had known terrible loss a quarter century earlier, and by editorial and sermon and aching memory, the coming day was going to be remembered as the worst disaster in Alaska history. Before that day had fully dawned, this would no longer be true.

Captain Bradley dropped his passengers off at their destination, the office building that housed the Alamar offices, their local business and communications headquarters, and then he drove off.

Alamar wasn't part of Exxon. It was an outside agent that assisted crews, including Exxon's, when they were in port. It was a place to order supplies, to pick up and drop off mail, from which to make phone calls and receive messages from the ship.

When the three sailors walked in the door, it wasn't necessary for Joe Hazelwood to introduce himself. He was well known from his previous visits. And if they didn't know him from that, they knew him by reputation. The Exxon captains were all supposed to be good, but many said that he was the best.

He was one of that lucky minority who had always known what he wanted to do. He had wanted to sail a ship. And now he was a captain at sea.

This was clearly his destiny. Joseph Jeffrey Hazelwood, one of four children of a Pan Am pilot, was born in Hawkinsville, Georgia, in 1946, but his family moved to Huntington, Long Island, where Jeff, as he was known, grew up and still lives. The town was on the water, and before long it was clear that Jeff was a natural sailor, a *great* natural sailor, fearless and confident and joyful at the challenge of danger. As a teenage Sea Scout on a sixty-five-foot schooner battered by a violent storm in Long Island Sound, he climbed the fifty-foot mast to haul in the damaged mainsail. Some of the other boys were crying or throwing up, but Jeff volunteered without hesitation for the rescue mission. "Jeff related to sailing like a pro golfer who swings a club for the first time," recalls a friend from Sea Scout days.

His choice of college seemed inevitable. In 1964 he entered the New York Maritime College at Fort Schuyler, in the Bronx. "The Fort" was strict and demanding. The students were called cadets and wore uniforms; more of them dropped out than graduated. There were noon military drills, hazing, and no drinking or marriage allowed. Hazelwood hated restrictions on his freedom, but he found some escape playing hard on the Trolls, the school's lacrosse team.

He began to find another outlet, too. His father, the pilot, had not permitted alcohol in the home, and the Fort prohibited it on campus, but with his friends in the Trolls, Joseph Jeffrey Hazelwood had begun to drink. He had begun to be a binge drinker. One of his former roommates told the press, "On a scale of one to ten, we were probably a fourteen in terms of drinking. We made the movie *Animal House* look like amateur work." By the Trolls' standards, though, Hazelwood was someone who knew when to stop.

His revels didn't seem to affect his seamanship, or the high regard of instructors and peers. Those who did well at the Fort hoped to get jobs with the companies running large tankers. The biggest of these was Exxon (then ESSO), and Joe (then Jeff, which he dropped) Hazelwood was one of the handful who were taken on.

The job was a prize. Joe's third-mate pay was twenty-four thousand dollars a year, very high for a starting salary in 1968. He soon was married and bought a house in Huntington. Not that he was able to spend much time there. His first duty was on the *ESSO Florence* in Wilmington, North Carolina, and from the very start it was clear that the employer was getting its money's worth. "Joe had what we old-timers refer to as a seaman's eye," says his first boss. "He had that sixth sense about seafaring that enables you to smell a storm on the horizon or watch the barometer and figure out how to outmaneuver it."

This appraisal was widely shared. And rewarded. Hazelwood had joined ESSO at the age of twenty-two, and by the time he was thirty-two he had been made a captain, the youngest in Exxon's fleet. He was put in charge of the *Exxon Philadelphia*, which ran the California-to-Alaska oil route that now, at forty-two, after a succession of ships, he found himself following again as skipper of the *Exxon Valdez*.

He had a number of little chores to do at Alamar. He placed some phone calls to what everyone in Alaska calls the Lower Forty-eight—that other part of the United States, between Canada and Mexico. He called Benicia, the Exxon West Coast fleet office, and talked twice to the company's office in Houston. He called Ed Murphy, the state harbor pilot who had helped guide the *Exxon Valdez* to its berth the night before; they had agreed to meet for lunch in town, and now Hazelwood asked Murphy to pick him up outside Alamar. He heard from his ship by radio and received some news that probably didn't seem very significant just then—the tanker was now supposed to leave an hour later than scheduled: ten o'clock rather than nine. It must have been about noon when he learned this. They would have plenty of time.

Alaskans are friendly, and the people in the Alamar office were genuinely pleased to greet the captain and his two aides. The sailors were glad to see familiar faces, too: Bob Arts, the Alamar manager, who left after saying hello, and Pat Caples, Gretchen Dunkin, and Carla Hilgendorf. They talked and smiled and got caught up to date a little. On previous visits, Carla Hilgendorf had helped supply him with fresh fish for the crew. He asked her if she could have some delivered to the ship before it sailed. She said she'd try. Then it came time to move on. They were getting hungry.

Ed Murphy was waiting outside and drove them to the Pizza Palace, about ten minutes away, where all four of them had lunch.

The current *Fodor's Alaska* credits the Pizza Palace, now renamed, as having "the best pizza in Alaska." Whether or not this distinction is correct, or was then, none of them chose to order pizza.

The waitress asked them what they wanted to drink. Roberson said he'd have a beer. There was no problem with this; the Coast Guard and Exxon rules forbade crew members ashore from drinking alcoholic beverages within four hours of assuming their duties. It was just past noon, and the ship was not supposed to leave before ten that night. Glowaki ordered a beer as well. Murphy, the driver, said he'd just have some iced tea, and Hazelwood said he'd have the same. During the meal another round of beer was ordered, but Hazelwood stuck to iced tea.

Though no one said so, it was an interesting choice. For Joe Hazelwood, as many of his fellow seamen knew, had been treated for alcohol abuse, and what and whether he drank was cause for some concern.

No one can say precisely why he drank, or if in fact there was a cause outside himself, but surely this superb mariner was frustrated and unhappy with the conditions of his career. He knew how good he was at what he did, and he felt that what he did was not sufficiently valued. It didn't count as much as other things, things that he disdained.

As *Time* would say in its lengthy cover story on Joe Hazelwood a few months after this fateful day, "Even as Hazelwood's reputation as a boozer grew, so did his image as the best captain in Exxon's fleet. Exxon's management, however, was increasingly unhappy with the talented young skipper, less for his drinking than because of his headstrong, independent manner. Like the old-time captains he modeled himself after, Hazelwood shunned paperwork, company politics and extensive contacts with the M.B.A. executives who were increasingly chipping away at the authority of shipmasters. 'Joe didn't have Exxon tattooed under his eyelids,' says a high-ranking Exxon engineer. 'He'd make his own judgments and act accordingly. That's why those at sea respected him and those on land thought he wasn't a company man.'" He felt that he'd scaled the highest peaks of his calling, but that those whom he served were too busy fencing their narrow valley to look up.

His drinking was obvious, and increasingly well known. In July 1984, in Huntington, he was arrested for drunken driving—hit-and-run driving at that. He was found and arrested in his own driveway, and when he refused to submit to a Breathalyzer test, his driver's license was revoked. (Later, after his conviction, the cause of revocation was changed to drunken driving.) In 1985, at the urging of his boss and close friend at Exxon, Captain Mark Pierce, he entered the South Oaks Hospital Alcoholism Clinic on Long Island for a twenty-eight-day inpatient alcohol rehabilitation program. A doctor found him "depressed and demoralized." He finished the hospital course and was discharged with the diagnosis "alcohol abuse episodic" and "dysthemia." The recommendation was "Alcoholics Anonymous and after-care."

A few months after he left the hospital, Hazelwood returned to work as skipper of the *Exxon Yorktown*, an oil tanker that moved along the East Coast. This made it much easier to attend Alcoholics Anonymous meetings in Huntington, which he did. It is difficult to imagine the laconic captain as a leader in this forum of highly personal candor, and he was not. But he swears that in the eighteen months following South Oaks he had only five alcoholic drinks. He can describe each one.

After that he drank more often, with a pattern of sporadic intensity. He tended not to drink at home, in front of his wife. But when he was away at sea it was another story—and that was where he should have been happiest. Skippering a ship was the great love of his life, but corporate bureaucracy had become a source of dark frustration. Why couldn't they just let him sail? Everything seemed dictated by accountants. All you heard about was cost. Each ship had been made a separate profit center, and was strictly examined as such. It didn't make sense. When he was captaining the *Exxon Chester*, an asphalt carrier, a fresh storm off Atlantic City snapped off the ship's mast. There were thirty-foot waves. The radio was out. Some of the sailors were starting to abandon ship, but Hazelwood was able to put up a makeshift antenna to radio shore, and then, by following the storm, to guide the ship safely back to New York. It was quite a feat of seamanship, with the safety of crew and cargo the first priority. But when it was over, Hazelwood had to withstand strong criticism from the number crunchers at Exxon. Why hadn't he continued on his planned route southward? It cost money to turn back to a safe port in a storm.

Cost, cost, cost. When Hazelwood first went to work for Exxon, there could be forty sailors on a ship smaller than the *Valdez*. When the *Valdez* was first launched in 1986 (at a cost of $130 million), its crew numbered thirty-four. On Good Friday, 1989, there were only twenty crew members, and plans had been made to cut this even further, to fifteen!

It wasn't only cost and cutbacks, either. It was a question of who was in charge. It wasn't the captain any longer. It wasn't any *person* actually, it was memos and directives and the incessant and growing demand for more paperwork. This was not what had stirred the heart of the Sea Scout. He had been so lucky in knowing what he wanted to do—but you couldn't do it anymore. He wanted to be a sailor, not an administrator, and the denial of his dream was deadly.

He tried not to let this show. The man who sat there sipping iced tea in the Pizza Palace was affable. But not many months earlier, he once again had been arrested and convicted for drunken driving. His wife now knew. His marriage was in trouble. He was thinking of taking a job as a harbor pilot on the Columbia River in Oregon. A harbor pilot. On a river! But he kept a smile on his face and drank some more iced tea.

Whatever his inner demons, he was well known and well liked within the sailing community. Bob Arts, the manager of the Alamar office, came up to the table and introduced his wife and child. On his way out, without the four sailors knowing it, Arts picked up the tab for their table. Exxon was a very good Alamar customer, but it was probably more than that. People *liked* Joe Hazelwood. He was a damn fine captain. Someone else came over and introduced the skipper of the *ARCO Juneau*. This was the way it used to be, like a family.

The four men left, growling affectionately at the vanished son-of-a-gun Bob Arts who should have let them pay for themselves. They drove back to the center of town, where Ed Murphy dropped his passengers off in front of a gift and flower shop, the Hobby Hut. They stood outside for a minute, talking about the errands they had to do, and agreeing that they'd all meet up later at a place called the Pipeline Club. Glowaki went off, and Hazelwood and Roberson went into the Hobby Hut. Soon after, Roberson left to find some magazines and mail some letters. Hazelwood stayed behind.

The owner of the Hobby Hut, Mrs. Emily Kaiser, knew Captain Hazelwood from previous visits. He would come in and order flowers (the Hobby Hut could wire them anywhere). And that's what he was there for now. Hazelwood had one child, a daughter, Alison, an honor student in junior high, and ever since she was born he had wired her flowers on any holiday when he was away from home, which was probably most. Since it was approaching Good Friday, he ordered a dozen long-stemmed red roses sent to his home with a note saying, "Happy Easter Alison and Sue, love Jeff." He paid right there, fifty-three dollars. He waited for the order to be verified, then looked around the shop, bought some cards that he put in his attaché case, and chatted with the proprietress. She was from Long Island, too, and they talked about what had changed, and what had not. He says he was in her shop for about an hour, and she says so, too.

He then went to two other shops: Sugar and Spice, and then Alaska Imports, across the street. He says he spent twenty minutes in each place.

Next he went back to the Alamar office. He wanted to thank Bob Arts for paying their bill. And he was following up on the conversation he'd had at Alamar earlier that morning with Carla Hilgendorf. Now, she said she was sorry; she'd checked on the fish for the crew but nothing was available. She also said that Bob Arts wasn't there—maybe he was downstairs at his wife's office. After talking for awhile, Hazelwood went down to the office, looking for Arts, but no one answered his knock. He tried the door. It was locked. He'd have to thank Bob Arts in two weeks, the next time the loop brought him back to Valdez. Of course, it did not occur to him that he would never be there again.

And then he walked back to meet the others in the Pipeline Club, right across the street from where he'd ordered flowers.

The Pipeline Club is now famous for what did or did not happen there in the late afternoon of March 23, 1989. At the time, it had merely a local renown. It was very popular with the citizens of Valdez. Its name was not misleading; it was much like a club, a dining room as well as a bar, a place to gather, play darts, have a drink, catch up on what was going on. People move to Alaska because they're individualists, but that doesn't mean that they want to be alone. They're escaping from society, not other people. Most are very friendly, and nowhere more so than within the dark and windowless confines of the Pipeline Club on a cold, damp March afternoon. On first entering, the lighting seems to come primarily from the jukebox, the video game, and the two spotlights aimed at the mutilated dart board. As one's pupils dilate, the place is gradually revealed to be full of people: the group that gathers for coffee every day, seven days a week, the old people looking for company, the women's alley cat softball team having a few drinks before their kids get home on the school bus, the man trying to read his newspaper by the fluorescent tubing of the jukebox, the dental assistant from down the street having a Bailey's and coffee before returning to the afternoon flossing, the sailors coming and going from the ships in port that day, the strangers, the regulars, the cribbage players, and, of course, the drinkers.

George Glowaki was already at a table when Joe Hazelwood came into the bar.

"I'm going to buy myself a drink, George," said Captain Hazelwood. "Can I get you one, too?"

Glowaki pointed to the gin and tonic already on his table. "No," he said, "I'm fine."

They were all aware of the four-hour rule: no alcohol within four hours of the ship's departure. But wasn't that now ten o'clock? It was still afternoon—late, but afternoon.

Hazelwood walked over to the bar and ordered a Stolichnaya on the rocks. The bartender, Lisa Harrison, said she didn't have that brand, so he asked for whatever the house brand vodka was, which turned out to be Smirnoff, eighty proof. The bartender didn't use a shot glass to measure; she just poured the drink over the ice in the glass.

Hazelwood took his drink back to the table and sat down with Glowaki. They talked and drank, and a little later Joel Roberson arrived. He asked if they wanted something to drink. They said no, they were fine, so when he came back and joined them he brought only a beer for himself.

It was good to get off their feet and swap stories. According to Hazelwood, "It's the curse of the seaman that all you talk about on the ship is what's going on ashore, and when you get ashore all you talk about is what's going on on the ship."

More people were coming into the Pipeline Club. Gretchen Dunkin, whom they'd seen that morning in the Alamar office, came over to say hello and wish them a Happy Easter. After she left they saw that their glasses were empty. Hazelwood went over to the bar and bought another round, beer for Roberson, gin and tonic for Glowaki, and vodka on the rocks for himself. More stories were told. Then Glowaki bought everyone a third round. When that was finished, they realized that it was very late indeed and that they had better get back to the ship.

But Glowaki thought it would be a good idea to take back some pizzas for the engineers who'd stayed aboard. So they all tramped over to the Pizza Palace. It was colder now outside. Large wet snowflakes were starting to fall. The walk didn't take long—less than ten minutes—but they were chilled and damp.

They placed their order at the Pizza Palace and then used the pay phone there to call for a cab. The restaurant was very crowded. People were picking up and waiting for take-out orders, and there wasn't enough room for everyone in the waiting area. So the three of them stepped outside to wait. After a few minutes back in the wet clinging snow, they concluded that this wasn't a very good idea. They had to get out of the cold, but they didn't want to go back into the crowded Pizza Palace. So they stepped into the next building, which was the Harbor Bar.

As Hazelwood tells it, "We didn't want to occupy this guy's establishment, so we went over and proceeded to order drinks." Standing at the bar, Hazelwood asked if they had any Stolichnaya, and turned and grinned at Glowaki, a Polish immigrant who hated all things Russian. Hazelwood was trying to get his goat. What he got was the house vodka, non-Soviet and on the rocks. The drink was served, sitting there on the bar in front of Hazelwood, his fourth admitted drink of the day, but he says that he doesn't think he drank it: he recalls only that he let it sit in front of him until they could see through the window of the Harbor Bar that their cab was pulling up.

The pizzas were ready and they took them and got in the station wagon cab. The taxi driver said that he had to pick up another fare who was also going to the terminal. He was waiting inside the Pipeline Club. So they drove back to the Pipeline Club, and the cabbie went in while the three sailors remained in the car. The new passenger, Allen MacGregor, a crew member of an ARCO tanker, climbed in and sat on the jump seat. Hazelwood was in the front. The drive back to the terminal took a little more than twenty minutes.

There is a gate at the terminal, and when the cab pulled up to it, everyone had to get out. This was the usual procedure. They gave their I.D.

cards to a guard and carried everything they had with them—the attaché case, their packages, the pizzas—to the security checkpoint. They had to open everything up for inspection, and then pass through a metal detector. While this was going on, the outside guard went through the cab, checking the seats and underneath them and then the trunk, to prevent any contraband or alcohol or drugs from being brought in. None was found. They spoke to the guards at the security check and their return time was recorded: eight twenty-four. Having passed the check, they returned to the cab and drove back in through the gate. They dropped off MacGregor at his berth and proceeded to berth five, where the *Exxon Valdez* was anchored. The crewmen got out, crossed a catwalk to the gangway, and climbed down to their ship. The gangway was steeper than when they had traversed it that morning, because now the tanker was much lower in the water, laden with fifty million gallons of North Slope crude oil.

As soon as he came aboard, Hazelwood could see that the tanker was in the final stages of readiness for departure. He spoke to several crew members, one of whom confirmed that the ship was scheduled to leave at nine after all, entered what they called the House (the tanker's living quarters), and then the captain walked up six flights of stairs to the starboard side, put his briefcase in his office, and climbed the short staircase, thirteen steps, from his office to the bridge. The third mate, Gregory Cousins, was there, as well as Pat Caples from the Alamar office and Ed Murphy, who again was going to act as steering pilot after they were under way. Caples was there to take the ship's mail to shore; she went with Hazelwood to his office, took the mail, and left the ship. On returning to the bridge, he was joined by several crew members, including Lloyd LeCain, the second mate, and Cousins, the third mate. Together they went through the precheck—all the things that had to be done before they could depart.

At nine forty-two the *Exxon Valdez* slid out of its berth. It was as if a huge section of the terminal itself had broken off and now was floating out to sea. The next stop would be Long Beach. They had to move very slowly, no more than six knots. There were small islands ahead, reefs, and probably ice. Of course there was radar, and the Coast Guard was watching them on *its* radar, but you couldn't be too careful. Once they were in Prince William Sound they'd be pretty much home free, but getting from Port Valdez to the sound itself took a little more doing. One had to pass through the Valdez Narrows, a route not encouragingly named. This long, thin inlet posed potential hazards, one of which was that of head-on collision—it was possible for two tankers in the narrow passage to actually run into one another. So two lanes had been established, one inbound to Valdez and the other outbound to the sound. These lanes could be discerned only through nautical measurement, and by buoys, but to a captain like Hazelwood they were as obvious as a floodlit freeway.

Hazelwood stood on the bridge with the third mate, Cousins. The second mate, LeCain, had gone to his cabin to sleep. He was supposed to relieve Cousins later. Hazelwood transmitted some information to shore by radio.

And then he left the bridge. It was Cousins' watch, and Hazelwood told him to call if he needed anything; the captain was going to his office. There was a lot of paperwork to do. Cousins could look out for things. And of course Ed Murphy was a top-notch pilot.

Leaving the bridge is not a casual thing. The Exxon manual said that a captain had to be on the bridge "whenever conditions present a potential threat to the vessel such as passing in the vicinity of shoals, rocks or other hazards presenting any threat to safe navigation."

Hazelwood did indeed have paperwork to do. He always did. It seemed he was never through. This time he had to make some calculations about the cargo. He had wanted to do this before departing, but they'd moved the time back on him.

While he was working he drank a bottle of Moussy, part of a store aboard the *Valdez*. Moussy is a mock beer, containing about one-half of one percent alcohol. It would take an awful lot of bottles for the alcohol to kick in. Perhaps the theory was that it was safer to let the crew drink this largely impotent brew than to be tempted by stronger contraband. In any event, Hazelwood had a second bottle. When Cousins called to say that they were lined up where they were supposed to be in the outbound lane, he returned to the bridge for a minute, and then he went back down to his paperwork. He got another call when the tanker was nearing Potato Point, at the end of the narrows. Ed Murphy, the pilot, told him that there was some ice up ahead; it would be necessary to maneuver around it. Once again Hazelwood returned to the bridge.

At close to eleven thirty, Murphy left the *Exxon Valdez* aboard a pilot launch, his duties done.

It was about time to call the next watch: at midnight Second Mate LeCain was supposed to replace Third Mate Cousins on the bridge.

LeCain was much better trained than Cousins, but he had been working very hard and it was decided that they would let him sleep a little longer. Cousins stayed on duty.

Hazelwood studied the ice reports and decided that the best way to avoid icebergs coming from the Columbia Glacier would be to move from the outbound lane to the inbound lane. Their speed now was about twelve knots, maneuvering speed. Hazelwood radioed the Coast Guard and told them that he was moving to the inbound lane and changing course to 200 degrees; they checked and let him know that the incoming ships were sufficiently far away to permit this.

But ten minutes later, Hazelwood told the helmsman, Harry Claar, to change course to one hundred eighty degrees and to put the vessel on autopilot. Neither move was reported to the Coast Guard. Cousins had been temporarily off the bridge, but soon returned and was told of the instruction. Hazelwood also told Cousins to make a right turn back into the outbound lane when the tanker reached a certain point near Busby Island, three miles north of Bligh Reef.

At ten minutes before midnight the helmsman's watch was changed. Claar was relieved by Robert Kagan, who had only recently been promoted from ordinary seaman to able seaman.

And then Hazelwood left the bridge again. At eleven fifty-three, he told Cousins that he was going below to complete some paperwork and to call him as soon as he had begun to turn near Busby Island. There would be a light to signal that position. They could see it already, off in the distance. When they got to the light, Cousins was to begin his turn. That looked to be about three minutes away. Cousins said fine, no problem. Then Hazelwood went below to his office. He began to work on some new calculations, for the long voyage ahead.

Cousins was doing some calculations of his own. He had been placed in charge of executing the turn, and he didn't want to make a mistake. So he, too, left the bridge and went into the chart room adjacent to it, where he carefully began to plot his position on the map—though the place where he was instructed to turn was already visible from the bridge itself. Hunched over his maps, he worked to calibrate the route as exactly as he could.

In his cabin, Hazelwood worked on. A storm was brewing in the Aleutians, and he was trying to figure out a way to get ahead of it. Up above him, Cousins was checking his maps just one more time. No one, other than the helmsman, Kagan, was on the bridge.

Eight minutes had passed since Hazelwood had given his instruction and gone below, but still the great tanker had not begun to turn; it was headed toward Bligh Reef.

The first alarm was sounded by the lookout, Maureen Jones, who rushed onto the bridge, crying out that the flashing red buoy near Bligh Reef, which should now be on their port side, could be seen instead off the starboard—as alarming as the discovery that one is going the wrong way on a one-way street.

Quickly, Cousins ordered Kagan to make a ten degree turn. Then he picked up the phone and called Hazelwood's cabin—he told the captain that the turn had been initiated. He added that there might be some ice ahead in their path. It was two minutes past midnight. Hazelwood listened to the message and said that he'd be up in a little while. He went back to his calculations.

The ship was not turning back quickly enough toward the outbound lane. It was on a collision course. This was observable in the Coast Guard radar, but it was not observed; the crew member on duty had left his seat to go to get some coffee. No one was watching the screen.

Cousins recognized what what was going to happen. Breathing quickly great grasps of air, he called for the rudder to be moved from ten degrees to twenty. Then, at the last minute, desperate, he ordered a hard right rudder.

In Hazelwood's office, the phone rang again. It was seven minutes past midnight. This time Cousins' voice sounded strange. There was panic in it. "We're in serious trouble," he said.

And at that very moment Captain Hazelwood could feel his ship running aground. There was a shudder, a series of harsh jolts. Someone later said that it felt like going over a speed bump. But they weren't on a highway: they were at sea.

Hazelwood ran up the stairs to the bridge. He saw Cousins and seaman Maureen Jones. He saw their faces. There was a floodlight on the side of the ship. He looked, but he didn't have to look. He knew. From the first jolt, as he was racing up the metal stairs, the sickening crunch was being processed by every neuron to his brain, decades of experience telling him the worst thing he could ever know.

There was a small bathroom on the bridge. Captain Joe Hazelwood leaned inside it and vomited into the toilet.

Then he tried to pull himself together. He looked over the port side and saw a geyser of oil shooting upward. He went over the starboard side and flipped on its floodlight. The oil was gushing there, too, great streams of it into the air. The tanker had disemboweled itself on the pinnacles of the reef.

He knew at once and absolutely that his life as a captain was over. But he was a captain still, and, though he could barely breathe, he resolved to act like one. He gave instructions to Cousins. He checked the engines. He called George Glowaki and told him they had run aground. He told Cousins and Jones to wake up all the crew and have them ready to put on their life jackets and heavy rubber survival suits.

He kept the engines on and tried to make things better, but nothing worked.

Nineteen minutes after the grounding, he called the Coast Guard and told them what had happened. Down below, beneath the water line, the *Exxon Valdez* was gushing oil at two hundred thousand gallons a minute into the cold clear waters of Prince William Sound.

2

The Warrior

Thousands of miles southeast of Valdez, in the upper center of the Lower Forty-eight, the Twin Cities of Minneapolis and St. Paul rise from the rolling Minnesota plain. Many times more people live within this metropolitan area than in all the state of Alaska. The skyscrapers of the two downtowns confront each other across the Mississippi, but they provide the only height on the horizon. The surrounding countryside is unrelievedly flat. And the place is about as far from a sea as one can go on this continent. In aspect and energy, this urban center could not be more unlike the peaks and tides and solitude of Alaska.

The only similarity is the climate. On Friday, March 24, the stubborn traces of winter lingered still. There were patches of snow and cruel winds. Dark low clouds obscured the sun. The temperature was just enough above freezing to turn the snow to slush. In St. Paul, by the federal courthouse, sallow natives who had not known nature's warmth for half a year picked their way gingerly around the forming pools.

One man seemed less cautious than the rest. Youthful, ample, and disheveled, he strode across the parking lot in search of his car, splashing as he walked. He wore no hat and his fair hair was victim to the wind. Though he had just left the courthouse, his tie was already loosened. Under one arm was a large cardboard file and under the other what seemed to be several dead ducks. These were in fact artificial. He had been arguing a case involving the infringement of a patent on his client's windsock decoy. Perhaps because it was Good Friday, the court proceeding had ended early. He threw the files and the fraudulent ducks in the back seat and set out to return to his office, in Minneapolis.

If the day was gray and the task at hand tedious, you couldn't tell it from the face of Brian Boru O'Neill. Unlined, confident to the point of cockiness, so exuberant that every change in expression worked its way into a grin, he appeared, even when sedentary, trapped behind a steering wheel, to be just that which in fact he was: good-humored, tireless, boyish, brash, alert as a falcon, totally indifferent to any opinion but his own. And if he smiled as he drove between pleadings and dictation, it was because, like his warrior namesake, King Brian Boru, the *ardri* of Ireland a thousand years earlier, he had just tasted battle. And he loved it.

Near the Minneapolis line, the freeway narrows to two lanes. The traffic slowed. O'Neill turned on the radio.

The news at first could not compete with his own musings on the skirmish just ended. How could they *say* that their duck was distinct! For God's sake, those ducks were *twins!*

The radio was just background, in and out of his consciousness as he refought his rebuttal and the traffic crawled along.

It wasn't much of a news day. Ollie North's lawyers were demanding that former President Reagan testify at the colonel's trial. The local Walker Art Center was selling its glorious landscape by Frederic Church.

And then:

The largest oil spill in U.S. history had just occurred off Alaska. Millions of gallons of oil had poured from a giant tanker, the *Exxon Valdez,* and into Prince William Sound.

There wasn't much more. The tanker had run aground on a reef and ripped holes in its hull. The announcer did not say how that had happened. The first reports dealt only with the size of the spill. Nothing this big had ever happened before. The effect on the environment could not yet be known.

Why wasn't this traffic moving! O'Neill wanted desperately to learn more facts. The news had gone on to the contras, and the other stations only had music. The traffic was still crawling. It might as well have been stopped. Off in the distance was the skyline of Minneapolis. O'Neill could see the massive building that held his office. If only he was there! He had to find out more.

He resisted an urge to honk the horn. He forced himself to think. And then the grin returned. He was remembering the names of people who would know what was going on.

B rian O'Neill was born (within a few months of Joe Hazelwood) in Hancock, Michigan, in 1947, but a year earlier, or later, it would have been someplace else. The family moved around a lot. Colonel O'Neill was in the Army Corps of Engineers, and each new project meant displacement for a family that grew to six children in thirteen years.

Brian was the firstborn. He entered kindergarten in Japan and third grade in Germany. Other grades were in both Washingtons, D.C. and Seattle, and in Pebble Beach, California. Brian graduated from high school in Fountain, Colorado, a suburb of Colorado Springs. There were one hundred forty in the graduating class, and every one of them knew Brian O'Neill. He was captain of the football team and lettered in basketball and track. Though vastly more traveled than most of his classmates, he fit right in, the high spirits and blunt speaking that were to make him such a difficult fit in a corporate law firm were far more acceptable to his high school peers. An instinctive outdoorsman, he loved Colorado, escaping whenever possible to go fishing or camping, happy, as the saying goes, as a boy out of school.

He was escaping in part from the responsibilities of being an oldest child. Five younger siblings can be a burden to a first born who sees the need to step in. And he did see that need, felt it deeply. There was a problem with alcohol in the O'Neill household, and the very bright and capable son had to be concerned not only with those in the family younger than himself. No wonder that the outdoor life held such attraction. It was blissful to be responsible only for one's own life.

Not all escape is geographic. In his teens, Brian O'Neill began a lifetime of heavy drinking. The sensitive soul beneath the brash shell must have wondered if dependence was inevitable, or if through will it might be overcome. Charming ways and easy banter masked a fierce resolve, a steely insistence that destiny was not inherited but could be altered through achievement.

When it was time to go to college, he chose to attend West Point. His law partners were later to say that that was the last place they could imagine such an unbridled spirit, but perhaps he saw a need for structure, whether at the military academy or, for that matter, within a tightly organized law firm. He might chafe at constraint—he was always getting demerits—but he also knew what he needed. Besides, military education was a family tradition. His uncles had been at West Point, and at Annapolis, too. The academic standards were high, and it was free. (O'Neill's grandfather had been the mayor of Ironwood, and Senator McNamara of Michigan was pleased to nominate that gentleman's descendant to the academy.)

O'Neill speaks happily of his military education. He says he liked his classmates, which suggests that they liked him. Officer-training discipline was strict, but he and his friends let off steam in the local taverns. The Point is within fifty miles of the Fort: perhaps Cadets O'Neill and Hazelwood leaned on the same bar one weekend night.

This did not affect academic performance. O'Neill graduated in the top quarter of a class of eight hundred twelve, one of the seventy-six cadet captains who ran the Corps of Cadets.

Nothing, of course, is really free. In exchange for the absence of tuition, he was legally obligated to spend the next five years in military service. This requirement rankled. O'Neill *liked* being in the army, but not the absence of choice in the matter.

One restriction of army life, however, had been lifted the moment O'Neill received his diploma. Undergraduates at the Point are not free to marry. Just after commencement, O'Neill marched up the aisle with Carol Sanger, who had yet to finish up at Wellesley. She was attractive and bright—bright in a way he hadn't much encountered before. The granddaughter of Margaret Sanger, the founder of the American birth-control movement, Carol Sanger was thoughtful, resolute, and informed. She had firm opinions on matters that her new husband had never even thought about. He was fascinated by her background, so different from his own. She seemed to be related to all sorts of interesting people, Michael Rabin, the violinist, the painter Milton Avery, the actress Suzanne Pleshette. Carol's father had a Ph.D. in English from Columbia. The Sanger family seemed to its newest in-law to embody urban culture. They were *somebody*, which was what he was going to be. *They* called *him* "the kid from Wyoming," a place in their minds sufficiently like Colorado to obviate the need for greater accuracy.

The bridegroom spent the first six months of his marriage at Fort Sill, Oklahoma, where he attended field artillery school. The bride stayed behind. Army regulations.

Though maritally this was inauspicious, Lieutenant O'Neill liked his first job. He liked his fellow soldiers. He liked ordnance. He particularly liked missiles, at the deployment of which he became quite expert.

The next assignment lasted eighteen months and was divided between Italy and Crete: Xania, Vicenza, forays to Padua and Verona. It might have seemed like an extended honeymoon—except that most of the time the bride still wasn't there. She was finishing her senior year at Wellesley. O'Neill became a captain, and learned even more about missiles.

When his wife received her degree (graduating Phi Beta Kappa) and rejoined him, O'Neill might have continued the only kind of life he had ever known: frequent changes in postings, less frequent but well-assured promotions in rank, growing command of his military specialty, some day command itself.

But that did not happen. Brian O'Neill had decided to go to law school. He took the Law School Admission Test and did well enough to be accepted at the University of Michigan Law School, then as now one of the best in the land. He asked for and received permission from the army to attend.

His motive in this abrupt career change was not escape from the army. He enjoyed what he was doing, and was good at it. He did not want to reject his military heritage. He did not want to waste his training. He was not after change for its own sake, or an end to uprooting. His motive was not money, nor was he after another degree to fall back on. He simply wanted to practice law.

"I wanted to be in a line of work which could make a social contribution," he now says, and though this proclamation is very standard on law school application forms, in O'Neill's case, given subsequent events, it is believable. He certainly believes it now. "I wanted to keep hands-on," he adds, "not just be somewhere where you could get promoted out of actually doing the work."

This is critical, and all too far from usual. Edna Ferber, the author of *Show Boat*, told the graduating class of an acting school that their success would depend largely on whether they wanted to act or merely to be actors and actresses. The point is universal. It's not the position, but the doing

that matters. Verbs, not nouns. One should want to be not A Doctor, but
to heal; not A Writer, but to write; not A Lawyer, but to practice law. Brian
O'Neill wanted to practice law. Like Joe Hazelwood on first sailing the
sea, he felt instinctively that this was what he was put on earth to do.

From the first day of law school he knew that his instinct had been right.
He *loved* it. He thought he had liked West Point, but now that seemed, as
they said back then, like kissing your sister. *This* was exciting. Compared to
his previous education, this one seemed so open and unstructured. He was
entranced by the Socratic method, a law school staple, where there's a dialogue between teacher and pupils and *no right answer.* This was as far from
the Point as one could get. He loved the give-and-take, the *freedom* of it all,
inextricable from the subject—the subject itself in a sense.

And he was good at it. Very good. He studied harder than ever before
in his life, a total immersion that was better for his grades than for his
marriage. O'Neill graduated fifth in a class of four hundred twenty. He
was managing editor of the *Michigan Law Review,* voted its most valuable
editor, and was one of five students awarded the designation of Greatest
Contribution to the Class.

By then his marriage was over. The couple had parted in the first year
of law school, and then divorced.

It was less easy to separate from the army. O'Neill had a five-year
commitment to finish serving, and law school didn't count. He still owed
three years of military duty. But it no longer had to be in ordnance. Now
at last he could practice law. And with his sterling academic record, he
had some choice in assignments.

He chose the Pentagon. He joined the staff of the Army General Counsel
Office. The army didn't *have* a General Counsel much before Senator Joseph
McCarthy went after it, and Joseph Welch was hired to defend. Welch tri-
umphed, then left, but the army being the army, the office stayed on. And grew.

But not too much. It was still small enough for an able newcomer to be
noticed. And no waiting around to cut your teeth. O'Neill sensed that he
could achieve *anything* in the practice of law, that it was the gateway to
great achievement, a glittering destiny of his own making. He didn't want
to waste a minute getting to it. The Pentagon job allowed him to start
right in on matters that would have been years beyond the reach of beginners in private practice. He participated in the appellate litigation that
succeeded in upholding the conviction of Lieutenant Calley for his role in

the My Lai massacre. He helped facilitate the admissions of women to West Point. He worked on a lot of base closings, defending the army's decisions before tribunals around the country.

Life was pleasant. O'Neill, single again, had an apartment on Nineteenth and S, just above Dupont Circle. He drove an MG to work and wore civilian clothes. His superiors liked him. He was enthusiastic and charming. He knew how to talk to people. When someone was needed for a meeting at the White House, he was selected.

The novice attorney was a natural networker. Soon he was a friend and tennis partner of the Secretary of the Army, Martin R. Hoffman. This was just a start. Their doubles foursome came to include Justice Rehnquist.

The most significant contact he made through tennis was Jane Severns, who was in charge of starting times on the clay courts of Fort Myer. She was six years younger than he, still in college. The daughter of a naval officer, she was slender, graceful, gentle, lovely. Within months of meeting they were married.

Their first big decision was where to live. But not what to do: Brian was going to practice law, and not in the army. The clock was ticking on his military indenture. The five-year obligation was nearly up. He couldn't wait. There wasn't a chance he would renew. He so hated the idea that he couldn't quit that as soon as he could, he did.

Where, then, to enter private practice? He burned with the desire to do well, to do *spectacularly* well, to make a name for himself, to make a new self. He had been wild with rage on learning that he hadn't been selected to clerk for Justice Rehnquist. Well, maybe it was better to start in at a law firm right away. He could, of course, stay on in Washington, where one of the largest firms, Wilmer, Cutler & Pickering, had already made him an offer.

But he had other plans. In addition to tennis, he also played squash. And one of his squash regulars was Hadlai Hull, the Assistant Secretary of the Army for Financial Management. Hull had been an officer of the Dayton Company (now Dayton Hudson) in Minneapolis, then a very big company and now much larger, one of the major retailers in the country. Dayton's primary law firm was also in Minneapolis, Faegre & Benson. Hull extolled its virtues to O'Neill. He urged him to go out there and talk to a senior Faegre lawyer, Gerry Flom. O'Neill did.

His first visit to Minnesota was in February, and so one must marvel that there ever was a second. He still winces at the memory of the cold and the wind. But first impressions can be overcome. O'Neill observed that all of the downtown buildings in Minneapolis seemed to be connected by enclosed passageways at the second-story level, each block linked by its own Bridge of Sighs. The secret of surviving the Minnesota winter apparently was never to go outdoors.

His hosts were certainly warm enough. In addition to Flom, he met with Jim Loken (now a U.S. Circuit Court Judge), Tom Kimer, and—the recruitment of new talent being far from unplanned—Jim Stephenson, who was also a graduate of West Point. The meeting went very well. O'Neill recognized tough, smart litigators when he saw them, and so did they. Everyone was friendly.

They had, of course, checked O'Neill out. His outstanding grades were merely a threshold. Virtually everyone at Faegre & Benson had been a law school star. And those in charge of hiring knew that that was not enough.

Whatever skills it brings to its clients' problems, the most important judgment call a law firm makes is over whom to hire. The young graduates working their way up the letterhead are not the employees, they're the product. They are what the law firm has to sell. They are the only thing that keeps, and, God willing, attracts, the clients. If the client is not pleased, there are other firms in town. And pleasing the client is not merely a matter of winning cases or finding loopholes. It's at least as important to answer the client's phone calls. And then to be pleasant. And if not pleasant, then at least tactful. And to look good and sound good and inspire confidence.

These minimal standards are not always met. A senior partner can weep on learning that the firm's new Yale Law School hotshot has just told a major client that his work must stay on hold because the hotshot is much too busy with another client "who's a lot bigger than you." And this nitwit was Order of the Coif, the highest law school honor. The horror stories abound. And the message from each is the same: good grades aren't enough. Someone first in his class could turn out to be a fool. Or lazy. Or so pompous that the client could sue for abuse. No, good grades are not enough. It's important to be smart, *necessary* to be smart, but that's not all. Big firms also want their lawyers to be smooth.

Brian O'Neill was smooth. He was tall and good-looking and (at the job interview) well dressed. He was diffident but assured. His easy grin did not deflect attention from his thoughtful remarks. Though outwardly relaxed, somehow you knew that he was tough. He was, in short, like most of his contemporaries in their new small offices down the hall: exceptionally presentable, the trim, keen, poised embodiments of what lawyers think businessmen like.

And he was enjoying himself. It was clear that he was being courted. The quartet with whom he was meeting had gradually shifted from interview to pitch. They were pitching their firm. This was a high compliment to O'Neill. While all firms take hiring seriously, Faegre & Benson's standards are particularly unbending. The firm tended to think of itself as a club, with admission difficult and errant conduct most definitely proscribed.

It was not difficult to paint a fetching picture of the firm. One could truthfully entice an ambitious young lawyer with the glitter of opportunity.

Minnesota is a prosperous place, and its Twin Cities particularly so— a thriving, growing sunbelt economy tucked away in the frozen North. It is the commercial and financial center of its region. Thanks to the proximity of the University of Minnesota, it is a vital center of high-tech and health care industries. Despite harsh climate and high taxes, it is the home office of a surprisingly large number of major American companies. Many of which are represented by Faegre & Benson.

The basic reference source of American law firms is the Martindale-Hubbell Law Directory. Each firm supplies its own description. The most recent edition states, under the heading FIRM PROFILE, the following:

> Founded in Minneapolis in 1886. Faegre & Benson is one of the 100 largest law firms in the United States. The firm consists of 270 lawyers practicing in virtually all areas of law from offices located in Minneapolis, Denver, Des Moines, Washington, D.C., London and Frankfurt. We represent both businesses and individuals. For many years, we have regularly represented many of the leading commercial, financial, service and industrial companies in the Upper Midwest of the United States, including the region's largest merchant, its largest bank and several of its largest hospitals. We also represent Fortune 500 companies internationally and in the United States in particular practice areas.

The firm's description of its client base is understated, like the little letters on the bottle of Scotch that say Purveyor to H.R.H. the Queen. Faegre & Benson does not have to shout; it has some of the juiciest plums in the orchard and everyone knows it. It represents some of the largest companies in one of the richest cities in the nation. It does not just represent them, it *defends* them.

For Faegre & Benson is a defense law firm. There are plaintiff firms, which sue, and there are others, like Faegre, that defend against the suits. Of course, when one company sues another, Faegre could find itself representing a plaintiff. And naturally it brought actions from time to time against *people*—defaulters on loans, for example. But its major clients were corporations, and its major role was to defend them. To defend them against people, to defend them against the government, to defend them against the disgruntled and the greedy: terminated employees, angry shareholders, dissatisfied consumers, the allegers of mistreatment and malpractice and libel and negligence and reckless disregard. Its sentries man the highest towers and guard against attack.

And who are those sentries? The ablest of defenders, recruited from across the nation and trained and drilled for years. Martindale-Hubbell lists every single one—just name, place and date of birth, and academic credentials. These latter, taken as a whole, are staggering, an aggregate of overachievement that has the desired effect on applicants and adversaries: It is intimidating. There is no one "best" law firm in any one city, no monopoly on excellence, but the Faegre listing, as even its rivals will concede, is really something. At first glance everyone seems to have been on the *Yale Law Journal* or the *Harvard Law Review.* There are so many Phi Beta Kappas that it looks like a requirement, and summa cum laudes and Rhodes Scholars abound. And as if Order of the Coif, or Article Editor, *Minnesota Law Review,* were not quite enough, there are all the postgraduation judicial clerkships, not merely the state supreme court and the federal judges of the District of Minnesota, but from virtually every U.S. Circuit Court in the nation, and then, topping that, those who clerked for U.S. Supreme Court Justices Frankfurter, and Warren Burger, and Tom Clark, and Antonin Scalia.

And then, finally, after all these variants on a single lofty theme, there is a short concluding paragraph, the coda to the movement, the LIST OF CLIENTS. It is relatively short, and very sweet. Not *all* the local giants, to be sure, but one can't ethically represent *both* the big banks, after all. The jewels in Faegre's heavy crown are Norwest Bank, ADM, Northwestern National Life Insurance (now ReliaStar Financial Corporation), Bemis, Cowles Media, Dayton-Hudson, International Multifoods, Medtronic, Piper Jaffray. These are some of the companies served by Faegre as primary outside counsel. In addition, there are many national clients that Faegre serves as local counsel: AT&T, Chrysler, Coca-Cola, IBM, Prudential. The list goes on and on. The most common local description of the Faegre client base is Blue Chip.

The number of lawyers in the firm was smaller when Brian O'Neill was being interviewed in 1977. But everything else—the stratospheric résumés, the awesome client list—was very much the same. So it was flattering to the young captain that an interest was being taken in him. More than an interest: an offer. The group had moved on to dinner at the Minikahda Club, the oldest country club in the area. The clubhouse is elegant and the dining room likely to be uncrowded on a weekday winter night. There was privacy. There was good humor. Drinks were served. Stories were told. There was wine with the dinner.

And also the offer. They asked O'Neill to join them as an associate in the firm. He accepted.

Law firm courtships are seldom consummated so swiftly. This was only the first date. In most cases there's a report back to the firm, and then a meeting, and then perhaps a second interview. On the applicant's part, it is common to talk to a great many firms, weigh the varying offers, perhaps negotiate a bit.

But this was simple. They just shook hands and had another round of drinks. O'Neill called home later and told his wife that they were moving to Minneapolis. His decision had been solitary and spontaneous, but not uncalculated. Hadlai Hull had advised him not to begin his private practice in Washington. Get your trial experience somewhere else, he had said. Minneapolis was someplace else. Faegre was a major firm with a bright future. His starting salary was as disproportionate to most of his contemporaries as was Joe Hazelwood's. Besides, he really *liked* these guys. And the weather would have to improve sometime.

It did, though not much before the O'Neills arrived that summer. They moved into a small but pleasant house near a lake in south Minneapolis. Everything was so much greener and cleaner than in Washington. The people were friendly, the streets safe. For newlyweds, it was probably encouraging to hear the area invariably described by natives as the Best Place in the World to Raise Children. National magazines extolled its virtues. And in fact the place was always near the top of all those ranking lists that chambers of commerce covet.

Perception doesn't become cliché without passing a lot of tests, at least one of which, hopefully, is truth. Minnesota *is* an unusually attractive place to live. It has plenty of problems that are the same as anywhere else, but the evidence suggests that once people move there, it's hard to get them to leave. The chamber of commerce clichés—the hardworking populace, the parks, all the lakes within the city borders, the cultural abundance (the Guthrie Theater, the Minnesota Orchestra, the Minneapolis Institute of Arts, the Walker Art Center, the Minnesota Opera, the St. Paul Chamber Orchestra), the health, the wealth, the relative cleanliness of the politics and the air, the astonishing level of civic involvement, the omnipresent *niceness*—all these local nuggets contain specks of real gold.

This is more than metaphor. The place was so nice partly because it was so rich. The cities were primarily white-collar, not industrial. Most people worked in offices, not factories. The biggest companies sold cereal and computers and pacemakers and grain, and spawned a vast supportive community of bankers, brokers, copywriters, teachers, curators, retailers, litigators, jobbers, researchers, artisans, insurers, healers, printers, realtors, and the writers of slogans, programs, and wills. There were not many smokestacks, but on weekends the cities emptied anyway as tens of thousands clogged the highways to their summer cabins.

Many of the big companies were still run, at least in part, by the descendants of their founders. These executives had known their counterparts from birth, and to a remarkable degree filled up each other's boards. There was a certain clubbiness to this, and no lack of certitude and confidence, but there was genuine benevolence, too, an abundance of hardworking civic involvement, obligatory attendance at dawn meetings several decades before the phrase *power breakfast* was coined, an expectation of personal and corporate philanthropy perhaps unmatched in any other place. If more stratified than anyone cared to admit, there was undeniably a sense of community. And life in that community, even in the 1970s, though there were some poor and some oppressed, still recalled the fictional depictions from the time when television was black and white.

The natives joked about Minnesota Nice, and outsiders called it conformity, but civility was in fact the norm and any rip in its fabric a vice. The stability of the corporate giants, the homogeneity of the populace (though considerably more diverse than may have been apparent to a young male associate in an establishment law firm), the relative prosperity, the Scandinavian virtues of cooperation and aversion to complaint, all had launched an ark that was not meant to be rocked. George Orwell thought that English civility stemmed from living on an island: without the fear of outsiders crossing a border, there was less need for swords or armor at home. Minnesota was a little like an island, too—the severity of its winter like a channel keeping others out.

This was the place where Brian O'Neill began to practice law. No one could have predicted where that practice would take him. Not making waves was understood in every quarter, but nowhere more so than among his new colleagues, the guardians of the guardians of the state.

At first, he seemed just like everyone else. His suits were dark and pressed, his shirts were white and starched. He had an office exactly the same size as that of every other new associate. The offices were not as large as those in some rival firms, and surely not as opulent. The decor, somber and just short of drab, seemed calculated to assure stern clients that their own fear of cost was fully shared. The place was not *shabby*, to be sure; it did have dignity. Each lawyer's name was painted in gold on a dark wood bar beside each dark wood door. The chairs were worn but resembled leather. The walls were decorated primarily with diplomas. The firm had seeped to several floors, but everywhere it was the same: lawyers had windows, while secretaries, files, and books were relegated to the space between the views. The firm was in the massive granite edifice of the Northwestern National Bank Building, owned by and also housing the firm's principal client.

Everyone worked hard. The computer did not yet reign and lawyers were not then told precisely the number of hours that they were expected to bill each year. But that was not necessary. This was a very competitive group, and everyone wanted to Get Ahead. Every associate wanted, after seven lean years, to be made a partner. This usually did happen (unlike the New York firms where only the very hardiest salmon completed the swim upstream), but not always. So the associates came in early and stayed late. Arrival at nine was the subject of comment, jocular but ominous. Squash racquets were placed inside briefcases, where they wouldn't show.

Lunch was brief and cheap but sociable, the associates usually eating with each other. They would go across the street to the salad bar at Dayton's (a client) or to the Dayton's or Target employee cafeterias or perhaps to Peter's Grill, where from a window booth one could see the senior partners entering the Minneapolis Club. This structure, darker even than

Faegre & Benson, was where the firm's annual dinner was held. The young lawyers were sometimes brought there for lunches with clients, and as they climbed the stairs to the Main Dining Room on the third floor they noted gravely the portraits of all the club's past presidents, from the founders in their wing collars near the lobby to their offspring and cousins ascending the stairwell. It was a source of pride to note not merely the many clients in this crowded gallery but some of the firm's own lawyers as well. This was clearly a place to aspire to. In the meantime, O'Neill and some of the other associates belonged to the more affordable Minneapolis Athletic Club down the street.

Faegre & Benson was organized by department, and O'Neill was in Business Litigation. He worked closely with Jim Loken. The neophyte's specialty became farm foreclosures, and his client was always a bank. He thought of it as good experience and a job that had to be done. Loken was tough and skilled and a very useful mentor to an aspiring young associate. There was a lot of time in court, which is hard for a novice to get, and if one foreclosure came to resemble another, learning the ropes made it worthwhile.

Things were going well for O'Neill. The firm liked his work. He liked his work. He and Jane loved Minneapolis. They had made friends. They moved to a somewhat larger house in a somewhat better neighborhood. They needed more room: now there was Brian Boru O'Neill, Jr. Life was good, and the future looked even better.

And then one day, shortly after the birth of his first child, O'Neill woke up not feeling very well. His back hurt. It *really* hurt. It was hard to move around. He tried to tough it out, but the pain kept getting worse.

The doctors were never sure what it was. Some thought O'Neill had Guillain-Barré syndrome, an inflammation of the nerves that can run the gamut from pain to death. But no one knew for sure.

He was hospitalized, at first in Minneapolis and then near the Mayo Clinic. He was debilitated, slept for very long stretches, and when awake was nearly always in discomfort. For more than a year he alternated between hospital and home.

He could not, of course, return to his office. The firm kept him on full salary, and asked for nothing in return but rest and recovery.

But he insisted on working from his bed. Despite the concern of his colleagues, his doctors, and his wife, he continued the production of the documents of foreclosure. He still boasts that in his year of grave illness he billed nearly fifteen hundred hours of legal work. Despite this achievement he recovered, and when he returned to work, his gratitude to the genuinely supportive firm was fully matched by its to him.

He was ready to resume his career, and he did. He took up where he had left off. Or did he? A year's painful convalescence, productive or not, can make a difference in a life. It can promote reflection. It permits a new outlook on life, and the isolation that fosters its growth. A long illness can be transforming. One can emerge from the chrysalis of malady a very different person—and not really know it at first. It's possible not even to be conscious of the change. But if change there was, then sooner or later it will show. Ambition may not be diminished, but perhaps the path it will take has been changed.

Not long after his recovery, O'Neill was back in court, zestfully foreclosing the mortgage on another farm. His client was a rural banker. On the other side was a young farm couple. The wife knew she was outmatched, but was desperate in the fight to save her home. She had an argument, which must have been painful to deliver in open court: the papers served on her husband were not valid because he had been too drunk at the time to know what they meant.

O'Neill responded gently at first. Just how drunk, he asked, was drunk? Quite a lot was the answer. Could she be more specific? She was: twenty-five or thirty beers.

O'Neill's tone changed. He had carefully prepared for this moment. He was fully armed, and at last had lured her into range. He repeated her answer. Twenty-five or thirty beers. He paused. And then he asked, "Why weren't they in the trash?" He knew there were no cans, at least none that she could produce. It had been checked out. He had her.

The blood went out of her face. She didn't know what to say. Beer cans, their house—her eyes were haunted.

And then something happened that was very unusual. Brian O'Neill felt ashamed. Deeply ashamed.

"She was wearing a McDonald's uniform," he later recalled. "She looked like hell. She was maybe twenty-seven but she looked like forty-five. She was working like a dog to save her farm, and what was I doing? I was trying to throw her out."

All of a sudden, he stopped trying to throw her out. Instead, he worked out a settlement where she could keep half the farm—the half with the house on it.

It would not be fair to say that everyone left the courtroom happy. The rural banker was furious. He would not use O'Neill again.

That turned out to be a futile gesture, for before long, O'Neill had decided that he wanted no more of farm foreclosures.

They talked it over back at the firm, and soon he had a new specialty. He would argue patent cases. There were a great many of these, referred by patent lawyers who weren't also litigators. Many of them didn't like going into court. O'Neill did.

And he liked something else, too. He regards his patent trials as "morally neutral litigation—two white guys pushing piles of money around. And not hurting anybody."

He says this today and says he thought it then. It seems a remarkable transformation from the ordnance officer of a few years earlier or, for that matter, from the eager beaver who shook hands on a new career without first calling his wife.

He *did* seem transformed after his illness, and disgust at counting beer cans was only one sign of the change. He had also started to dress differently. On joining Faegre he had recognized a dress code, unwritten but obligatory as that of the Point, and to this he had readily adhered, alternating his blue and gray suits. All of a sudden he started showing up in blue jeans. And T-shirts. And *boots.* Not the boots of soft leather that only just cover the ankle and are cinched by a buckle and strap. These were cowboy boots, and he wore them every day.

Today most firms have a "casual day." Not then. And certainly not Faegre & Benson, whose *messengers* were supposed to wear ties. There were partners at Faegre who found a blazer out of place.

And here was this—well, you couldn't call him a hippie (a word some were still using then) because his hair was too short and he was undeniably *clean,* but he did, as some put it, look like a goddamn lumberjack.

He was spoken to about his appearance. He said that what he wore didn't matter. Didn't *matter!* He wasn't supposed to *discuss* it. He was supposed to show *fear.* He certainly wasn't supposed to grin. He was supposed to *comply.* Instead, he did nothing. The boots stayed.

And so did O'Neill. There were no consequences to his insubordination. Glares in the hallway, but really that was all. It was instructive. The patent cases were highly profitable. "We made a mint," O'Neill says. He may have dressed like a fishing guide, but he was bringing money in the door.

But then he started taking cases for free. This was not in itself objectionable. Good firms usually donate some services without fee—to the indigent, for example, or on behalf of some worthy cause. This practice is called *pro bono,* from *pro bono publico*—for the public good. Faegre, as a leader of the local bar, had always encouraged a certain amount of *pro bono* work. It was what you were supposed to do, and a source of considerable pride.

But the *pro bono* matter that O'Neill brought into the firm did not involve drafting a lease for a day care center. It wasn't like that at all. It was the most visible legal role in the most bitter controversy in the state. It was a raging civil war, and O'Neill was asked to command one army— one navy, really: a navy of canoes. The opposing fleet was made up of motorboats.

Between Minnesota and Canada lies the Boundary Waters Canoe Area, a vast aquatic region of awesome pristine beauty. Some of the locals thought there was money to be made in the tourist business by allowing motorboats into the Area. Environmentalists wanted only canoes. The matter had landed in federal court, and the Sierra Club, which was playing a leading role in the litigation, asked O'Neill to be its lawyer. *Pro bono,* to be sure.

He accepted, and the explosion inside his firm reflected the one that was rocking the state. Minnesota, placid Minnesota, where people really did put a premium on being nice, was divided by anger and recrimination. It was the clearest form of a classic battle: jobs versus the environment. In a sense it was a civil war, splitting the indignant citizens of northern Minnesota from most of the rest of the state. And it was a class war, too, since northern Minnesota residents have not shared fully in the prosperity to the south. Their region once had supplied seven-eighths of the iron ore in the world, and now that those veins were depleted they were looking desperately to the tourist industry. They saw the canoeists as elitists, unconcerned with the livelihood of others. The canoeists, for their part, regarded motorboats as noisy, polluting, and vulgar, the obscene despoilers of peace and beauty. People were on one side or the other. Both U.S. Senate seats were on the ballot then in Minnesota. The leading candidate for one, a Minneapolis congressman endorsed by the Democratic-Farmer-Labor party, lost his primary election in a stunning upset partly because he had sided resolutely with the canoeists. The incumbent in the other Senate seat was defeated later that year, at least in part because he had tried to compromise the issue. Neither side *wanted* to compromise. Each wanted to win.

O'Neill wanted to win for the canoeists. Some in his law firm wanted him out of the case. It wasn't that they were for motorboats. But they were against controversy. The case might be *pro bono,* but the name on the pleadings was still Faegre & Benson, and there were those who might actually think that the firm was *siding against business.* Some *clients* might think that. Let the Sierra Club find another lawyer—and actually pay for the legal work, while it was at it. Some partners spoke angrily to O'Neill about his representation.

But rebuke did not deter. O'Neill plunged ever deeper into the case. He knew perfectly well that throughout the office there was plenty of opposition to his role and, increasingly, to him. It didn't seem to make the slightest difference. His visibility in the case, if anything, increased. And to make matters worse, he eventually won.

O'Neill was now a hero to environmentalists, and not just locally. Even his enemies conceded his tenacity and skill, and his new allies saw him as their best hope of prevailing in all sorts of other matters (most of them for free). He took on another pro bono case.

No money, mused his colleagues, but at least an end to controversy. They were wrong. In place of canoes, O'Neill now was defending wolves. It is safe to say that the wolf was not an object of universal veneration, particularly by farmers and ranchers, who didn't want their livestock eaten. They were busy shooting the predators, but O'Neill went to court and won an order preventing this. He wasn't finished. He fought for years to keep hunters from shooting at wolves as well. He argued that wolves were an endangered species, and he became a national hero to those who wanted to preserve the rapidly dwindling wolf herds.

These efforts were not popular with hunters. More Minnesotans own rifles than motorboats—a great many more. O'Neill was making enemies.

This was the West Pointer, the networker of Pentagon brass, the scourge of the mortgagee. Even his friends were wondering what had happened to him. He had always seemed so, well, *regular.* They had seen the grin, but not the granite. Had it always been there? If not, it was now. He had discovered environmental law, and the warmth of the spotlight, and the most effective fulcrum of his growing talent. In federal court, with a new national base of impecunious clients, he was being all that he could be.

His next cause made even more enemies. This time he was on the side of rats. Or so it seemed. He succeeded in enjoining the Environmental Protection Agency from using strychnine above ground to kill rodents, having demonstrated the effect of the poison on plant life. It was a stunning victory, but not applauded in every quarter.

There were those at Faegre & Benson who genuinely thought that O'Neill had gone mad. What was he thinking of? They no longer cared that so much of his work was for free. Fine, keep it up! Find some hospice to represent! But just stop doing this to the firm! Canoes! Wolves! Rats! Whom would he try to save next?

It was mosquitoes. O'Neill's next cause was on behalf of the only thing hated not by some Minnesotans, or even by most, but by all of them. The Land of Ten Thousand Lakes produces insects so large that they are nicknamed "the state bird." Picnics and barbeques end at dusk as citizens flee indoors from the first whining dive of their primordial enemy. And yet Brian O'Neill, as if oblivious to this betrayal of his *volk,* actually sued the Mosquito Control District to stop its spraying to kill mosquitoes. His argument was that the insects provided food for ducks and birds. To Minnesotans, it was as if some quisling had thrown open the gate to the fort.

In fairness to Faegre & Benson, somewhere amidst these tumultuous crusades, Brian O'Neill had been made a full partner. This bestowal, despite the absence of necktie, retainers, or docility, was a tribute not only to O'Neill but to the firm, which could have rid itself of all the stress simply by withholding its offer. That would not have been fair, and it did not happen. Nobody disputed the fact that O'Neill worked like a dog. And he was good. Busy as he was protecting vermin, he also found time to spend with his patent cases—which he usually won. Even his notoriety was a two-edged sword. It wasn't all bad to have an environmental hero in the firm. It softened the image a bit. It lent credibility to other kinds of representation. His presence somewhat placated a populist federal judge who otherwise looked with disfavor on large corporate firms. More to the point, environmental law was a growing profit center. O'Neill was bringing in clients who could pay. And even some of the *pro bono* victories had been rewarded by court-directed fees.

There were those who felt that a partnership was settling O'Neill down. It represented more security for his growing family (a daughter as well as a son). It meant he was making more money. Surely he must be feeling more collegial toward his colleagues. His most exasperating *pro bono* forays seemed to be over or winding down. Those in the firm who had advocated patience were beginning to feel vindicated.

This was the state of affairs when O'Neill, in the middle of a duck-decoy patent case, first learned of the *Exxon Valdez* oil spill.

3

Semper Paratus

A fter his ship had run aground, the first call Captain Hazelwood made was to the Coast Guard. He reported briefly what had happened. This conversation took place no more than twenty minutes after the accident, perhaps half past midnight.

Just a minute or two after that, in Valdez, the phone rang in the quarters of Chief Warrant Officer Mark Delozier, who had been serving in the Coast Guard for more than twenty years. He wondered who could be calling at that hour. It turned out to be the man standing radio watch at the traffic center, and he sounded a little out of breath. He said that the *Exxon Valdez* was aground on Bligh Reef, and that Delozier should get right over to the Coast Guard command office.

Others had preceded him to the office, and their faces were grim. The local Coast Guard commander was on the radio talking to crew members aboard the *Exxon Valdez*. The details got worse and worse. The lieutenant commander, Tom Falkenstein, finally told Delozier that they'd better get out to the ship. It was about time. Although the Coast Guard was charged with policing the waters into which vast quantities of oil were now being discharged and had been informed of the extent of the disaster, the officers' discussion about the matter had already lasted several hours. Finally, together with a third man, Dan Lawn, from the Alaska Department of Environmental Conservation, and two crew members, they put out in a launch and headed in the dark for Bligh Reef.

Visibility was very bad, but the small boat had radar. They didn't need it to spot the ice. Delozier could see a four-foot chunk right by the hull. They carefully steered around the ice, but the water as they neared the stricken tanker contained an even greater hazard. Before he could see anything, Delozier could smell the fumes. It was oil all right, and he couldn't get over how intense the odor was. Delozier looked quickly to be sure that no one was smoking. He was afraid there could be a fire—or worse yet, an explosion.

And now, with their lights, they could actually see the oil and feel its sluggish weight against the passage of their boat. It was all around them. It was so *thick,* more than a foot and a half of it covering the surface of the sea. And the oil was bubbling, too. The launch passed through the hellish sight and sound and smell and finally reached the grounded tanker on its reef. It was easy to see, all its lights ablaze. However tormented the foaming sea around it, the giant vessel remained motionless. Its vast length neither rose nor fell with the waves that struck its base. It was like some mountain newly formed, rooted to the earth below, oblivious to the hissing and the danger.

The crew members stayed with their launch, and Delozier, Falkenstein, and Lawn went aboard. It was about three forty-five in the morning—more than three and a half hours after the grounding. They went immediately to the wheelhouse. Hazelwood was standing up against the window, looking out. Commander Falkenstein spoke to him first, and the others huddled around. Delozier noticed that Hazelwood was smoking, and, fearful of the oil fumes, asked him to put his cigarette out, which Hazelwood quickly did. The conversation continued, and Delozier noticed that even when he was speaking, Hazelwood kept his chin in his hand and that his fingers often covered his lips. The Chief Warrant Officer thought he knew why. He could smell the odor of alcohol. He was sure of it: the smell was very strong. Was he trying to cover that with his hand?

Delozier and Falkenstein walked out to the starboard bridge. As soon as they were out of earshot, Delozier asked his commander whether he had smelled alcohol, too. He said that he had.

"We need to do something about this," Delozier said.

"What do you suggest?"

"We should call back to the base and have someone come out here and begin some testing."

Falkenstein looked thoughtful, and Delozier went on. He talked about the new regulations coming in place that dealt with drinking, and the need for quick action: the longer they waited the less accurate the test would be. So Falkenstein called the Coast Guard station in Valdez and requested help. While they were waiting for it to arrive, they began interviewing crew members. They were trying to find out exactly what had happened; they had to make out a report. In answer to Delozier's questions, Hazelwood said that the only alcohol he had consumed ashore had been a beer—at lunch. Or maybe it was later, at a bar.

From the start, the Coast Guard investigation was not happily fated. The trip out to the *Exxon Valdez* had been remarkably delayed, and now more hours passed before the second boat responded to the call for further assistance. It arrived about six o'clock. Delozier was delighted to see it, and as soon as Trooper Mike Fox had come on board, he asked him if he was ready to proceed. Proceed with what? Fox asked just what the problem was. When told that they wanted to test some crew members for alcohol, Fox said that he wasn't prepared to do that. He had been told on shore only that he was to come out and take care of an unruly person. He hadn't brought any alcohol-testing equipment with him. All he could do was try to test for eye-hand coordination.

So they had to call back to shore once more. And this time they tried to make sure that there was no misunderstanding. While they were waiting a second time for testing equipment, Delozier busied himself with a number of tasks, including a surreptitious search of Captain Hazelwood's cabin. First he went into the stateroom. He looked in the trash can. He searched the bathroom. He peered into the small refrigerator. He looked under the bed. He went through the doorway into Hazelwood's office and searched that, too. In the office wastebasket he found two empty bottles of Moussy. He noted this, and quickly rejoined the others. They resumed their interviews of the crew.

Then, for the first time, though they had been aboard the tanker for nearly six hours, Commander Falkenstein mentioned to Delozier that perhaps there might be already on board some kits for the testing of blood alcohol. A call from shore had put this idea in his mind. Delozier asked Hazelwood, who said that, sure, they had the kits. He went and got them. When Delozier said that he wanted to start taking samples of the crew, Hazelwood pointed out that that would be against company policy: only qualified medical personnel could draw blood samples from members of the crew. Delozier wasn't sure what to do.

Shortly thereafter, a small two-seater helicopter landed on the deck of the *Exxon Valdez*. Its passenger was Petty Officer First Class Scott Connor, the Coast Guard's medical liaison at Elmendorf Air Force Base in Anchorage. He had been on the Valdez base that day and, despite having given the blood alcohol test fewer than half a dozen times in his career, was directed to get out to the grounded tanker with ample material to take blood samples. First he called the Anchorage base to double-check exactly what was needed for such tests, and then, since he didn't have the materials at hand, he went to the Valdez community hospital and picked out the supplies he would need. (The Coast Guard motto, after all, is *Semper Paratus*, "Always Prepared.") He dashed out to the airfield, but then had to wait for half an hour until the helicopter was ready to go.

They flew up over the mountains and out to sea. It was past ten o'clock in the morning. It was light enough to see from the air the dark oil spill spreading out from the grounded tanker, a devil's halo in the grayish dawn. They landed on the deck and Connor climbed out of the helicopter; he soon discovered that he had stepped into a puddle of crude oil. The heel of his shoe was pulled off by the sticky surface.

A crew member brought Connor up to Captain Hazelwood's quarters. Three of those who were going to be tested were sitting there waiting: Greg Cousins, Bob Kagan, and Maureen Jones. They had already submitted to urine tests. So had Hazelwood, but he wasn't present now and Delozier wanted to take his blood test first. They sent for him, and he said he was willing to be tested. He held out his arm and Connor drew three vials of blood—more than was necessary. Connor was using the tubes from the kits that had already been aboard the *Exxon Valdez*. Each kit had a red-stoppered tube and a gray-stoppered tube. But he had brought his own equipment as well and thought that to be extra-safe, he'd better take another sample. So he used a vial from his own kit, a gray-stoppered one. That made two gray stoppers and one red for the Hazelwood sample. When they were filled and sealed, the tubes for each crew member were put in a separate Styrofoam box, which was then also sealed.

As soon as the blood had been taken, each donor and Connor signed a document affirming that fact. Delozier signed it, too, as a witness. These documents also were sealed within the Styrofoam containers. This was the beginning of what was known as the chain of custody—the paper trail designed to keep anyone from tampering with a sample. To maintain the chain of custody, whoever has signed for the blood samples has to stay in constant possession of them. If the samples are stored or refrigerated, it must be behind locked doors, with the custodian keeping the key. If the sample is handed over to another custodian, it has to be signed for anew.

Hazelwood's blood sample had been taken at about ten forty-five in the morning—seven hours after Delozier had first smelled alcohol on his breath and nearly eleven hours after the grounding. Delozier told Connor to deliver the samples to Lieutenant Stock in Anchorage. The helicopter had been standing by, and this time it took off right away. They landed at the Coast Guard base in Valdez. As it turned out, there was no need to hurry: Connor's plane wasn't leaving for Anchorage until the following morning. So here he was at noon on the Valdez base with four Styrofoam containers stuffed into a somewhat awkward bag and wondering what to do with it. He was part of the chain of custody. He wasn't supposed to leave the samples just anywhere, unless he locked them up. And preferably in a refrigerator. There was one for that very purpose at the marine safety office on the base. Samples were often locked up there before being shipped. Connor went over to the secured refrigerator, but when he got there he found there was no key. The man who had the keys was on one of the Coast Guard boats that was out creating a security perimeter around the *Exxon Valdez* (a perimeter that presumably kept expanding with the spread of the slick). Nobody knew where any duplicate keys would be.

Connor waited, but no keys showed up. Finally, about five o'clock, still clutching the bulky bag, he left the base and checked into his hotel in Valdez. He wished that that refrigerator hadn't been locked. He opened the window of his hotel room and placed the bag on the sill. This was intended to simulate refrigeration. The Alaskan air was cool, but you couldn't really call it cold. After about an hour, Connor went back to the base. The man with the keys still had not returned. More waiting. After awhile, Connor had an idea. He went down to the galley and entered the large walk-in refrigerator and put his bag on the lower shelf, in the corner. On his way out, he asked the cook to be sure to lock the refrigerator before he closed the galley down for the evening. Then he went back to his hotel room. At least now he could keep the window shut.

The next morning he picked up the bag and flew to Anchorage. Apparently the cook had not locked the refrigerator door, but the samples seemed to be all right. He kept the bag on his lap throughout the flight. His wife met him at the airport, and as soon as they were home he placed the bag in the refrigerator. About two hours later, he received a call from Lieutenant

Gary Stock. Could he bring the samples over to his office in the Federal Building and hand them over? Connor felt intense relief. He hurried to the office. Stock opened the bag, then opened the containers, and looked into each one—most carefully at Hazelwood's, for rumors were already rampant that he had been drinking. When he was satisfied that there seemed to be no evidence of tampering, he picked up a pen and made Scott Connor very, very happy. He signed the chain of custody card, which meant that now *he* had to watch the bag until it was sent off for testing.

At first Lieutenant Stock wasn't sure quite where to send it. He was not very experienced with blood samples. In fact, his Coast Guard experience with biological emissions had been limited to urine samples. Now he had been told to have these blood samples tested, but no one had told him where. In the past he had sent narcotics to be tested at the state trooper lab, so he called that number and talked to someone there. He asked this voice if the testing could be done locally. The response was that if what was wanted was a complete spectrum analysis of all drugs and alcohol, if you're looking for every type of narcotic, then you're best off to go to California. The Chem West laboratory, in Sacramento, was recommended.

When Lieutenant Stock called Chem West, he was put in touch with Dr. Jill Henes. She said they could indeed do the testing he required, just send the samples out to California.

It was, however, now late Saturday afternoon. The samples would have to be packaged. The packager was closed. So Stock would wait until Monday to send out the blood samples.

Lieutenant Stock believed strongly in the chain of custody. No window sills for him. The samples were going to have to be securely locked up for the weekend. He had a friend, the unit urinalysis coordinator, who knew of a warehouse with a refrigerator and a lock. There was only one key and he actually had it. He handed it over to his friend. When Stock got to the warehouse, he was delighted to see that the key fit not a small built-in lock like on a desk but a big, hefty padlock. The samples would be secure. He carefully put the key in his billfold.

On Monday he retrieved the samples and took them to the packager. He kept his eye on them while they were being wrapped. They were Federal Expressed to the Sacramento lab and received there Tuesday afternoon—four full days since Captain Hazelwood had held out his arm for blood to be drawn. Now all that remained was for that blood to be tested.

4

Finding a Client

As soon as Brian O'Neill returned to his office, he started calling around. He now had a national network of contacts in the environmental movement, but most of those he spoke with didn't have much more information than what you could get on the news. The spill was big, all right, but the damage hadn't fully occurred. The vast pool of crude oil, eleven million gallons of it, had not moved very far from the site of the spill. It still wasn't clear in just which direction the current would take it. That direction meant everything. For the only time in the long and wrenching drama that they were about to share, Alaskan fishermen and Exxon executives uttered the same fervent prayer. They prayed that the current would flow south and take the oil out to sea. If the oil moved southwest, toward land—it was unthinkable. Because that was where the salmon fisheries were: at Prince William Sound, Cook Inlet, Kodiak, and Chignik.

Just staying where it was, relatively immobile, the oil had already touched the herring fisheries. While not as great an enterprise as catching salmon, netting herring was still big business. In fact, it's so lucrative that the Alaska Department of Fish and Game, in order to prevent extinction of the resource, has declared a very short season for the catching of herring. It is certainly the shortest hunting or fishing season on earth: a season opening, often as short as one hour. Remarkably, that seems to be enough.

43

Within this limitation, one boat can catch $150,000 worth of herring. Permits to participate in this frenzy were traded for as much as $300,000.

Bizarre as this may seem, it is as nothing compared to the fact that the fleeting season was scheduled for late March. And on the very day it was to have been held, the *Exxon Valdez* oil reached the herring. There was no alternative. Just before it was to start, the season was canceled. And with it the livelihoods and hopes of the herring fishermen, and the communities that depended on their catch. The loss was catastrophic. And the herring schools were, one might say, small fry compared to the vast salmon fisheries whose fate now rested on the pending flow of a current.

If the extent of the damage was yet to be known, there was a good deal of consensus over fault. Everyone was saying that the captain had been drinking. There were jokes about it on TV.

O'Neill's phone was ringing off the hook. It was known that a great many birds and sea otters were already dead. He seemed to be talking to every environmental activist in the country. Many of them beseeched him to get into the case. This was like urging Patton to cross the Rhine. He really needed no prodding. All his life he had been seeking some achievement that would define that life, redeem it from its origins and failings. It was clear to him from the little he already knew that this was going to be the biggest environmental case of all time. He wanted desperately to be in it. And in a major way. All those years of *pro bono* victories, however acclaimed, had been merely preparation for this. And he *was* prepared now, at the top of his powers—still youthful, already experienced. He could do it. He knew.

But he also knew that he had no client. He had concluded that none of the groups he was talking to—not the Audubon Society or the Defenders of Wildlife or the Sierra Club—would be found to have the requisite legal standing to sue. *They* thought differently, that they could get into court on behalf of dead fish or birds or other wildlife. But O'Neill didn't think so. He understood what this lawsuit would be like. What was sought was not an injunction over harm to a form of wildlife. That was no longer possible— the lethal force was already released. The suit would be for *damages,* and you can't give money to a fish. The suit would have to be on behalf of the fishermen. (In Alaska, the word "fisherman" includes the many women who earn their livings in this arduous manner.) And the defendant would be Exxon, one of the biggest corporations in the world. No expense would be spared in the defense, and if the battle were to be joined, let alone won, the rival armies must be equally armed. Not perfectly equal; that was neither possible nor necessary. Alexander had routed the vaster armies of Darius, but not single-handedly. He had needed his own cohorts, too.

O'Neill needed a client. He needed a fisherman. He needed *lots* of fishermen, who had suffered personal loss. He needed a grail at the end of the crusade to justify the cost of keeping troops for years in the field. His green network was only of limited value. He needed to sign up Alaskan fishermen as clients. The days flew by as the oil barely moved, and the phone calls became more frustrating and desperate.

One person O'Neill spoke to was another first-rate environmental lawyer in Minneapolis, Chuck Dayton. Dayton passed along the name of a former clerk in his firm, Peter Ehrhardt, a graduate of the University of Minnesota Law School, who now had his own small firm in Alaska in a town called Soldatna, not far from waters affected by the spill. O'Neill made notes as he spoke on the phone. He had other names, too, from other phone calls, of lawyers in Alaska who might help him contact fishermen. Most of them were in Anchorage. But Dayton's lead stayed on the list.

O'Neill had decided to fly up to Alaska himself. He couldn't do any more from where he was. He had yet to meet a salmon fisherman, or anyone who knew one. He needed to be on the scene.

If he wanted the firm to pay for the trip, it was better first to ask permission. The member of the Management Committee to whom O'Neill felt closest was Jim Fitzmaurice, an exceptionally good litigator. O'Neill went down a floor to see him.

He stuck his head in the office door and saw that Fitzmaurice was on the phone. Indeed, not long before, Fitzmaurice had been on the phone to Exxon, inquiring about the defense team that would fight the oil spill claims. Fitzmaurice had once represented Exxon in court, and very ably, and so he thought it couldn't hurt to mention his availability in the present time of distress. His contact at Exxon was polite, but unmistakably inclined to pass. It is interesting now, years later, to speculate on the consequences to Exxon had it only said yes to Fitzmaurice. Had he been even a minor member of its corporate legal team, then neither O'Neill nor anyone else at Faegre could have represented the other side. This would have prevented the most dramatic transformation in their lives, and as for the impact on Exxon—well, let us permit that tale to unfold.

O'Neill was standing in the hallway waiting for Fitzmaurice to get off the phone. The next office belonged to a young new partner, Gerry Nolting. The two were friendly but not really close; they were, after all, in different departments. O'Neill was in Business Litigation and Nolting in General Litigation, where he tried commercial and insurance cases. They didn't get to spend much time together. Now, Nolting's door was open. O'Neill popped in.

He started to say hello and then he noticed the map. Above Nolting's desk was a very large framed map of the state of Alaska. It occupied much of the wall. O'Neill asked what it was doing there. Nolting explained that his brother lived in the town of Palmer, north of Anchorage, and that the two of them went salmon fishing there every year. The map was a reminder. Of salmon fishing.

O'Neill and Nolting talked for the next three hours. Much of the conversation seemed directed at the map. Nolting seemed to know the area well, and something about the fishing, too. He was convinced that the currents were going to move the oil slick to the southwest, around the Kenai Peninsula and into the waters of Cook Inlet. This was the heart of the salmon fisheries. The impact would be catastrophic. The two men pointed to the map, and planned, and conjectured, and agreed.

Each lawyer's excitement was fueled by that of the other. They had something in common. Nolting was far less ebullient, and had never tried an environmental case. But the reason he *had* the map above his desk was because when he looked up at it from his litter of documents it reminded him of past escape, of freedom and great natural beauty, of a place he loved and knew and whose despoliation seemed a sin. He wasn't as dramatic as O'Neill, but O'Neill knew fervor when he saw it. And like O'Neill, from the moment he heard of the spill, Nolting had known that it would lead to the biggest environmental case of all time and that he wanted urgently to be a part of it. The two never said, "Let's work on this together," but after the first five minutes, and for the next five years, that's what they were doing.

They spent the rest of the afternoon and much of the evening placing more calls to Alaska. They phoned everyone they knew there, and quite a few whom they did not, to say that they were very interested, and to ask whether they could come up there and sit down and talk. A number of people said yes.

One of those they spoke with was Alan Beiswenger, a partner in the firm of Robinson, Beiswenger & Ehrhardt, in Soldatna. Like his partner, Peter Ehrhardt, who had already been brought to O'Neill's attention, he was a graduate of the University of Minnesota Law School. He had there-

fore heard a lot about Faegre & Benson. (He had, in fact, once interviewed for a job there.)

And they had heard of him. A young Faegre partner, Becky Rom, was
a friend of Beiswenger, and had recently had dinner with him in Alaska.
He had mentioned then that his firm had just become involved in an oil
spill case. It was this lead that O'Neill and Nolting were anxious to pursue. Beiswenger was happy to tell the callers what he knew: About two
years earlier, in July 1987, a British Petroleum tanker, the *Glacier Bay*,
had run aground, with substantial leakage of oil. The consequent lawsuits
were known as the *Glacier Bay* cases. Beiswenger said his firm was seeking millions of dollars, on behalf of some salmon fishermen.

At the revelation of this client base, O'Neill and Nolting both looked
up from the speaker phone. Their eyes met. They were talking to a
friendly voice that was telling them that it already had a base of salmon
fishermen as clients.

The voice went on. The third partner in the firm, it explained, was
Chuck Robinson, himself a commercial fisherman, and he represented
the Kenai Peninsula Fisherman's Association, a group that included six
hundred holders of commercial fishing permits.

The eyes, now speaking volumes, met again.

And so, about two weeks after the spill, permission for an exploratory
sortie having been granted, Brian O'Neill and Gerry Nolting flew up to
Alaska. They changed planes in Anchorage and then took an eight-seater
to Kenai, about ten miles from Soldatna. They were met at the airport by
Alan Beiswenger. He drove them to Soldatna. The trees along the route,
birches and firs, reminded the newcomers of Minnesota. But they were in
quite another world. Beiswenger stopped the car so that they could see
the vast flock of snow geese that had just landed. They stopped again for
the caribou by the side of the road.

That night they had dinner with Beiswenger. He talked about his firm.
He spent much of his own time on divorce work, he said. He didn't try to
build up his firm as something bigger and fancier than it was. He was
proud of what they had.

He should have been. It was a small-town practice—divorce, criminal
law, "whatever walked in the door"—but the three partners were as
proud of what they did as any Faegre lawyer. They were intelligent, sensitive, decent, and hardworking, and each had found in Alaska a life on the

terms he had wanted. Chuck Robinson was a graduate of UCLA Law School. He could probably have been a partner in a big California firm. He was happier where he was. He supplemented his lawyer's income by salmon fishing, and many of his fellow fishermen had become his clients.

The next day they met with Peter Ehrhardt and his investigator, Joe Malatesta, at Ehrhardt's office. They were somewhat startled by the strong resemblance of the tall and bearded Ehrhardt to Captain Joseph Hazelwood, whose photo was by then in all the papers. The firm of Robinson, Beiswenger & Ehrhardt was housed in a building that formerly had been a medical clinic. The visitors were not much impressed. That opinion was kept to themselves. This was indeed the other end of the status scale from their own gleaming tower, but such things mattered very little to them. What they cared about was finding clients so that they could sue Exxon. They were genuinely entranced with Ehrhardt, a pulsating dynamo who, if not actually bigger than life, was surely more colorful than their colleagues back home. His language was even further removed from the world of corporate law than his office. He was, to them, refreshingly blunt. (One of his aphorisms is "Any lawyer from East of the Mississippi is a lazy fuckhead." Fortunately, Minneapolis hugs the western shore of the river.)

Ehrhardt was also impressed by them. It took him only a few minutes to chuck his initial suspicion. He hadn't known what to expect. Like many small-town plaintiff lawyers meeting partners of a large corporate defense firm, he had been cocked and primed for condescension. He knew what his office looked like, and from his student days in Minnesota, what theirs did, too. They were from what he still calls a "big, big firm." But: "I liked those guys right away. They didn't talk down to us. I had expected more arrogance, but they seemed pretty excited about being here, and humble about their own experience."

Ehrhardt was perfectly willing to let O'Neill and Nolting look at his firm's *Glacier Bay* files. They were shocked by what they saw. Each had been accustomed to long, cool corridors lined with built-in sliding drawers to which omnipresent paralegals and secretaries relegated in perfect order, cross-referenced and color-coded, every single record and note and memo and brief pertaining to their own litigation. When they wanted something, they picked up a phone and a few minutes later there it was.

What they saw here was a room strewn with cardboard boxes. Some of the boxes contained only a few sheets of paper, and others were overflowing. You had to go through each box before you could be sure what was in it. Some of the fishermen claiming loss had documents to back up their case, and some did not. It all seemed random and disorderly. It was a mess.

Peter Ehrhardt understood this as well as they did. He and Robinson were doing most of the work in the *Glacier Bay* case, and he was swamped. He knew that he needed help. Big cases needed big resources: a large legal crew working full time. His small firm had other work to do—the clients who walked in the door with tales of defective products or marriages. He and his partners couldn't devote all their time to one case. They saw that they didn't have the staying power for a protracted case against a big company. By big company he meant British Petroleum. He was concerned not with the epochal conflict on the horizon but with the case he already had. He wanted their help in that. "We hoped they might get involved in *Glacier Bay*," says Ehrhardt. "Maybe Exxon, too, but frankly I was too worn out to think of Exxon."

If ever a deal was waiting to be made, this was it. The firm that needed help with *Glacier Bay* had the access to Exxon: the clients, and the capacity to get many more, as well as local presence and fisheries law expertise. The lawyers lusting to tackle Exxon had the resources to handle *Glacier Bay*: money, experience in organizing very large litigation, and skilled litigators who could come up to Alaska and work on the case full time. And at their own firm's expense. Faegre had what Ehrhardt called "staying power."

In representing groups of individuals against very large corporate defendants, staying power is critical. Most of the firms who take such work are small. They try the cases on a contingent fee basis, which is to say they will be paid a percentage of the recovery—if and when the case is won. The *when* is as important as the *if*. The contingent fee is often one-third of the recovery, and can be astronomical, but the lawyers don't have any money coming in until the case is won. Which can take years, and then if there's an appeal, more years. No money coming in, and lots of it going out: the cost of overhead (rent, salaries) for the law firm, the cost of travel and duplicating documents and hiring experts, and so on. There is also the cost of the lawyers' time. Lawyers charge by the hour, and theoretically every hour spent on contingent work is displacing an hour that could be billed to a client who would pay at the end of the month. With some lawyers this theory is correct. But even with firms in which all the work is contingent, the lawyer's time is obviously of value. Clearly, protracted contingent fee litigation represents a very great risk to the plaintiff firms.

No one understands this better than large corporate defendants. A favorite tactic is delay. The ticking clock costs them money, too, because they're paying their lawyers on a regular basis, but, with money coming in from their real business, they can afford to, and lawyers' fees are probably far less than a final judgment against them would be. With enough delay, that judgment may never come. There is a point at which even the most dedicated plaintiff team will have to throw in the towel. When debt becomes intolerable, they will have to settle the case, often for far less than they know they could get if only they could make it to and through the trial. So, generally speaking, defendants are not in a hurry. And they have considerable ability to string things out, requiring vast amounts of written questions answered, depositions taken, motions answered, and hearings held. Delay is their strongest card, and they play it.

The firms that end up handling contingent fee suits usually are those that can least afford to. They don't have deep pockets. The firms that *do* have deep pockets, or at least a high monthly income stream, tend to represent defendants. And if they do represent plaintiffs, contingent fees are very rare. Pay-as-you-go seems more prudent. Contingent fee cases are a gamble, and the big firms don't like to gamble. The small firms often have no choice. They're representing people, not companies, and usually people without much money. You can't send them a bill each month because they can't pay it. It's contingent fee or nothing.

Glacier Bay was a contingent fee case. No fisherman would ever have to write a check to Robinson, Beiswenger & Ehrhardt. If the judgment was in their favor, each fisherman would receive a check for his or her share—or, rather, for two-thirds of that share. The first third would be taken off the top by the contingent fee firm.

If it won the case. If it ever got to trial. If it could wait around for years. If it could shell out huge sums of money.

Peter Ehrhardt looked at the two eager Faegre lawyers and knew at once the cure to all his ifs. So he gave *them* an if: if Faegre would finance and organize the case, and contribute a team of full-time lawyers to it, he would work with them, share his client base, and split the fee. They could even have the lion's share of that fee. They could help round up more fishermen plaintiffs, too, and that larger pool could be fished again by both firms together when it came time for the *Exxon Valdez* case.

O'Neill and Nolting understood that they were being asked to provide all the up-front money and most of the bodies for what could be the two biggest oil-spill cases in history. They also knew that this was their best chance to represent a significant group of plaintiffs in the case that they saw as their destiny. They said that they'd let Ehrhardt know.

On their way out, they met Chuck Robinson. His strength of character was immediately apparent. And if they wondered what this gifted and charismatic African-American lawyer was doing in Soldatna, Alaska, working part time as a salmon fisherman, they soon came to understand the answer. Like his partners, and so many Alaskans, he was following the path not that others had thought suitable for him, but rather the one that he had chosen for himself. They were somewhat surprised to see that this Alaskan lawyer/salmon fisherman was an African-American, but few in Soldatna seemed to think that that was unusual, or even to think of it at all.

O'Neill and Nolting spent most of the next week in Anchorage. Before leaving Minneapolis they had made a number of appointments. As they kept them, one after another, new opportunities presented themselves. The lawyers with whom they met had heard of Faegre & Benson, too. Everyone recognized the vast resources of the firm—so lacking in the plaintiff bar. One Anchorage firm had excellent contacts with the state of Alaska. Surely that state would be bringing a major action of its own for the damage to its wildlife, commerce, and waters. It seemed possible that Faegre could represent Alaska in this endeavor. Was that better than representing what was then fewer than seventy fishermen in Soldatna and Kenai?

It wasn't even close. Alaska presumably could pay its bills on a regular basis. It would be a prestige client that could lead to other things. It would require no financing from Faegre. It was out of the question.

From the moment they had met with Ehrhardt they had seen the opportunity at hand. It wasn't just the stupendous pot of gold at the end of the rainbow. That was speculative, and far, far away. What mattered most was that those worried fishermen provided perfect entrée into the case. Those bulging cardboard boxes were the key to the door that led to the heart of the biggest lawsuit of all time. These were real people who they believed had been damaged by a polluter beyond any previous precedent. Though the road would be long and rocky, this was the straightest path to history. They would team up with Robinson, Beiswenger & Ehrhardt—and their clients.

Of course, they would have to convince their own firm. This was a task that might well have seemed at least as formidable as taking on Exxon. They were going to have to ask one of the most established, solid, hard-nosed, cost-conscious, careful, conservative, corporate defense law firms in the country to shell out huge sums of money and release a platoon of its lawyers from income production for many years in order to represent poor fishermen in a contingent fee case against one of the largest corporations in the land. Most Faegre lawyers would not have considered even asking the question. Many would have assumed that the answer would be not only negative but apoplectic.

The race is to the swift. They returned from Alaska at the end of the week and asked to meet with the Faegre & Benson Management Committee the following Monday. The meeting was scheduled.

It has been said that the phrase "law firm management" is an oxymoron. That was not true of Faegre & Benson. In most law firms there is a management committee, which tends to the administrative decisions of the firm. Sometimes the management committee is relatively powerless, a transitory necessity for the cutting of checks and coordination of staff. That was not true of Faegre & Benson. In some firms membership on the management committee is casually determined or democratically selected. That was not true of Faegre & Benson.

The Management Committee of Faegre & Benson was an almost mythic entity that controlled the firm. The key to both mystery and mastery was its role in determining compensation. In this it was, and is, unique. In most law firms the management committee decides each year how much every partner will be paid. Faegre & Benson was no exception. The Management Committee determined compensation, but unlike any other firm, *it did not reveal the results.* No one was told how much anyone else was making, and that information was not available. It was a secret. Each lawyer was told his or her *own* salary, of course, and could have whispered the figure to colleagues. But few did. Among other things, the person you told, even though the same age and years of servitude, might be making more than you. You might be making less than your peers. In a perfect news blackout, the embarrassment risks of disclosure are high. So Faegre partners walked the halls with their suspicions, but confession and even speculation were rare, and actual proof was out of the question. When a senior Faegre litigator was divorced and some details of his earnings were disclosed in the court opinion, lines formed in law libraries to read the advance sheets of the decision. But any sort of disclosure was very rare. Basically, no one knew.

Except, of course, for the Management Committee. Its capacity to impose and maintain the rule of secrecy caused amazement in other firms. And perhaps envy as well. For when *they* released the income figures publicly within their own firms, it often marked the onslaught of a year of bickering and recrimination. Most law firms are partnerships, and the annual earnings are divided up among the partners, though not in equal shares. It is a zero-sum game. If someone makes more, then someone else makes less—at least in terms of percentage of the whole. And this is what leads to pain and anger. In many cases the outrage is not so much over the salary received as its comparison to one's peers. Some lawyers think of themselves as being in a "class," which consists of all the other lawyers in the firm who were hired at the same time. To be paid less than a member of one's class can be interpreted as an insult. "How could *he* be making more than me?" There are those who actually would prefer to receive less annual income if it meant they could also be first within their class. Lawyers being lawyers, complex graphs and endless memos are constructed to refute the infamy. Those lawyers who work long hours think that that should be the basic test for compensation. Those who also manage to attract clients to their firm believe that this achievement should weigh heavily in salary deliberations. (Arguing over which lawyer *really* attracted the client is a frenzied subculture of its own.) And those who worked long and hard on a particular matter don't see that they should fail to be rewarded for their labor just because the client never paid the bill. Everyone has an argument fervently held. Any partner who has served on the management committee of a large law firm knows that the annual task of cutting up the pie is a sure route to misery, if not madness. To protect themselves from the memos and the glares, they strive to be as objective as possible. Theirs is a defensive game. Be able to justify your conclusions. Rely only on what can be quantified. Give so much weight to hours worked, and so much to dollars billed and paid, and so on. Make it scientific. Tell the whining ingrate that *you* didn't set his salary, the *graph* did, and that the graph is perfectly objective. Do it all by the numbers.

The Faegre solution of salary secrecy helped to create a very different climate. There was much less resentment and suspicion of favoritism than in more disclosive firms. It is true that Faegre & Benson was a hardworking firm with a great client base, and its lawyers were very well paid by local standards. But there were other firms all over town with lawyers making hundreds of thousands of dollars a year who were seething because the guy in the office next door was making three thousand dollars more that year than they. At Faegre there was much less of this sort of thing. One could guess at one's own disparity, even be certain of it, but at least be content that the shame was not widely shared. This permitted a spirit of collegiality, the goal of all firms, to infuse Faegre to a greater degree than at most of its rivals. It allowed for fellowship and cooperation (and the inevitable hint of conformity), which made an outspoken individualist like Brian O'Neill seem so threatening to some peers. There was still some backbiting and dissatisfaction, but the greatest threat to collegial harmony was absent. (The only Minnesota firm larger than Faegre, Dorsey & Whitney, had solved the salary problem in a different way—the lock-step method, where every person in each class was paid the same amount, ascending with seniority; it was a system whose merits became more apparent to a partner with the steady passage of time.)

The secrecy rule at Faegre had another advantage: the Management Committee did not have to go strictly by the numbers. It could afford to be more subjective. Numbers *mattered,* of course, hours billed and the rest, but so did other things. If someone's numbers were down because of illness or divorce, that could be taken into account; if someone had won the trust and confidence of a major client, that did not have to be irrelevant; there *were* contributions to the firm that could not be quantified—spirit leadership, past service, future promise—but that could be rewarded.

The firm disseminates regularly to the partnership a printed document titled "Factor to Be Considered." (This means, of course, to be considered in determining compensation.) There are ten factors. They are as follows:

1. Ability as a lawyer, including both technical proficiency and the willingness and ability to play a lead role on major projects.
2. Standing in the profession and the community, including activities undertaken to discharge his or her responsibilities to the profession and to society.
3. Time and attention given to the practice of law, including willingness to devote extra effort, work inconvenient hours, and confront particularly difficult problems.
4. Billings properly allocated to the lawyer's time.
5. Ability to satisfy and develop clients to whose work the lawyer may be assigned, including prompt and conscientious responsiveness to client's requests for service.
6. Attraction of new clients and effort devoted to building good will for the firm.
7. Work done which, though it may not be profitable, is significant to the welfare of the firm.
8. Training and developing younger lawyers in the firm.
9. Extent to which the lawyer is helpful and responsive to other lawyers in the firm and helpful in the internal administration of the firm.

10. Development of new areas of expertise that expand the ability of the firm to serve its clients and attract new clients.

This is an extraordinary list. It is highly subjective. Most firms could not get away with such criteria. That Faegre does is due to secrecy. As long as no one knows anyone else's compensation, the way it was determined cannot really be attacked. The cornerstone of what has worked is nondisclosure.

To get away with the extraordinary practice of salary secrecy, one needed an extraordinary management committee. The seven partners able to make such unappealable and unknown decisions had to be trusted by the rest of the firm. Their fairness, judgment, and competence had to be almost universally respected. They could, after all, be paying themselves twice as much as anyone else. The fact was that they paid themselves the same as other leading lawyers in the firm, and, without being told, this result was assumed by their partners. The members of the Management Committee were held in high regard.

Not that they were elected to their posts. At least as amazing as the secrecy rule was the fact that the Management Committee was self-propitiating. When it came time for a member to step down—and that could be after twenty years of service—his replacement was made by the Management Committee itself, which then announced the name of the new member to the firm. There was no vote of the partnership. (In recent years, the firm began to elect, by a vote of all the partners, members of the Management Committee, and for designated terms. The secrecy rule still prevails.)

The Management Committee, therefore, was like an absolute monarch. If it turned down a request, there was no appeal.

This was the august body before whom O'Neill and Nolting would appear the first workday after returning from Alaska. The two aspirants spent the weekend drafting and redrafting the memo that spelled out their proposal—unlike any other that had ever reached the rulers of that kingdom. They knew how unprecedented their request was, how antithetical to more than a hundred years of firm tradition. They couldn't help but speculate on how their audacity might be received. While the powers of the Management Committee did not include decapitation, its denial of their petition would seal their fate for life.

Who were these members of the Management Committee? There were seven of them. The chairman at that time was James A. Halls. He was a banking lawyer. One might as well have said he was a banker. He seemed like a banker, albeit a *friendly* banker, and he thought like a banker. O'Neill and Nolting realized that they were coming before his committee to request what could be construed as a very considerable loan—uncollateralized, and for a project that entailed some risk. The supplicants might be forgiven if they imagined that their proposal would be seen in a less daunting light by a fellow litigator. And there were only two litigators on the Management Committee.

The first was John French. At Faegre & Benson, where everyone was smart, people used to say "John French is *really* smart." It was not disputed. It was hard to know what French would think of the O'Neill-Nolting proposal. He had been one of the two members of the committee who had given them permission to fly up to Alaska and look around. Of course, there was a big difference between looking around and underwriting the Long March. Moreover, French was the dean of the local antitrust bar. A significant part of his practice was protecting large corporations from the grasp of class action plaintiffs. At this he was very, very good. And his belief in what he did was genuine. So how could he now commit his firm to backing fishermen against a corporate giant? Well, there were some grounds for hope. He was fair and reasonable. He went out of his way with great frequency to help and encourage younger members of the firm. O'Neill and Nolting still thought of themselves as younger members of the firm. You never knew.

The other litigator was Jim Fitzmaurice, head of the General Litigation Practice Group. A kind and thoughtful man, this former marine was also a very tough litigator. He loved his work and he liked O'Neill, and he certainly was able to see the possibilities in the Alaska proposal. On the other hand, he had spent his lifetime in face-to-face combat with the plaintiff bar. It is an association that permits respect but not affection. And although Fitzmaurice was the committee member to whom O'Neill felt closest, even his vote was not a sure thing.

Nor was that of Tom Crosby. Thomas M. Crosby, Jr. (Andover, Yale, Yale Law) was one of the Faegre partners whose portrait was hung in the gallery of past Minneapolis Club presidents. Farther down the staircase wall of pictures was that of his uncle, John S. Pillsbury, Jr., himself a Faegre partner until he left to head a large insurance company. And farther down from that, the closer one came to the origins of the club itself, were other relations who had been presidents of the club—George Crosby, his uncle; Albert Crosby, his cousin; and both his grandfathers, Franklin Crosby and John S. Pillsbury.* There were some collateral relations on the wall as well. The Crosby family had helped to found what later became General Mills, and when Tom's father married Ella Pillsbury, it was a union of the state's two most prominent milling families, each of which had played an early and abiding role in the life of the state. Minnesota's largest radio and television station, WCCO, bore the initials of the old Washburn-Crosby Company. Though not known to O'Neill or Nolting, Tom's wife is the great-granddaughter of one of John D. Rockefeller's early partners, and her family consequently had come to own a very substantial number of shares in Exxon. Tom Crosby did not seem a likely *provocateur* of the largest bastions of capitalism.

His true specialty was giving good advice. Secure in birth, fortune, and personal achievement, he had no ax to grind. He was dispassionate. His concerns were family, community, and Faegre & Benson. It remained to be seen, of course, what he would think about *Exxon Valdez* as a new landmark for his firm.

The other members of the committee were Gale Mellum, a leading securities lawyer; Gerry Flom, the head of the Corporate-Finance Practice Group; and Jim Stephenson, the newest member of the committee and head of the Banking Practice Group. (Stephenson was the West Point graduate who had helped recruit O'Neill to the firm.) All three were exceptionally good at what they did, but what they did was wholly on the other side of the fence from what O'Neill and Nolting were asking them to do. This was to be David versus Goliath, and their professional lives had been devoted to advancing the cause of Goliath.

Monday arrived, and O'Neill and Nolting were ushered into the meeting of the Management Committee. The committee members were friendly and polite. But not one of them was a pushover. All of them were shrewd and tough, and exceedingly cognizant of their firm's image and its client base.

O'Neill and Nolting handed out the memo that they had prepared to advance their proposal. It had very little to do with the *Exxon Valdez* case. It was concerned primarily with *Glacier Bay*. Faegre & Benson was being asked to send a team of lawyers and support staff off to Alaska for perhaps

---

*His younger brother, David, is slated to be the club's next president.

several years to join with Robinson, Beiswenger & Ehrhardt in representing what was hoped would grow to be one hundred fishing permit holders seeking compensatory damages for the losses they had suffered from the *Glacier Bay* oil spill. The estimated cost to the firm for this effort was $400,000. The estimated recovery to the plaintiffs was up to $6 million. Fees from this award would be divided with the Robinson firm: a sixty-forty split in favor of Faegre. This money would be the firm's share of compensatory damages, which was the the reimbursement of the fishermen for the proven losses. *Exxon Valdez* was something of footnote (though it was clearly understood that the client base in one case might have damage claims in the other).

There were a number of questions, carefully asked and earnestly answered. After that, O'Neill and Nolting were asked to leave and told that the Management Committee would consider the matter.

Which it then did. It was not a casual discussion. It was divided into two parts. First, the committee members analyzed this proposal as they would any other—the technical phrase, which no one used, is cost-benefit ratio. As they discussed the *Glacier Bay* case, it became increasingly more clear that the benefits outweighed the costs, even when allowing for the risks.

O'Neill had known his audience—his jurors, really—and anticipated that the very idea of a contingent fee would be a critical threshold test. So he had met it head-on, and in a hard-nosed way that he hoped would be appreciated by the committee. He had set forth three criteria that would have to be met before a firm accepted a contingent fee case: liability, causation, and the ability to pay.

The committee applied these criteria to the *Glacier Bay* case. Clearly, there was liability. A tanker, through provable negligence, had had its hull smashed and spilled great quantities of oil. It was equally easy to find causation: the oil had prevented some fishing and killed some fish, and this had reduced, if not eliminated, the incomes of some fishermen. The degree was debatable, but not the causation itself.

The third criterion was ability to pay. This frequently was the toughest test to pass. Even if there was not the slightest doubt of providing liability and causation, you had to have a defendant who could come up with the damages—many millions of anticipated damages in the *Glacier Bay* case. But this seemed not to be a problem. The British Petroleum tanker had been insured, and there was another monster fund to pay out proven claims.

The discussion of contingent fees was affected by a recent victory of the firm. A lawyer in a town in the Red River Valley had signed up a number of sugar beet farmers and was suing the United States Department of Agriculture for crop payments that it had declined to make. It was as if Robinson, Beiswenger & Ehrhardt had been dropped in Crookston, Minnesota: the local lawyer was perfectly able, and had signed up a promising client base, but lacked the resources to carry on against a giant, in this case the federal government. So he had contacted a friend at Faegre & Benson, John French, who had headed a team that took over the case and split the fee.

It had worked out very well. Faegre won the case, and the firm's fee, after the split, was about a million dollars—the largest litigation fee earned by the firm up to that time. This was not only a lot of money, it was three times the TDV of these. The letters TDV stand for time dollar value: the value of all the hours that a firm puts into a matter, at the full value that every lawyer and paralegal charges for their work. It is an important concept, and occasionally a cause of some frustration. Good defense lawyers charge high hourly rates and usually get them—but no more. They charge by the hour, and there are only so many hours in the day. There is a ceiling on how much they can make. It is a very high ceiling, to be sure, but a ceiling nonetheless. Sometimes defense teams can charge a premium for an unexpectedly successful result, but generally speaking, full TDV is the best that they can get. Getting *beyond* the TDV, getting a *multiple* of it, is quite rare and highly attractive, especially when it does not involve great risk. This can happen when you charge contingent fees. The firm had crossed this Rubicon in a big way in the Sugar Beet cases and the sky had not fallen. Why not now march on to Rome?

One big reason was that the defendants this time were not government bureaucrats—they were large corporations. The Management Committee was now onto the second and more difficult phase of its deliberations. It had not been very difficult to analyze the case on its merits and to evaluate it as a business opportunity. They knew how to look at numbers, and these numbers looked good.

But there was more to the decision than numbers. Much more. There was the question of the tradition and the future of the firm. Regardless of profit, was this the sort of thing that they should do?

If the Management Committee had been meeting twenty years earlier, when the firm was run by two strong leaders—Paul Christopherson and Robert Christianson—it was problematical whether a contingent fee proposal against a major corporation would even have reached the committee (which then had only one other member) and absolutely certain that it would have been rejected out of hand.

But much had changed in twenty years, and not only at Faegre & Benson. The world had changed. Members of this Management Committee were in close touch with the corporate executives whom they served, and they had heard some of those executives excoriate Exxon because of the spill. Some of the CEOs were environmentalists, too.

It is hardly likely that Faegre would have represented large numbers of indigent plaintiffs suing a grain company or a bank. But multinational oil extractors were not part of the Minnesota business community. They were off somewhere else, far away.

Perhaps the best thing O'Neill and Nolting's proposal had going for it was that it was narrowly focused. It was essentially a proposal to get involved in the *Glacier Bay* cases. Exxon was not ignored, but it was quite subsidiary. *Glacier Bay* was the spotlighted opportunity, and it was right at hand.

They went for it. The Management Committee, by consensus, approved the proposal and its budget. The ebullient duo was told to assemble a team and start packing.

Never was a command so readily obeyed—at least by those to whom it was directly given. But other bodies were needed, too. It now became necessary to select those lawyers and staff who would move with them to Alaska for an unknowable period of time, but certainly years. Whoever agreed to go would have to leave right away; the Robinson firm, delighted that help was on the way, was anxious that it arrive at once.

O'Neill set out to pick his team.

5

Finding a Lawyer

For the first few days after the spill, no one was quite sure whom to blame. There was an immediate and heartfelt desire to blame *somebody* for what had happened. Right from the start there were wire-service photos of oil-covered birds, of otters and grizzlies no longer sleek or powerful, of wildlife trapped in the suffocating black slime; there were aerial photographs of the vast and spreading spill, a metastasizing cancer beyond any cure. The pictures made most people feel either sick or angry. This wasn't a natural disaster, like an earth-quake. All this destruction had been caused by man.

But *which* man? If the accident had been caused by human error, just who was responsible for that? This was clearly a crime against nature, and how can there be a crime without a criminal? There is an abiding need to hold some person responsible.

Reporters from around the world converged on Valdez. They talked and they drank with the locals, often in the Pipeline Club. They picked up rumors that the Coast Guard had tested Captain Hazelwood to determine his blood alcohol level. Someone had smelled liquor on his breath. Someone had seen him drinking in Valdez shortly before he returned to his ship. He had not been on the bridge when the grounding occurred.

The National Transportation Safety Board announced that it would hold hearings on the causes of the grounding. Captain Hazelwood was asked to appear.

He was still in Alaska. He had remained there partly to be available to answer questions. But not to the National Transportation Safety Board. He didn't like the NTSB. He didn't like it at all. He derived this view from his father. The NTSB had rebuffed the elder Hazelwood's efforts to stay on as an airline pilot despite a mandatory retirement rule. The son still seems atypically angry when he speaks of the board.

In the days following the spill, there seemed to be nothing other than the *Exxon Valdez* disaster on television or in the papers. The pictures of entrapped wildlife were shocking. Nobody was talking about anything else.

Captain Hazelwood knew what was being rumored about him, about his role in this mess. He saw the look in people's eyes. If he appeared at a hearing, would he be asked about his drunken-driving record? His treatment at South Oaks? Would he be questioned under oath about what he had had to drink in Valdez? And who would be asking those awful questions? The hated NTSB!

So he did not testify. He fled Alaska. He shaved off his beard so that he would not be recognized, and together with Greg Cousins flew back to New York via Seattle. He returned to his home on Long Island—but not for long.

The *New York Times* was reporting that in 1984, after an accident, Captain Hazelwood had pleaded guilty to driving while intoxicated, and that he had been convicted of drunken driving in September 1988 and had his license revoked. His driver's license had been suspended on two other occasions during the last five years, the *Times* said. The match was close to the tinder, and the tinder was soaked with oil.

And then the blaze erupted. The results of the blood test came in. The test showed that Hazelwood had a blood alcohol level of .061. Under federal law it is illegal for a crew member to operate a vessel if his blood alcohol level is over .04. Captain Hazelwood's test result was fifty percent higher than that. It was still lower than the drunken-driving threshold under Alaska state law, but that wasn't the point. The point was that the blood test was taken about eleven hours after the grounding. If the alcohol blood level was .061 *then*, what would it have been at the time of the spill?

At Exxon they had been waiting to see what the blood test would show. When the results came in, Captain Hazelwood was summarily fired. The reason given publicly for the dismissal was that he had violated the company's alcohol policy.

Hazelwood heard about his firing on the radio. He was angry that no one had called him first, that he had had to learn of it in that way.

But soon he had no time for anger, for anything other than a desperate search for help. A warrant had been issued for his arrest. The state of Alaska had filed criminal charges against him. He had been charged in Valdez District Court with three counts: operating a motorcraft while under the influence of alcohol, reckless endangerment, and negligent discharge of oil. Though misdemeanors, the first two charges were each punishable by up to a year in jail, and fines were possible for all three. And there might be other prosecutions as well. The Coast Guard said it was considering bringing charges. The FBI said that it was conducting a criminal investigation into the spill.

The police were looking for Hazelwood, but no one could find him. It was known that he had left Alaska and had returned to Long Island, but he wasn't at his home, or with his parents, either.

It was not only policemen who were trying to find him. An astonishing number of reporters were searching for the captain, too. There was no bigger story. The name Hazelwood was in the headlines, it led the evening news. It was the staple of the talk-show monologues, the butt of jokes on the air and repeated in bars and offices and coffee shops. David Letterman: "Excuse number ten of the Exxon tanker captain: I was trying to scrape ice off the reef for a margarita; number seven: I wanted to impress Jodie Foster; number six: I kept drinking beer to wash away the taste of cheap scotch. . . ." The *Boston Globe* dug up an old pretrial deposition in a harassment suit against Exxon in which the plaintiff, a former second mate, had stated, "There's a bad joke in the fleet that it's Captain Hazelwood and his chief mate, Jack Daniels, that run the ship." The oil spill itself seemed like the end of the world, a big black blob off the coast, an *American* coast, like a monster attacking the shore. Whoever had caused this must be a monster, too—a monster or a joke or both. The clamor grew in volume as the search for the missing culprit intensified.

Hazelwood was hiding at the home of a friend on Long Island. It was agony to watch the television screen: David Brinkley, CNN, every push of the button. When his face was shown, he couldn't help running his hand over his chin—yes, the identifying beard was gone.

But he couldn't hide out forever. He needed help. They were saying that he had fled from Alaska, that he was a fugitive from justice. The district attorney reportedly had instructed him not to leave Alaska. Hazelwood insists that that isn't so: no one told him that he was not supposed to leave. He hadn't fled, he had just gone. He was hurt and confused and frightened and angry. He needed help desperately. He needed a lawyer.

He realized with relief that he already had one. At the Maritime Academy he had known a cadet named Michael Chalos, a few classes behind him. They had played on the same lacrosse team. He knew that he was a lawyer now, in Manhattan. Hazelwood's brother had worked for him. Just after the grounding, the captain had called Chalos to defend him against Coast Guard efforts to revoke his license. Now he dialed the number again.

Michael Chalos was not a criminal lawyer. He, and the successful firm he had helped to build, specialized in transportation law—maritime and other matters in which his background and expertise proved helpful.

He talked to Hazelwood, heard the urgency in his voice, and agreed to represent him. The two would work together virtually every day for many years to come.

When Chalos took the case, he had no illusions about his mastery of criminal law. He knew relatively little about it. But he knew who did. Tom Russo had recently joined the Chalos firm after thirteen years as a criminal prosecutor in the Queen's County District Attorney's office. As head of both the homicide and rackets bureaus there, he had had more than his share of high-profile cases (Son of Sam, John Zacarro). It is a highly stressful way to practice law, and he had wanted a change. He had known Mike Chalos in law school, and when he joined his firm, it was with a feeling of relief. No more headlines, flashbulbs, arraignments, or bail. Russo was looking forward to a nice, dull cargo-charter case.

And then, not many months after joining the firm, he found himself representing the most publicized criminal defendant in the land. Whatever he thought of the vagaries of fate, he threw himself into his new assignment. He clearly was destined for the job.

He called a lawyer in the Alaska District Attorney's office. He said that his client was not a fugitive from justice and that he was willing to return to Alaska to face the charges. But there were two questions he needed answered. The first concerned the amount of bail, and the other Hazelwood's personal safety.

The second inquiry was a reasonable concern. The public was clearly outraged by the spill. Much of the hostility was directed at Exxon; windows were shot out of an Exxon station in Seattle, and the caller claiming responsibility said that Exxon had been too slow in its response to the spill. Others felt the same way. Hundreds of environmentalists rallied in front of the federal Courthouse in Anchorage. In Juneau, demonstrators marched on the state capitol, and when one speaker said that "Exxon deserves to be in jail," he was loudly cheered. Congressional committees were demanding to know what had really happened. President Bush was being asked to close down the Alaska pipeline. Desperate to pour . . . well, *something* on troubled waters, Exxon placed full-page ads in most of the papers in Alaska, and a great many in the Lower Forty-eight, apologizing for the spill. But passions remained very high.

This was why Tom Russo was asking that Hazelwood's safety be assured. But the Alaska district attorney was unwilling to talk about that, or low bail, either. He didn't want to talk about anything. His office regarded Hazelwood as a fugitive. No promises; just bring him back.

Russo had heard that tone from district attorneys before, and he knew what it meant. He decided that it wouldn't be a very good idea to surrender his client in Alaska after all. It seemed more prudent to handle the matter right where they were. He contacted the Suffolk County district attorney and succeeded in negotiating terms for the captain's surrender in the jurisdiction where he lived.

So early on the morning of April 4, Captain Hazelwood and his lawyers drove into the parking lot next to the Suffolk County district attorney's office. They were shocked to find that the lot was filled not with cars but with journalists, more than a hundred of them. Hazelwood had heard tales from his wife and his parents about the hordes of reporters surrounding their homes, ringing the bell, going through the garbage. But that seemed like nothing compared to this. There were so *many* of them—a mob swamping client and lawyers with shouts and lights and cameras, a thick spill of its own, drowning and suffocating its victims. Captain Hazelwood had recently finished reading *The Bonfire of the Vanities,* and he couldn't help but feel like Sherman McCoy as he tried to make his way through a mob to his arraignment.

Presiding over the matter was Judge Kenneth Rohl. Hazelwood, Chalos, and Russo went to see him before actually going into court. As soon as they walked into his chambers and saw the fish and wildlife prints on the wall, they thought they might be in trouble. They were. The judge wouldn't comment on the deal that had been struck with the district attorney's office.

So they all went into the courtroom. It was overflowing with reporters, some standing back against the wall. There were so many lights that the fire alarm kept going off.

The district attorney announced the terms that he had agreed to and was recommending: bail in the amount of twenty-five thousand dollars, a fifth of which was payable in cash, and voluntary return by Hazelwood to Alaska, escorted by New York state detectives.

The judge let him finish, and then made a speech of his own. It was something.

"These misdemeanors are of such a magnitude that has never been equaled, at least in this county," he sternly, if awkwardly, intoned.

"He's got to think about that. We have a man-made destruction that has not been equaled, probably, since Hiroshima."

And with that he rejected the proposal of the prosecuting attorney, and instead set the bail for Hazelwood at one million dollars. Five hundred thousand of that had to be paid at once in cash.

In reliance on their agreement with the district attorney, Hazelwood's lawyers had brought with them five thousand dollars in cash. They could scarcely have imagined that one hundred times that amount would be required.

So Captain Hazelwood had to go to jail. Pale and shaken, he was handcuffed, led by deputies through the predatory throng, and then to the Suffolk County jail. He was put into a large cell filled with the most serious offenders. Every one of them was looking right at him, but when the sliding door clanged shut, Hazelwood says that his strongest feeling was one of relief that at least for one night he was safe from the press.

He smiles when he talks about it. "Going to jail is like going to sea," he says, "except the jail doesn't sink." Regardless of his bravado, it cannot have been a happy experience, despite the rise in Hazelwood's very local prestige when the eleven o'clock news came on. Nothing on earth, no feat of daring or rapacity, could have more favorably impressed his cellmates than the announcement of the million-dollar bail. None of them had ever dared a deed with such a consequence. They looked at him with the highest possible respect. He was *bad*.

The million-dollar bail made a big impression elsewhere, too. It was clearly excessive for what was, after all, a misdemeanor. People thought the judge had gone too far. His rhetoric also backfired. The Hiroshima line made headlines, but many thought it unfair. In the Associated Press wire story about it, the judge's remarks were followed by the reporter's comment that "the U.S. bombing of Hiroshima at the end of World War II killed or injured nearly 130,000 people and leveled 90 percent of the Japanese city. No known life has been lost in the oil spill."

Chalos and Russo had worked all night, and the first thing next morning they appeared before the supervising judge of the Suffolk County Criminal Court, Justice Thomas Stark, urging that the bail be reduced. The new judge agreed. "The award of bail is not commensurate with the seriousness of the crime or the effect of the crime on the community," he said. The district attorney added, "We can't take out our wrath on one individual," a simple precept that was to become a major issue.

Justice Stark reduced the bail to twenty-five thousand dollars, bond or cash. It was posted, and Captain Hazelwood walked out of the jail and over to the waiting car of his lawyers. They drove off together, on a journey far longer than any of them could possibly have imagined.

6

To Alaska

W ho wants to move to Alaska?

The answer, demonstrably, is a great many people, most of them young. Currently, six babies are born in Alaska for every person who dies. The Land of the Midnight Sun is very youthful, and filled with new arrivals.

Why do they move there? In a surprising number of cases the answer is escape. Escape not from tyranny—few of those seeking asylum on our shores dream of doing so in Alaska—and not from poverty, either. Wages have been high in Alaska in recent years, and the pipeline engendered a boom. But there's also great opportunity (sometimes much greater) in many parts of the Lower Forty-eight not to mention Hawaii, where it never gets cold.

Most of those opportunities, however, are connected to large organizations: corporations, agencies, affiliates, banks, funds, programs, firms, studios, bureaus, HMOs. And this is the key to the northbound flight. Some people don't *like* being part of a team, not even when it's possible to rise within it. They are loners. They're ready to work, and work hard, but for themselves, or at jobs that they can leave with very little fuss if they should decide to do something else. They don't want to work for anything big enough to have a Department of Human Resources. They want to *be* a human resource. They want to be on their own. They most decidedly do not want to network. They want to wear what they want to wear, and they see anything else as a uniform. They don't want once a week to be allowed a Casual Day; they want a Casual Year.

And in Alaska they've found it. Go North, young man, and woman, too, and be a salmon fisherman rather than a cog, and if you must be a lawyer, do that in Soldatna, with no senior partners and the chance to walk home for lunch. It's *structure* they hate, and regimentation, and social pressure and social climbing, and pretense and conformity and career disincentives to saying what one really thinks.

It is no secret that the Lower Forty-eight are busily headed in the other direction. More and more people work for fewer and bigger colossuses, and downsizing means only a loss of jobs, not constraints. The brass rings of modern life are not grabbed, they're paid for, and there are those for whom the price is too high.

Because the price is paid in the way we live our lives. And the bigger the prize the bigger the price. The better educated one is, and the brighter one's prospects, the more likely is entrapment in routine, bondage to possessions, exclusion from leisure, and submersion of self. What one does becomes what one is, and hours are evaluated, not lived. It's what drives great captains to drink. Private life and the thoughtful work that flows from it are jettisoned on crowded career tracks by the spectacularly misnamed "upwardly mobile."

And nowhere is this descent into amber more evident than in the practice of law. It is a very crowded profession. Nearly half the lawyers in the world live in the United States. There are close to one million American lawyers, one for every two hundred and seventy clients, otherwise known as citizens. And the ratio is narrowing. Law school admissions offices continue to be overwhelmed.

Why so many young people want to become lawyers is something of a mystery. A few years back, when some law school deans commissioned a survey to find out why their gates were being stormed, they were astonished to find that high on the list was the image fostered by the TV series *L.A. Law.* Perhaps. But that show is long off the networks and still the hordes are applying—and not to *Baywatch* school, either.

They may just want to be lawyers. It's a very commendable choice, though to state that is to invite ridicule. There's no audience so stony that it can't be brought to life by yet another lawyer joke. Dewey, Cheatem &

Howe. Most people, including most lawyers, resent *some* lawyers. They're overpaid, they overcharge, they chase ambulances, they tolerate lies, they never get to the point. Just which gripe one picks from the endless litany depends on each person's exposure to the legal system, but it's a fairly safe bet that that exposure wasn't pleasant.

Yet law as a profession performs a noble task. It makes freedom possible. The Statue of Liberty lifts the torch, but that might as well be a law book she's holding under her other arm. Because freedom, once found, has got to be defended, and the battlefields of human rights are frequently the courts.

People point out with pride that this is a nation of law, yet everyone jokes about it being a nation of lawyers. We can't have it both ways; it's a package deal. The rule of law, which made the torch a magnet, is maintained not by guards but by guardians, guardians for hire. All the tiresome quibbling of those guardians is a small price for what they keep intact.

And there's a hidden bonus to all this: the lawyers themselves, a huge internal army with no commander save each client, a vast reserve force on which the national life does draw, an unbelievable number of men and women who are trained to analyze and argue and to see the other side. It's *good* for a country to have people—even a million of them—who are skeptical, questioning, verbal, resourceful, independent, tough, conciliatory, resolute, stubborn, realistic, and informed. The lawyer's most maddening phrase is "on the other hand," but that's the magic incantation that keeps all tyrants at bay.

But now the profession is becoming a business. It is subject to the same forces as everything else in the postmodern world. These are largely economic forces. They require regimentation of what were the fiercest individualists in the land. They've changed the quality of life of those who defend the freedom of others and had sought it for themselves.

The young lawyers who are snapped up by the big firms are those who show the most promise. They are paid a lot of money. They are reminded of the loftiness of their calling and the tradition of their firm. They begin their careers eagerly.

Faegre & Benson was no exception. Those who were hired had been academic stars. They'd been singled out since fourth grade for glittering careers. Every test and prize and honor was a signpost on that path.

They were used to competition and success. From the first day at work every one of them went to it with a vengeance. They worked long hours, they jogged before dawn to get their motors running, they performed.

And as the years passed, they were rewarded. With money, and in responsibility. They learned to argue cases, organize evidence, draft momentous documents, calm clients. Soon they were training the neophytes who followed them.

They became partners. They bought better houses. They sent their children to good schools.

They bonded with the colleagues in their practice group. They went to parties. They went to lunch with new friends of the same age from within the client base.

But mostly they just worked. Their hours of toil were not reduced as they rose within the firm; quite the reverse. The walls of each office enclosed most of their conscious lives.

And what of those lives? Those living them began to wonder. For the practice of law was changing, and the changes were swift and foreboding.

It had to do with money, the root of all upheaval. As the economy took off and the need for legal services raced ahead of it, the profession grew more competitive. There was more money at stake, and less client loyalty. To survive, a law firm had to put its best foot forward, and its best foot was not its decor, it was its lawyers. To snare the best coming out of law school, beginners' salaries soared, and then the law firm was stuck. When the floor is raised, the elevator takes off from there.

But salaries were only part of the new cost of running a large firm. Rent shot upward, too, as firm size doubled and tripled and doubled again. New space was always being added, sometimes whole floors at a time—and in the most expensive buildings in town, close to the financial and business centers. A big law firm usually can't build its own building out in the suburbs like its clients do; it must be near the courthouse.

The overhead each month is staggering. A firm like Faegre & Benson may well have more people making a salary of $200,000 a year than virtually any of its clients. But it doesn't mill flour or manufacture pacemakers. It has no inventory. It has no real book value. It has only lawyers. It's in the business of selling legal services, and it sells them by the hour. It's horrifying to calculate how many thousands of hours must be billed each month just to pay the rent. A law firm can't raise its hourly rates much higher than its competitors and hope to stay in business. There's only one thing to do: work more hours.

Most law firms now tell their lawyers how many hours they are expected to bill each year, and there is not the slightest confusion over what "expected" means. And the goal is a floor, not a ceiling. Surpassing it becomes a grueling contest.

The score is posted regularly. Most firms distribute sheets each month showing how many hours each lawyer has worked, how many of those hours have been billed, and how many have been paid. This data incites peer pressure, managerial comment, and individual frenzy. The fate of each soul is proclaimed by the computer.

Of course, what comes out of a computer depends on what goes in. And so the paradigmatic moment in the modern practice of law occurs when a lawyer closes the office door and begins with bitter desperation to fill out the waiting time sheets.

The time sheet is the daily record of how many hours a lawyer has worked. It puts the lie to those who say that scholars can't write fiction. There is a separate time sheet for each day of the week, and weekends are included. (They afford the best chance to get ahead of one's colleagues.) A lawyer records the date, the name of the client, the matter number, the amount of time worked, and a brief description of that work.

This is not as easy as it sounds. Ideally, a lawyer is recording the work all during the day as he or she goes about doing it. That's what one should do. Of course, one should eat right and exercise, too, but not everyone does. Despite good intentions, lawyers can put off the time sheets for many reasons: travel, meetings, too busy, not busy enough, forgetfulness, or simply the unpleasantness of the task. But at the end of the month, the time sheets must be handed over to the keepers of the computer. (In some firms, lawyers are not paid until their time sheets are in.)

And so each lunar cycle finds many lawyers staring at blank forms and trying to remember what went on. They look at their calendars and appointment books and recent correspondence and try to recreate the past. In this, some are fully as creative as Proust. They are less fortunate, however, because in their efforts, evidence is required. One can't just write down, "Tuesday, five hours, Gotham Bank." One has to describe just what work was done for the bank. Because all the time sheets of all the lawyers who worked for the bank that month will be amassed and collated, and the resultant print-out of work performed may be sent to the client with the monthly bill. So if one has written, "Five hours—preparation of memo," someone at the bank may ask "What memo?" No good law firm will tolerate a lie. One has to be very careful.

Many time sheets permit only a minimum unit of time to be recorded, say, nothing less than fifteen minutes. This is to avoid the administrative costs and likely ridicule of billing for a two-minute phone call. But people do make two-minute phone calls. These can be recorded as having lasted fifteen minutes. There are those who see this requirement as an opportunity. If one makes eight client calls in an hour, one can bill two hours. One *must* bill two hours; it's the rule.

Another opportunity is found in travel. It is a common practice to bill the traveling lawyer's time as portal-to-portal, that is, from the moment one leaves home for the airport until the moment one checks in at the hotel. So lawyers who fly a lot get to bill a lot of hours. They accept with equanimity the announcement that the flight has been delayed.

Sometimes this hand can be overplayed. There is the legendary story of the young New York lawyer who billed his client for twenty-five hours on one day's time sheet. It seems that after working all day he had boarded a plane to Chicago, and the difference in time zones made his calculation technically accurate. The client's reaction to paying for twenty-five hours in one day is not recorded.

There are other stratagems as well. Vagueness can be helpful; the single word "preparation" may do the job if no one asks about preparation for what. There are lawyers who feel they've done two full hours worth of work in one, and so bill two. (There are probably far more lawyers who record less time than they've actually worked because the economics of the particular matter don't justify billing the client more.) There are those whose memories truly are faulty, and who try in all honesty to remember with whom they spoke three Tuesdays earlier. There are those who think that *thinking* about the case, no matter where, should be billable. There are those who are working for a set fee and who, on perceiving that the value of their hours will be less than that fee, simply add more hours. It costs the client nothing but helps them meet their time quota.

Most of the time is honestly recorded, because most law firms are vigilant and most lawyers honest or at least cautious. But the process of filling out those time sheets is for many the sharpest focus of their personal discontent. An astonishing number of lawyers volunteer the opinion that this is the worst thing they have to do. An attorney may look back on a month of small triumphs—settling a case through resourcefulness and calm, wisely persuading a frightened client to abandon some hazardous course, finding on reflection the key to an agreement that will last. But however creative or helpful this counsel, it will be weighed in units not of merit but of time. At so many dollars per minute. And that is why so many lawyers, including the hardest workers, hate—really hate—the very thought of time sheets. It reduces their worth to a value other than that which they hold for themselves. These leaders of the bar once had heroes, too, and whether those heroes were Holmes or Darrow or someone else, they weren't revered for their hourly rate.

Oscar Wilde wrote that a cynic is one who knows the price of everything and the value of nothing. That would make ours the most cynical age in history. Because not only the legal profession but every corner of our swollen economy as well is busy reducing human endeavor to quantifiable units. People work not to smell, but to buy, the roses. The fabric of our society is appraised by the price of each thread. Increasingly, and in every field, the rewards are only economic. The quality of human life seems not so much lessened as irrelevant. Every aspect of life, however plush, seems like the residue of ruthless accounting, even language. Civility and thoughtfulness are vanishing in part because their cost can't be justified. The talk-show host commands monosyllabically, "Explain," when what is meant is, "Could you please tell us what you mean by that?" The reason for such abrupt discourse is that every second of network time is golden. "Please" alone costs a fortune. Those who type "say again" unto the Internet rather than "Could you please repeat that?" are saving time, which is money, but they are not saving civil discourse. They are not saving their own lives.

What does all of this have to do with Alaska? It helps explain why people go there. It explains, perhaps, why outstanding lawyers with safe berths in a prestigious and thriving law firm would abandon professional routine and urban comfort for years of struggle in Soldatna.

For Faegre & Benson, too, had changed since Brian O'Neill had joined it. In the dozen years that he had been there, the firm had grown from eighty-nine lawyers to two hundred thirty-five. Starting salaries had soared. Business was booming. That was the problem: some people *thought* of it as a business, rather than a profession.

Even the old cozy offices were gone. All the dark and polished wood and slightly shabby carpeting had disappeared in a fireball on Thanksgiving night in 1982. The massive granite bank building and everything in it had been atomized by raging flames. Nothing was left—even file cabinets vanished in the searing conflagration. But the insurance was current and adequate. It was folding chairs and partitions and temporary squatter space for quite a while, but carefully the lawyers re-created much of the vast documentation that had been destroyed. From the day after the devastating fire, they were back in business.

By early April 1989, when Brian O'Neill roamed the halls of the firm seeking cohorts for Alaska, those halls bespoke the resurgent success of the firm. A new bank building had arisen on the site of the old. A soaring tower of rosy Kasota stone designed by Cesar Pelli, it contained the now numerous floors of Faegre & Benson. These did not even remotely resemble the vanished stolidity that had preceded them. It seemed like a completely different firm: light and airy, touches of pale marble and light wood, open and accessible and efficient. Just like every other firm.

Those who toiled in this pastel hive were really very fortunate. They had been spared much of the competitive excesses of other successful firms. The secrecy rule was still firmly in place, which kept resentment at a minimum. The collegiality enhanced by Rebuilding the Firm After the Fire was easier to retain because of the compensation scheme. Where there are lawyers, there will be bickering, but by and large Faegre & Benson had been immunized against much of the infighting and unease that marks the modern practice of law in so many other firms.

Even so, it was not paradise. Better than most is not perfection. No large firm can fully escape the transformation of the profession. There were a number of lawyers who were finding their lives constricted. There were those who were hopefully considering teaching law or writing books or perhaps seeking a judgeship. Virtually no partner ever left Faegre & Benson for another large law firm, but there were other alternatives. In dozens of tasteful offices, beneath the best diplomas in the land, there were recurrent furtive dreams of somehow making it over the wall.

And who should come along but Brian O'Neill. Pitching nothing less than flight to Alaska. Exodus perhaps for years. It seemed like an adventure. There were those who were intrigued.

Departure had its risks, of course. Anyone who went off to the tundra would miss the chance to work alongside many of the firm's leading lawyers. They would lose the chance to show their skills to the best clients in town. It might be a career mistake. Out of sight, out of mind. Brian O'Neill was a very controversial character. Would proximity to him be detrimental? Staying put was safe; Alaska was a risk.

But, as lawyers say, on the other hand. When the dean of the Harvard Law School came to Minneapolis to address his school's alumni there, a member of his entourage approached a local lawyer, looked at his name tag, and gushed: "Oh, 1963! That was a *great* class. We have *two* billionaires in that class!" What was life all about? What was happening to the profession? Was money all that mattered? A sensitive young lawyer could look around, and then choose Alaska.

O'Neill didn't ask just anyone to go. He was a realist. The stars, or those with wagons hitched to stars, would stay put. Besides, he wanted people who would do as they were told, which for the most part meant younger lawyers. Now, his speech loaded with Alaskan metaphor, he says he wanted a team of sled dogs. There is no question of who would be standing behind and above those dogs, cracking the whip.

But each team has a lead dog, too, a tireless performer out in front whose stamina and character set the pace for the rest. From the very start, that was Gerry Nolting. This canine comparison is not meant to be dismissive, for his contribution to the great adventure is immeasurable. And though he surely knows his own worth, he seems quietly devoid of ego.

He was the perfect partner for O'Neill. They could not have been less similar, fire and water. The water had considerable depth, which meant, of course, that it seemed still or at least very quiet. Where O'Neill was flamboyant, Nolting was methodical. A number of those who worked with him in Alaska have used the same phrase: "He would chew through the mountain to get to the other side." In the drama that was just beginning to unfold, his role was never scripted for center-stage, but absent his efforts, the dazzling production could well have floundered out of town. He was steady and resolute, quietly resourceful, from the first search for backers to the last curtain call. Of those Faegre lawyers who began the long journey, he virtually alone would end up with his marital status unchanged. He seemed the least probable candidate for a trek into the unknown, yet when the team reached its destination, it knew how very much was owed to him.

Nolting, of course, was never asked to go to Alaska. He was in from the beginning, though O'Neill selected the others.

The only other partner asked was Steve Schroer, just a year younger than O'Neill. A native Minnesotan, born in St. Cloud, he had received a second law degree at Cambridge University in England after serving on the *Columbia Law Review* and as law clerk to Judge Murray Gurfein on the

Second Circuit Court of Appeals. He had once envisioned a career as an opera singer. More pertinent to O'Neill, Schroer had, while at Cambridge, written a lengthy treatise on the economic and legal aspects of commercial salmon fishing. This happy coincidence was most alluring to the land-locked lawyers. Schroer was asked to join the team. He accepted. He had gone through a divorce, had not found in his business litigation practice a real substitute for La Scala, and was ready to try something new.

Lori Ann Wagner (Phi Beta Kappa, Wisconsin Order of the Coif) was still in her twenties and had been at Faegre & Benson for only three years. She was a litigator and dealt with intellectual property as well. She had been horrified and angered at the news of the spill. Further, what was proposed struck her as an opportunity for adventure. She signed on as soon as she was asked.

Sarah Armstrong was even younger, an academic star the University of Minnesota Law School. She was only a first-year associate at Faegre but had been working with O'Neill in environmental litigation. When he assembled his prospects and asked, "Who wants to go to Alaska?" hers was the first hand up.

These were the lawyers who made up the first team—with one addition. On the eve of departure, O'Neill asked Ruth Nissen, a second-year law student who was clerking at the firm, if she wanted to go along, too. She did.

Support staff would be needed as well. Preparing the fishermen's claims would require an extraordinary effort of collecting and processing data. Secretaries and clerks became part of the team: Chris Johnson, Kathy McCune, Katie Roessler, and, later, Leanne Mischke.

There was no time to lose. Everyone had to leave right away. The deal with the Robinson firm was for immediate assistance. There was hurried packing (fortunately, the Minnesota wardrobe was well suited to Alaska). For the single members of the team, the imminent flight was exciting. For the married, there was the ache of farewell, tempered perhaps by some imprecision about how long they would really be away.

In terms of first impressions, the team arrived in Alaska at just the right time. It was warm. It was sunny. It was bright; in fact, it was bright for most of the hours of the day. From the plane, the glittering water and awesome mountains far surpassed those quickly researched pages in *National Geographic*. Landing did not spoil the illusion. The people seemed happy and rugged, and the air was amazingly clear. It was glorious. It *was* an adventure.

And then they arrived at the Redoubt Arms in Soldatna. They had rented rooms in the apartment building, sight unseen. When they saw the place, their hearts sank. The building catered to long-term transients, fishermen in for the season. The accommodations were cheap and clean, but that was it. Some were reminded of their college dorm rooms, particularly as this establishment had posted rules of conduct on the walls. The first of these admonitions was, "No Cleaning Fish in the Rooms."

They were in fact living dorm-style. Each gender shared a suite of separate bedrooms and common living room and kitchen. The furniture was minimal and functional and had seen use by a good many fishermen. These rooms were a place to sleep and, arguably, to eat, but there was nothing, absolutely nothing, to lure even the indolent to linger at home.

Not that any of them *was* indolent, or that there was any time to be so. Their very first task on arriving in Alaska had been to open a Claims Office. It was here that fishermen were to come and have their claims for damages evaluated. If it looked as if they had indeed suffered provable loss, that would be pointed out to them, and a new client might be signed up. This type of work formerly had been performed within the constraints of the crowded Robinson office. But no longer. There really wasn't enough room there for the Faegre team, not to mention the new hordes of plaintiffs whom O'Neill was hoping to attract.

So a Claims Office was opened in a storefront in Soldatna, between an optician and the Public Assistance office. It was furnished with long folding tables and metal folding chairs. The space was partitioned into separate rooms, so that each fisherman could be interviewed privately. The cardboard boxes had been carried over from the Robinson office and their contents were photocopied and organized and fed into the computers that the team had brought from home. In many cases, the data in the boxes were incomplete. The fishermen had to be called back in and reinterviewed. Then all the new data had to be integrated with the old, and a whole set of questions developed so that they could proceed more efficiently in the future.

They had to know exactly how much money each fisherman should claim as loss, for the nature of the litigation had now changed. The Robinson firm had filed a class action suit and was seeking to have the class certified. That could no longer be. The Management Committee of Faegre & Benson had been quite clear on this point: no class action suit. The plaintiffs would have to sue for actual damages: the lawyers would have to prove how much income each fisherman had actually lost because of the *Glacier Bay* oil spill. The Robinson firm had to acquiesce in this, but warned the Faegre lawyers that they were letting themselves in for a lot of work.

In class action suits, the lawyers file the case on behalf of everyone in a certain class, or category. For example, all the salmon fishermen in Cook Inlet. It isn't necessary to identify them by name, or even to know who they are, or how many. If the class is certified, the lawyer then asks for a certain amount in damages. It's an aggregate, often an estimate. And if the case is won, or settled, the money gets sent to the members of the class, who are largely unknown. So the lawyers take out ads in newspapers describing the settlement and asking class members to come forward. Since these ads are often presented in a typeface discernible only by diamond dealers, the number of plaintiffs who come forward may well be far less than that on which the aggregate claim was based. There are many different views on how to distribute this money, but no question that the legal fees come off the top, often a third of the total, plus expenses. And this has led to charges of abuse. If an unscrupulous lawyer succeeds in having a very large class certified by the court, he or she could then settle the case for a fraction of its plausible worth. If this is done early on, very little money has been advanced, and the third of the settlement is largely profit. A very nice profit, too, if the class and its claim were huge, even though the settlement was less than ten cents on the dollar. The lawyers who play this file-and-settle game may be relatively few, but they have given class actions a bad name in some quarters. One of those quarters is the corporate boardroom, where such litigation is seen as a form of legalized extortion. Despite their disdain, some corporate counsel actually *like* class actions because they think a whole mass of plaintiffs can be bought off cheaply, at little more than the cost of a trial, and with no risk of further cost.

Faegre & Benson's insistence on direct action litigation probably reflected the corporate view of class action suits. But there were sound business reasons for this approach as well. If the fishermen had suffered substantial damage, and that could be proved, then each individual's recovery would be higher than as members of a speculative class. In a class action, Faegre could be sold out by co-counsel from other firms who were in a hurry to settle. Class action suits were fine for millions of consumers who each had suffered a fifty-dollar loss. But here there were thousands at most, and their claims were large and provable. Do it the old-fashioned way: prove up each claim. Show the actual loss that each fisherman had suffered. So the Claims Office was open for business from seven in the morning until seven at night, seven days a week.

Organizing the claims was only part of the task. The larger part by far was signing up new plaintiffs. Only about sixty fishermen to date were being represented by the Robinson law firm. There were many times that number out there somewhere in the area. The problem was finding them. It was a big area.

O'Neill started buying ads. There were some in the local newspaper, the *Peninsula Clarion,* but most of the budget went into radio. On trucks and in boats and trailers, on docks and in kitchens and bars, people stopped flipping the dial when they heard that they might have some money coming. If they fished in the area and their livelihood seemed to have been affected by the *Glacier Bay* spill, they should come in for a free evaluation; come in to the Claims Office, right next to the optician. The ad was run frequently.

The fisherman started coming in. At first many were deeply suspicious. The ad mentioned Faegre & Benson, and word was that this was a really big firm. These were people who had gone to Alaska to escape many aspects of modern life, and slick city lawyers embodied much of what they had fled. Yet the sandy-haired guy who seemed to be in charge was certainly friendly enough, and dressed in a way that made the fishermen feel comfortable, in fact superior.

The biggest initial attraction at the Claims Office, however, was undoubtedly the female staff. They were astonishingly good looking. Sarah Armstrong, for example, resembled a somewhat younger and more attractive version of Daryl Hannah. There were other knockouts, too. Whether by design or happy accident, the standard of beauty was very high. And this was Soldatna, where men greatly outnumbered women and unattached females were few. You couldn't keep some of those fishermen out of the Claims Office.

Still, not everyone was ready to sign on the dotted line. One night there was a big local meeting in town. O'Neill was making his case to represent them. Someone in the audience stood up and expressed the widely shared view that their side would never prevail, not in *Glacier Bay,* let alone later on, should they proceed against Exxon. "Exxon's about the biggest and the richest company in the country," he said, "and so they're bound to hire the best lawyer there is."

"You got it almost right, friend," said O'Neill. "They're the biggest, and the richest, and so I don't doubt that they're going to hire the *second* best lawyer there is."

"That did it for me," says another fisherman. "That guy O'Neill had confidence, optimism, and a sense of humor. I signed right up." And so, over the weeks and months, did many others. In growing numbers they began to bring in their records. Boxes filled with paper that smelled like smoked fish were dragged across the floor of the Claims Office and the contents transformed into coherent claims adhering to a uniform order.

The fishermen came to find that these lawyers weren't so bad. They didn't talk down to anyone, they worked like dogs, they were very quick on the uptake, and they seemed to be having fun. The lawyers, for their part, were revising their notion of fishermen. Hemingway had not proved to be an accurate guide. The people who walked into the Claims Office seemed much more like small businessmen, which is exactly what they were. Many were middle-aged. One out of five were women. Almost all were tough and good-humored and possessed of quiet self-esteem. They were for the most part educated people who were traveling a solo route through life.

Some of these fishermen had been doing very well. Fishing permits sold for as much as $300,000, and earnings each year could be several times higher. Some had become millionaires. The average fisherman's income was about $150,000—and this was for one month of work each year. But the work they did was risky, arduous, and amazingly intense.

The lawyers soon learned that there were two distinct categories of fishermen, the set-netters and the drift-netters. Each category required its own permit and sought the same catch: salmon.

The life cycle of the salmon is one of the great miracles of nature, remarkable beyond even the metaphors it has spawned. Most salmon are hatched in inland rivers. Some have been found in the upper Yukon River, three thousand miles from the sea. When they are less than a year old they begin their migration downstream to salt water. They thrive in the ocean and grow large—some, the king (or chinook) salmon, as big as one hundred pounds, but most, like the sockeye, from five to nine pounds. After perhaps four years far out at sea, they reach the time and urge to spawn but will only do so at the spot where they were hatched. So, traveling great distances, they somehow reach the very stream from which they once emerged and proceed to swim against the current until they reach the headwaters, which is their fixed goal. It is an amazing journey. Swimming upstream is fully as hazardous as it sounds. Their river course is often studded with rapids and falls, not to mention bears. No matter. They manage to leap several times their own length to overcome these obstacles. Most do not make it, and those that do, the Darwinian survivors, are nearly skeletal, for they do not eat once returned to the river, and their fins are broken and battered from the struggle. But they have made it, incredibly, right back to the ancestral pool. And there they spawn. And then they die. They drift downstream and soon perish. But the eggs they leave behind will hatch, and the same amazing cycle will begin anew.

When the large and, presumably, lustful salmon near the shore in search of their ancestral river, they encounter, in recent times, two hazards more menacing than anything in nature. The first is the drift-netters. These are fishermen, usually two at most, in small boats with big nets, which scoop up the fish in great number. And should the salmon make it through or by this obstacle, they will find waiting a second hazard, the set-netters. These fishermen operate from the shore, spreading their nets down to the migrating mass in the sea.

It is a very competitive business. Some set-netters can make millions per year, though the drift-netters (known as drifters) probably have a higher average income. With the set-netters, everything depends on location, location, location. The sites are assigned with great precision. Proximity to a stream outlet is critical. Permits there go for a premium. Other venues are less auspicious: "starvation beach" is a well-known local example.

And as if the salmon didn't have enough problems, drifters have taken to using spotting planes. These aircraft radio to the drifters the exact location of a promising golden swarm—but in code. Others might be listening in.

It is all a lot of trouble, but there is money to be made. The salmon, whether sockeye or chinook, have been in high demand worldwide. They are one of the few edibles to have escaped life's gustatory trade-off, being, as every mother and nutritionist knows, both good to eat and good for you.

The fishermen's claim for damages was very simple: the *Glacier Bay* oil spill had caused them to catch fewer salmon. Even assuming this cause and effect, they still had to have evidence of how many fish they should have caught and how many they actually did catch. The Minnesota team working twelve-hour days in the Claims Office had reduced all the documents and interviews to neat and clear charts, one for each fisherman. Basically, these covered each day's fishing in the period following the *Glacier Bay* spill. One column told what the projected catch should have been, and the next what that catch actually turned out to be. If it was lower, which it was, then the difference was the damage claim. If, instead of 16,000 pounds projected, the catch was 7,232 pounds, then the lost catch was 8,768 pounds for that day. At $1.80 per pound, the damage claim for that day would be $15,782.40. The number of fishermen plaintiffs had grown to many hundreds, and the catch of each of them had been itemized and calculated in this fashion for every single day.

The immediate problem is apparent. How does one accurately "project" the number of fish that should have been caught that day? The Faegre lawyers relied in part on official estimates, and on the number of salmon that had swum past the fishing sites in the past. And how did one know the number of salmon? Because they had been counted. And how does one count salmon moving quickly under water? With sonar counters. The Alaska Department of Fish and Game had installed these devices in the streams. A light beam went across the stream, under water. When a fish broke the beam, it was automatically counted.

It was quickly pointed out that while the sonar count was about one million fish, the fishermen and their lawyers were projecting numbers based on *two* million fish. Those opposing these projections came up with a simple but effective phrase: "You can't catch the same fish twice."

This was not arguable. But the plaintiff lawyers had another response: the sonar counters were inaccurate. The Faegre lawyers, scarcely knowing what a harbinger of future cost and complexity they were unleashing, had found and engaged what they believed was the world's foremost expert on sonar fish counters, Professor Jack Suomala of MIT. They quoted him as saying that the sonar devices had greatly undercounted the fish. Fish didn't swim by in single file in order to be counted, they argued. It's not like lining up for airport security. Instead, they swim abreast—perhaps as many as six alongside one another—so the sonar only counts one.

This was one of many problems that the Claims Office lawyers were facing, and some of them couldn't be solved merely by hiring an expert.

There was, for example, the matter of rivalry between the drifters and the set-netters. One group could, after all, only catch the prey that had escaped the other. So, since Chuck Robinson, when he wasn't practicing law, was a set-net fisherman himself and represented the association of set-netters, the rival group, the Upper Cook Inlet Drifters Association (UCIDA) was represented by an attorney in Anchorage. He had filed a class action suit on behalf of the drifters, though it had yet to be certified. Nolting went to Anchorage and convinced the other firm that an actual damage suit would be more beneficial. So the drifters threw in their lot with the set-netters, and Faegre & Benson ended up representing them both.

Another problem seemed even more formidable. In fact, it seemed unsolvable: a total blockage in the pipeline of money to the fishermen. This was the problem of the turned-off TAPS fund.

When enormous reserves of oil were discovered in Prudhoe Bay, Alaska, in 1968, the happy companies that shared the bounty of this discovery had to decide how to get their oil to its markets. Some people wanted to build a pipeline all the way through Alaska, then all through Canada, and then into the United States. For a number of reasons, this did not happen. But a pipeline was built between the oil sites at Prudhoe Bay and the town of Valdez, eight hundred miles to the south. Valdez is the northernmost ice-free port in the United States, so the oil could be shipped by tanker.

Everyone knew, of course, that putting so much oil in tankers created the potential for a catastrophic spill. So the Transatlantic Pipeline Authorization Act—known as TAPS—contained a plan to pay for the costs of such a spill. It was very simple. For every barrel of oil that they shipped, the oil companies were required to put five cents into a fund. The fund was capped at $100 million, and even at a nickel a barrel, the cap had already been reached. The idea was that after a major spill, the claimants should not have to wait around for years until some court determined their damages. They should be paid right away, from the $100 million fund. If a court should eventually find that some defendant—an oil company or a shipper—was responsible for the spill, then that defendant would have to pay the damage verdict back into the fund. The whole point of the fund was to make sure that those who had been damaged by a spill would get some money quickly.

But several years had passed since the *Glacier Bay* spill, and no one had received a cent. The problem was that the law required the insurer of the ship to come up with the deductible—the first $14 million—and the insurance company had refused to do so. That refusal was before the court, but in the meantime no money was being handed out.

O'Neill and his team were anxious to help. Some of their clients were desperate, their savings exhausted since the spill. They needed money right away. It is true that if they got it they could be plaintiffs no longer: a condition of accepting TAPS money was the abandonment of other legal claims. If they could hold out to trial, they might get more. Still, money was money. A bird in hand. And Faegre & Benson's share would be the same no matter where the award came from. It wasn't only fishermen who had nothing coming in. The Faegre team was spending a fortune and had sent nothing back home but faxes. There were grumblings from the south. A quick cash infusion would be welcomed all around.

So these outsiders tried to figure out how to get the TAPS funds flowing. Everyone in Alaska had given up. But at night, after the Claims Office had closed, when the Minnesota team was sitting around the kitchen table in one of their two sour suites, eating O'Neill's pasta and drinking Washington State wine, they would all talk about the impasse. There had to be a way.

There was. Like most solutions, it was perfectly obvious after someone had thought of it. Gerry Nolting thought of it. The roadblock wasn't the insurer. It was the law. The statute required the insurer to kick in first. So, just change the law. And make the change retroactive, to just before the *Glacier Bay* spill.

How does one change a federal law? It helps to have some voters on one's side. O'Neill and Nolting had a good many voters: the fishermen and their families and their friends. This was more than a mere blip, given Alaska's exiguous electorate.

Soon, postcards and letters and phone calls were landing in Washington from their launch sites around Cook Inlet. They were landing in two places—the offices of Alaska Senator Ted Stevens and his colleague, Congressman Don Young. The epistolary volley was followed by the arrival of the troops; O'Neill and Nolting flew from Alaska to plead their case in person. "Plead" does not quite cover it. Both carrot and stick were deployed. And it was not that hard a sell, asking elected representatives from Alaska to send nontax dollars back home. So it came to pass that the law was amended retroactively.

If only everything were that easy. But some matters did not lend themselves to quick and creative solutions. Some were like quicksand. In terms of time and money, the most formidable task so far was now at hand: the taking of depositions.

Those fortunate enough never to have been deposed, and who therefore imagine that the word applies only to the fate of unpopular monarchs, may require some explanation. "Deposed" means being questioned—on the record. Depositions are like minitrials, but with neither judge nor jury. The person being deposed shows up at a specified time and place. The opposing lawyers ask a battery of questions. The person being deposed is represented by counsel, too, who may give advice about answers or object to the questions. A stenographer is present, and everything is taken down. The purpose of the deposition is twofold: to save the court's time (without depositions, trials would be vastly longer than at present) and to permit each side to elicit the information needed to develop its case before trial.

There is another reason for depositions, though no one admits to it. It is to bankrupt the other side. Depositions consume vast quantities of lawyer-time, and therefore are very expensive. Some defendants demand many depositions, all day long, for a protracted and crowded period, in order to exhaust the plaintiff's resources—fiscal and physical—and force a cheap settlement. This often works.

It didn't work with the Faegre team—not that the defendants didn't try. The TAPS fund was represented by Wilmer, Cutler & Pickering, one of the largest and one of the best firms in Washington, D.C. (It was the same firm that had made young Captain O'Neill his first civilian job offer, and had he accepted it he very likely now might have been opposing the fishermen.) The Wilmer, Cutler lawyers noticed (which is legalese for scheduled) twenty depositions in a single day, every day, for two weeks. This strategy may have arisen from the assumption that the plaintiffs didn't *have* twenty different lawyers. That assumption was correct. Frantic phone calls were made to Minneapolis. Young Faegre associates quickly boarded planes. The Robinson firm put its usual work on hold. On the first day of the depositions, each of the twenty conference rooms was graced by the presence of a qualified plaintiff lawyer. Some, to be sure, were less conversant with fishing terms than others, but the shot across the bow had been returned. After the second day, the rest of that deposition schedule was canceled. Henceforth, depositions would be scheduled more reasonably over time.

But still there would be as many of them. The list of plaintiffs had grown to eight hundred. And other players in the drama would be deposed as well. Before all the oil spill cases had reached the courts, the Faegre team would take part in a thousand depositions.

Most of them were very much alike. In fact, there came to be an almost nightmarish aspect to it all for those caught up in the banal repetition. And one can only imagine what the typical salmon fisherman thought of the process. Summoned by a very official-looking document, with the name of the court affixed, to an office assigned for the purpose, he encountered the glacial stares of some of the most expensive lawyers in the land. And they looked it: dressed to kill. At the fishermen's end of the table were lawyers who increasingly resembled the fishermen themselves, except that they were younger and more haggard. Now safely distanced from the Faegre home office, they were dressing like the natives. The TAPS fund could send a fresh team of lawyers to each deposition, but the fishermen could not. O'Neill's team was stretched very thin indeed, rushing from deposition to deposition, objecting to or exasperated by the same apparently pointless questions ("How big is your boat?" "What time did you set out?"), sick with exhaustion, bored by redundancy, aghast at the certainty of months and years of the same.

And thus was the time spent in Soldatna. Problems arose and were solved, and a remarkable amount of work was somehow done. Life was very crowded, but not grim. There was time for play as well. As if the heavens had acquiesced in the protracted hours of the Claims Office, the midnight sun shone for many hours after closing. There was time for softball and running, and hiking in the glorious country that surrounded the flat little town. The Minnesotans played the Robinson firm in basketball, despite a very significant height advantage for the local team. O'Neill, a zero handicap golfer, and some of the others used the local course. There was a bar with a band—the Night Watch—where sometimes they went as a group. Kathy McCune was only twenty and afraid of being carded, so O'Neill, who was obviously of drinking age, always held her hand when they went through the door and the couple would be passed through. Some of the young women went out dancing quite a bit, often returning home only a few hours before it was time to be at the Claims Office for another long day. (Each morning before opening the office, Sarah Armstrong had to sweep the moose dung off the front porch.)

Also, though it would seem the last thing in the world to which their labor had disposed them, they all regularly went fishing. They fished the streams for salmon. It was the best place there was to do so. People came from all over the world to fish the Kenai River. The largest salmon are the kings, and the largest king salmon seem to favor the Kenai River. Their preference has been acknowledged by the Alaska Department of Fish and Game, which everywhere else certifies any fish over fifty pounds as trophy class but has ruled that on the Kenai it must be seventy-five pounds. There are just too many sixty-pounders. Some close to that were hauled in by the delighted Minnesotans, struggling under the summer sun at one in the morning.

The transplanted lawyers went commercial fishing, too, on several occasions. Loyal to the Robinson firm, they were set-netters. They helped lower the nets into the water and watched them spread. It was amazing when the fish appeared—an endless gleaming hoard glimpsed just beneath the surface, swelling the huge net in seconds. The fish were quickly hauled in and the net cast again and again, like a giant panning for gold.

There was a movie theater in town, the TV sets in their apartments had cable, and some out-of-town papers could be found at Carrs grocery store in Kenai. But basically, aside from work, there wasn't much to do. Soldatna had a population of about five thousand and so did nearby Kenai, but both looked like small new strip malls on the outskirts of some factory town (but without the factory). None of those who had so eagerly answered the summons to adventure had foreseen how wrenching would be the dislocation in their lives. They genuinely liked their clients, but life here was so very different from back home. The Twin Cities are a major cultural center for their vast hinterland; there had been restaurants and boutiques and parties and thousands of young professionals like themselves. Here the big treat was the occasional birthday dinner at The Four Seasons, the best restaurant in the area, where perhaps they dined on fish that they'd helped catch.

Their isolation brought them closer to each other. They usually took their evening meal together, crowded around the kitchen table in the Redoubt Arms. This was the best time. They all praised O'Neill's cooking. His halibut was a treat. They drank and talked and laughed and planned. But there were no opening nights at the Ordway in St. Paul, no Neiman Marcus, no Bach Society, no glitter or gossip or reminder of home. For those with children, there were no T-ball games, no homework on the kitchen table, no first toddling steps, no *Goodnight Moon.*

They were lonely, and they were away from home, and they were young. The women were besieged with suitors, and some were more involved than others. Sarah Armstrong met and became close to one of the plaintiffs, Dean Osmar, who was celebrated throughout Alaska as the daring winner of the Iditarod, the classic annual dog-sled race of a thousand miles from Anchorage to Nome. Within a year of her arrival in Soldatna, Katie Roessler was married to Joe Malatesta, Jr., the son of the investigator at the Robinson firm. Almost every life seemed altered by the exodus. Chris Johnson went to work for a judge in Kenai, and only very recently departed for Texas. Lori Wagner would be separated and ultimately divorced. Steve Schroer, who had been divorced before going to Alaska, started dating again. And Brian O'Neill and Ruth Nissen, who had left spouses back home, began a relationship that would lead to marriage. Gerry Nolting spent a lot of time commuting back to Minneapolis to be with his wife and daughter and, eventually, daughters.

They did not spend all their time in Soldatna. When the fishing season ended, some fishermen returned to their homes in Washington and Oregon. The team members flew out for many depositions there.

And of course they got to go home. Nolting, who had an infant daughter, went nearly every weekend. The others, too, made fairly regular trips to see family and friends and to catch up on things in the office. It soon became apparent that some colleagues had their reservations about the Alaska venture. The team had been gone a long time. Its efforts had been very expensive—many hundreds of thousands of dollars already. There were those in the home office who noted that all the money was going out and none was coming in. This venture had the approval of the Management Committee, but that didn't mean that everyone else thought it was a good idea. Some were appalled that the firm's august name had been featured in radio ads. Soliciting clients! When the wayfarers stopped into the office, the looks they received were not always friendly.

Their biggest concern, though, was back in Alaska. A few months after their arrival there, the Exxon oil had finally moved around Kenai Peninsula and into Cook Inlet. The salmon fisherman's nightmare had become reality. Would there ever be another fishing season? Those who had paid small fortunes for the permits now lived in fear.

There were those who were ready to address those fears. From the time that the *Exxon Valdez* had run aground, lawyers from all over the nation had descended on the area in numbers and with avarice unmatched since the Klondike gold rush of 1897. They were as hardy and rapacious as the prospectors who preceded them, though much better dressed. And every one of them was busy panning for clients. Like the oil itself, they spread thickly and relentlessly along the troubled shores of the inlet. Some fishermen whose season had been ruined by the spill now sought solace in the region's drafty bars, but they no longer had to buy their own drinks. The affable strangers who did the honors were, in a manner of speaking, fishermen themselves, and their season had not just been closed. Quite the contrary.

There were hundreds of lawyers after Exxon plaintiffs. You could see them everywhere, on the streets and in restaurants, and occupying every room in the best hotels. They invaded the waiting rooms of all the local law firms, seeking alliances. They were on the shore and by the docks, greeting fishermen. They sensed that Exxon would be the biggest defendant of all time, and they hustled and jousted to get to be part of the action.

Though the mating dance of their competitors was swirling all about them, O'Neill and his team stuck primly to their work in the Claims Office. They were working on the *Glacier Bay* case. They were not asking anyone to sign up with them to sue Exxon. Of course, they didn't have to. They already had eight hundred clients, the heart of the local fishing community. Those very same people could sue Exxon, too, when their lawyers were ready.

It might be better, though, to get *Glacier Bay* out of the way first. The Exxon oil had indeed made its way up the inlet, with disastrous impact on the fishermen. The entire drifter fishing season had to be canceled in 1989. The *Glacier Bay* spill had been in 1987. It would be difficult, psychologically as well as tactically, to argue that the Exxon oil had polluted clean water at the same time one was arguing that those waters had not yet recovered from the *Glacier Bay* spill.

So, though the shoreline was being transformed by the biggest cleanup of all time, an effort that would cost Exxon about two billion dollars, and everyone was talking about nothing else but the monstrous spill, the Minnesota lawyers stayed in their makeshift office and threw themselves into preparation of the *Glacier Bay* case. It may not have seemed possible, but even more depositions were added to the crowded schedule.

As it turned out, very few of the *Glacier Bay* clients ever got to court. The TAPS fund had started kicking in. The effort to persuade the Congress to amend its law retroactively was now paying off—literally. In the summer of 1990, the TAPS administrators offered O'Neill's clients cash compensation for their claims.

Many didn't think the offers were high enough. The prevaling feeling was that the TAPS fund was heavily influenced by the oil companies who (involuntarily) funded it, that it was being used to pay off the fishermen cheaply (rather than quickly, as intended). Regardless of this perception, however, half the fishermen—about four hundred—agreed to take the TAPS money and drop out of the *Glacier Bay* case. Some thought their claims were not as strong as others, and some just needed the money right away. They received between thirty and fifty thousand dollars apiece.

Those who had turned down the TAPS money were resigned to going to trial. But then something happened that they had not foreseen. The early Exxon claims were before the same judge who was presiding over the *Glacier Bay* claims. He had seen how quickly half those *Glacier Bay* claims had disappeared through the payment of TAPS funds. Perhaps this might happen in the Exxon case as well. He asked the lawyers in the Exxon matter if they thought this was a good idea.

The plaintiff lawyers had to tone down their response a little for the judge. These wary advocates were the cutting edge of the national class action bar. Many saw the whole TAPS mechanism as a tool of the oil industry, a crafty way to chisel on payments. They managed to get this point across to the court.

The TAPS fund people were stung. Their integrity had been called into question. This was outrageous! They then proceeded to go back to the *Glacier Bay* holdouts and offer them more money. Much more. This time, the average payment was between fifty and eighty thousand dollars apiece. About three hundred of the *Glacier Bay* plaintiffs took the money. That left only one hundred still willing to go on to trial.

Why had the TAPS fund sweetened the offer? Perhaps to show that it was serious about compensating fully for actual loss. Perhaps because the plaintiffs' turndown of the first offer had signaled the sincerity of their claims. Perhaps because the TAPS administrators wanted to handle the Exxon claims, too, and saw their second offer as a way of answering the plaintiff lawyers' objections.

Whatever the motive, the money was paid. There was a lot of it. Faegre & Benson's fees for the two TAPS payouts were close to four million dollars. This more than paid for all the long hours that the Alaska team had worked. And the money came just in time to help fatten the year-end bonuses of all the partners back in Minneapolis. This year, at the firm's annual dinner in February, their reception would be warmer than before. The naysayers would be silenced, at least for the time being.

Not that the team could now take it easy. With the TAPS fund out of the way, the trial loomed ahead. It was almost a year away, but when they thought of all the things they had to do to get ready for it, there was the gut-wrenching fear that they could not make it in time. This wasn't like sending carefully prepared damage claims off to a TAPS committee and seeing what offer came back. This was a *trial*. With a jury!

And a judge. The presiding judge in both the *Glacier Bay* and Exxon cases was the Chief Judge of the United States District Court for the District of Alaska, the Honorable H. (for Hezekiah) Russel Holland. An imposing presence—six foot three, gaunt, and flamboyantly bearded—he was then fifty-four and had been a federal judge for a number of years. One courtroom reporter says that he resembles Abe Lincoln with a white beard, and he does—except that, beard and all, he looks and moves like a far younger man. There is an almost palpable alertness to him.

Their fate would be in his hands. They scrutinized every source, trying to figure out whether he was friend or foe. What they learned was not encouraging. True, he had in common with O'Neill both Michigan birth and graduation from its law school. But from that point the resemblance diverged.

Judge Holland had ascended to the bench along the most time-honored path; he had been the law partner of a future U.S. Senator, the very same Ted Stevens who had helped O'Neill and Nolting amend the TAPS legislation, and who had been pleased to recommend his friend's appointment to President Reagan. When Stevens first was sent to Washington, Holland had taken over his law practice, which included the representation of a good many oil companies, some of them major, like Mobil. He had remained a member of the Petroleum Club.

This was not auspicious. Still, he did have the reputation of being a good judge, hardworking and fair. Good lawyers know that good judges are far less influenced by their associations than by the facts of a particular case. O'Neill and Nolting had met Holland several times at pretrial

meetings in Anchorage, where his court sat. He had been warm and cordial—it seemed to them that he was relieved to find two big-firm corporate counsel amidst the more flamboyant class action types crowding his
courtroom. If this was so, it was not entirely comforting. If the judge favored defense lawyers, they were in trouble.

Well, the judge would do what he would do. In the meantime, they had
to hustle to get ready for the trial. They were back into depositions, sometimes involving the same fishermen who had been deposed before. They
had to get everything right. They found new expert witnesses, and went
to see them, and sat down with the experts who already were on board
and whose technical jargon could be maddening. First you had to understand what they were saying and master the terminology yourself, and
then, patiently, politely—for these experts were the masters in their
fields—help prune their language gradually into cogent English, get them
to speak in words that the jurors would comprehend, and then accept.

The most critical job was deciding which plaintiffs to use. There were
one hundred fishermen left in the case. But the trial would not involve
them all. There would be only sixteen plaintiffs. Both sides had agreed to
this. Rather than go through the time, trouble, and expense of having all
one hundred plaintiffs appear in court serially to be examined and cross-
examined and have their claims scrutinized through the opposite ends of
the adversary telescope, there had been a temporary outbreak of common
sense. The sixteen plaintiffs who would appear and have their claims ad-
judicated were standing in for everyone else. They were representative of
all the different types of fishermen who were still seeking redress. Some
were set-netters, and some were drifters. The drifters were further divided into subcategories. Some were long-time fishermen, and some
were inexperienced. Some fished every day of the season, and others less
regularly. Some used one kind of boat, and some used another. Every
variant that could lead to a distinction in the claims brought forth a different person to be included within the sixteen.

It was easier to decide on the categories than on who the actual plaintiffs should be. The lawyers for both sides, by mutual agreement, had a
say. Some claims within a class were stronger than others, and some fishermen made better witnesses. There was a lot of give-and-take. O'Neill
struggled to include as many women as possible, but most had accepted
the TAPS payments, and he was able to produce only four for the trial.

The trial was scheduled for Anchorage, before Judge Holland, the latter part of August 1991. But first the plaintiffs put on a trial of their own. In July they went through an elaborate and secret procedure aimed at simulating what they were likely to find in court.

There was a time when trial lawyers would select jurors and argue the case relying primarily on their own instincts. No longer. In large, complex cases, many advocates, however skilled, now hire outside experts to test market the product before the trial itself. The focus groups and feedback that are used to sell cereal and candidates are now employed to try out legal arguments and select jurors as well.

A whole cottage industry of experts has arisen to replicate a trial before it has occurred. O'Neill and Nolting engaged the jury consultant firm of Tsongas & Associates, from Portland, Oregon. Meeting with Joyce Tsongas and her team in Minneapolis and Portland, the Faegre lawyers sought to find the themes that might prevail at the trial, now only a month away. When these had been laid out and discussed and honed, and the most promising selected, it was time to try them out on a mock jury.

Three juries, actually. The Tsongas team went up to Anchorage and selected jurors, using exactly the same techniques that the federal court would employ. They selected thirty-six Alaskans, and separated them into three different juries of twelve. Each of those juries then sat and watched a video of the trial—of the opening and closing statements, anyway, and summaries of the exhibits. On tape, O'Neill was the lawyer for the plaintiffs and Nolting made the arguments for the defense. After the tape had ended, each of the juries deliberated and finally came up with a verdict. That is to say, three verdicts.

All of them were bad. Not merely bad, disastrous. O'Neill and Nolting were shocked. Two of the mock juries awarded no damages at all to the fishermen. The third gave only a minimal amount.

Like drowning men, their past lives passed before them—the last two years of their lives, anyway. Was all the work, all those hours, all that money, for nothing? What would their partners think if they zeroed out? What would their *clients* think—all those fishermen who had turned down the TAPS settlements, in part because they had faith in their lawyers.

They *couldn't* lose. Panic turned to desperation and then worked itself up to resolve. There was still a month. So they'd bombed out of town. Rewrite!

Wasn't the point of jury consultation to ferret out the bad news before it was too late? So with much renewed attention, they listened to their experts explain why the juries had rejected their pleas. Each jury had been painstakingly debriefed in an effort to find the problem.

There was more than one problem, according to the data, but by far the most serious was that the jurors thought that the fishermen were greedy. The *Glacier Bay* claims were for losses in a single fishing season: 1987. Yet the spill had caused fishing to be canceled on only two days of that season. And despite the spill, it had been a wonderful season. The fishermen had set an all-time record for the size of their catch. So how had they been damaged?

O'Neill thought he had answered that in his video presentation. He had pointed out that this was no ordinary season; the fish had appeared in astonishing numbers. It seemed that all the salmon in the sea had decided to come home and spawn. Some fishermen caught twice as many fish as in the past. O'Neill had argued that this meant not only that the canceled two days had cost them a mint, but also that the days when they did fish would have been even more profitable had it not been for the effects of the spill.

The jurors hadn't bought it. The best year ever should have been even better? This looked a lot like greed.

The lawyers were certain that their claims were fair. So it now became a question of restating them. New themes were developed. Everything had to be personalized. The fishermen had to be seen not as greedy entrepreneurs but as people, people like the jurors, families mortgaging their homes to finance one successful season, fathers and sons, fathers and daughters, risking everything on one season, and when the season of a lifetime miraculously did occur, failing to reap the full reward for all that they had risked.

The lawyers learned to describe fishing like farming. You needed one good year because lean years were sure to follow. And when a great year did occur, it couldn't be seen as ample return for one year's effort but rather as a once-in-a-lifetime opportunity.

Another problem that had troubled all three juries concerned the price of fish. A significant part of the plaintiffs' claim was compensation for the lowered prices they had received. In 1987 the fishermen had netted the largest salmon catch in history, but the price paid for salmon by the canners had sharply fallen. Of course, said the jurors: supply and demand. The market was glutted, so the price went down. That's what happens. No, no, no, said the plaintiffs (at least to each other); you've got it all wrong. Cook Inlet sockeye salmon was so unique that increasing its quantity would not reduce its value. Though this was fervently believed by the lawyers, they conceded that it would be a hard sell. And, indeed, the jury wasn't buying it. Perhaps the processors could verify the unique-taste theory. But other strategies had to be developed to convince the jury that lower prices had been caused not by more salmon but from a fear of oil contamination.

A third problem was the jurors themselves. Some of them didn't like fishermen. The debriefings had suggested just who these might be. As Joyce Tsongas put it, "You don't select a jury, you de-select a jury." That's what all this work was for. The data showed that sports fishermen could be hostile to commercial fishermen, who were, after all, netting the prey before it could reach their lures. Notes were taken on which jurors to reject.

The plaintiffs alone spent hundreds of thousands of dollars on jury-selection experts. These may well have been the most effective dollars spent. Nothing in a trial—no argument, no surprise evidence—matters more than selecting the right jury. Now that selection has been made less chancy through consultants and simulation. Is this fair? Does it skew the search for justice? Our system assumes that justice is served by vigilant adversaries striving mightily to win. Jurors never have been picked at random; both sides have always striven to detect sympathy or bias. Are they not supposed to do so with accuracy? Those who are disgusted by the expertization of societal choice—the focus group before deciding whether to veto the bill—may find some solace in the fact that human beings continue to escape the categorical boxes in which some experts place them. The most scientifically selected juries still provide surprises, as we shall later see.

The month passed very quickly. They weren't sure that there would be enough time. The themes had to be redone, the exhibits revised, the experts questioned, new opening and closing statements written and rehearsed. With less than two weeks until the trial, the team went up to Anchorage and installed itself in the Quality Inn, which had hard-line computer capability and therefore could be linked to the main data base back in Minneapolis.

By mid-August the sun shone nearly all the time, but days passed when they didn't even see it. And when they did leave the Quality Inn, it was to take themselves and two years' worth of work on the ten-minute walk to the courthouse. It was time for the trial.

They were in Courtroom Number Two, which was the one always used by Judge Holland. They shook hands with their opposing counsel, Mike Woodell and Bill Ingelson from the firm of Bradbury, Bliss & Reardon, of Seattle and Anchorage. Trying the case for the plaintiffs was Brian O'Neill.

Every seat in the courtroom was filled. Many people were waiting out in the hall. Some of those in the spectator section were fishermen, of course, but a remarkable number were lawyers. The word was out that this case could be a harbinger for all the Exxon litigation coming up. Judge Holland was presiding over both matters. The damage issues were very similar. The inclinations of an Alaska jury might be revealed. And this trial would give both sides of the rapidly expanding oil spill bar a chance to look over this so-called hotshot who was going to single-handedly argue the plaintiffs' case. Everyone was watching carefully, and some were taking notes.

The jury selection took only two days. O'Neill thought he had rejected the problem jurors that the consultant had warned about, the sports fishermen and all those people in local businesses that were dependent on the prosperity of the oil industry. But you never could tell.

O'Neill put the sixteen plaintiff fishermen on first. Each took the stand and was questioned by O'Neill about their damages and then cross-examined by the opposing lawyers. Their risks, dreams, dependents, and mortgages were not ignored. The fishermen's testimony took up a lot of time. It was necessary and important but far from being the whole case.

Perhaps the key issue was that of price. All the research indicated that the jury would doubt that low fish prices should be blamed on the oil spill. So next O'Neill called his witnesses from the State of Alaska Department of Natural Resources, who testified that fish buyers had been very concerned about the spill; if oil from the fish got into the chain of commerce it could destroy the market.

This was the argument that O'Neill kept hammering home, in his opening and closing statements and by the witnesses and experts he questioned throughout the trial: the drop in salmon price was due to the oil spill, not surplus quantity. Both American canneries and Japanese buyers were afraid of what would happen if oil were found in the fish they had to sell to consumers. It would be economic catastrophe. To hedge against this risk, they had lowered the price they were willing to pay for the catch. Also, the careful search for contamination had slowed down the canning process, and this had affected the canners' capacity to pay.

O'Neill called to the stand several processors who supported these arguments. And he called on expert witnesses as well. A fishery economist from the University of Washington talked knowingly about price and laid the blame for its decline on the spill. Other experts followed him to address the slippery subject of all those conjectural salmon that somehow had gotten away. Jack Suomala, the sonar expert, and Dr. Don Rogers, a fisheries biologist known locally as "Dr. Salmon," talked about how to really count fish.

After every expert and witness and objection had been heard, and the closing arguments, so often rehearsed, given for the final time, the twelve jurors rose and left the room. And with them went the trial. They were the trial now, they were everything, especially the verdict they were about to make. They were the repository of all that had been argued and asserted and denied. They alone would say which experts should be believed. They alone would determine how much each fisherman would get. They alone were the finders of fact. Theirs was the job of declaring the truth.

Until they came back, there was nothing to do. There was busy work, there was cleanup, but basically the only task was to wait.

It was not as easy as it sounds. No one knew how long the jury would be out. It could be days. One couldn't just stay seated in the courtroom. Everyone left, but they were careful to leave word of where they could be reached as soon as the jury returned.

For O'Neill and Nolting the anguish of waiting was protracted not only by time, but distance. They couldn't wait around for the verdict. As soon as the jury was gone they left Anchorage and flew back to Minneapolis. Each had an urgent reason for returning, something more urgent even than the trial. Nolting's wife was about to go into labor, and he wanted to be at her side. O'Neill was getting divorced. His marriage had been in serious trouble even before the oil spill cases, but absence in Alaska had not helped. He and Ruth Nissen had fallen in love. She was bearing their child. They wanted to marry, and the court date had been set for the divorce from Jane.

Other members of the team had stayed behind. Steve Schroer was to call the second he had any news. He made sure that the courthouse staff always knew where he was. And then he and the others just continued to wait.

The worst thing about the waiting was the rumors. Everywhere the Minnesotans went there were other lawyers from all over the country, and each of them had an opinion about the case. Some were more tactful than others, but it was impossible to escape the impression that O'Neill and his team were going into the tank. The lawyers for the oil companies were one thing, but it was dispiriting to hear this from the plaintiff bar. And yet there was no question about it. They heard it by innuendo and they heard it directly. These newcomers from Minnesota were overreaching. They were asking for too much money. They would never get it. They wouldn't get a fraction of it. Maybe twenty percent of what they were asking for. Maybe nothing at all. They were asking the jury to repeal the law of supply and demand. A smaller claim is a surer win. These guys didn't know the score.

The jury had gone out on a Tuesday afternoon. Wednesday came and passed, and everyone said that some delay was to be expected. With Thursday it was the same. On Friday people were a little testy. The weekend came. The jury did not meet on the weekend. The lawyers went to their rooms, and went out to dinner, and ate too much, and didn't eat at all, and encountered stares and smirks from their colleagues in the lobby, and wondered what the hell the jury was up to.

Monday came. There really was a limit to human endurance, and there were those who felt certain that they had reached it.

In Minneapolis it was five thirty in the evening. Gerry Nolting was working in his office. O'Neill was gone for awhile, something about the divorce. Nolting's phone rang. He wondered if it was his wife; it was about time.

It was Steve Schroer in Anchorage. His voice was strained. He said, "Gerry, I'm calling from a pay phone. Get a pen and pencil quick."

"Cut the shit," said Nolting. "Tell me: is it good or is it bad?"

"It's tremendous," said Schroer.

And it was. The fishermen got just about everything they had been asking for. Theirs was a stunning victory, far better than what most lawyers were predicting. The jury had bought all O'Neill's arguments! Half the damages awarded were for the decline in the price for fish. When they were debriefed, the jurors repeatedly talked about the fact that the abundant season of 1987 should have been a once-in-a-lifetime opportunity. Even the lawyers' language had become the jury's.

Only sixteen plaintiffs had been involved in the case. The other eighty-four were still waiting in the wings. But the victory of this first group had been so sweeping, the precedent so clear, the test group so representative, that further resistance by the defendants would be futile. Settlement of the remaining cases soon followed, and on terms very close to the jury verdict.

It was all over very quickly. The fishermen represented by O'Neill ended up with fifty-one million dollars. The fees to Faegre & Benson for its *Glacier Bay* representation, after the Robinson firm and other firms had taken their cut, and after expenses, were eight and a half million dollars—twice the value of the many thousands of hours they had worked. This was by far the largest single fee that the Minneapolis firm had ever received. There was jubilation in the halls, a very merry Christmas in the offing, and heartfelt, if fleeting, praise from even the sternest skeptics.

Most of the praise was going to O'Neill, the man of the hour. But he seemed less ecstatic than those who now pumped his hand. He saw his victory as only the first step toward the infinitely larger quarry of Exxon. He was exhausted, and knew that more years of even greater exhaustion lay ahead.

And he knew that victory had costs as well as fees. His divorce and remarriage had occurred before the final settlement was signed. He was happy with Ruth, but there was pain at the estrangement from his children. He knew that his restless, rootless life consisted mostly of immersion in work.

When asked about the dislocations in his life, he looks bemused and quotes a Yukon poem by Robert Service, "The Men That Don't Fit In."

There's a race of men that don't fit in,
A race that can't stay still.
So they break the hearts of kith and kin
And they roam the world at will.

Perhaps. But O'Neill was not about to roam the world. The path ahead was indeed a long one, but it went on in a straight line. It led to the great goal of his life, of which, ever since he first heard of the *Exxon Valdez* spill, he had never lost sight. The victory others were cheering was only the qualifying round. The main event was far, far in the future. But now he knew the way was clear.

7

Swimming Upstream

*G*lacier Bay was forever behind them. Their first goal, their
major goal, was now at last their only goal: the *Exxon Valdez*
case. However distant, it still loomed large on the horizon, a
monster daring any to approach.

No sooner had the Minnesotans embarked upon this final quest than
they found their way blocked by strong opposition. The lawyers who con-
fronted them were equal to the battle over limitless stakes—and deeply
suspicious of this youthful team now entering the contest. When the Faegre lawyers first encountered these high-powered eastern trial counsel,
the looks they received were intimidating, and meant to be. Not exactly
sneers, but surely the hint of condescension, the unasked but unmistak-
able question of who the hell are you to be playing in this league. Those
thinking that question were the scarred and hoary veterans of decades of
major litigation, the survivors of many a protracted siege. They weren't
about to let these newcomers prevail.

They were very tough. So tough indeed that one could only wonder
what the Exxon lawyers were going to be like. For these stern gatekeep-
ers, standing in the path of O'Neill and his friends, were not, in fact,
members of the defense team. They were plaintiff lawyers, the leaders of

the national class action bar, with their own fishermen clients and technically on the same side of the case.

On the same side, and with the same foe, but you couldn't really call them allies. All the time that O'Neill and the others had been conquering the slopes of *Glacier Bay,* these other plaintiff lawyers had been chiseling footholds in the hard surface of the vastly higher Exxon peak. They were not themselves a team, but rather a large and acrimonious collection of individualists, even among themselves fiercely disputatious. But on one point clearly all agreed: they didn't want anyone else sharing their base camp.

That's what happens in the really big cases. Drawn like flies to honey by the sweet golden smell, they arrive from every direction. And their most ferocious battles are not with the defendant but over the protection of their own hard-won pieces of turf. They know above all else that there are only so many slices to a pie, and if someone else comes in for an additional slice, that newcomer's share could well come out of their own.

Their real fight is often with each other, over who will get the larger share. For at the end of the road, if things go well, there will someday be a verdict, an award to be divided among all the plaintiff teams. Who gets what will be determined finally by the court. Each share will be awarded partly by the number of clients they represent, but a less precise factor will be how much each lawyer contributed to the case. This is to some degree a matter of opinion, but there are things a resourceful lawyer can do to help ensure a larger portion of the award. It is very helpful to have a visible role in the leadership of the case, in the trial itself and in the preparation for the trial. Who does what in these regards will be decided by orders of the court, but the court cannot rule in a vacuum. The plaintiffs themselves must try and work out a pecking order of participation, and, if they can do that, seek to get the court's assent.

So there is an extraordinary amount of jockeying for position. From the day after the *Exxon Valdez* spill, and for more than two years thereafter, this is what had occupied their time. It was not a pretty sight. Elbows were applied. All the time that the Faegre team had remained holed up in the Claims Office in Soldatna carefully analyzing each fisherman's claim in turn, all the hours spent on planes in search of experts, all the endless days of defending depositions, had been differently employed by the other plaintiff lawyers. They had been busy, too, but not in actually trying a case. Theirs had been a full-time internecine struggle to find and keep some incremental advantage, the staking out of claims to a putative mother lode, what looked to be the biggest case of all time.

The same analysis that had led the Management Committee of Faegre & Benson to authorize the suit in the *Glacier Bay* case had been used by the national plaintiff bar in appraising its chances against Exxon. The same three tests had to be met: liability, causation, and ability to pay. It was easier to apply these tests in the *Exxon Valdez* case. It was more than easy; it was stimulating. Liability? This was the hardest. The captain had been drinking, and they would argue that Exxon was accountable. Causation? That was open and shut. The fishing season had not been *affected;* it had been *closed.* And last, of course, in the ascending scale of attractiveness, was ability to pay. This was *Exxon!* One of the largest corporations in the world. The twenty-sixth largest financial entity of any kind in the world, including countries. The deepest pockets in the history of litigation. And if *punitive* damages should be awarded, there was no end to how high that could be. Billions. Many billions. The class action lawyers had lived their lives for such a moment, and now the opportunity was here at hand. They had found their clients. They had filed their suits.

Most important, they had formed their committees. It was what they had been doing for the last two years. Litigation committees are the key to positioning for vying lawyers bringing suit. Getting on a committee is itself an important step. Being assigned a key job on the committee is even better, an important chit to be noted when the money is being handed out. *Chairing* a committee is of course the best of all, a title to be pointed to when the time for apportionment comes.

But first one had to be *on* a committee, and so many were applying for the chance. The number of committees grew, but there were more bodies than berths. There was a Discovery Committee, a Legal Committee, a Damages Committee, a Settlement Committee, and, of course, an Executive Committee.

These were all in place by the time O'Neill and his band arrived. The committee appointments had been made. Nevertheless, these new arrivals were knocking on the door. They wanted to be part of the action. Far more, though the entrenched plaintiff lawyers would have been apoplectic had they known it, O'Neill was not auditioning for a respectable supporting role: he intended to be the star of the production. From the moment in his car, with the decoy ducks on the seat behind him, when he first heard on the radio about the spill, he had grasped the grail that fate had offered. He knew exactly where he was going.

But did *they?* The chairmen of the committees, those who through extraordinary effort were already at the head of the line, could be pardoned for some reluctance at the arrival of these outsiders.

To begin with, the entrenched leaders of the plaintiff group were unashamedly class action lawyers. The newcomers had a direct action case. They actually knew who their clients were. Would the directness of their aim be compatible with the amorphous net of all the others?

Even worse was *who* they were. They were Capulets in Montague country. They were defense lawyers. They were from Faegre & Benson. The other plaintiff lawyers had heard of this firm. Some had opposed it in the past, sometimes successfully and sometimes not. But all shared the same opinion: this was the enemy. At any rate, these were the lawyers of the enemy—these were the gray suits who charged by the hour and had no sense of humor. No doubt they were very good, but this wasn't the sort of thing they would be good *at.* White Men Can't Jump. And even if they could turn themselves into plaintiff lawyers for the oil-spill cases, and even if they were great at it, they weren't from the same side of the street. They were from a different culture and a different class. They were viewed with deep suspicion by those ready to impute disdain.

On the other hand. Many trial lawyers are emotional, but they don't go by emotion. They weigh the odds. The veteran plaintiff lawyers who had invested much time in Alaska, and some cash, now weighed the odds. It soon became clear that there were several good reasons for admitting the applicants into their ranks.

First, *Glacier Bay.* These people had just won a case. An oil-spill case. And they hadn't merely settled it favorably. They had gone to *trial.* In front of Judge Holland, the very same judge who was hearing the *Exxon Valdez* case. And they hadn't merely won; they had won *big.* Much more money than anyone had expected. They had deposed hundreds of fishermen. They seemed to understand all about damages. They could turn cardboard boxes full of oily invoices into neat little charts and graphs. They unquestionably knew how to try this kind of case.

That achievement had earned much respect. The plaintiff class action bar contained some lawyers of consummate skill and extensive courtroom experience. But it contained some others who had never in their lives tried a major jury trial to its conclusion. They might be praised as veteran litigators, they may have grown rich in their profession, but some of them were not all that familiar with a courtroom. These lawyers were skilled at finding the clients before anyone else did, and then settling the case before the expenses had really mounted up. To them, the company of those who had actually managed a big case to and through its successful jury conclusion was more than a little comforting. At the very least, *Glacier Bay* was a lucky talisman; better to keep its sorcerers close at hand.

A second reason for accepting Faegre & Benson was that it, too, had deep pockets. It wasn't that the other plaintiff lawyers were poor; a number of them made far more money every year than any Faegre partner. But theirs was for the most part individual wealth. Faegre & Benson was a large and prosperous law firm, with a good steady income stream from noncontingent corporate clients. More to the point, it was *willing* to finance a significant part of the case. It had kept a very skilled team in the field full time for two years in order to win *Glacier Bay.* Plus God knows what it had spent on experts and data processing. It had backup. It had staying power. Its winning team was now committed to the same effort, perhaps augmented, in *Exxon Valdez.* No matter how much money these other lawyers may have had access to, it's hard to turn down someone who is willing to help foot the bill.

Third, there was Brian O'Neill. He had tried the whole *Glacier Bay* case by himself. Many of the Exxon plaintiff lawyers had sat there in court and watched him. They had egos and they were competitive, but they had to admit that that O'Neill knew the score. And they knew a winner when they saw one. O'Neill was their kind of winner: cocky, confident, relentless, a consummate showman who never lost sight of the ball. He might be grinning all the time, but you could tell—and this was the greatest compliment—that deep down he was really *tough.* How did a guy like that ever end up in a defense firm?

So chairs were scrunched together and other places set at the plaintiff table. Brian O'Neill was made chairman of the Damages Committee, and Lori Wagner a member. Gerry Nolting was put on the Liability Committee.

Their admission to the inner circle was a major contribution to the struggle against Exxon, but it's a good bet that it would never have occurred had it been left to a vote of the eighty-four plaintiff firms already in the case. It is doubtful that that disputatious horde could have reached unanimity over what day of the week it was. There were those in the throng around the trough to whom proven ability in a newcomer was something of a disqualifier. There was enough competition among themselves as it was. The slices of the pie were getting mighty slim.

Fortunately for O'Neill and his confrères, the top leadership of the plaintiff class was considerably more enlightened. The cream had risen to the top, though not easily.

In August of 1989, a Case Management Plan had been submitted to the court. Though apparently as close as all the plaintiffs were able to come toward consensus, it was not a perfect arrangement. It offered—in fact, parodied—a scheme of shared management, "a team of eight megalomaniacs to head the case."

The author of this harsh assessment is David Oesting, of the estimable Seattle firm of Davis Wright Tremaine. He is one of the great heroes of the *Exxon Valdez* case. Close to O'Neill in age, a native of northern Wisconsin and graduate of Washington University Law School in St. Louis, he had moved to Seattle to practice law in large part because the openness of the place appealed to him. He was an outdoorsman who loved fishing and hunting and the absence of societal restraint. Seattle then seemed to offer more opportunity in those regards than most other urban centers.

Not that the firm he joined was a storefront in a logging camp. Davis Wright Tremaine can fairly be characterized as the Faegre & Benson of Seattle. About the same size (it has two hundred seventy attorneys), it is a big-time, blue-chip corporate defense firm. It represents an impressive share of major Northwest companies. Its lawyers are first-rate and its usual adversaries are just the sort of plaintiff class action lawyers who were beseeching the court for a piece of the Exxon action.

So how did a partner in this firm come to be representing a class of fishermen, landowners, and processors in the *Exxon Valdez* case? It was a combination of ability and opportunity. And timing. David Oesting had made a name for himself in commercial and bankruptcy trial work. He was highly regarded within his firm. But Seattle was growing too crowded for him. Everyone in the country seemed to be moving there. One day he learned that the number of registered voters in Seattle was greater than the total population when he had moved there not long before. He didn't like the trend. So in 1980 he had moved his family to

Alaska, where he opened the small Anchorage office of Davis Wright Tremaine. He had thrived there, personally as well as professionally.

When the plaintiff lawyers were beginning their involvement in the *Exxon Valdez* case, one of the ablest of them, and certainly the most prominent, was Mel Weiss, of the New York firm of Milberg Weiss. He was the leader of the national class action securities bar, and phenomenally successful, earning millions of dollars a year. He knew as much as anyone about big class action cases, and he knew that he needed local counsel. He also knew David Oesting. The two had been adversaries in the litigation following the biggest municipal bond failure in history—the legendary W.P.P.S.S. case. Oesting, of course, had been on the defendant's team. But the opposing trench is a good spot from which to judge the effectiveness of the enemy, and Weiss had been battered enough to realize that Oesting knew how to catch and return a grenade. He wanted him on his side in *Exxon Valdez,* and he got him. Presumably the Davis, Wright managers went through the same analysis that had caused the Faegre & Benson Management Committee to depart from its habitual defense practice for this one wildly promising fling.

Having come down from the turret to join the mob across the moat did not change Oesting's notions of how a battle should be fought. Like O'Neill, he brought past habits of organization and diligence to his new pursuit. As he looked around at his squabbling colleagues, he was dismayed. All this jockeying for position was not advancing the case.

So when Judge Holland looked at the eight-headed monster being proposed to run the case, and then rejected it, Oesting knew exactly how he felt. He went to see the judge with a new proposal of his own. He suggested that the judge himself should choose the leaders of the plaintiff team. Just have everyone interested in the job come forward and apply, with Judge Holland making the decision. The judge could see the merit of this proposal. He subsequently announced that all those wanting to be lead counsel for the plaintiffs should file a two-page statement saying why they thought they were qualified.

A great many lawyers felt compelled to respond. One of them was David Oesting. And in December of that year, when Judge Holland announced the names of the two lawyers who would serve as Co-Lead Counsel for the plaintiff side of the case, one of them was Oesting.

The other was Jerry Cohen of Cohen, Milstein, Hausfelt & Toll, of

Washington, D.C. He was a legendary figure in the class action antitrust bar. It is safe to say that *he* had not been a defense lawyer previously. A former chief counsel to the Senate Antitrust and Monopoly subcommittee, he had co-authored a book titled, *America, Inc.: Who Owns and Operates the United States.* He had helped win the biggest victories in the biggest cases: against Union Carbide in the Bhopal, India, chemical disaster; against paper companies and corrugated box manufacturers accused of price fixing; against Conoco in an air-pollution case; against Pan Am, TWA, and British Airways. He had won the court victories allowing the United Farm Workers to organize for the first time. The Exxon case was shaping up to be the biggest of all, the capstone of his career. He was one of the oldest lawyers in the case and highly regarded for his kindness and wisdom. His clients were Alaska Natives: Eskimos, Indians, and Aleuts.

It would have been very difficult for Judge Holland to have appointed only one lead counsel if that person was a prominent member of the defense bar. And if a plaintiff lawyer had to be appointed as co-counsel, Cohen was an understandable and popular choice. In any event, two heads were better than eight.

While Oesting and Cohen came from opposite sides of the litigation tracks, each knew better than many of their colleagues the enormity of the task that lay ahead. And how little progress had been made toward their common goal. Many had staked their claims, but few had started digging. What was needed were lawyers who really knew how to do this thing, and, even more, who really knew how to *work*. The Co-Lead Counsel were very much aware of the *Glacier Bay* case, not only the lovely verdict but all that it had taken to get to that verdict. That was the sort of thing that this case needed, too. So they extended helping hands to O'Neill and his team, who thus embarked upon an increasingly upward path. The assistance was self-serving but (or therefore) quite genuine. Oesting and Cohen were not the only enlightened benefactors. There were other powerful lawyers who recognized that O'Neill's team was less likely to take another slice than to add to the size of the pie. Notably among these prescient allies were Mel Weiss, once again welcoming defense lawyers to the plaintiff team, and Richard Gerry, of Bixby, Cowan & Gerry, of San Diego and Anchorage, a personal injury lawyer who had cut his teeth working for Melvin Belli and was a former president of the American Trial Lawyers Association. The door was opened wide and held there by some very formidable new friends.

O'Neill needed all the help he could get. As soon as he and Lori Wagner were put on the Damages Committee, they had set to work with a vengeance, eager to prove themselves. They soon discovered more opportunity than they needed. It was not unlike the first look at the cardboard boxes in the Robinson office. The same reaction set in now: is *this* all that's been done? The damages cupboard was bare. Not a fraction of what they had achieved in *Glacier Bay* had even been attempted in *Exxon Valdez,* although the class action lawyers had been encamped in Alaska fully as long as they. And the Exxon case was incomparably larger. It was painful just to think of all that remained to be done.

There was nothing to do but begin. One good thing, O'Neill thought, was that *Glacier Bay* had been one hell of a rehearsal. By trial and error, but with increasing confidence, they had learned how to create damage claims that would hold up in court. No doubt this achievement had helped in his selection as chairman of the Damages Committee. But the previous work now looked simple indeed compared to what was required in the larger, looming case. The Exxon spill had eventually spread over twelve hundred miles of coastline—the same as the distance from Cape Cod in Massachusetts to the outer banks of North Carolina. Throughout this enormous area, the effects of the spill were unequal; damages varied greatly from place to place. There was much variety in the type of fish caught, too, and in the price of each type. This was not one inlet of salmon fishermen, it was a whole universe, diverse and complex. Unless all the different categories could be set out and tabulated in some uniform manner, it would be impossible even to discuss settlement with Exxon, let alone argue effectively for compensatory damages at trial.

So O'Neill came up with the idea of the Damage Matrix, which was a sort of Domesday Book of plaintiff claims. And like the survey of William the Conqueror, it took years to prepare. No scholar however pedantic, no monkish scribe fervent in his labor, would have welcomed this ghastly task. For a man of action like O'Neill it must have been torture; even for a woman of immense resolve like Lori Wagner it seemed daunting. Yet for the next two years she devoted all of her time, and he half of his, to this tedious, difficult, maddening, and absolutely essential task. The Damage Matrix divides all the claimants into groups, for example, Kodiak fishermen, and within each group determines each year's loss by subjecting its components to a uniform formula: price times the number of permit holders times the number of pounds of fish caught. When this new world was finally mapped, the heavy tome became the most carefully guarded document on the plaintiff side; it is still top secret. Its completion was a monumental task. The Damage Matrix is to most other damage claims what the census is to headcounts.

It has been noted that its preparation consumed half of O'Neill's time. The other half was not spent recovering. There were so many other things to do. To begin, the number of plaintiffs he represented had almost tripled. When word of the *Glacier Bay* recovery trickled down the coast, everyone asked who the lawyer had been. Other attorneys were making promises but this fellow O'Neill had already delivered the goods. So he no longer had to buy radio ads. People swarmed to sign up, and Faegre & Benson ended up representing twenty-two hundred fishermen suing Exxon. Each of the new plaintiffs had to be questioned and then all their claims worked up. This work was done by Sarah Armstrong and her crew in the Claims Office back in Soldatna, but all the new parties to the action meant more work for O'Neill, too.

One of the things that soon became clearer than ever before was the extent of suffering that the fishermen had endured because of the spill. The files were records of heartbreak. The years of lowered or absent income had wrought hundreds of tales of personal tragedy. Destitution, bankruptcy, drunkenness, and divorce were all too common. Some fishermen had suffered strokes; in one case a multiple sclerosis condition had been badly aggravated by the stress of the spill, resulting in permanent disability. None of the seemingly endless stories of individual and familial distress was legally relevant exclusively to economic damage. But together they touched the hearts of the counsel, whose job it was to review the files, and served to renew their efforts to establish the case for economic redress.

Also terribly time-consuming was the search for experts. O'Neill and Wagner couldn't compile the Damage Matrix without expert scientific and economic help. There were so many variables in computing loss: the destruction of the food the fish lived on, the effect on global food prices of the spill, the highly contested estimates of how many fish had been killed. Did salmon find their spawning grounds through sense of smell, and, if so, did oil fumes affect that? There were so many questions. But two were paramount: what the price should have been, and how many fish there would have been absent the spill. These questions had to be answered differently for each salmon run, of which there were hundreds, and for each type of salmon, of which there were five.

All these variants could be addressed only by experts. And, relying on the courtroom aphorism that an expert is someone from out of town, great distances had to be traveled in search of convincing authority. O'Neill and Wagner met with scientists in Seattle and at Yale and Cornell. They traveled the land to meet with experts on toxicology; they huddled in far-off labs and classrooms and airports with economists, fisheries biologists, real estate appraisers, anthropologists, sociobiologists. They spent over a million dollars on studies. And they spent even more precious, dwindling hours reading and understanding and questioning the studies, and then building them into their Matrix.

While O'Neill and Wagner were reading economic studies on late-night flights, Gerry Nolting was expanding his role on the Liability Committee. Liable means responsible. The question the committee had to answer was why Exxon should be held responsible for the spill. When Nolting arrived, there was still a lot of talk on the committee about the physical condition of the tanker itself. Some thought that worn-out equipment made the case for liability. Nolting saw it differently. He had two theories that he felt were stronger. First, Captain Hazelwood's drinking, and Exxon's failure to monitor it and give him an on-shore assignment; and second, the fatigue of the crew. Nolting thought that Exxon's cost-cutting moves had left the tanker undermanned, with the seamen who remained working longer hours than was compatible with safety. The two theories explained the accident: Hazelwood's drinking had caused him to leave the bridge, and the crew member who remained there was too tired to make the right decisions.

Other committee members came to share this point of view. These were simple propositions and potentially very appealing to a jury. The problem was in proving them. It would have to be shown not only that Hazelwood drank enough to be noticed, but that Exxon *had* noticed it— or should have—and then did nothing. This meant talking to the people who had sailed with him, to those who had seen him in port, and to all his supervisors at Exxon. Each of them would have to be deposed—an incredibly lengthy list. And they were scattered all over the country and beyond (one was now stationed in Singapore). Nolting spent most of his time on depositions, half of it on the road.

The fact that they were now *taking* depositions of Exxon people doesn't mean that they didn't have to *defend* the depositions Exxon was taking of their thousands of client-fishermen. By the summer of 1992, the scorched-earth policy they had seen in *Glacier Bay*—bankrupt and exhaust the plaintiffs under the sheer weight of depositions—was now being employed by the Exxon lawyers, in staggering numbers and at astonishing cost. And this time it was clear that they wouldn't turn around and go back just because the other side had fielded a team. When the well-tailored hordes swept across the northern tundra, the fishermen's handful of defenders sent a desperate message back to their fort for help. Just in the nick of time, it came. Forty lawyers from Faegre & Benson, partners and associates both, young and old, were rallied together and sent off to Alaska to fight. Some had never before represented a plaintiff. There was a lot of rapid acclimatization, with neckties shed in the cause of client confidence. And then the battle was joined. In deposition after deposition, in all the meeting rooms and offices throughout the sullied landscape, the smooth and expensive Exxon lawyers discovered, to their astonishment, that their adversaries were remarkably like themselves. Just as experienced, just as good, and, if truth be told, just as dissimilar from the fishermen. But they were formidably effective in the defense of these unaccustomed clients. All the resources poured into the depositions by Exxon were impressively met in kind, though God knows who was left to represent the Norwest bank back home in Minneapolis.

A number of the lawyers active in the case would later compare all the liability problems of proof to the film *Rashomon,* Kurosawa's classic case for the elusiveness of truth when all we have is testimony. It is a good analogy. But, looking at the deposition warfare, yet another film by the same director comes to mind, *The Seven Samurai.* For the Alaskan fishermen had hired warriors as well trained and professional as their foes. This was the point at which the villagers' resolve was supposed to break, crushed by the adversaries' numbers. A humble settlement was meant to follow. That did not happen. The Faegre support troops more than held their own, did their job and then returned home, some limping but with great war stories, and perhaps a warmer glow than combat had brought them in the past. Their bruised peers in the enemy camp, who had expected defenseless peasants, might well have paused for a moment to wonder just where the hell all these Samurai had come from.

This is not to suggest that the only professionals were from Faegre & Benson. The years they all spent in the field together served to remove any doubt among the plaintiff lawyers about relative merit within their ranks. There were phoneys, laggards, and hangers-on, to be sure, but there were tireless artists as well, and everyone knew who they were. In a camp divided by previous allegiance, stalwarts of both the plaintiff and defense bars saw in this temporary allegiance proof that ability can flourish anywhere. An unsurpassed example of diligence, for example, was Matt Jamin from a small firm in Kodiak, Alaska, indefatigable on behalf of the Alaska municipalities he represented, doggedly working up land damages.

No one contributed more to the common effort than David Oesting. As chairman of the Law Committee, he was in charge of all briefing, all legal research, the entire procedural strategy, jury instructions, and all the motions that had to be argued before the start of the trial itself. There were hundreds of these. Many were part of the process known as discovery. Each side wants to discover everything the other side knows. Each side objects to giving up its documents. It is a paper fight, and the referee is the court. Discovery motions are not glamorous; Tom Cruise will never argue one. But they are absolutely essential to the far more dramatic trial. The zingers and retorts, surprises and tricks, that shock or please the jury all stem from the midnight perusal of documents that were themselves obtained after endless discovery motions had been made. Oesting argued or supervised most of these motions, and much, much more. He oversaw the administration of the entire disparate plaintiff team. He brought order to the process. He established a standardized time-keeping process, a remarkable achievement considering that some plaintiff lawyers, who charged a percentage of recovery rather than an hourly rate, had never before filled out a time sheet. He established a budget process. He levied and collected an assessment against each law firm in the case, to keep the work regularly funded. He actually won agreement of his plan for determining what percentage each firm would receive of the final recovery. He was everywhere, all the time. If anyone was in charge, it was David Oesting.

But Oesting's greatest contribution to the case was yet to come. A year of frenzied and dogged activity had left the plaintiffs even more aware of how much work remained. Painful as it was, they had to look ahead to the trial itself. Most particularly, a lead trial counsel had to be selected. This was no mere plum; it was an orchard. One person was going to argue virtually the entire plaintiff case. This would be one of the largest and most visible trials in legal history. Whoever was selected to argue the case would be the focus of incredible publicity. For any lawyer, however distinguished, it was the role of a lifetime.

It was a role widely coveted. Among these veteran litigators could be found no lightweight egos. Many saw themselves as uniquely suited for the part. And even those who admitted some personal limitations felt strongly about who should *not* be allowed to reach center stage. It should not be a newcomer. It should not be some corporate defense type. It should be someone from the original cast. Having played, even starred, in another production wasn't good enough. This was a *plaintiff* case; choose from the plaintiff bar.

But of those doing the choosing, the one with the greatest say was himself a defense lawyer. David Oesting at first could see some merit in choosing a defense lawyer—himself. By the standards of some of his temporary colleagues, he was a modest man, but his was not false modesty. He knew what he could do. He could try this case, as he had many others. But that would mean dropping all the administrative tasks that he had been handling. It wasn't a question of handing the reins to someone else; he honestly didn't know who else could do all that he had been doing.

He did have a good idea, though, of who else could try the case. Those confident of their own ability are more likely to acknowledge excellence in others, and David Oesting knew that Brian O'Neill was very good. He had not sat through the *Glacier Bay* case, but he had spoken with those who had. He didn't really need to speak to them: he'd seen the verdict and knew that a victory of that scope could scarcely have been an accident.

Since then he had been working with O'Neill, working closely, and on a daily basis. The guy knew how to organize a damage claim. More to the point, he knew how to *sell* his damage theories. He had sold them to the Damages Committee, and to the other lawyers in the case—a tougher jury than any court could summon. He had sold them with a smile, and behind the smile a total command of the facts, and behind the facts the kind of toughness that never has to bluster, and behind the toughness the most important thing of all, beyond even massive self-confidence, the only really indispensable talent: the total will to win.

There was something else, too. O'Neill *wanted* to try this case. However implausibly, he already saw himself as the lead trial counsel. You could tell that not merely by the evident aura of command. You could tell it from the way he wasn't just doing his part of the job, he was trying to stay on top of everything else, too. He'd grab the transcripts from some of the other lawyers' depositions and throw them in the bag to read on the way to meet some economics professor on some campus out in nowhere. He didn't *need* to read them. On the other hand, maybe he did. Because he saw the case as his already. He had always felt that way. And now every time you told him something, or made a point, you could see him taking it in, and you knew what he was thinking. You could almost hear him arguing it in court.

There were a lot of people who could try this case. Some were very good. A couple were great. There were choices that would go over with the team a lot more easily than a not-very-old defense lawyer most of whose plaintiff work had been on behalf of wildlife. This time the wolves were on the other side. There would be plenty of griping about the selection of someone so far removed from the plaintiff bar. There were safer choices.

But there was no better choice. In fact, the more Oesting thought about it, there was no other choice at all. This disciplined and rational man decided to go with his instinct, though of course it wasn't really instinct at all.

In January of 1993 O'Neill and Oesting met at the Davis Wright Tremaine office in Seattle. There were only the two of them. They talked about who should try the case. Oesting shared his conclusion that there were only two candidates, and they were both in that room. But he knew which one should get it, and that was O'Neill. He said he would get the others to go along.

He did. At a meeting of the Executive Committee a few months later, on the twenty-sixth-floor office of Davis Wright Tremaine, some two dozen lawyers filed into the big conference room, the more agile or powerful finding seats at the table and the others pulling up chairs with their backs to the window, foregoing the view of Puget Sound. Mel Weiss, perhaps the most prominent class action lawyer in America, was there of course, and some thought he would be the lead. Dick Gerry was there from San Diego. In fact *everyone* was there, all the key players in the case.

Without making a fuss about it, Oesting announced that O'Neill was going to try the case. That was all right, wasn't it? A variety of grunts were taken as assent.

And so it had come to pass. Later, more than a year later, when it became necessary on the eve of trial to get it in writing, Judge Holland signed Order Number 192 in the case of *In re: The EXXON VALDEZ*. To this day, O'Neill, though he is never at a loss in court, is unable to say the words "order number one ninety-two" without obvious emotion in his voice. The order reads:

1. An In-Court Trial Team is hereby appointed to prepare and present plaintiff's case to the Court and the Jury consisting of Brian B. O'Neill, Jerry S. Cohen, H. Laddie Montague, Matthew D. Jamin and Richard F. Gerry.
2. Brian O'Neill is hereby appointed Lead Trial Counsel for such Team.
3. Lead Trial Counsel shall have the authority to make all final decisions relating to the presentation of this case to the Court and to the Jury in Phases I, II and III as provided for in the January 5, 1994 Second Amended Trial Plan approved by the Court in Order No. 173.
4. Agreements made by defendants with Lead Trial Counsel relating to the presentation of this case to the Court and to the Jury in Phases I, II and III shall bind all plaintiffs in this action.

There was no question of who was in charge. Other lawyers would spell him on occasion, but only briefly and only when he chose. Every decision was O'Neill's to make, all authority his own. He was going to try the case. His dream had not yet come true, but his opportunity had.

Order Number 192 was signed by Judge Holland on March 23, 1994, exactly five years from the day when Captain Hazelwood set out on his tanker for the last time. The five years were like five centuries and five minutes, a different lifetime, really, passing in a flash, unfathomable to those who had not shared it.

Now only the trial lay ahead.

8

Voir Dire

Of all the things that people don't like about lawyers, the most maddening—not the most serious, but the most *maddening*—is the way they talk. Why can't they just talk like everyone else? They have their own language. Sometimes it's Latin, sometimes it's something else, but always it's mumbo-jumbo, a private insider's code that only other lawyers understand. It's like speaking a foreign language in your own country, when you don't have to. What's the point? Intimidation? Bonding?

So the very first part of the *Exxon Valdez* trial was not called Picking the Jury, which is what in fact it was. It was called *voir dire*. This is a Norman phrase with a Latin root, and it means "to speak the truth." It scarcely seems synonymous with jury selection, but perhaps in medieval times some Norman magistrate charged with resolving disputes told the assembled villagers to answer his questions honestly. If they didn't, he couldn't pick a jury. You needed jurors who could at least try to be fair, who weren't related or hostile to the defendant, or both. So all prospective jurors were asked if they knew the parties to the dispute, and whether they had already made up their minds, and whether they had a conflict of interest, and whether they thought they could be open-minded and fair. Before they answered these questions, the magistrate sternly would remind them *voir dire,* to speak the truth.

In the many centuries that followed, very little about this changed. There were some minor additions to the process, such as lawyers, but picking the jury still involved screening out conflicts and bias. And it was still called *voir dire,* though many of the lawyers who intoned those words had not a clue as to their meaning.

So the first few days of the *Exxon Valdez* trial were devoted to *voir dire.* At nine thirty-five on the morning of May 2, 1994, in Courtroom Number Two of the Federal Courthouse in Anchorage, a cross-section of Alaskan citizens, more than a hundred of them, filled up the courtroom seats and wondered if they'd be selected. For the most part, they had mixed feelings about such a prospect. On the one hand, this was certainly the most celebrated case in Alaska's history (perhaps America's as well), and to be part of it, to help *decide* it, was exciting. On the other hand, the trial would probably last for months. That was a big slice out of someone's year, and, in some cases, income. The jurors were paid only forty-three dollars and eighty cents a day. And this case was awfully intimidating—all those well-dressed lawyers up in the front of the courtroom were certainly intimidating. Would their questions be difficult to follow? Was this going to be technical? Was this going to be *hard?*

Each of the prospective jurors had been chosen at random from the list of all registered voters in Alaska. Some had traveled great distances to be present in the Anchorage courthouse. They knew that they were going to be questioned, probably several times, in writing and in person, and that eventually only twelve of them would be selected to serve as the jury.

The lawyers who would be asking all these questions were up in the front of the courtroom. They all *looked* like lawyers. They all looked good. They were all dressed the same. It was hard to tell which lawyer was on which side.

Had the prospective jurors been forced to guess just which of these blue-suited picadores was on the side of the fishermen, they probably would have picked Michael Chalos. Some of them would later say that he reminded them of Columbo, the television detective whose shambling mien entrapped many more elegant foes. He certainly didn't look as if he was representing Exxon. And, indeed, he was not. He was representing Joseph Hazelwood. The interests of the Exxon Corporation and its former captain were not entirely the same (though their fate was largely linked for the purposes of this trial). Exxon Corporation and Joseph Hazelwood had been separately named as defendants. So Hazelwood had his own attorney, the old school friend to whom he had turned in the horrible days after the spill. He was not only Hazelwood's friend and lawyer: he was his employer, too. Unhirable as a mariner, the former captain was now working for Chalos's small firm as an investigator. Born in Greece and less glitteringly educated than other leaders in the case, Chalos's diffident good humor masked (until jocular turned jugular) big-time street smarts and an unswerving focus on the welfare of his client. Exxon was a partial ally, Hazelwood a lifetime friend. And he was more than capable of looking after that friend. Working with Tom Russo, he had been largely successful in defending Hazelwood against the criminal charges. The Alaska jury had found the captain not guilty of the charges of recklessness and operating a vessel while intoxicated. He had been found guilty only of the misdemeanor of "negligent discharge of oil," and that was—and still is—on appeal.

And then there were the Exxon lawyers. None of them reminded anyone of Columbo. Exxon had not picked its trial team from the Yellow Pages.

The leader of Exxon's team was Patrick Lynch of the Los Angeles megafirm of O'Melveny and Myers. In his early fifties, Lynch had a long record of brilliant defense work for very major clients: the National Football League, Gallo, IBM. His law firm, the oldest in Los Angeles, had more than five hundred lawyers, including William Coleman, a former Secretary of Transportation, and Warren Christopher, then Secretary of State. The client list would inspire envy from even the largest New York firms: Columbia Pictures, Paramount Pictures, Federal Express, Manufacturers Hanover Trust Company, Wells Fargo Bank, and on and on.

There were two other principal Exxon trial lawyers, both from the same firm in Nashville, Tennessee. The more senior, in his sixties, was James F. Neal, who had founded the firm of Neal and Herwell, which, less than a quarter century later, could truthfully describe itself in Martindale Hubbell as a nationally recognized firm specializing in white-collar criminal defense work and complex civil litigation. Having honed his skills as a Watergate prosecutor and as Chief Counsel for the U.S. Senate Select Committee on Undercover Operations, Jim Neal seemed to specialize in defending very big clients in very big trouble. He had defended Governor Edwards of Louisiana against sensational corruption charges. He had skillfully eased the Ford Motor Company off the hook in the Pinto cases. He had defended Elvis's doctor. He had saved from prison the Hollywood defendants in *The Twilight Zone* helicopter crash case. Despite the incredible sums at stake in this case, he certainly didn't seem intimidated by being in this Anchorage courtroom.

Neal not only had a remarkable record, he had a remarkable colleague. Helping him try the case was his younger partner from Neal and Herwell, James Sanders. The jurors, who evidently watched a lot of television, thought Sanders looked like Michael Landon, long hair and all. About O'Neill's age, he, like his mentor Neal, had been born in rural Tennessee and had spent most of his life in his home state. He had maintained a cozy backwoods drawl. Simple country lawyers whose clients include Coca-Cola and Union Carbide can probably charm fillings from teeth, and no better lawyer than James Sanders would take part in this case. It was a high tribute to his skill that he had been asked to play a major courtroom role. Lynch and Neal were brilliant and famous lawyers, among the very best in the land. But the trial would be so long and the issues so diverse, that some division of labor had been thought helpful. Each of these stellar litigators would spell the others, and concentrate on his own assigned area of the case.

The plaintiffs had only one lawyer. Brian O'Neill, in the course of the trial, occasionally would let another attorney stand in for him to question a witness, but basically he himself was it. He would be on virtually all the time, giving all the opening and closing statements himself, questioning most of the plaintiff witnesses, cross-examining almost all those witnesses called by the defense. The defense lawyers could take turns if they wished, but O'Neill always would be there, an omnipresent force continuously in action. Some of the prospective jurors had heard that the plaintiffs were only going to use one trial lawyer, but they weren't quite sure just which of those guys it was. They were about to find out.

The judge, who *looked* like a judge, and who was so obviously and completely in charge that he didn't even need that gavel, spoke good-naturedly to the crowd that filled the courtroom.

"Good morning, ladies and gentlemen," said H. Russel Holland. "The court case set for trial is in the case of *In re: The EXXON Valdez*, Case Number A89-095 Civil. This case is to be a jury trial. Counsel, is there any reason why we should not proceed with jury selection?"

There was not. And so the matter was under way. The judge made some introductory remarks. He knew that many in the juror pool knew little or nothing about what was expected of them, and so he began with the most important point, which was their own importance. "It is the function of the Court, that is myself, to determine matters of law which arise during the trial of this case. It is the function of the jury to ascertain the facts of the case. Of these two functions, judge and fact finder, the jury's function is in a very real sense the more important of the two."

The judge then told them that they were going to have to fill out written questionnaires under oath, aimed at eliminating from the pool those who could not be expected to be impartial. Those who remained were then going to be questioned in the courtroom by lawyers from each side, and further screening would take place. Since all these questions went to their objectivity, it would help if they knew the facts of the case. So the judge had asked the lead lawyers for each side to stand up and address the panel of jurors "for the purpose of informing you in a general fashion what this case is about." He then called on the first lawyer, who was Brian Boru O'Neill.

The jurors never again would have to ask themselves which one was the plaintiff's lawyer. O'Neill came out swinging. Regardless of what the judge had intended, he was not merely explaining the case, he was *trying* it. With startling audacity, brio, and candor, he lit into Exxon:

"In 1985, Exxon Shipping Company top management knew that Captain Hazelwood was drinking on board ship and had returned to ship drunk. Captain Hazelwood went through treatment for alcoholism in 1985 and Exxon knew that. Exxon reinstated Captain Hazelwood, after he had gone through treatment, as a supertanker captain and he started drinking again, and officials at Exxon knew that after he had gone through treatment he had started drinking again, and that he had relapsed back into his alcoholism.

"A week before the wreck of the *Exxon Valdez* there was an ugly drinking incident in San Francisco, and an Exxon employee, one week before the wreck, reported Captain Hazelwood to her superiors and his superiors, and despite knowledge of this treatment, his resumed drinking and this ugly drinking accident one week before the wreck of the *Exxon Valdez*, Exxon management did nothing.

"A week later, after drinking throughout the afternoon and the evening of March 23, 1989, Captain Hazelwood took command of the *Exxon Valdez* out of Valdez, Alaska. Then, without explanation, he pointed the *Valdez* at Bligh Reef, dead ahead, increased the speed of the vessel and left the bridge of the vessel. And for six critical minutes after he had left the vessel, there was no officer on the bridge of the *Valdez* and *Valdez* didn't turn and it ran—it ran aground spilling eleven million gallons of toxic crude oil."

Having described to the jurors not the issues but his conclusions, sternly, as if these were accepted facts, O'Neill did then briefly allude to the bias matters on which they would be questioned. These were not set out in an absolutely neutral fashion: "We're going to ask you whether you're opposed to our system as it is now. Our system as it is now provides for punitive damages." In this same manner he noted the other issues and then sat down.

He could see from their faces what the other lawyers thought of his performance. Whatever their impact, his remarks had not been prompted by the passion of the moment. They were quite deliberate. For months his jury experts had pushed the merits of "primacy and recency." In consultant-speak, this means that juries are most impressed by what they hear first and what they hear last. O'Neill was counting on it. So the first words these jurors heard from him—from anyone—were words of attack on Exxon.

The next lawyer who spoke to the jurors was Michael Chalos, defending Hazelwood. And he *did* defend Hazelwood from the indelible opening charge of alcoholism. Whatever else he had planned to say in the brief space allotted to outlining the issues was now displaced by the urgent need to rebut O'Neill's opening salvo. He accused O'Neill of having sensationalized the facts. He strongly denied that his client, Hazelwood, was an alcoholic. He denied that there had been an ugly drinking incident a week before the grounding. He denied O'Neill's dramatization of the accident; what Hazelwood had sought in steering the vessel "was no harder than making a right turn on the corner with your car."

He was followed by Pat Lynch, representing Exxon, who archly distanced himself from the O'Neill approach to jury instruction. "It seems that after hearing Mr. O'Neill that we are at the end of the trial here, but what we are actually doing is starting the process of selecting a jury. . . . So I will not talk to you as if I wanted you to decide today when you leave this room that the plaintiffs have no case. And I will not ask you to listen to all and prejudice all the evidence that you are going to hear, and I will not try to bias every question that you will be asked to answer on this questionnaire this afternoon as if it were put there by the Court to help you preindict Exxon. . . . My job is not to argue the case to you for a decision this afternoon. It is to give you a little information about what we think will go on in this case and what the issues will be in this case to help you fill out the questionnaire."

He then described the issues in a manner only slightly less emotive than O'Neill's. "The plaintiffs and their lawyers are interested in recovering more than full and fair compensation, much more. They are asking you, in the guise of the interest of protecting the public or somehow promoting oil-spill prevention or something, to award them very large sums of money which they pocket, which are called punitive damages." Punitive damages were to the defense what alcoholism was to the plaintiffs: a cancer eating away at the innards of our society, the worst possible evil. And when it came to alcoholism, Lynch was dismissive: "There will be very compelling evidence in this case that alcohol had nothing to do with this spill, that Captain Hazelwood made a very simple, very direct comment to a qualified seaman . . . It was a command to turn right at the next corner." Since alcohol had nothing to do with the spill, Exxon's monitoring policy was irrelevant. In any event, that policy was a thoughtful attempt to balance the rights of the individual against the rights of the public.

Having made his points, Lynch asked the jurors "not to jump to judgment as the introduction you heard from plaintiff's counsel would suggest, but as prospective jurors to keep an open mind."

The judge then had some remarks of his own, and it is certain that the jurors were paying attention. He talked about how long he thought the trial was going to last. He said he hoped it would be done in three months, but it could be four. The trial would take place every weekday from eight in the morning until two in the afternoon, with two fifteen-minute breaks. This was not a criminal case, where a jury can be sequestered in a hotel and guarded by marshals. These jurors were free to go home every night. Judge Holland was very clear, however, that they could not discuss the case with anyone—not their families, not their friends, not anyone at all. Nor could they read about it in the papers, or watch the news on television. It might be difficult to maintain this isolation for months to come, but it was vitally important.

That was it, for the time being. The jury was excused to the jury room, where they filled out their questionnaires and then went home. The lawyers stayed right where they were. They waited for the last questionnaires to be picked up. And then each team grabbed its smudgy copies of the questionnaire and set about the frantic task of going through them all before the next day's session. Each side had the same goal: to find and eliminate its enemies. At this stage of the jury selection, it wasn't difficult to remove those jurors who clearly should not have been there. Some of them worked in the oil industry, even for Exxon. Others were commercial fishermen. These obvious conflictees were swiftly weeded out. Both sides agreed to their removal.

What then remained was more difficult. There was still a fairly large pool of prospective jurors—more than forty. Starting the next morning, each would appear, in turn, in court to be questioned very briefly (no more than ten minutes) by both the plaintiff and defense lawyers. For a prospective juror to survive these nets and continue the swim upstream, both sides had to say "pass for cause" to the court, which means approved for some reason. If one side had some reason why the juror should *not* serve, the lawyer would say "challenge for cause." The reason for the challenge would then be stated, the lawyer for the other side had the right to argue against it, and the judge would decide whether to pass or excuse the juror. Those who passed would form a new pool, which would later be whittled down by each side, with no reason required, until only twelve remained: the jury.

It was a lot of trouble, compressed into a very short time. For two full days each side would have ten minutes per juror to probe and perceive bias, and to quickly calculate which way it cut. It was an inhuman process, a conveyer belt of land mines that just kept coming, all looking much alike at first but some of them fully armed. The lawyers had to somehow sniff these out, split-second decisions before the belt moved on. It was a frustrating job, exhausting and stressful, requiring constantly the most heightened attention in a desperate effort to read another person's mind. The process was messy, hurried, and wildly chancy, like bobbing for apples and somehow avoiding those that had worms.

It was the most important part of the case. If you could pick the jury right, that would matter more than anything else. All these high-powered lawyers knew that, they knew it absolutely, in their bones, had learned it painfully time and time again in many hundreds of trials. Picking the jury wasn't just the first inning, it could be the ball game. The most brilliant arguments, the most convincing witnesses, the most devastating evidence, could weigh far less than some juror's thumb on the scales of justice. The next two frenzied days would be their only chance to prevent that. Both sides were telling the truth when they said that what they really wanted was an open-minded jury; they were far less eager to plant allies than to eliminate foes.

The first day of jury selection began. It didn't take long to discern a pattern in the questioning. O'Neill, who always got the first crack, would ask about people's experience with alcoholism, and whether the fact that Exxon paid a lot of taxes to Alaska had made the corporation sacrosanct. The second question signaled a real problem. The oil industry was the biggest employer in Alaska. The clean-up effort by Exxon had produced even more jobs. Further, the state taxes paid by the oil companies were so great that no Alaskan had to pay any income tax at all. Better still, the state paid *them*—more than a thousand dollars every year to each Alaskan, thanks to oil revenues. This might explain why Exxon had not sought to have the trial moved to some other state. Many had expected that the defendants would do so, to have the trial as far removed as possible from the site of the damage. But Exxon had done jury research, too, and knew that a good many grateful Alaskans *liked* the oil companies. How much they liked them was something that O'Neill's questioning was trying to find out.

He had another standard question, too, and it usually surprised each juror. He asked them why they lived in Alaska. He always asked it in a friendly way, but he was deadly serious. The jury consultants had said this was critical. If a juror chose to live in Alaska because of the natural beauty of the place, then perhaps they would be willing to punish those who had despoiled their environment.

Punishment was everything. If the jury didn't believe in punitive damages, then O'Neill had wasted the last five years of his life. And some people did *not* believe in punitive damages; the studies showed that. So O'Neill put it to them directly: "Do you hold any views one way or the other on the subject of punitive damages?" There was also a follow-up question: "Do you get scared off in dealing with billions of dollars?" This question was aimed at more than an answer. The jury consultants had said that if jurors actually said the word "billions" a few times, they would be more comfortable with it when the time came to award damages.

The defendants had some standard questions of their own. No matter who was doing the questioning, one defense question was always asked: "If you had a belief that the facts were such that your belief differed from the rest of the jurors, do you feel like you have the strength of character to hold out and tell people what your beliefs are, independent of what they may say to you?"

The defendants might as well have put up a billboard. The ubiquity of this one question proclaimed in large capitals their belief that most jurors were likely to find against them. But the parties had agreed that a damage verdict had to be unanimous. So with every juror they were looking for the holdout, the stubborn or principled individualist who would not budge regardless of pressure.

Since the lawyers for both sides knew just what they were looking for, and were very, very good, there were a number of spirited clashes over the suitability of specific jurors. Chalos, for example, challenged for cause a woman who had been married to an alcoholic (nine DWI arrests) and scarred by the experience: "I hurt inside because I was thinking that maybe it was me why he was drinking." It was not unreasonable for Chalos to suppose that her lingering resentments could be focused on his client. He didn't want this juror.

But O'Neill did. "Alcoholism is a part of life," he argued. "If we're going to strike everybody in the community who had some knowledge or interaction with the disease of alcoholism we're not going to get a jury." The judge ruled for O'Neill; the woman stayed in the pool.

(It was soon clear that the lives of most of the potential jurors had been touched, and often not lightly, by alcohol. *Voir dire* means to speak the truth, and juror after juror did so on the subject of drink. Their testimony is an astonishing catalogue of the damage done by alcoholism in our society. One learns of spouses and parents and children who were alcoholics, of arrests and pain and divorce and death. The jury pool was randomly selected. The testimony of its members is more telling than any statistics on the ubiquity of abusive drink.)

Sometimes the decision to strike was very easy. When O'Neill asked one woman, "Do you think you could be fair?" her answer was, "No. I don't." There was no need for further questions.

When an Exxon lawyer would challenge a juror for cause, O'Neill would usually fight that challenge like a tiger, regardless of the odds of prevailing. When a young fisheries technician said that he viewed Exxon unfavorably, O'Neill argued that this was merely the expression of "the doubt of a decent, God-fearing human being who is troubled by issues that trouble all of us." The judge didn't buy it. When an assistant bakery manager said that Hazelwood's drinking after his supposed rehabilitation should be held against him, and that his own parents' alcoholism made it hard for him to be unbiased on the subject, O'Neill found no problem with that. "Ninety percent of the population holds that view," he argued. Again, the judge ruled for Exxon and excused the juror.

Sometimes, of course, the parties were in agreement. Several of the jurors quickly satisfied both sides. Linda Hood, who had been born in Anchorage fifty years earlier, was pleasant and had no opinion about almost anything that she was asked. This was apparently the key to selection, though there was some concern over the fact that she worked in a center for sleep disorders, and sleep deprivation would be a major issue in the case. Rose Martin, an air force wife who worked part-time as an elementary school monitor, was similarly pleasant and noncommittal and was speedily selected as well.

When someone said they had no opinion about an issue in the case, it was difficult to strike them for cause. You were supposed to state a reason for striking, and with no comments it was hard to find reasons. This made O'Neill a little nervous. He knew that after all the adverse publicity, if Alaskans had formed opinions they were likely to be hostile to Exxon. He knew this, and he knew that defense counsel knew it, too. On the second day he blurted out his frustration. "The jury the defendants would like would be a collection of people who never read the newspapers because they're the only ones that will not have read about the spill."

He said this during a particularly sharp exchange. Pat Lynch had asked a prospective juror a very direct question: "If you were in my position, representing the shareholders and employees of Exxon Corporation, would you want a juror like yourself to sit in this case?" She had given a very direct answer: "No." O'Neill was adamant that this should not be a disqualifier. "The ordinary person formed some views as to the spill. The good juror is the one who can say, despite what I read, because I do read the newspapers, and this was on the front page of the newspaper, I can still be fair." The judge did side with Lynch and excuse her, but not because she had formed some opinions; he was concerned by the fact that her brother-in-law was a set-netter. Throughout the proceeding the judge seemed less concerned with prejudgment than with conflict. He was a very practical man.

It was in fact difficult to imagine that any Alaskan had no views at all on the grounding, and easy to be skeptical when the absence of opinion was expressed. Each side had to rely on things that are not taught in books, nor even by consultants. They had to rely on their gut instincts. Which way will this sweet grandmother vote?

And what on earth was one to make of the formidable presence of Bruce A. Dean? On the questionnaire, he had signed his acronym, BAD, much to what can only be called the initial confusion of defense counsel. (He had the same letters emblazoned on his jacket, too.) The unemployed miner made a fierce appearance, with a striking walruslike moustache and piercing eyes behind his aviator glasses. It was hard to know what to make of him. When O'Neill asked him what he liked about mining, he replied, "I just like blowing stuff up. Making a big mess, not having to clean it up." To establish rapport as a fellow marauder, O'Neill inaccurately replied that "I spent thirteen years in the army, and we had a good time there" (a service record that of course included law school). Both sides approved Dean for the jury, O'Neill because Dean had laughed at his jokes, and the defense perhaps because Dean, the miner, had expressed some concern about environmental regulations. Dean provides a good example of how little one can know about a person from a few minutes of interview or even an eighty-two-question written survey. No one in the courtroom other than Dean himself could know that only a few weeks earlier, the police had raided his house and seized the marijuana plants that he had been growing there. Beneath his breezy manner was the very real fear of arrest. And if they had known this, what would they have done about it? Which way would it have cut? Would O'Neill have struck him as being potentially sympathetic to those accused of substance abuse? It was hard to know. It was hard to know anything about these jurors.

Take Rita Wilson, for example. Would it have made any difference if anyone had known that the forty-four-year-old elementary school secretary was taking prescription medicine to treat her bouts of depression? There was no question asked, written or oral, that would have produced that information. Even so, there were in her testimony hints of a troubled and insecure person. When the judge told her to speak into the microphone, she said, "I'm sorry." When she said that the spill was in 1985 and O'Neill, correcting her, noted that it was 1989, she replied, "It was '89? See? I'm a terrible citizen." When O'Neill suggested that perhaps she shouldn't skip over the news sections of the paper, she said, "I know, this is embarrassing."

As always, O'Neill asked about punitive damages. He asked twice whether Rita Wilson could—should the facts justify it—award them. And both times she said yes. She also said, in response to his follow-up, that "billions is a hard concept for me."

So presumably was self-esteem. When Sanders had his turn to question her, and asked about the effects of the oil spill, she blurted out, once again, "I feel like a terrible citizen because I don't have, you know, I don't have any opinion about it."

Both lawyers approved Rita Wilson, Sanders probably because she had no strong opinions. If this was his reason, he was wrong. But very lucky, as it would turn out.

They were trying to finish the jury selection in two days, and so the second day in court was very long indeed. It was the only time during the trial when O'Neill publicly admitted fatigue. He was, of course, the only person asking questions for his side, while the defense lawyers all took turns. But his inhuman task had its rewards. The *voir dire* is the only time when counsel may speak directly to an individual juror, pay a compliment, tell a joke, look the subject in the eye, smile warmly, inclusively, conspiratorially, establish at least a spark of rapport that can be kindled later in the trial. The defense lawyers were charming and personable, too; the southerners laid it on with a trowel. But there were four or five of them; O'Neill was working alone. He was the only lawyer in the case who had the opportunity to interact on a personal level with every member of the jury. Further, every member of the jury knew that he had approved their selection. They didn't know that about anyone else. Some knew that Sanders had wanted them on the jury, or Neal, or Lynch, or Chalos, or Doug Serdahely from Anchorage, also representing Exxon. Each of them had taken part in the *voir dire*. Everyone likes to be approved, but if the jurors felt any gratitude for their selection, it was split five ways among the defense team and undividedly directed to O'Neill.

Some had very specific cause for gratitude. When a juror did admit to some preconception, it usually was adverse to Exxon. It was O'Neill's job to insist that regardless of any qualms, this was still a fair-minded individual. The actual bickering over inclusion primarily was done out of juror earshot, but O'Neill's support and approval were very poorly disguised.

For example, when Janette Garrison, a school custodian, stated under oath her belief that another court had already found Captain Hazelwood guilty of being under the influence of alcohol at the time of the grounding, Sanders argued for her exclusion from the jury. O'Neill said that if the misconception was clarified, he was sure that she could keep an open mind. The judge went with O'Neill.

They almost finished by the end of the second grueling day, but not quite. There were still a few more names to call. They had to finish up the next morning.

The first name called was Ken Murray, a counselor at Alaska Junior College who had been laid off and was spending much of his temporary leisure working with his local Rotary. Murray, an African-American, had moved with his schoolteacher wife from Tennessee to Alaska because they thought the Anchorage school system offered more opportunity for their children. Although Sanders joked that he and Neal themselves were products of the Tennessee public school system and hoped that wouldn't be held against them, both sides approved the inclusion of Murray.

The last juror to be examined presented an unusual choice. He had some problems with the concept of punitive damages, and he also had some negative feelings about Exxon. One might have imagined unanimity between the lawyers in striking him for cause. Even the judge seemed troubled. But both parties passed him. Perhaps they were inspired by the old adage that the enemy of my enemy is my friend.

They now had questioned everyone. Twenty-four people had survived within the pool. All that remained were the peremptory challenges: Each side was able to strike six jurors, with no reasons given.

Though very tired, they had worked through the night to come up with their lists of strikes. The two sides took turns reading their decisions.

The first juror O'Neill struck was David Poisson (an ironic target for one representing fishermen), an insurance salesman who had stated with some fervor that jury awards, and for that matter attorneys' fees, often were excessive. The first defense strike was of Terry Dodds, whose answer to a written question had been, "I am unlikely to forget the personal and financial devastation wrecked upon my family and friends due to the oil spill." The court had not excused this juror, and now the peremptory challenge was a way of overruling the judge. There was more of this sort of thing. It was really a matter of bookkeeping, the last chance to get the liabilities off the balance sheet. So it was not surprising that the juror hostile both to punitive damages and to Exxon would be peremptorily struck; the only real question had been which side would strike him. It was

O'Neill. Perhaps the defense would have permitted him to remain. Exxon might well have approved the selection of Ida Tarbell to the jury if she had been sufficiently opposed to the concept of punitive damages.

Once all the strikes had been made, the parties were, in Churchill's phrase, at the end of the beginning. There were now twelve names, a jury, *their* jury, their universe in the difficult months to come. There were nine women and three men. Their ages ranged from thirty-four to sixty-seven. Ten were white, two were African-American. Only one juror, Murray, the unemployed college counselor, had a college degree. The others were a school secretary, two school janitors, an unemployed miner, a McDonald's worker, a retired factory worker, a retired bookkeeper, a hospital clerk, a court clerk, a mother who took care of her grandchildren, and a young man who took care of his asthmatic mother. It was a group of average citizens, as it was supposed to be, charged with finding the facts, which would then become The Truth. The jurors were informed of their selection and told to return three days later, on Monday morning at eight, for the beginning of the trial itself.

9

The Opening

There were really three trials. As soon as one ended the next began, with the same jury and only a few days off in between. The three trials had been agreed to long in advance by the parties and the judge. They weren't actually called trials; they were called Phases. Phase One would determine whether the spill had occurred because Hazelwood and/or Exxon were reckless in the operation of the tanker. Phase Two would determine how much money would be paid as compensatory damages to the fishermen and others for the harm that they had suffered from the spill. Phase Three would decide whether Exxon and/or Hazelwood should pay *punitive* damages as well, and, if so, how much.

Phase One was the key, for if the jury did not find recklessness, there could be no Phase Three: there could be no awarding of punitive damages. This, of course, would be a disaster for the plaintiffs, their own grounding. There would still be a Phase Two, to be sure, with compensatory damages being awarded, but that dispute was over how many millions of dollars should be paid. The Phase Three fight, if Phase One even permitted it to occur, would be a fight over *billions* of dollars to be paid by Exxon as punitive damages. That was why O'Neill had tried to lure each juror into actually mouthing for the first time the magic word "billions." The Alaska jurors were not like the late Senator Everett Dirksen, who famously proclaimed, "You spend a billion dollars here, and a billion dollars there, and pretty soon it adds up to real money." Anchorage was not Washington, D.C. These people had trouble even *saying* "billions," and comprehending what it meant. It was a thousand million dollars. Even that was hard to take in. These were people who drove like blazes to get the video back to the rental store before the six o'clock deadline because they couldn't really afford the three-dollar fine.

Not that they would be handing out any money in Phase One. Their only job at this phase of the trial was to find whether recklessness had oc-curred. Not just whether Hazelwood was reckless, but whether Exxon had been, too. If so, that would be the key to the vault.

The jurors showed up, as instructed, at about quarter to eight on Monday morning, May 9, 1994. They gathered in the jury room. Just after the hour they would be escorted into the courtroom and over to the jury box.

It was the same courtroom where they had endured the *voir dire*. But now it seemed quite different. It was crowded to full capacity, and not with prospective jurors. There were a great many lawyers from both sides of the case. There were Exxon officials, and some fishermen, too. There were journalists in abundance, print and wire service and television: from the *Anchorage Daily News* the *New York Times* and from Dallas and Australia and the BBC and ABC and Reuters. There were VIPs and well-placed friends, and others who had managed to wangle a seat. There were no tickets for admission; it was supposedly first come, first seated, but both sides sent young staff members to the courtroom early each morning, be-fore the lines had formed, to hold down seats with jackets or purses until their allies arrived. Other than this, getting in was partly a matter of luck. Tourists might find themselves in front-row seats, while plaintiff lawyers or oil company executives waited in line outside the courtroom.

(In some cases, attendance at the trial required considerable sacrifice. When Peter Ehrhardt came up from Soldatna and announced his inten-tion of watching the trial, O'Neill said, "Not unless you shave off your beard!" The Alaskan lawyer did indeed bear an uncanny resemblance to Captain Hazelwood. Since O'Neill would be arguing that those who claimed to have seen Hazelwood drinking in Valdez could not possibly have mistaken someone else for him, he didn't want this seeming clone to be out there in front of the jury. Ehrhardt was outraged by the demand to shave—he had had that beard for thirteen years. But O'Neill was adamant, so off it came. "God," said Lori Wagner on seeing the bare pink face. "Now you look like James Taylor!")

Those lucky enough to be admitted were astonished by the appearance of the place. People said it looked like a disco. There was an abundance of high-tech equipment. The most spectacular of the numerous communications toys was a television screen measuring approximately six feet by six feet and mounted on wheels so that it could be rolled over to face the jury box when exhibits were required. Lest this daunting screen prove insufficient, two thirty-seven-inch Mitsubishi backups had also been provided, one at each end of the jury box. There were the feeder mechanisms for these displays, and the intertwined and taped wiring that connected video command to response. The entire courtroom had been reconformed so that the cutting edge of technology could be employed. Television monitors had been installed everywhere: on the judge's bench, on the lectern from which the lawyers spoke, on the witness stand, on the counsel tables at which the lawyers and Hazelwood sat. So many monitors, but no cameras. Judge Holland, in accordance with federal guidelines, had ruled against the network request to televise these proceedings. All the apparatus that had been installed was for internal use only.

That installation had been hugely expensive, and unlike anything seen in a courtroom before. The planning had begun long before the trial. Both sides had approved the highly innovative plans, and had shared in the expense. Two weeks before the trial, a technical consultant charging what O'Neill calls "a couple of grand a day" came up to Anchorage to see that everything worked and that the legal staff knew how to work it. The technical advisor, Gary Hilton from Invision Corp., was later, in Los Angeles, to apply many of the same techniques first tested in Anchorage in one of the few cases to be more celebrated, the criminal trial of O. J. Simpson.

The real innovation was not the size or ubiquity of television screens, but the amazing uses to which they could be put. In the annals of courtroom procedure, this truly was something new. If someone understood the new technology, there was nothing that could not be made to appear immediately upon a screen. It wasn't just documents or photos that could be swiftly displayed, it was videos as well. And not only an entire video, but any portion of it that one wanted to see, immediately. The immediacy was the miracle. You didn't have to play the whole tape of *Casablanca*, for example, to get to the line where Claude Rains says, "I'm shocked, shocked to find that there's gambling going on here." You only had to apply a scanner, taking only seconds, to put that on, or any other line: "Play it, Sam," or "I came for the waters," or "You're a rank sentimentalist," or anything at all.

Of course, they didn't play *Casablanca* in the courtroom. They played depositions, hundreds of which had been taped over the preceding years. And now the tapes were on CDs, which made the other new technology possible. With CDs, you could have bar codes. If one worked hard enough, every line of every deposition could have its own bar code. And if the legal assistants worked late enough every night, they would be ready every day to retrieve, by subject, any line of testimony that a courtroom witness had previously uttered in a deposition. No one had ever been able to do this before, and while it may sound a lot less interesting than *Casablanca,* in its own way, it was going to constitute an entire second front.

People were waiting for the trial to begin. They looked around at all the strange equipment, they searched for celebrities in the audience, they whispered to one another the identities of those hawk-eyed lawyers up at the front of the room, who were quickly scanning their notes before the judge arrived. If there was one focus to every stare, it was the bearded man dressed in blue, sitting erect in his chair at the counsel table, his head never turning to the spectators. Joe Hazelwood would be in the same place every day of the trial (except for Phase Two), facing the jury. Five years had passed since the grounding, and if appearances count, it could well have been ten. He was nearly bald now and his regrown beard had streaks of white. He seemed perfectly calm, even at peace. His face was impassive, and he appeared to regard the proceedings with nothing more than ingenuous interest.

A door opened and the jury began to file in, and people throughout the courtroom turned their heads and stared almost obscenely at the twelve downcast figures as they stiffly entered the crowded, quiet room and with self-conscious scraping of chairs arranged themselves in the partitioned jury box.

Then the judge entered. Whenever this happens everyone rises and remains standing until the judge is seated. It is a very simple thing, more custom than duty, and it happens in every court and almost nowhere else. People stand for a President or a Pope, to salute their country or to express their faith. They stand for a judge because the true majesty of this land is the law.

Judge Holland gave some introductory remarks. These were not directed to the courtroom audience, which he gave no sign of noticing. His words were to the jury.

He informed them that Exxon had admitted, for the purpose of this trial, that Joseph Hazelwood had been negligent in leaving the bridge of his vessel on the night of the grounding. Further, Exxon admitted that such negligence was a legal cause of the oil spill, and that it, Exxon, was responsible for this act of negligence.

But though Exxon admitted that Joseph Hazelwood had been negligent, Joseph Hazelwood did not admit it at all. And, the judge continued, regardless of who was or was not negligent, both Exxon and Hazelwood denied the claim for punitive damages.

Having set the stage, the judge then summoned the actors. It was time for each side to give its opening argument. First on, as always, was Brian O'Neill.

God knows how many fists were clenched beneath the defendants' table. If he had begun the *voir dire* with a scathing denunciation of his corporate foe, what would he do now when he was *supposed* to start arguing his case? Well-tailored shoulders were braced against the onslaught.

The harsh blows never came, at least not right away. With boundless good cheer and booming voice, and not a moment's hesitation or anxiety, seemingly oblivious to the notion that he, too, was on trial, O'Neill seemed pleased at his good fortune to be just where he was.

He said that he wanted to make some introductions. He introduced his partner, Lori Wagner, and Dick Gerry, and Laddie Montague, a plaintiff lawyer from Philadelphia, and Jerry Cohen, and commented that "as we move along, I'm going to let them do something, too," resolving any doubt as to just who was in charge.

And then he got the defendants' fists to clench again, and perhaps caused pills to be surreptitiously swallowed.

"I want to introduce you to some of my clients," he said. "My clients include ten thousand fishermen and four thousand Natives, the municipalities in the spill area, native corporations in the spill area, and natives who live in remote villages whose subsistence lifestyle was impacted by the wreck of the *Exxon Valdez*. Now, I can't introduce you to all fourteen or fifteen thousand of those folks, but I'm going to introduce you to a few.

"We have from Prince William Sound, the herring fisherman Snooks Moore, who is right there behind the TV set." Everyone looked and Snooks Moore hesitantly rose.

O'Neill pointed out all the others. "Kory Blake, Prince William Sound herring fisherman. Jamie Henderson, a Prince William Sound herring fisherman, all the way in the back. Tom Cochran, a Prince William Sound herring fisherman. Jere Eidem, who fishes for black cod and fishes in Upper

Cook Inlet. Bobby Correia and Liz Schmidt, who are Upper Cook Inlet fishermen, herring. Richard McGahan and his son Richard, Junior. Dave Horn, Timmy Keener, Dean Osmar, who is a fisherman and who was the 1984 Iditarod champion.

"Lois Munson, Ken Duffus, Ron Cusack, Kerry Nelson, Patty Wright, Jim Gray.

"Now as I said, the classes that are before you also include Natives who subsist, and I have from those classes with us here today, Eleanor McMullen. Back behind the TV set. Larry Evanoff, Gary Kompkoff, and Lois Munson.

"The municipalities, the cities in the case, include Kodiak Island Borough, Ouzinkie, Port Lions, Old Harbor, Larsen Bay, Seward, Cordova. The classes before you include all of the property owners in Prince William Sound; the Natives come from the villages of Tatiklet, Kodiak, Larsen Bay, Karluk, Port Lions, Akhiok, Ouzinkie, Ivanoff Bay, Chignik Bay, Chignik Lagoon, Chignik Lake, Perryville."

The defendants may have been rethinking their decision to keep the trial in Alaska.

"The plaintiffs in this case represent the full fabric, the full tapestry of life in and around Prince William Sound and indeed Alaska life. Now, how did we all get here? How did you get here, how did we get here, and how did the Exxon defendants get here? How did we get to the point to where twelve citizens will be judging the actions of one of the biggest corporations in the world? A disaster happened, and why did the disaster happen? The disaster happened because of the recklessness of Exxon Corporation."

And just how was Exxon reckless? This was, of course, the multibillion-dollar question, and O'Neill devoted the remainder of his opening remarks to answering it.

He had a very simple answer—and lots of factual allegations to back it up. That answer, and Exxon's rebuttal to it, were the heart of the case, really the case itself. And as O'Neill went on, defining in detail why he felt Exxon had been reckless, it became clear to everyone in the courtroom just what kind of case this was, quite apart from its size. For it was in many ways the biggest case of all time. Each side had spent years preparing for it and unbelievable sums of money doing so. O'Neill estimates that, if one includes the cost of lawyers' time, the plaintiffs together had spent $125 million to be in Courtroom Number Two, and the defendants several times that amount. Vast forests had been felled to fill Kafkaesque warehouses with legal documents. Academia had been scoured for its most lucid experts. Hundreds of lawyers had left their homes to wander in the frozen North in search of proof.

And proof of what? As O'Neill continued his remarks, it all became clear. This monumental matter, this legal mastodon, this landmark trial, this culmination of unparalleled effort and wanton expense, was, as O'Neill's words suggested, at its heart and to a great degree nothing really more or less than the world's largest drunk-driving case.

That was it. In Phase One, the most critical part of the trial, there were no complicated legal theories, no Latin phrases, no formulas or precedents brought forward. This was a drunk-driving case. O'Neill's unfolding argument was that Exxon was reckless because its captain had commanded the tanker while drunk and the company should have known that this would happen. "Exxon was reckless when it ignored the serious problems of an important employee."

O'Neill's speech was devoted primarily to evidence of just why Exxon should have known of Hazelwood's drinking. He began by describing the Graves memo, a 1985 report to Exxon officers of Hazelwood's drinking before he sought rehabilitation, and the IDR (Individual Disability Report), which was the report to Exxon of Hazelwood's twenty-eight-day stay at South Oaks Hospital for the rehabilitation program.

Why, the defense must have been wondering, was O'Neill talking about such old stuff—the Graves memo and the IDR report? Because he was about to develop a theme. "These are the only two Exxon documents that we'll ever see about this subject," he told the jury.

At first, it had been frustrating to find so little in the Exxon files to help make the case that Hazelwood was drinking. There were only two documents. It had gradually dawned on the plaintiffs, though, that the absence of proof proved something else. These straws could be spun into gold. Why *weren't* there more memos in Exxon's files? Why was that cupboard so bare? Was it because Hazelwood had in fact remained sober or because Exxon didn't want to know that he had not? O'Neill, of course, felt that he had the answer. More than an answer, a theme—a recurrent theme, restated throughout each movement of the trial, working its way up to a deafening crescendo at the very end.

But this was the very beginning, and O'Neill was carefully laying out his facts. Each note was sounded separately, no need for melody yet. The first point was that by placing a recovering alcoholic on a tanker that was at sea for ninety days at a time, Exxon had doomed any chance of his recovery. "You're taking him away from aftercare. You're giving him a lot of responsibility and tedium at the same time."

Another note: "You'll see the chairman of the board of the Exxon Corporation tell the Congress of the United States that Captain Hazelwood was the most closely monitored man in the fleet. He should have been." And then, for just a moment, a hint of the theme. "Exxon will not produce to you one piece of paper out of the millions of pieces of paper in its files, not one piece of paper that shows that that captain was monitored."

And then more notes, a flood of notes, staccato. Each one dealt with Hazelwood's drinking between his rehabilitation and the grounding. Investigators had been hired and every rumor followed up to glean this relentless recital of sporadic alcohol abuse. "Now I'm going to tell you what happened, and many of the facts that I'm going to tell you that we're going to prove in this courtroom, this is the first time they will have seen the light of day." There followed the naming of those Exxon employees with whom Hazelwood drank on ship, and those Exxon employees with whom he drank on shore, and those who smelled alcohol on his breath, and the Exxon official to whom these things were reported. O'Neill claimed that assigning Hazelwood to command the *Exxon Valdez* was itself reckless in light of these reports, and done only to save the few thousand dollars extra that it would have cost to assign someone without a Prince William Sound pilotage endorsement.

It must have been painful for Hazelwood to hear each alleged drinking incident recounted in such cold detail: two vodkas in the Portland airport, the where and when and witness of every relapse.

It was O'Neill's job, of course, to build his case. So he intoned about "a fellow named Steve Day, who's an Exxon superintendent who saw empty Henry Weinhard beer bottles on the vessel" while it was in the shipyard being fixed. One cannot help but look back many years, to the early days of O'Neill's career. Was this moment so very different from the farm foreclosure proceeding that he felt had transformed his career? The poignant look of the farmer's wife was supposedly the turning point on his personal road to Damascus. So much time had passed since then, so much acclaim, so many victories on the side of the angels, or at least endangered species. But change can be illusory. Hazelwood had found that out, and now so did his adversary. Across the span of time and distance, Brian O'Neill was still in the business of counting his opponents' beer bottles.

The last drinking incident that he recited had taken place just one week before the grounding. The *Exxon Valdez* was undergoing repairs in San Francisco Bay. An Exxon employee named Mary Williamson shared a launch with Hazelwood. She felt he was abusive to her, and she was pretty sure that she smelled alcohol on his breath. She reported this to her Exxon superiors, O'Neill said, and yet Hazelwood was not asked about it and was permitted to set off on his fateful voyage to Valdez.

As if this final chance to prevent the disaster was too much even for him to bear, O'Neill turned from recitation to unleash the full force of his very considerable rhetorical powers. How could they have permitted Hazelwood to command a tanker? "His alcoholism was as clearly charted as Bligh Reef. Exxon knew he was drinking again and somebody should have said stop at this point in time, and nobody did and the *Exxon Valdez* readies itself to be loaded to go to Valdez, Alaska, and be loaded with fifty million gallons of toxic crude oil, and who else was aboard the floating time bomb? A helmsman, the guy who steers the ship, named Robert Kagan who has trouble steering, hearing and seeing, and a complement of officers, Hazelwood, Cousins and Glowacki, all of whom at some point in their careers have violated the Exxon alcohol policy."

Pausing to take a deep breath, O'Neill moved on to the last fatal day ashore in Valdez. He retraced the captain's steps and counted his drinks, coming to the very impressive total of sixteen. This was at some variance from Hazelwood's admission of three vodkas on the rocks. Since O'Neill was of the view that the drinks had been doubles, he was counting each one twice. That still left quite a gap from sixteen. O'Neill's explanation was that the captain had made additional trips to the Pipeline Club during the day—when he was supposedly in the flower shop, for example.

He then described what happened after the captain had returned to his ship. To begin, O'Neill argued, rules and laws had been broken. The Exxon bridge manual had a requirement—watch condition C—that two officers be on the bridge. This had been violated. It was against the law to drink alcohol within four hours of assuming sea duty. This had been violated. There was a law that said that ship crew members must have had six hours of rest in the twelve hours before they assumed their duties. This had been violated.

Then he came to the grounding. He described how Captain Hazelwood moved from the outbound to the inbound lane in order to avoid ice sighted in the Narrows. He said that "Hazelwood changes the vessel's course from two hundred degrees to one hundred eighty degrees, putting it on a collision course with Bligh Reef, and doesn't tell the Coast Guard that he's changed the course." Hazelwood then put Cousins in charge, O'Neill said, and told him to turn when he came abeam of Busby Island. "Two minutes before Busby Island, Hazelwood leaves the bridge. Two minutes. He doesn't wait the two minutes for the turn. . . . Why? Captain Murphy smelled alcohol on his breath . . . and we know what he did that afternoon. After the captain went below, Cousins spent six minutes in the chart room. "Now remember that Cousins was told by the captain to turn in two minutes. And the turn doesn't happen. The turn doesn't happen for quite a while. The captain should have been able to tell that the turn wasn't happening.

"So for six minutes prior to the accident, Captain Hazelwood, disabled because of his alcoholism, is below, a tired Cousins is back in the chart room. There isn't an officer in control of the vessel and the vessel hits Bligh Reef and that's why we're here.

"The wrong person gave the wrong order to the wrong person at the wrong place at the wrong time, and it was all made possible when Exxon gave the keys to the car to their captain."

He was coming to the end of his remarks.

"Now, Prince William Sound is a beautiful and special place. It is one of the last best places on earth, and this last best place on earth is not only renowned for its beauty, but it provides their livelihood and it provides their dinner table. For a native who lives in a remote village, when the tide goes out the table is set. The oil on the vessel comes from the North Slope. It is the people's oil, not Exxon's, and the extraction and transportation of oil is inherently dangerous. And it is very profitable. Wealth was given to Exxon in exchange for responsibility. The public's trust was given to Exxon in exchange for responsibility."

That responsibility, he argued, had not been discharged. The failure to monitor the captain, the ignoring of the evidence of his relapse, the use of overworked and tired sailors on vessels, were all signs of abdicated responsibility.

And this, he said in conclusion, "wasn't just negligence, it was recklessness; it was recklessness to the captain, it was recklessness to *them*"—he flung out his arm toward the fishermen whom he had earlier introduced—

"it was recklessness to *them*"—he pointed to still others—"it was reck-lessness to the people of Alaska, the biggest mess by the people that had the wealth and power and size to do better. Thanks."

Applause is not permitted in a courtroom, but there is a certain kind of si-lence that is hard to mistake. There was no sound of movement, no whisper, no cough. The judge said that this seemed to be a good time for a recess.

Twenty minutes later, when people were back in their seats, it was Exxon's turn to speak. The opening statement would be given by Pat Lynch. The tall, angular lawyer went slowly to the lectern. He was no fool and knew he had an uphill battle. Whatever else he felt about O'Neill's re-marks, he recognized that they had been effective. He made his living de-fending with great skill the largest corporations in the land, and he had no illusions whatsoever about how they were regarded by the public. In the popular culture—in movies, on television—large companies were with increasing frequency cast as villains. When King Kong was remade, it was not so much the giant ape that was portrayed as dangerous as it was the giant multinational oil company that captured him—a company much like Exxon. Well, there was nothing that Lynch could do about that sort of thing. His job was to give this sort of thing, the trial itself, his best shot.

His best shot was to admit that Exxon had made mistakes—but that these constituted negligence, not recklessness. Indeed, as he pointed out in his opening remarks, Exxon had already agreed to compensate people for the damage they had suffered from the spill.

"I stand here in a posture which in my years of practicing law I've never been in before, and that is that . . . the client I represent begins by saying that it is responsible for this accident, begins by saying that this terrible oil spill which undoubtedly had harmful effects on the fishermen plaintiffs and the Native plaintiffs and the other people that Mr. O'Neill mentioned, they are entitled to compensation and Exxon Corporation should pay them compensation, and Exxon Corporation fully expects that you will decide what they should be paid."

But, he noted, it was quite a step from that to punitive damages, and the burden of taking that step and proving recklessness was on the plain-tiffs. There was a big difference between negligence and recklessness.

"If you try to think in common, ordinary terms about the difference, you might think about things that I think all of us have experienced.

"You know, you can imagine driving along in your car and trying to adjust the radio or your rear-view mirror or something, or looking up at the rear-view mirror to see if your eyebrows are right, and somebody unexpectedly stops in front of you, or something happens and you get into a traffic accident; that's simple negligence. A person that has that happen to them is responsible to pay the costs associated with the accident. Probably most of us, one way or another, have been involved in something like that.

"Recklessness involves something much more than that. It involves something like looking at a train as you're approaching the intersection and deciding to race the train as you're approaching the intersection, knowing full well that you're putting people on the train at risk, and people in your car at risk, but deciding to take that chance. It's consciously taking the chance to cause an accident. It's thinking about it and deciding, I'm going to take a shot at that. That's the kind of conduct plaintiffs need to prove to prove recklessness."

So the big question for the jury was this: "Was Captain Hazelwood acting like a man racing a train through an intersection?"

To this question, he had an answer: nothing that Hazelwood had done leading up to the crash was reckless. Putting the ship on autopilot had not been reckless. Lynch compared that to putting a car in cruise control, or even using a computer. "Some people trust computers. Some people don't trust computers. I'm using a computer for my opening statement. Mr. O'Neill did not use a computer for his opening statement." This particular analogy may have been more accurate than helpful.

Trusting Greg Cousins to turn right, Lynch argued, had not been a reckless act by Hazelwood. Again, he used a curious analogy: driving with one's son and saying, "When you get to the light up ahead, turn right." Not every parent who has taught a child to drive may have retained the same confidence.

So why *had* the accident occurred? "I think one thing that happened was, Mr. Cousins wanted to show Captain Hazelwood what a good mate he was. He decided to do some things over and above Captain Hazelwood's order." So he went to the chart room to write down a fix at Busby light. That may have been why "instead of starting to turn right as the ship was abeam of Busby Island, it continued for seven minutes on the course of one hundred eighty degrees." However, in the end, "no one can reconstruct exactly what happened."

And though Lynch denied that Exxon was trying to put the blame for the grounding on the Coast Guard, he had to admit that Coast Guard error "was part of the picture." Not a happy part. The passing of Busby Island by the *Exxon Valdez* did appear on Coast Guard radar, but there was no one to see it. The man in charge had gone for coffee. And when he returned, he busied himself with changing some tapes and had his back to the radar screen. If Coast Guard folly were the only issue in this case, the trial would scarcely have lasted past noon. But Lynch knew well that implicating others did not absolve his client, and so he moved on to other things.

He moved on to the subject of alcoholism. He allied himself with the forces of enlightenment and rehabilitation. "The plaintiffs have tried to hang a label of alcoholism or drunk on this case so they can get punitive damages. And in attacking and trying to parlay that into a showing that Exxon was reckless in dealing with Captain Hazelwood, they're trying to do more harm to people who have a problem with alcohol, trying to undo a lot of what has been done, twenty years to try to bring this problem out of the closet, to end the day when people who had a drinking problem were called drunks and were fired and were left to wait on the trash heap for whatever could come their way."

So when Hazelwood, despite his past treatment for alcoholism, was assigned to captain a tanker, there were reasons for that. There were, said Lynch, three reasons. First, "the only practical way to get people to voluntarily seek help was to tell them that if they did so they wouldn't be penalized in their job." This concept was incorporated in the Exxon Alcohol Policy, and the company was complying with that policy. Second, keeping a former alcoholic from captaining an oil tanker may have been against the law. "In 1976 the Attorney General of the United States ruled that a person who has been treated for alcohol problems is a handicapped person and is entitled to the benefit of laws protecting the handicapped from discrimination." Third, there was the concern that keeping Hazelwood from command "would drive the problem of drinking underground."

Despite all this, it was of course still necessary to monitor Captain Hazelwood. But that monitoring, Lynch said, had to be confidential in nature.

He elaborated. "They didn't go around coming in every week saying, 'Captain Hazelwood, take the pledge, have you had anything to drink?' But they watched his job performance carefully." It scarcely seems possible to have more disparate views of monitoring than those advanced by Lynch and by O'Neill.

Lynch concluded with a summary of his case. "I'm not saying there was no negligence. I'm not saying Captain Hazelwood should have left the bridge. I'm saying he made a mistake. He committed an error, and other errors were committed, and the totality of these errors, any one of them—take any one of them away, and the ship veers off this way and safely heads for San Francisco or Long Beach. It was only the combination of all those errors that kept it headed this way toward Bligh Reef, and that was not the result of a drunken captain. That was not the result of any accident that had to happen. This was an accident that didn't have to happen, and wouldn't have happened except for a chain of mistakes from Exxon people, Mr. Cousins, Captain Hazelwood, others ... the Coast Guard and others. It's a tragedy.

"The plaintiffs, Natives and the fishermen are entitled to full compensation for their loss. This is not a case in which punishment is warranted. Thank you, Your Honor."

Following him, without introduction, was Michael Chalos, representing Captain Hazelwood. Neither as charismatic as O'Neill nor as analytical as Lynch, Chalos had no master at getting to the point. His first words were these: "There are two myths that surround the grounding of the *Exxon Valdez*. The first myth is that Captain Hazelwood was a relapsed alcoholic. That is wrong. The second myth is that the accident came about because Captain Hazelwood was impaired by alcohol. That is also wrong. Please allow me to expose both myths for you."

As for the first myth, "they want you to believe that my client was a skid-row bum. Well, he was none of that. He was none of that. He voluntarily went in 1985 to seek treatment for a condition which was diagnosed as 'dysthymic disorder.' That's a form of depression. That was the primary diagnosis that was placed on him. The secondary diagnosis was 'alcohol abuse, episodic now.' What that means is that when he got depressed he drank to excess, so they had to deal with the depression so that he *wouldn't* drink to excess. That's what he went in for. Unlike what plaintiffs would like you to believe, he was never diagnosed as alcohol dependent. . . . No one said he couldn't drink socially, and that's what he did."

As for myth number two, that the accident had occurred as a result of Hazelwood's drinking, Chalos had an even stronger response. It was, in fact, the cornerstone of his entire defense.

It had to do with the blood samples. Though the results of Hazelwood's blood test had been .06, which is less than the common standard for automobile drunk driving, O'Neill was arguing that since the test was taken about eleven hours after the grounding, Hazelwood must have been far beyond the drunkenness threshold when he left the bridge of his ship. It was known that O'Neill had experts who would testify to this.

Chalos's response was to discredit the test. If the test was the best proof they had that Hazelwood was drunk while in command, then they had no proof, Chalos contended, because the test was no good. The chain of custody had been broken.

He was very convincing. Chalos, who is proud of having been born on the island of Chios, also home of the poet Homer, was moved to create his own vivd odyssey, in which the stoppered vials, rather like Ulysses, endured a protracted journey fraught with peril. With considerable zeal, he retraced for the jury the fate of the blood sample from the time it was drawn until it had been tested a number of days later. He talked about Scott Connor, the Coast Guard corpsman who had taken the sample and then put the blood into three vials. Two had a gray stopper and the other a red stopper. The gray stopper indicated the tubes had a preservative in them, which was intended to keep the blood from fermenting and thereby giving a falsely positive reading. Connor put the samples in a Styrofoam bag and sealed it, and then flew to Valdez. The chain of custody then required a locked refrigerator but instead the samples ended up on a windowsill (which, Chalos pointed out, was on the first floor), and then overnight in the unlocked general galley refrigerator ("next to the tomatoes, the lettuce, the carrots, the onions, whatever else was in there"). The next day Connor returned the samples and flew to Anchorage, where, instead of handing them to his superior officer, he took the samples home.

"Unbelievable! He takes them home! Keeps them there for a couple of hours, then . . . he brings them to his superior officer who's supposed to be the genius, and this guy immediately breaks the seals, takes the seals off. 'What'd you do that for?' 'Oh, I just wanted to see the color of the blood.'" Chalos shared a can-you-believe-it look with the very attentive jury, and then continued, shearing further links from the chain of custody.

He described how the samples had then languished unattended in a remote warehouse for several days before being shipped in an unrefrigerated package to the lab in California.

And there, he said, the worst outrage of all had occurred. In the lab, the vials came into the possession of Karen Metcalf. "Her job, her only job, is to make sure of the size of the tubes and the color of the stoppers." And what she then logged in were tubes of a different size than what Connor reported he had taken, and with three red stoppers. "Three red stoppers! What happened to the gray stoppers?" The red stoppers meant no preservative, which would falsify the results "if in fact it was Captain Hazelwood's blood.

"So okay, so the story would be bad enough if that was it. But that's not it. Listen to this. About a month after the lab has the samples and after they've been tested already, a Mrs. Judy Pete, who happens to be the wife of the man that runs the laboratory, without explanation, and very mysteriously, I might add, goes to Karen Metcalf and she says, 'You made a mistake when those samples were received. That wasn't the correct designation.' Karen Metcalf says, 'No, I didn't make a mistake. There were three ten-millimeter tubes with red stoppers on it.' Mrs. Pete says, 'No. I want you to change the records, the official records. I want you to change them, cross out the—what you wrote before and write in two gray-stoppered tubes and one red-stoppered tube.' Karen Metcalf says, 'Well, I didn't think I made a mistake, you know. I don't know why she was asking me this.'

"I tell you why she was asking her that. Connor had given a statement to authorities that had probably gotten to them, and they were trying to conform the records to what Connor was saying.

"Ladies and gentlemen, there's serious doubt, serious doubt that the blood that was tested was Captain Hazelwood's blood. . . ."

He left the subject on a note of dark suspicion. "The best I can say is that blood test is—and I'm going to use an understatement—it was botched. But I think it was a lot more than botched." Even the most trusting of the jurors might at that point be imagining, at the very least, a furtive hand reaching up to the windowsill. Chalos returned to the counsel table. The opening statements were over.

10

Denial Is Not the Name of a River in Egypt

The moment had come for the first witness to take the stand. But O'Neill didn't begin with a witness. He opened with a video. For twenty-seven minutes the same images glowed throughout the highly wired courtroom, on big screens and small, with no bad seats in the house. The video was a series of clips of top Exxon executives testifying before Senate committees and appearing on national talk shows— *Face the Nation, This Week With David Brinkley,* the *MacNeil/Lehrer News Hour*—in the first frenzied weeks after the spill.

Some of the testimony was harmful to the defendants in the present case, such as Exxon president Lee Raymond telling David Brinkley that if there had been an error in judgment, it was in returning Captain Hazelwood to sea duty after his alcoholism treatment. Many of the statements would provide the opportunity for furious rebuttal by O'Neill throughout the trial, such as the statement to a U.S. Senate subcommittee by Frank Iarossi, head of Exxon Shipping Company, that Hazelwood was "the most closely monitored man" in the fleet.

The point of the video was probably to highlight the inconsistencies of Exxon officials with their later trial testimony. It certainly laid the

groundwork for much subsequent courtroom contradiction. And it exploited fully a problem of Exxon's. Immediately after the spill, the company's top officers had not hidden from the angry public roar. They had
made themselves available in the most public forums to answer questions
about the spill. They had spoken calmly, frankly, and with shared indignation over what had occurred. The impression was left that it was
Hazelwood's fault, not theirs. But a company's public-relations goals just
after a disaster are very different from its litigation needs five years later.
Sometimes one acts against the other, such as the video of Chairman
Rawl saying on the *MacNeil/Lehrer* show that Hazelwood's actions constituted "a gross error," words that come dangerously close to the concept of recklessness. And another useful aspect of this very first barrage
of video artillery was its reminder, through grim Senators and indignant
network stars, of just how major and how horrifying the spill had been. It
reopened the wound.

And then it was time for the witnesses. All the disagreements in the
case were over facts, and the jury would decide which facts were true in
large part because of which witnesses they chose to believe. Each witness
would be called by one of the parties. All the plaintiff witnesses went first.
Each would be questioned in a helpful manner by a plaintiff lawyer. Then,
in cross-examination, the defense lawyers would get to ask questions—
less helpfully, trying to discredit the witness or the testimony or both.
After that, the plaintiff lawyer got to ask a few more questions, to try to
repair the damage. When all the plaintiff witnesses had been called, the
defense could call *its* witnesses. Each side's roles then were reversed, and
the same process was played out.

Most people in the courtroom were wondering who the very first witness would be. Trial lawyers were thought to put much store on first impressions. O'Neill already had warned that he had revelations never before disclosed. Would the first to take the stand be someone with a
particularly lurid tale of drunken debauchery and excess?

The first witness, as it turned out, was an aged photographer. And he
was questioned not by Brian O'Neill but by Lori Wagner. This may have
been a little disappointing to those expecting fireworks, oratorical or evidentiary. But it did not lack premeditation. There was a reason for his
being there, for being first. It was not his dry humor, though that was evident. (When asked how long he had been doing marine photography, he

replied, "Interminably.") He had been called as a witness so that his photographs could be shown to the jury. A few months after the grounding,
he had been hired by the state of Alaska to take pictures of the damaged
Exxon Valdez. These photographs now were shown. The jury was shown
on its three screens the location of places on the vessel that would figure
in their deliberations—the bridge that the captain had left, the gangplank
that supposedly only the sober could traverse—and was introduced to
nautical terms such as *starboard* and *aft.* They also saw the shocking size
of the ship's wound. The great gaping hole still had rocks, which looked
like boulders, imbedded in its serrated rim. It was like a huge dead sea
beast, as frightening in its size and vulnerability as the underwater pictures of the *Titanic,* a somewhat shorter vessel. The jurors could not
doubt the violence of the impact.

The photographs were very effective, and so, too—the plaintiffs
hoped—was the fact that the witness was being questioned by Lori Wagner. Nine of the twelve jurors were women. So Lori Wagner had been
conspicuously present at the counsel table. There was nothing token
about her participation in the case, however; no one else had matched her
tireless and brilliant work in creating the damage matrix. Throughout the
trial, she played a critical role in preparing O'Neill for each day's session.
She was the principal gatekeeper for all those seeking access to O'Neill.
But there were other hardworking stars who were not sitting at the counsel table. The gender card *was* being played, deliberately and with her
concurrence. She didn't just sit there, though; she questioned the first
witness, and during the trial would be one of the very few plaintiff lawyers
to displace O'Neill.

She questioned the next witness, too, which was made more difficult
by virtue of the fact that he wasn't there. Many of the witnesses in this
trial did not want to come to Anchorage to testify, but had to. They had
been subpoenaed. Not to show up would be a crime. But the subpoena
powers of the court were limited to a one-hundred-mile radius from the
courthouse. If you lived farther away than that you could not be served.
Joel Roberson, one of the two crew members who had spent the day before the grounding with Captain Hazelwood in Valdez, now lived in
Texas. He could not be subpoenaed. But he had been deposed. And his
deposition could be, and now was, read aloud in court.

Nothing in this trial was simple or unplanned. You didn't just stand up and read the deposition to the jury, questions and answers both, as is often done. Instead, someone played the part of the missing witness— took the stand, pretended to be the witness, and when asked a question, read the same answer that had been given in the deposition.

Perhaps not exactly the same answer. The role of substitute witness afforded a dramatic opportunity, and the plaintiffs took it. You didn't have to say the words exactly the way they had originally been pronounced. There was no law against changing inflection. And inflection was important. When asked whether it was possible for Hazelwood to have had more than one drink at the Harbor Club, Roberson had replied, "I would certainly think that, yes, this was possible, certainly." This line can be read aloud in many ways; emphasizing the last word strongly enough would alter the meaning. Considerable time had been spent on choosing stand-ins who could convey the desired impression, and on rehearsing over and over again the way they gave their answers.

Not that the plaintiffs needed to play games with inflection: Roberson's testimony was useful to their case even on the printed page. He testified that Hazelwood had said that the grounding was his own fault. And when asked by the Coast Guard what the problem was, Hazelwood had replied, "You're looking at it." He also said that after the grounding he had smelled liquor on Hazelwood's breath—though he added that this was after the Coast Guard had come aboard and not before that. When asked if he had ever seen Hazelwood drinking aboard the ship, he gave an answer that each side could, and did, work with. He said that Hazelwood had poured for him a glass of orange juice and an unidentified colorless liquid which the Captain claimed was confiscated alcohol but which Roberson said was tasteless. (On cross-examination, Sanders had elicited from Roberson the possibility that Hazelwood was playing a joke on him.)

The next witness was on videotape. Lisa Harrison lived more than one hundred miles away, and so didn't have to be present. She had been the bartender at the Pipeline Club who had poured Captain Hazelwood's drinks on the day before Good Friday in 1989.

Her testimony may have been on tape, but it was dynamite. It was startlingly inconsistent with the version given by Hazelwood and the two crew members who had been with him. Their story was that Hazelwood had ordered and consumed three drinks during their one late afternoon visit to the Pipeline Bar.

Bartender Harrison's recollection was very different. She said that Hazelwood had made *two* visits to the Pipeline Club, not one. Her shift that day was from ten thirty in the morning until late afternoon—six thirty. She said that Hazelwood first came in around noon. He had a quick drink and then left. She said he returned around two with another man, and the two each had a drink and left.

It is true that her memory of the supposedly second bar appearance, in which Hazelwood drank with at least one companion, was less damaging than Hazelwood's admission—one drink versus three. But he *had* admitted having three drinks that afternoon, and so was stuck with that. And now the bartender had described another, earlier, visit during which the captain had drunk a vodka at about noon. But Hazelwood was having lunch at noon, and there were a number of witnesses to that. He *could* have been there at two, as the bartender also claimed. His version was that he had been in the flower shop at two o'clock, but he said he was there for an hour, which jurors might find a long time to be buying flowers, and the shop was directly across the street from the Pipeline Club. The florist supported Hazelwood's version: he was there for about an hour. But Lisa Harrison's account raised many doubts in jurors' minds.

She raised another issue, too. She said the drinks of Smirnoff vodka that she poured for Hazelwood were doubles—at three ounces apiece, and eighty proof.

The cross-examination did not change her story. She was certain that Hazelwood came in at noon and then again at about two, and was gone for good by two thirty. She certainly didn't see him again, and she worked until six thirty. She was sure of that because the place was so uncrowded—that day at any rate. At this point in the testimony she stops, and muses, and says something that suggests the maelstrom that was about to hit the Valdez area: "That was my last slow day as a bartender."

Her testimony concluded the first day of the trial. The proceedings always ended at two. The lawyers then began a far longer workday than the one just concluded, getting ready for the next session. The jurors went home, admonished to talk to no one, not even to each other, about the case.

The first witness to be called the next morning was another bartender, Emma Lee, and she also appeared on videotape. She had relieved Lisa Harrison at six thirty. And, she claimed, Captain Hazelwood had walked in the door and she had served him a drink. She said he was by himself, stayed no more than fifteen minutes, and then left.

She said she had no doubt about whom she had served. She knew who Joe Hazelwood was; he usually came to the Pipeline Club when he was in town.

If the two bartenders were both right, then Hazelwood had made three trips to the club instead of the one he described. The aggregate testimony seemed incredibly damaging. The best that cross-examination could achieve was the bartender's opinion that the captain had not seemed to be drunk.

The next witness was not on videotape; her deposition testimony was read by a stand-in. The plaintiffs had cast this role with extra care. They found more helpful to their case the testimony than the person giving it. So they had put in her place a member of their legal team, a woman whose calm and precise enunciation of the missing witness's words achieved a triumph of diction over content unmatched since Eliza Doolittle's description of her poor aunt's tragic end.

The witness whose testimony was being read was Janice Delozier. She was a dental assistant in Valdez whose office on the day of the grounding was closed between one o'clock and three. She had decided to kill the two hours at the Pipeline Club. She testified that she was one bar stool away from Hazelwood when he ordered his vodka on the rocks, and that she saw him order a second drink as well.

If believed, this testimony was particularly damaging because it corroborated the claim of the bartender that Hazelwood had been at the Pipeline Club hours earlier than he now claimed. Was she describing merely a second visit, or even a third?

Mrs. Delozier had never seen Captain Hazelwood before that day and did not know who the bearded man was. So how then had she remembered his order—his two orders? Her own explanation was that "I have a very good memory, and have been told so a lot."

The reader similarly blessed will find the name Delozier vaguely familiar. It is the surname, as well, of Mark Delozier, the Coast Guard warrant officer who first boarded the *Exxon Valdez* after the spill, detected alcohol on the captain's breath, and suggested that a blood test be taken. The same Mark Delozier who then had surreptitiously searched Hazelwood's quarters. *That* Mark Delozier. He was related to Janice Delozier by marriage. He was her husband. In fact, the very evening she returned from her observations in the Pipeline Club, he was summoned from their bed by a phone call to attend the stricken ship, where his own sensory acuity would be displayed. When he returned, very considerably later, he shared with her his suspicion that the accident had been alcohol related.

Several days later, according to her testimony, Mrs. Delozier found herself in a flower shop, the very same one from which Captain Hazelwood had wired Easter flowers to his family, the shop of Emily Kaiser. While the proprietress was complaining about her Easter sales, Janice Delozier happened to glance down at a newspaper on the counter. At the top of the page there was a headline about Captain Hazelwood. Next to it was a photograph. She looked at it carefully. The memory so often celebrated kicked in once again.

When her husband returned from his office that evening, she said that she needed to tell him something.

"I told him—he knew I was already having coffee at the Pipeline. I relayed to him, 'Remember the day I had the two-hour lunch break?' He said, 'Yes.' I said I was at the Pipeline with the gang, and he said, 'Yes.' I said, 'Well, this guy came in, et cetera, et cetera.' I said, 'And Mark, as God is my witness, it was Joe Hazelwood.' That's what I said. And he kind of sat back in the La-Z-Boy, you know. He didn't do any handsprings. He just said, 'Are you sure?' And I said, 'Yes.' And he said, very slowly, very carefully, 'Tell me a little slower this time what you just told me, tell me again.' And I did. And I said, 'I do not want to get involved in this. I just want to tell you, I don't want to be involved in it.' And he more or less gave me his word, which was neither here nor there."

It was apparently here, as her surrogate now was testifying in open court, a bubbling brook of local incident, describing in Chekovian detail the decor and denizens of the Pipeline Club. And putting one more nail into what plaintiffs hoped would be the coffin of Hazelwood's version of his day.

The next witness was actually present, and was questioned by Lori Wagner. Captain William E. Murphy, who went by the name of Ed, was the state harbor pilot with whom Hazelwood had temperately lunched in Valdez. That evening he had piloted the *Exxon Valdez* out of the harbor, and then departed the tanker in a small boat half an hour before the grounding. He made a good appearance in court. He was obviously a highly professional mariner, like his friend Joe Hazelwood. He was there under oath to give testimony damaging to that friend, and he did not seem happy about it.

He was already aboard the tanker when Hazelwood returned from shore, and Murphy admitted to having smelled alcohol on the captain's breath. On the other hand, he verified that the Valdez lunch had lasted from noon until one thirty, which meant that even if the bartender was right about an earlier visit, she was surely wrong about the time. This was important; if she was wrong about that she might be wrong about anything.

He also verified that the captain had been gone from the bridge for a considerable length of time, and that that was unusual.

Lori Wagner pressed him to express his conclusions about the causes of the grounding. He stalled at first, but then stated that "somebody screwed up . . . it's real apparent to me that there were serious mistakes made." Wagner then pressed him again, asking just who had made the serious mistakes. He would not answer this directly, but he admitted, "There is quite a lapse of time where apparently no action was taken when the ship was clearly standing into danger." That was as far as he would go in ascribing fault. "The ship was steered toward a known danger until it struck the known danger." His testimony seemed torn between exceptional professionalism and loyalty to a friend—an admirable, if tortured, polarity.

The cross-examination of Captain Murphy by Jim Neal shows why a Nashville lawyer is worth hundreds of dollars an hour. He managed to mitigate much of the damage. Between their opening and closing statements, the lawyers weren't really allowed to *say* anything. They could only ask questions. But if one asked enough questions about Moussy, as Jim Neal did, one could establish clearly that it is a nonalcoholic beer that *smells* like real beer, and so perhaps *that* was what Captain Murphy had in fact detected.

And then there was the litany. Each side had its litany. With O'Neill it was a litany of all the steps of monitoring that Exxon didn't do. With the defense it was the absence of any outward sign of drunkenness in Captain Hazelwood. In questioning Murphy, Neal provided a good example:

"Now, when you saw Captain Hazelwood for the first time up on the bridge, did he appear—did he in any way appear to you to be intoxicated?"

"No."

"Did he in any way appear to you to be impaired?"

"No."

"Did he appear to you in any way to be slurring his speech?"

"No."

"Did you observe him swaying or misstepping?"

"No."

"Was he slurring his words?"

"No."

"Did he appear to you to be at that point in time in any way intoxicated or impaired?"

"He gave no such appearance."

And so Captain Murphy left the stand having reluctantly and despite corrective revision added some slight weight to the plaintiffs' main assertion, that the captain's drinking had caused the crash.

And now it was time for Brian O'Neill to resume his role in the spotlight. He stepped up to the lectern and could scarcely have uttered more arresting words.

"Plaintiffs call Captain Hazelwood as an adverse witness under the Rules of Examination."

Captain Hazelwood left his place at the counsel table and went over to the witness stand. The clerk said, "For the record, would you please state your full name and address and spell your last name, please."

"Joseph J. Hazelwood. Address is Huntington, New York."

"Spell your last name."

"H-A-Z-E-L-W-O-O-D."

"Thank you."

The clerk drew back and O'Neill then took his place. He looked directly at Hazelwood, who calmly returned his gaze.

It was the first time that the two men had met. Gerry Nolting had deposed the captain; it was thought best that Hazelwood not encounter his true adversary until the trial. O'Neill's look was one of sympathy, and behind that a considerable agenda. Hazelwood looked quite openly back, and conveyed nothing.

They were the two central players in this drama, and to a very considerable degree they were the same person. They were the same person altered by circumstance. They were free men who wanted above all to remain free. Each possessed the bounteous blessing of knowing exactly what he wanted to do with his life. Each was exceptionally gifted in that mission. They both disdained the forces that kept them from their excellence, the regimentation of their lives, the subordination of their individual selves.

Each hated the pressure to conform. One of them triumphed over that pressure, had used the standard of the conformists to win their support. The other—well, the other was in the dock, his dignity retained through knowledge of a skill that he would never be allowed to show again. And the dock was in a courtroom in Anchorage, Alaska, U.S.A., in a state that stood for what both men wanted even more than career, a goal more elusive than one of them knew—freedom.

And of course they had this in common, too: both lives had been damaged by alcohol, though perhaps neither man was a stranger to denial.

O'Neill was a pacer, and he circled his prey. His words were entirely sympathetic. "Captain, I realize that this is difficult for you, and if you'll stick with me, it will be over. . . . If you don't understand a question or think the question isn't fair, you tell me—okay?"

He was positioning himself as the captain's friend, with Exxon their common foe. His very first question was, "How did you first find out about your termination from Exxon Corporation?" The answer was that he had heard about it on the radio. No one at the company had called him. No one had talked to him. When asked his reaction to this, Hazelwood said that it had made him angry.

The captain would be testifying over the next three days—far longer than any other witness. His appearance provided the best opportunity for each side to promote its own version of events. Had his drinking been so prevalent that Exxon should have known about it? Had he been adequately monitored? How much had he drunk that day in Valdez? Why did he leave the bridge? What had caused the accident? All the disputed facts revolved around this one man, what he had done and what he had not done. His story was the case itself, and at the outset of his recital of the story, O'Neill had rekindled at least a spark of the captain's anger at Exxon.

The courteous questions gradually drew out the tale of Hazelwood and drink. After a period of sporadic alcohol abuse, he had undergone a twenty-eight-day rehabilitation program at South Oaks Hospital in 1985. When he left, it was recommended that he not drink. He attended some Alcoholics Anonymous meetings.

And he spoke about his past drinking on the phone to Ben Graves from Exxon, who after hanging up wrote a report to some senior Exxon Shipping officials recounting Hazelwood's admission that before his rehabilitation he had occasionally drunk aboard ship and sometimes returned to the vessel after drinking. This report remained in Exxon's files.

But Hazelwood had been reassigned to sea duty by Exxon. Before this was allowed to happen he met with an Exxon Gulf Coast port captain named Sheehy, who wanted to have a little talk with him first. They met at a hotel out by the international airport at Houston. They sat down at one of the tables off the lobby.

Just where they met was very important, at least to the lawyers in the case. It was a matter of ongoing and vigorous debate. There had been tables with umbrellas over them, at which food and drink were served. Hazelwood refers to this atrium area as a sidewalk cafe. O'Neill calls it a bar. In fact he called it that in his opening statement. When seated at the whatever, Hazelwood had ordered a club soda and Sheehy a beer. To O'Neill this was shocking.

"This meeting at this lobby, lounge, bar, restaurant, this meeting when Mr. Sheehy ordered a beer, was that the first contact in person that you had with anybody from Exxon Shipping Company, or Exxon Corporation following leaving the South Oaks medical facility?"

Of course it was, and O'Neill was indignant that poor Captain Hazelwood, who had been through so much in this case, "which is more than should be visited on anyone," should be summoned virtually from treatment to a saloon in order to discuss with Exxon his rehabilitation.

Not that O'Neill thought it was much of a discussion. "There was no discussion between you and Mr. Sheehy of South Oaks, aftercare, AA, or drinking; is that a correct statement?"

It was, said Hazelwood, but Captain Sheehy had given him a copy of the Exxon Alcohol and Drug Policy, and "he looked me square in the eyes and told me in no uncertain terms that there would be no violations permitted of the Exxon alcohol policy."

But for O'Neill what mattered most was what had been left unsaid, and that went for the other Exxon port captain, Tompkins, with whom Hazelwood also met.

"Was AA discussed?"

"No."

"Was aftercare discussed?"

"No."

"Was the subject of your personal drinking discussed?"

"No."

"Was the subject of drinking on board vessels or returning to vessels after having drunk discussed?"

"No."

"Were you told not to drink?"

"With the exception of the parameters of the alcohol policy."

"Were you told you were going to be monitored?"

"Well, in his inimitable fashion, Mr. Tompkins kind of indicated to me I was going to be watched."

"Did he tell you you were going to be watched?"

"He didn't verbalize that, no."

"So he did not tell you you were going to be watched?"

"No."

"Did he tell you you were going to be monitored?"

"No, it was just, 'Look forward to working with you.'"

"Did he tell you or discuss with you anything that Exxon could do to facilitate attendance at Alcoholics Anonymous?"

"No. That subject wasn't brooked."

"Now, there were these two meetings?"

"Yes."

"And then you rejoined the fleet?"

"Yes."

"Now, have we covered the subject matter of these two meetings fairly?"

"Yes."

It was as if he was trying to *help* Hazelwood, who had suffered so much, help him to see how little help the company had given him in the fight to stay sober.

But Hazelwood did start drinking again. O'Neill now was forced to ask for the details, but he did even this in a friendly way, with delicacy of feeling, eliciting the fact that the captain had concealed his renewed drinking from his wife.

It then became necessary to ask about every instance in which Hazelwood had had a drink, from his treatment to the grounding. Every instance that the plaintiffs knew about, that is, but that list was extensive. They had hired investigators to talk to the ship's crew, they had followed up the most improbable rumors, they had pursued every lead. And they had slowly compiled a list of those who had seen the captain drink, or joined him. The way to share that list with the jury was to question the witness about everyone on it. Of course, this wasn't very pleasant for the witness, but O'Neill tried his hardest to lessen the strain through good humor.

"Now, coming back from this vacation to Portland, you flew back and you met a guy on the airplane, and as a result of some bet or another, you lost a bet with regard to a beer, or you won a beer?"

"I don't know who; we had a bet about the luggage. We had to transfer planes in Salt Lake. One of us bet our luggage would make it and one of us said it wouldn't."

"Was it a Delta flight?"

"Yeah."

"Been there, done that. God, that was such a pit. I shouldn't say that about Delta, but I think I have some privilege in the court when they sue me." He grinned and shook his head. That Delta. Then he continued.

"When you got off the airplane in Portland, and Captain Stalzer met you?"

"That's correct."

"And you had a couple of vodkas with Captain Stalzer?"

"I heard—I don't know. I bought this fellow a beer, and I had a drink."

"And then you went to dinner that night?"

"About seven hours later."

"And was Stalzer at dinner?"

"Yeah, he, myself, and the chief mate went to dinner."

"And Stalzer is an Exxon captain?"

"He was the alternate master on the *Valdez*."

"And you had wine with dinner?"

"Yeah, I think the three of us split a bottle of wine."

"On this trip to Portland, did you have a beer with Cousins in his apartment, or your apartment?"

That was the way it went, for a very long time. Every drink, every can of beer or glass of wine or shot of vodka, single or double, downed or sipped in airport lounges or in company apartments near dry-dock ports or restaurants or bars, solitary drinking or festive occasions, had been traced and now was revealed in open court. By the end of the day the jurors probably were either bored or thirsty. But, of course, there was method in this accretion of intemperance facts. This was a vital part of the case. The point of the detail was not so much to paint Hazelwood as a drunk as to discredit the notion that Exxon had monitored his drinking.

O'Neill kept coming back to this every chance he got. Why hadn't Exxon monitored him? Hazelwood said he thought he *was* being watched—by his supervisor, Paul Myers. "Once I started working for him, I started calling him Lamont Cranston, he was like a shadow. I couldn't shake him." But if this were monitoring, he said, it was the only case of it he knew.

Why didn't Exxon know about all this drinking? That was O'Neill's most basic question. And he underscored it by reading a list of names of

Exxon employees to Captain Hazelwood, Exxon *employees,* as he put it, and then asking after each name "whether from the time you got out of South Oaks until the time you left San Francisco for the fateful voyage you drank with them?" It seemed like a considerable list.

"Carlos Hogan?"

"Oh, yeah."

"Nate Carr?"

"Uh-huh."

"Mr. Cousins?"

"Yeah."

"Brian Dengel?"

"Yes, sir."

"Kevin Dick?

"Yeah."

"Patrick Enright?"

"Uh-huh."

"Kathy Haven?"

"Uh-huh."

"Charles Kimtis?"

"Yes."

"James Kunkel?"

"Yes."

"Joel Roberson?"

"Yes."

"Thomas St. Pierre?"

"Yes."

"Captain Stalzer?"

"Yes."

"Robert Sturgis?"

"Yes."

The point of this recital, which O'Neill prayed would be obvious to the jury, was this: if all these people were Exxon employees, and if Captain Hazelwood's drinking was being monitored by Exxon, why were the Exxon files bare?

It then became necessary to retrace the captain's steps in Valdez during what everyone in the case seemed to be calling "the fateful day," March 23, 1989. This had been done many times before. Perhaps the only steps more painstakingly retraced in modern times were those of Lee Harvey Oswald.

Hazelwood stuck to his story. He and his friends had met for lunch in Valdez, and he had drunk iced tea. After lunch, at about one thirty, he had spent an hour in the flower shop and then perhaps another hour browsing in nearby stores, and then more time returning to the Alamar office and after that looking for someone who wasn't home. He had gone to the Pipeline Club at about four thirty, where he met up with the others. He had drunk three vodkas on the rocks—singles. They left the Pipeline Club at about six thirty and stepped into a bar to avoid the cold and snow while waiting for a pizza to be ready. While in that bar, Hazelwood says he ordered another vodka but doesn't think he drank it. The mariners returned by cab to the ship, checking in at eight forty.

O'Neill remained friendly, but there was a question that he had to ask. Several questions, really, all flowing from the interview that Hazelwood had given to Mark Delozier on board the vessel on the afternoon following the grounding. The version of events that Hazelwood had given Delozier was somewhat different from what he was saying now. He said then that he had looked into the Pipeline Club at three. He had said later in the interview that the beer wasn't really at lunch, it was at a bar, the Harbor Club, just before returning to the ship. When Delozier asked him about any other alcohol consumption, he said that he'd only had the Moussys, which were alcohol-free, and he'd had a couple of those after he was back on board but before sailing.

Quietly, O'Neill asked, "Did you tell him about the vodkas you had?"

"No."

Almost helpfully: "Why not?"

"Well, the whole context of this interview was taking place in a trying condition. . . . At that time we were trying to get lined up for lightering, we had another rising tide, and I just wanted to get rid of him. I didn't want to waste my time with him to reconstruct the events of the previous afternoon, which weren't very important to me at the time."

O'Neill listened respectfully to this response. "Would it be fair to say with regard to what you drank that day, you were less than frank with him?"

"Yes."

As if satisfied, O'Neill went on to the next subject: the grounding. He retained a respectful tone, though he did play to the courtroom the audio tape of Hazelwood's distress call to the Coast Guard, just after the accident. In this tape the captain's voice sounds incontestably slurred. Further, he tells the Coast Guard that he's grounded north of Goose Island when in fact he had hit Bligh Reef. When O'Neill asked whether he had mistaken his position, Hazelwood said, "No. I had a position on the chart . . . but my mind didn't want to accept it."

O'Neill asked another question about the grounding. "It hasn't been asked before and I'm going to ask it frankly. If you had been on the bridge . . . even after a number of drinks, that vessel would have turned and missed the reef, wouldn't it?"

He received an honest answer. "I can think of no reason why I couldn't have turned it."

O'Neill was coming to the end of his direct examination of Hazelwood. By the standards of his past attacks, O'Neill's treatment of the captain had been courteous and respectful. He did not descend from that high ground now, though his last two topics were unavoidably more personal.

The first dealt with legal fees. Hazelwood's legal fees. O'Neill asked, "How much are you out-of-pocket, yourself, with regard to attorneys' fees in this case?"

"Attorneys' fees?" said Hazelwood. "As of today, none."

"And that is because your attorneys' fees are being paid by Exxon Corporation or Exxon Shipping Company or both?"

It was. Other questions produced the fact that Hazelwood was presently employed by the Chalos law office in New York, and that Exxon was a client of that office.

O'Neill said no more, but looked sympathetically at Hazelwood. He believed, and hoped the jury would, too, that Exxon through this arrangement still maintained economic control over Hazelwood, despite his having been fired by the company, and that in consequence, he could not freely testify against the company.

The second topic, the last of this direct examination, dealt with whether Hazelwood was a drunk. "Drunk" is the word O'Neill uses, though not just then, and AA employs as well, to describe an alcoholic. It was vitally important to O'Neill that Hazelwood be seen as an alcoholic. If he were someone who once was depressed and therefore drank too much, and now was cured and could drink moderately, then all the wealth of detail that he had introduced, the glass and bottle counting, would lose its luster with the jury. If Hazelwood was not an alcoholic, a beer at the Portland airport was not going to sway many minds. If he was, and Exxon had known that, or should have known that, then—well, the word at which O'Neill was shooting was "reckless."

If Hazelwood was an alcoholic. O'Neill had an ace to play in this regard, only he couldn't play it. But perhaps he could let the jurors know that it was in his hand. Shortly after the grounding, Hazelwood and Cousins had surreptitiously left Alaska, flying to Seattle and then on to New York. The plaintiff investigative team had talked to the stewardesses on the first flight. They said under oath that both men were drinking on the flight—one stewardess said that Hazelwood consumed as many as five drinks. Though if ever there was a time to get blotto this flight between disaster and arrest was it, the stewardesses' testimony would have gone a long way toward establishing that Hazelwood was in fact an alcoholic. But Judge Holland had ruled that this testimony was not admissible. In a pretrial hearing he said that the subject of the testimony was collateral to the issues in his court. The plaintiffs were wildly upset over this ruling, but there was nothing they could do about it. It is one small example of the extraordinary powers that a judge possesses, well beyond what he does during the trial itself.

O'Neill approached the subject of Hazelwood's alcoholism with an initial feint at levity.

"Have you heard the expression Denial is not the name of a river in Egypt?"

"I've heard it, yeah."

"You've heard it at AA meetings?"

"I've heard it elsewhere."

"Have you heard it at AA meetings?"

"I guess I have, yeah . . ."

"Would it be fair to say that as a result of your experience in AA meetings, that you know that a symptom of the disease of alcoholism is a lack of honesty or truthfulness with regard to that question?"

Chalos objected, but the judge said the question should be answered.

"I assume that's one component, yeah."

"And you've said that there was no binge drinking or heavy drinking at or about the time of the incident." A pause. "Did you drink after the incident?"

"No. I think the last drink I recall having is March 23, 1989."

"Did you drink on the airplane with Mr. Cousins from Anchorage to Seattle when you came back after the incident?"

All the lawyers knew of the judge's ruling on the stewardesses' testimony. They were all looking at Hazelwood. So was the judge.

The captain answered the question.

"No."

"Are you certain of that?" When a lawyer under these circumstances follows up with a certainty question the intent is very clear. O'Neill was risking judicial rebuke, or worse, in order to let the jury know that he thought the witness was lying.

"Yes," was the answer.

One must say that O'Neill did not give up easily. He edged himself to the extremity of a very precarious limb.

"Now let's just assume—for the sake of discussion—let's just assume for the sake of discussion that you did. Wouldn't you say that it was a manifestation of an unhealthy attitude towards drinking?"

Chalos objected, and the judge forcefully sustained the objection.

And that, really, was all that O'Neill wanted to ask Captain Hazelwood—just now, anyway. He would have another shot at him a little later, but this opening gambit was designed to be civil, and it had been. More than civil, considerate. *Sympathetic.* Really Hazelwood's friend. He ended up almost with a supplication.

"Have I been fair in the questions?"

Chalos, who is no fool, immediately objected. The judge sustained him.

O'Neill looked puzzled, as if his quest for kindness had been misunderstood.

"Captain," he said, "I want to thank you for your patience. I realize what a difficult thing it was, and I have no further questions. Your Honor?"

His Honor said it was now time for cross-examination. First came Jim Neal, on behalf of Exxon.

Neal had seen, of course, just what O'Neill had spent much of his time trying to establish, and so now his questions were designed to show that Hazelwood *had* in fact been monitored by Exxon.

"Mr. O'Neill talked about no monitoring and so forth. After your leave of absence, compare the times you meet with your supervisors after your leave of absence at South Oaks with the times before, that is in number. Did you meet with them much more frequently after your leave of absence?"

"Yes."

"More contacts?"

"Yes, much more."

As if hard of hearing: "Much more?"

"Yeah."

"After your leave of absence at South Oaks, did it appear to you that you had contacts with your supervisors that other masters didn't have? Say, at fleet conferences or something like that?"

"Fleet conferences, with Mr. Koops, I would have to say yes, and the West Coast fleet, it was Mr. Myers. They had changed around the port captain business, so he became my supervisor as opposed to Mr. Koops, so there was more interaction between Mr. Myers and me than I witnessed with other masters that were attending."

The questions clearly had been designed to produce a sense of surveillance. The problem with this valiant effort was the paucity of hard fact. The *feeling* that one was being followed was not as convincing a sign of monitoring as documented interviews would have been. Once again, there was reference to the ubiquitous Paul Myers, aka Lamont Cranston, the radio figure whom perhaps some jurors would remember. "He was my shadow. Every time I turned around, he was there." Absent greater specificity, this sort of thing only got one so far.

An incident was related in which Hazelwood's cabin was searched for alcohol by another Exxon captain, Ivan Mihajlovic. (None was found.) But Mihajlovic was a friend of Hazelwood's who had heard a rumor of drinking and had dashed over to the ship to see for himself; no one had sent him. He was part of no company program. There was another search, too, by an Exxon employee, after Hazelwood had supposedly ordered beer over the ship's radio, but nothing was found on board, and the beer apparently had been delivered and drunk on shore. But Hazelwood testified that when he met with Paul Myers, his "mother hen," his "Lamont Cranston," neither the radio order nor the recent search was discussed, or even mentioned.

Neal, of course, was not Hazelwood's lawyer; his client was Exxon. So he made it very clear that the Exxon Navigation and Bridge and Organization Manual said that a captain *must* be on the bridge "whenever conditions present a potential threat to the vessel such as passing in the vicinity of shoals, rocks or other hazards presenting any threat to safe navigation."

He followed up on this. "Now is it your opinion that on March 23, 1989, at eleven fifty-two in the evening, those conditions did not exist?"

"That's my opinion."

Neal also asked about Hazelwood's former salary from Exxon. The revelation that he had been paid $100,000 a year for six months' work, with no prohibition of his supplemental income during the six months off, was probably designed to rebut the idea that Hazelwood was Exxon's victim.

In response to other questions, Hazelwood talked about having won the Exxon Fleet Manager's Safety Awards in 1987 and 1988, and expressed his high regard for Greg Cousins's ship-handling skills. Then Neal was through with him.

The major defense examination of Hazelwood was by his own lawyer, Michael Chalos, who spent a great deal of time repairing some of the damage that had been done to his client. Once more the steps of the fateful day were trod for the benefit of the jurors, some of whom by now, no doubt—though they'd never been to Valdez—could find their way from the Hobby Hut to the Pipeline Club blindfolded. The point of this revisit was correction. Hazelwood was asked about the hat he had worn, and his description of it was quite different from the bartender's testimony. As for Janice Delozier's testimony, Hazelwood said that no photograph of him had been taken, let alone published in a newspaper, at the time she claimed to have seen it in the flower shop. This single fact, if correct, could only detract further from the credibility of a witness whose husband had begun the charge that Hazelwood was drinking.

And speaking of Coast Guard corpsman Mark Delozier, Chalos asked about his interview of Hazelwood after the grounding. O'Neill had pointed out the many factual errors in what the captain had told Delozier. Chalos helped Hazelwood to explain why he had erred.

"Captain, what was your state of mind when you gave that interview to Mr. Delozier?"

"State of mind was somewhere between shock, terror, worry, everything rolled into one. I guess it comes under the umbrella of trauma."

There were a number of corrections to impressions that had recently been made. The rules forbade drinking within four hours of assuming one's post, but Hazelwood had been told that his ship would leave at ten, and then the time had been moved up to nine; no matter what the late-shift bartender said, he had not been in the Pipeline Club at seven; there was a reason for leaving the bridge—he had to finish up some paper-work; he had seen Cousins take the vessel off autopilot; on a difficulty scale of one to ten, the turn he instructed Cousins to make would only rate a two; the Coast Guard should have warned them of danger; if the captain's orders had been accurately followed, there would have been no grounding; the mistaken location and slurred words on the Coast Guard radio tape were the result of trauma and hyperventilation; the initial admission of guilt was merely a captain's way of assuming responsibility; Exxon was paying his fees involuntarily—employment law required it; Chalos was not Exxon's controller of Hazelwood, he was his lifetime friend; Hazelwood was not an alcoholic.

This last point received considerable emphasis. Chalos concluded from his answers that Hazelwood had consumed alcohol only eleven times in the sixteen-month period before the grounding.

"Do you consider yourself an alcoholic, Captain?"

"Not then nor now."

"When you boarded the vessel on March 23, 1989, were you impaired by alcohol?"

"No."

"Did alcohol play any role in the grounding of the *Exxon Valdez*, Captain?"

"No."

"Thank you very much."

When Chalos stepped down, Hazelwood may have thought that his own testimony had been concluded, too.

But he wasn't through. His real courtroom ordeal was about to begin.

O'Neill came over to the lectern. "If I may cross-examine, Your Honor?"

"Yes, you may," said Judge Holland, who then went on to explain to the courtroom the unusual procedure. The normal direct/cross-examine/redirect did not apply here. Both parties had wanted Captain Hazelwood put on early in the trial, so the plaintiffs had called him, questioned him directly, then the defense lawyers had done the same. Since they had not been bound by the scope of O'Neill's initial questioning, the judge thought it only fair now for O'Neill to be able to follow up on all the defense questions. So Hazelwood stayed right where he was.

O'Neill came out snarling. There was no more Mr. Nice Guy. The courtesy he had shown the captain earlier was gone, and in its place came the slashing, pacing, pitiless attack of a predatory jungle cat, toying with its prey between bites. The civility of his earlier questioning had been tactical, drawing facts, not blood, leaving no mess for the defense team to clean up. But they had finished now; the floor was his, and now the moment, too.

His very first question was, "Captain, how much time did you spend getting your testimony ready? How many hours?"

When Hazelwood said that he had spent about six hours, O'Neill asked him whether he'd read over his own depositions, and his interview with Delozier. The captain replied that he had.

O'Neill then asked, "It's important to be honest, isn't it?"

"Yeah, I would assume so, yes."

O'Neill then launched into the discrepancies between what Hazelwood had just testified to in court and his earlier depositions and interview. For example, Hazelwood had said that he entered South Oaks voluntarily, hoping to cure his depression. That testimony was central to Exxon's case; the company alcohol policy said that those who self-identified, who came forward and admitted their problem, would not be penalized for doing so. The theory was that this encouraged problem drinkers to seek help. It was a cornerstone of Exxon's explanation for keeping Hazelwood on as a seafaring captain.

Now that cornerstone was pulled nearly out of the foundation. O'Neill was asking about Captain Pierce, an Exxon employee who had called Hazelwood and asked him to seek help for his problem. Hazelwood had then entered South Oaks.

"So you didn't self-identify?"

"No."

"You got caught?"

"I—I don't know how Captain Pierce came to call me."

"Now ... do you know as you sat there and testified about it that Exxon Corporation, that it was in Exxon Corporation's interest to say that you had self-identified because it helps them with regard to their argument that they properly reinstated you in a vessel—you knew that, didn't you?"

Hazelwood said that he hadn't thought of it in those terms.

Both his veracity and his sobriety were under relentless attack.

"Have you ever lied about your drinking?"

"Yes."

"We know that you've lied to your wife on occasion?"

"Yes."

"And you lied to Mr. Delozier on occasion, too, didn't you; on one occasion that we know of?"

"Yes."

"Your wife was in favor of help with regard to South Oaks?"

"She was in favor at the time to anything I was doing to help myself."

"And all the way through the grounding, all the way through March 23, 1989, for three years you never told your wife you had resumed drinking, did you?"

"I don't think the subject ever came up, no."

There was no respite. O'Neill asked if Hazelwood knew the "third tradition" in Alcoholics Anonymous. When the captain said he did—it was "the desire to stop drinking"—O'Neill said simply, "Plaintiffs' Exhibit 127."

"What is 127?" said the puzzled Hazelwood.

It was, he soon learned, a bar list. A list describing some of the seamier bars in San Francisco, an attempt at raunchy humor that had been given to Hazelwood by a friend, and which he'd kept, and which O'Neill had discovered.

"And you had this for a year in your cabin?"

"Somewhere around there, yeah."

"Are these particularly nice joints that are described in here?"

"Some are, some aren't."

"Pretty hard-core lot, aren't they?"

"No."

"You want to read some of the excerpts from it out loud and we'll make a judgment on that?"

There was no stone unturned, or unslung. O'Neill's look was priceless at the revelation that the *Exxon Valdez* was now back in service under a new name, the *Sea River Mediterranean*. He made it seem like finding a Nazi in Argentina.

The worst moment for Hazelwood, and a turning point in the trial, came in the midst of this barrage. O'Neill had a copy of a very standard agreement between Exxon and Hazelwood that neither would use their trial testimony in any arbitration between them. O'Neill's job was to make this sound suspicious, and he was up to the task.

"Did you want the freedom to come in here and be able to tell a version of the facts or a story and not be bound by that version of the facts or story in the later arbitration proceedings?"

Hazelwood, much battered by now, was exasperated. "That didn't really enter into my mind. You're the ones who dragged me in here."

O'Neill, the pacer, was already some distance away, his back to Hazelwood. He stopped suddenly in his tracks. He held the pose. He wheeled around. He came up close to the witness. His voice was low, but quite audible.

"*We* dragged you in here?"

"Uh-huh; got my deposition."

O'Neill was very steady.

"Let's follow that sentence. I represent fishermen and Natives?"

"Certainly, yeah."

"And who was the captain of the vessel that spilled the oil that disrupted their fishing seasons and their subsistence?"

"I was."

A pause, and then: "*You* dragged us in here, didn't you?"

There was no response.

It was perhaps the climactic moment of the trial. The courtroom was absolutely still, and O'Neill extended the silence, like a diva her ovation, by just standing there, immobile, before he renewed his questioning. He has said since then that if Exxon had apologized for the spill early and often enough, its fate might have been altered. That may be. Its reticence may only have mirrored a corporate belief that actions speak louder than words. But sometimes words are longed for, particularly words from the all-powerful. Silence in the face of disaster to many people signaled not asperity but arrogance, the belief that being in oil means never having to say you're sorry.

The captain was now trapped in this perception. He was trapped by his own inartful words. He had complained of having been dragged into this courtroom, had complained to a brilliant improviser who could not have wished for better material. Not seeing who had brought them there was perhaps the major issue. For those who felt so, the trial had suddenly become much more clear, and Hazelwood's role in it as well. The captain had caused a sea change.

Perhaps O'Neill should have sat down right then, but he had a few other things that he'd prepared, and there would be no other chance to use them.

So he used Lamont Cranston. That was Hazelwood's euphemism for Paul Myers, his watchdog. Of course, O'Neill didn't think that Myers had been a watchdog. He saw no evidence of that. He smelled coaching.

"Now, in response to West Coast questions about monitoring, you twice used the phrase 'Lamont Cranston'?"

"Uh-huh."

"Whose image was that? Was that suggested to you by somebody else in preparation for this testimony, or was that your image?"

"It was my image."

"And how does the whole expression go, with regard to Lamont Cranston, 'the Shadow'?"

"'Only the Shadow knows,' I believe."

O'Neill smiled. There was more than one trout in this stream.

"What does the Shadow know?"

Hazelwood was trying. "Everything."

Reel it in. "He knows 'what evil lurks in the hearts of men, only the Shadow knows.' Isn't that the expression?"

After letting his words sink in, O'Neill moved from metaphor to video. A fortune had been put into new equipment, and there was no point in wasting it. So when O'Neill was asking about what drinking activity had been reported to Paul Myers, he contrasted the answer Hazelwood gave with instant videos of the captain giving quite another story.

"Would it be fair to say that each time the story changed, you had an opportunity to talk with your lawyer, didn't you?"

Hazelwood now was beyond any artifice. "It would be fair to say. That's who I spend my time with, it seems."

Confession was no deterrent. O'Neill merely moved to a new target. He seized on each inconsistency and transformed it into a lie. His sharp questions became the Bligh Reef of the captain's credibility.

"About the events of the day before, I compressed them all. I just wanted to get rid of him."

"You compressed whatever drinking you did into one beer?"

"I guess I . . . yes, you could say that."

There remained not a trace of the sympathy he had once bestowed on Hazelwood.

"Let me ask you something. I was listening when you testified, and you made yourself out to be a victim. I didn't hear you say during your testimony that you were sorry. Did you?"

The tone now was one of scorn.

"Your position as you sit here today is that you just did everything super; isn't it?"

Finally, Neal stood up and objected, saying that this sort of thing had been going on long enough. He sounded like a living will. And even O'Neill then had to agree that the time had come to pull the plug. Holding a sheaf of notes to indicate that he *could* have gone on and on, he went back to his table and sat down.

For a minute, no one knew quite what to do. Hazelwood looked longingly at the counsel table. The judge said that under the circumstances, perhaps the defense lawyers should have a little more time, after all.

Neal said that he only needed one minute. He was very angry.

"Captain Hazelwood . . . I did notice the rather clever questions of Mr. O'Neill, and did you perceive from those questions that he was accusing you of lying to help Exxon?"

"That was the sum and substance that I got, yes."

"And did you perceive that he was accusing me of seeking to have you lie by virtue of his questions about after you'd talked to Exxon lawyers you'd said such and such things? Do you remember that?"

"Yeah, I don't think he personalized it to you, but in general."

"I am the Exxon lawyer that's talked to you, haven't I?"

"Yes."

"Is my position correct that you wouldn't lie to help Exxon?"

"Certainly not."

"Captain Hazelwood, I've asked to interview you a couple of times?"

"Yes."

"In the presence of your counsel, right?"

"Yes, sir."

"You've been kind enough to let me do that?"

"Yes, sir."

"Did I ever suggest any way in the world that you tell anything but the truth?"

"No, sir."

"Thank you."

Chalos was nearly as brief. For a few minutes he threw himself into the effort to rehabilitate his client's credibility, but the judge had asked him to be brief and so he just settled for this:

"Captain, Mr. O'Neill asked you, then he didn't want to hear the answer: Are you sorry for what happened on the night of March 23, 1989?"

"Certainly. I'm devastated, but he never asked me."

"He didn't ask you?"

"No."

"Captain, did you testify truthfully here today and yesterday and at your deposition?"

"Yes."

"No further questions, Your Honor."

And then, after three tough days, Hazelwood was excused as a witness. He left the stand, but in a sense he now stayed there for the rest of the trial.

11

Experts

The remainder of the plaintiffs' case consisted of a steady stream of witnesses, most of whom were either whistle-blowers or experts. It wasn't hard to tell just which of these a witness was. The whistle-blowers were usually seamen, professional mariners who somewhere along the line had seen Captain Hazelwood take a drink and now were in the spotlight under oath to talk about it. They testified as well to other infractions of duty. Some of them were there reluctantly and others with zeal, but none seemed very comfortable. They were plain speaking, taciturn, seafaring folk who didn't look at home on *land,* let alone in court. Frequently, the facts had to be pried from them by the well-dressed pearl fishers who circled the dock.

The experts, on the other hand, were hard to shut up. Their volubility stemmed from lifetime immersion in fields so specialized that the opportunities to speak before large groups were rare. Besides, they were being paid to be in court. Paid very handsomely, in many cases. For experts who not only are learned in their fields but articulate on the stand are worth their weight in gold, and get it.

The first witness to follow Hazelwood was neither a true whistle-blower nor exactly an expert, but rather a little of each. Dr. Sivanchandra Vallury was a senior psychiatrist at South Oaks Hospital, and the physician who had treated Joseph Hazelwood. His appearance was by deposition. He couldn't remember the details of his treatment of the captain, nor specifically the course of conduct he recommended, but under questioning, Dr. Vallury stated that what he generally recommended to patients was a lifetime of abstinence from alcohol.

The next witness also appeared by deposition, but though his words were not spoken in court by him, they were poignant nonetheless. Lloyd LeCain was the second mate who was supposed to have relieved Greg Cousins shortly before the grounding. He had been sleeping, and Cousins had let him sleep. Several testified that LeCain was a far more qualified seaman than Cousins, the third mate. Many people believe that if LeCain had not been sleeping, there would have been no spill—no spill, no loss of wildlife, no lost income for the fishermen, no billions spent in cleaning up the mess, no nightmare for Captain Hazelwood, no trial. But no one had wakened LeCain, and there was a trial, and now his words were being read. The words were divorced from the person but not from his pain. Apparently, no one had asked the "What if" question more than he.

"What is your present employment today?"

"I'm selling real estate. I'm not with Exxon anymore."

"How long have you not been with Exxon?"

"About four or five months."

"What were the circumstances of your leaving Exxon?"

"I have post-traumatic stress disorder and I was retired from Exxon."

"You have the disorder from the accident?"

"That's correct."

Not surprisingly, LeCain did not put the blame for the grounding on Cousins, the man whose place he should have taken. He didn't directly put the blame on anyone, but his testimony was not flattering to Robert Kagan, the former steward who was serving as helmsman when the impact occurred. He said he felt that Kagan needed extra supervision. He went further. He said that Hazelwood and Greg Cousins and the chief mate, James Kunkel, had felt that way about Kagan, too.

It didn't take long to verify part of that statement. The next witness was Chief Mate Kunkel, who was even more critical of Kagan than reported, saying that the helmsman was very poor at changing from one course to another without supervision, that he had sailed with him in the past and concluded that he had to be watched. He had shared these views with the other *Exxon Valdez* officers, including Hazelwood.

All the warnings about the helmsman's need of supervision seemed to make Hazelwood's absence from the bridge seem more serious, perhaps even reckless. Kunkel was asked about Condition C, the Exxon regulation requiring two officers to be on the bridge, one of them a senior officer.

There was something else that the plaintiffs wanted to talk to Kunkel about as well. He was the ship's fatigue officer. He had had the duty of reporting to the captain any crew members who hadn't had enough rest. "Enough" was not conjectural; it was a matter of law. A federal statute required an officer to be off duty for six of the twelve hours prior to his taking a watch while departing a port. Kunkel admitted to having fallen short of this standard himself in the past, and to not being certain whether Cousins and LeCain had met it on the night of the grounding.

The six-hour rule was a critical issue in the trial. If Condition C had not been met, that was clearly Hazelwood's fault but not necessarily Exxon's. After all, Condition C was an Exxon rule. The company itself was the authority requiring two officers to be on the bridge. But the six-hour standard was a federal law. It was Exxon's duty to see that it was obeyed. No person knew for certain exactly what had caused the grounding. But precisely because the incident was not readily explainable, the fatigue of the crew would supply a plausible answer. There were those in the plaintiff camp who saw in the fatigue issue the best chance of eventual victory.

This faction was placing much of its hopes on the next witness, David F. Dinges, Ph.D. There was no question as to which category he was in. Dr. Dinges was an expert. He was an expert on the subject of fatigue.

Why not? If there can be experts on how to count salmon in midstream, there certainly can be experts on fatigue. In fact, it was slightly more specialized than that. Dinges said that he consulted "primarily in the area of human performance as it relates to fatigue."

The role of the expert is to dazzle the jury. You start with a subject that no one knows anything about—like fatigue. Everyone *knows* what fatigue is, of course; everyone gets tired at least, but what do we *really* know about it in a scientific way? Then someone comes in with credentials to die for, more expert in the subject than anyone else on earth could possibly be, with degrees and published papers and consultancies and testimonials, and, most important of all, *confidence,* not condescension exactly but an aura that suggests that he won't sneer at you if you are very attentive and believe every single word that he says.

So:

"Could you name some of the governmental agencies with whom you have consulted?"

"The National Institutes of Health, the National Aeronautics and Space Administration, the Federal Aviation Administration, the National Transportation Safety Board, the Office of Naval Research, the Air Force Office of Scientific Research . . . I'm sure there are many more."

"You belong to any—are you a member of any foundation boards?"

"Yes, I am."

"Which are those?"

"I'm a member of the National Sleep Foundation, I'm Associate Director of the Institute for Experimental Psychiatry Research Foundation and have recently been appointed to the board of directors of the American Sleep Disorders Association."

At this point the jurors are trying hard not to look fatigued, because if they're not careful, this expert might study *them.*

The expert had already studied the facts of this case. He had concluded "that Mr. Cousins suffers from performance impairing fatigue that led to mistakes that led to the grounding."

This, of course, was devastating. But it is always this way. One side calls in an expert, and the expert says something that is devastating to the other side. Why would someone bring in an enemy?

The other side, however, does not roll over and play dead. That is not how it works. The other side knows how to deal with experts. Kill them. Metaphorically, that is. Discredit them. You can never, ever attack their expertise, because their credentials are too glittering, and they know a special language that you don't and can make a monkey out of you, but you can attack *them.* You can say that they're saying what they say not because it's true but because they are being paid to say it. You may not want to use those words, but there are ways to get the point across. Another way to discredit the expert is to use his own words against him. Most experts publish a great many papers—that's one of the reasons they can call themselves experts—and the flip side of this profligacy is contradiction;

something they wrote long ago may be at odds with present testimony. If found, it can be used to transform the expert into a mortal.

Pat Lynch had cross-examined experts before and clearly knew how it should be done. *He* wasn't that impressed by Dr. Dinges having been a consultant to the NIH or the FAA.

"You have never conducted any research involving people who work on ships full time, have you?"

"No. I have not."

This was merely a preliminary jab. It was followed up by a more forceful blow to his credibility. Lynch elicited the fact that Dr. Dinges had been retained by plaintiffs to study the issue in 1993. At that time, Lynch asked,

"Had you formed an opinion commensurate with the opinion you gave to the jury here this morning?"

"I hadn't formed an opinion, no."

At that, Lynch produced a printout of an article in the *Boston Globe* of May 28, 1990, in which Dr. Dinges was quoted as saying that the *Exxon Valdez* was a classic fatigue accident.

Dinges said that the newspaper had only quoted his earlier *belief;* three years later, after studying the material, he had been able to form an *opinion.*

Lynch, of course, was praying that the jury's reaction to this explanation would be the same as his own. He had cast several palls on the witness, but the expert's confident assertion that Cousins's fatigue had been a cause of the grounding was not likely to be forgotten by the jury.

The next witness, on video, was the champion whistle-blower of the trial and apparently possessed of a nose that oenophiles would envy, since he had detected alcohol on the breath of Captain Hazelwood a number of times and could distinguish the smell of Scotch and Bourbon. James Shaw had been an Exxon port steward, helping supply the galleys of ships that came into his port. He had spent a lot of time aboard ships that were commanded by Hazelwood, and had come to know and like the captain.

On three separate occasions Shaw had smelled alcohol on Hazelwood's breath. He had heard about a fourth incident that involved the captain drinking aboard ship. All these sniffings occurred after Hazelwood had left South Oaks. Moreover, Shaw had reported his observation to other Exxon employees, at least once to the port captain. This testimony, if believed, could be fatal to Exxon's claims that it had carefully monitored Hazelwood and would tolerate no lapse on his part.

But the party most wounded in court that day was Joseph Hazelwood. Shaw testified that one of the drinking episodes could not be directly observed because the door to the captain's cabin was locked while he was cavorting behind it with an unidentified woman. True or not, this was painful testimony for a man who had no choice but to sit there in open court, not meeting any stares, his face expressionless, conscious that his wife and daughter were following every aspect of the trial. One of the issues in this case was punitive damages. Arguments would be heard over whether Hazelwood as well as Exxon should be punished. Whichever way that decision went, it would be after the fact. Whether or not additional penalties were appropriate, punishment had already been meted out to Joseph Hazelwood; in addition to having been fired and made infamous, he was being subjected to accusations of marital infidelity, and all the world was watching.

Other crew members came to the witness stand, each in turn praising the captain's professional skills and then testifying to the number of times they had seen him drink. No one claimed to have seen helmsman Kagan drink, but the comments on his nautical qualifications were very far from flattering. Kagan himself took the stand and said that after the grounding Hazelwood told him that he had done a hell of a job. There were countless questions put to experts and crew as to whether the tanker should have been put on autopilot or on LPU, which stands for load program up and accelerates the vessel's speed.

There were several days of this sort of thing, and then it came time for the Coast Guard to testify. Mark Delozier, whose wife had testified to seeing Hazelwood ordering drinks in the Pipeline Club, appeared by deposition, as had she, with the full account of how he had smelled alcohol on the captain's breath, had instigated the blood tests, and clandestinely had searched the captain's cabin. He was followed by his Coast Guard colleague Scott Connor, who had drawn the blood and then transported it via windowsill and produce bin to his superior officer in Anchorage.

Connor's testimony produced a bombshell. He said under oath that he thought he had seen an opened bottle of Jack Daniels bourbon on a shelf in Captain Hazelwood's cabin, as well as some empty beer cans in the trash. His description was astonishingly lurid: "There is a ship on the rocks and oil is bubbling out of the side, and I'm brought into the captain's quarters and there's a bottle of whiskey, bourbon on the shelf. . . . It was like what my dad found in my drawer of my desk. Out there for everybody to see. And you knew it was trouble attached to it, but who am I to ask?"

Indeed. His sighting of the bottle was more dramatic than credible. He claimed that it was on a shelf in the captain's bedroom, in full view of everyone. Yet no one else had seen it. This was the room where the blood samples were taken; there were plenty of people around. The room had been searched by Mark Delozier, and that watchdog of sobriety had reported no Jack Daniels bottle.

Even Connor wasn't absolutely sure. "You know, I hope I just don't have this superimposed with some other event in my life."

His testimony and that of his fellow corpsmen did not paint a picture of perfection. Lieutenant Stark, for example, who had mailed the blood samples to the California lab, said that he had attended college at St. Cloud State University, "which is a branch of the University of Minnesota," though it is not. Someone who was mistaken about where he went to college perhaps gave unintended meaning to his assertion that the blood test chain of custody "is not rocket science."

As Michael Chalos had promised in his opening statement, the lab technician from California testified that one month after she had recorded the blood samples as to their condition on arrival, her superior had her change that record to the description that the Coast Guard had sent. This testimony, following that of Coast Guardsmen who made Inspector Clouseau seem like Sherlock Holmes, must have been deeply frustrating to the plaintiffs. Their case might depend on whether Captain Hazelwood had been drunk the night of the grounding. Witness after witness was admitting that he had not *seemed* to be drunk. The plaintiffs had a blood test, of course, that said the opposite. They *needed* that blood test. It was essential to their case. And now they heard—and the jurors heard—a tale of bungling and incompetence in the delivery of the samples for testing. What good was the test if the chain of custody had been broken?

The next witnesses helped restore the plaintiffs' faith in the jury system. The time had come for the top Exxon executives to take the stand.

Villainy was as important as drink to the plaintiff case. Their goal in this trial was punitive damages. For the jury to want to punish Exxon, it would help to have some bad guys. The plaintiffs wanted to characterize the Exxon brass as arrogant, untruthful, and uncaring. Part of that task—the appearance of untruthfulness—had been made easier for them by the inconsistency of Exxon'statements.

Exxon really had no choice. Sounding inconsistent was better than admitting guilt. And early on, just after the grounding, Exxon officials *had* said things that in the context of this trial were self-defeating. Their trial posture was very different, and of course this gave the plaintiffs, and most particularly O'Neill, a field day.

Lee Raymond, the president of Exxon Corporation at the time of the spill, appeared by videotape. It was not a very long tape. The plaintiffs felt they had better alternatives. If the goal was to contradict or embarrass someone's response to David Brinkley, this could be far more dramatically done with a living, breathing Exxon official in the witness chair.

They soon had one. Lawrence Rawl, recently retired, had been the CEO and chairman of the board of Exxon at the time of the grounding. He was questioned in the courtroom by Brian O'Neill, whose opening line was, "We've got to quit meeting like this."

Rawl just smiled. He certainly didn't look like the hard-nosed villain whom the plaintiffs might have preferred. He looked like, and was, a company man who had spent forty-one years working for Exxon, rising from a roughneck on a drilling rig in South Texas to chairman of the board of an entity so vast and rich that it might as well have been a country. His accession had not resulted from luck; he was smart, tough, resourceful, resolute, hardworking, good-humored, and in thought, deed, and manner entirely representative of the Exxon corporate culture. For a company large enough to have, in effect, its own airline had also reached a state of self-sufficiency that enabled it to develop and maintain its own culture. This helped insulate it from much of the ferment that surrounded it. Exxon operated in more than eighty countries and did not regard itself as less than their equals. Loyalty to the company was to its officers akin to patriotism. There was almost a religious tinge as well. The mission of the company was seen as essential to the maintenance of civilization. All the world was able to move and work by virtue of the fuel that was extracted from the earth's depths and then distributed around the surface of the globe.

The stewards of this enterprise believed in the long term. Time was on their side. Theirs was an epochal mission, and haste as grave a sin as panic. They believed in being rational. Calm and deliberation were the highest virtues, other than keeping one's word. The world outside their culture was volatile and harsh. They dealt with feudal despots, fierce revolutionaries, and political opportunists. No matter. Rapid change was all about them, but if they maintained their culture that did not matter. In the long run certain natural forces would assert themselves as always. It was a matter of waiting.

Of course, this put them at some variance from their own national culture. To their contemporaries they seemed frozen in an earlier moment of that culture, deaf to the frenzied chatter of modernity. And indeed that is what modern life seemed to them, merely chatter—talk, talk, talk—people reinventing themselves every hour and then talking incessantly about it. The officers at Exxon didn't understand a word they were saying. The company employed many translators all over the world so that it could communicate with sheikhs and commissars; its officers had no one who could translate the alien culture that surrounded them at home.

There is something very attractive to being immune from the pressures of the moment. Exxon viewed with contempt those managers of other companies who would sacrifice future growth for the next quarter's bottom line. They didn't understand those executives who lived or died for favorable press. Their own mission did not include being loved. They genuinely saw their job as keeping the world running.

Of course, one had to respond to a crisis. Lawrence Rawl had rushed into action before the Coast Guard had reached the *Exxon Valdez*. He canceled an Easter visit to his son in Massachusetts and flew to New York, where he thought the company offices would have better communications with Valdez. His first priority was to mitigate the spill, and he threw himself into this effort.

Spreading faster than the spill was the public reaction to it. Exxon had endured wars, nationalization of its pipelines, antitrust attacks, and explosions, but nothing in its history was comparable to this. There seemed to be little else on television. Black headlines and acerbic editorials assaulted them daily. Environmental spokesmen vied with one another for the apex of denunciation. Leaders of the government demanded an explanation.

As chairman and CEO, Rawl was the chief spokesman for the company. He rushed to do his duty, as if capping a fire in a well. It was not that easy. He soon found himself in the hearing rooms of the U.S. Senate and the House of Representatives, and on floodlit sets trying to explain things to Sam Donaldson and his colleagues.

He said things then that he would later regret. He said that it was an error of judgment to put a recovering alcoholic on the bridge of a tanker. He said a number of things about drink. And now he found himself in a legal setting, where under the laws of agency an admission that Hazelwood was drunk might mean that Exxon had been drunk as well.

Rawl's position on the stand was that his earlier public statements had been wrong. He had been misinformed. "If I had more time to get information I wouldn't have said those things." With regard to Hazelwood, "I've learned a lot of things since then that says he wasn't drunk at the time."

Rawl was a very good witness: affable, calm, and concerned. Under the circumstances, no one could have seemed more credible. But the circumstances were awful. For good reason or not, he had changed his story. He was being examined by a rhetorical master with a legal scalpel in one hand and a public relations hatchet in the other. The courtroom had been transformed at horrendous expense into an electronic showroom as if for this very confrontation. Rawl's earlier statements, since recanted, were flung on screens throughout the chamber in order to mock the newer version. He never lost his tolerant composure, his face remained the same as the one ten times its size flickering before the jurors. But that, of course, was the problem: one man, two stories.

And a relentless inquisitor. O'Neill had at his fingertips the capacity to find and display in seconds even one sentence out of hours of televised testimony, and he pressed the button again and again, gleefully.

The most damaging sentence that the jurors got to see was his previous statement that putting Hazelwood back in command of a vessel after he left South Oaks was "a gross error." This is of course very close to the legal definition of "recklessness." Rawl was resourceful; "My definition of gross, of course, may be different than yours." But that TV screen was awfully big.

Highlighting inconsistency was only one of O'Neill's goals. He also aimed to portray Exxon as uncaring, an arrogant giant that needed to be punished. To this end he brought forth a newspaper clipping. Not long after the spill, Rawl, in speaking to a group of security analysts, had commented in passing, "It's not clear to me why people are so angry at us." A reporter from the *Chicago Tribune* had heard and printed the line. O'Neill quoted it, but did not pursue the subject. He used it as his closing line, before sitting down.

Rawl's lawyers knew of course exactly what O'Neill was up to. And they knew that their client's culture played into his hands. Rawl and his peers believed that actions spoke more loudly than words, whether or not that is true today. The company had voluntarily spent billions of dollars on cleaning up the mess that its tanker had made. It had thrown every resource into this effort. That's why Rawl couldn't understand why people were still angry. He had spent a great deal of time since the spill trying to redress this wrong. Wasn't that enough? In fact it was not. People wanted to hear from the highest sources that their own pain and distress were understood, and shared.

So when Pat Lynch cross-examined Rawl, he focused on people's anger. He drew out a response that was true and helpful, but which had not previously been expressed.

"Did you think it was understandable why people would be angry about the spill?"

"Well, certainly. I was, needless to say, angry myself about the spill, but I could see particularly the people that lived there in that pristine environment, that oil all over . . . just to see it would make them very angry, and I could sympathize with them. In fact I can honestly say I was devastated. My wife was depressed, my kids. . . . There wasn't an employee, certainly in the U.S. but around the world, that didn't feel very, very badly. Not personally, they didn't feel personally responsible as I did, and as the shipping company did, but they felt, you know, it was just terrible, and they felt for the people that were damaged by this thing."

He went on to speak of all the Exxon employees who had worked side by side with Alaskans to contain and eradicate the spill; it was that cooperative effort that made the persistence of anger so troubling. Rawl spoke with obvious sincerity, and it is likely that some of the damage caused by O'Neill's questions had been repaired.

The problem was that O'Neill had a second shot at him. The reedirect examination of Rawl was brief but brutal.

Right off the bat, O'Neill asked, "Would it be fair to say that in the week or so after the spill, you did not come to Alaska?" Rawl said that was correct.

O'Neill went on. He specialized in this sort of thing—emphasizing those things that the defendants had not done. Had Hazelwood apologized? No, because no one had asked him if he was sorry. Had Rawl come up to Alaska right after the spill? No, because he was coordinating

Exxon's efforts out of New York. Both the captain and his former employer may have had perfectly good reasons for the omissions under attack, but not in terms of trial tactics.

They did not grasp the value of symbolic gesture. Rawl undoubtedly thought that he was better able to help the Alaskans where he was, rather than wasting time coming to where they were. This response was rational, but it was also wrong. Actions do not always speak louder than words. Sometimes a gesture is needed. When a Northwest Airlines jet collided with another plane at the Detroit airport with many passengers killed or injured, the board co-chairman of the airline, Al Checchi, flew at once to the scene of the disaster and met with the families of the victims. There was no lessening of grief, but no doubt his presence was taken to heart. Exxon's failure to respond similarly in its great disaster was a reflection less of its character than its culture. Airlines compete with one another incessantly over each individual customer. Despite considerable consumer activity of its own, Exxon was primarily in the business of oil extraction, refining, and distribution. It is not that it didn't have customers, or care about them, but rather that the skills most valued in the oil industry were not those of consumer cultivation. Someone who spends his days competing for passengers with the friendly skies of United is much more likely to know how to be friendly.

Exxon presumably had a public relations department, but the company itself seemed not to be interested in public relations. It may be admirable just to want to be oneself and not to pay someone to help make a good impression, but this form of integrity can carry a price. Exxon was paying the price every day in court—and even outside the courtroom itself. The federal courthouse where the trial was held was designated as smoke-free. A number of the jurors liked to smoke. They had to step outside the courthouse to indulge their habit, and those who stood there puffing away before the session resumed had an unimpaired view of the Exxon officials arriving. It was quite a sight. It wasn't that they pulled up in a fleet of limousines—they probably couldn't have even if they had wanted to; Anchorage doesn't have that many limousines.

They pulled up in vans. Rather, first one van appeared. It stopped in front of the courthouse. It waited. After a while, the other vans arrived. Their approach had been cleared by the scout. The vans disgorged the company executives who were to testify, and the lawyers, and the wordsmiths, and the consultants. And bodyguards. It was clear to the jurors that these were bodyguards. They had those plastic things in their ears like the Secret Service. They dispersed at once across the lawn between the vans and the courthouse, looking for trouble. Their eyes covered everyone between them and their destination, including the jurors. And then they drew close to their charges and the group coalesced and entered the building.

There was nothing wrong with Exxon hiring bodyguards. Oil companies regularly do business in places where this is essential. In Alaska, where guns are ubiquitous and drink abundant, it was not unreasonable to suppose that some person would journey across his ravaged land in search of vengeance. It was prudent to be prepared. But it didn't have to be so obvious. It didn't have to look so *paramilitary*. It startled and amused the jurors on the courthouse steps, and that wasn't really what the defendants should have had in mind.

The last major Exxon official to testify was Frank Iarossi, who had been president of Exxon Shipping Company at the time of the spill. When the grounding occurred, Lawrence Rawl had never heard of Joseph Hazelwood—one name out of the hundred thousand who worked for Exxon. But Frank Iarossi had heard of Hazelwood, had been familiar with his situation for quite some time. He, not Rawl, was in fact Hazelwood's real boss. It was Iarossi who had made the decision to return Hazelwood to sea duty after he left South Oaks. It was Iarossi who had ordered that Hazelwood be monitored. In a sense, Iarossi was the most important witness at the trial.

In his videotaped testimony, Iarossi defended the decision to return the captain to his command. He said it was basically a question of risk analysis. There were risks on either side of the question. On the one hand, there was the risk that the captain of a tanker might lapse into alcoholism and thereby endanger his vessel.

On the other hand, if Hazelwood were fired or assigned to shore duty, that example might inhibit other drinkers from coming forward and self-identifying themselves as alcoholics and voluntarily seeking treatment. "We didn't know how many future Hazelwoods there would be, and our concern was that if we backed away from the policy, we would never see self-identity of any of the potential other risks that might be out there." Further, he was worried about violating the law. He had been advised that alcoholism was considered a disability and that federal statute prohibited denying someone a position based solely on a disability.

The decision reached through this weighing of risks obviously had been wrong. No one on either side of the case believed that if Exxon had it to do over, the same decision would have been made. The captain, not the tanker, would be grounded. But hindsight needs no lookouts. The real question was whether the decision had been reasonable at the time. If not, was it more than unreasonable? Was it reckless? There was no more fundamental issue in the case, unless of course it was the degree to which the captain's drinking was monitored after he returned to sea duty.

Iarossi was subjected to many questions on this point. He said that he had understood that the fleet manager and the port captain would be doing the monitoring, that when Hazelwood was in port they would meet with him and look for signs of drinking; they would talk with some of the crew members about this, too. None of these monitors had ever told him that Hazelwood was drinking again. There was nothing in the file, either, to indicate this.

His testimony, of course, had been preceded by eyewitness accounts under oath of Hazelwood drinking aboard ship or in port. Many more of these would follow. The point of this steady stream of sightings was not that Iarossi was lying, but rather that he should have known.

Iarossi was the man who had fired Hazelwood after learning the results of the blood alcohol test. The press release accompanying this dismissal quoted him as saying that "the decision to terminate the employee was made because he violated company policy concerning alcohol." Now, in court, he was testifying that Hazelwood had been fired because he violated the company policy against leaving the bridge. When asked about the discrepancy, he said that the press release had been wrong. He had been too preoccupied with the spill to check his statement more carefully. "Of all the things that I needed to do at that point in time . . . this was the least important to worry about—how we got the wording right."

That says it all. To him this was a question of "wording," this amended reason for firing Hazelwood. Why quibble over it? What difference did it make? He had been going for days without sleep trying to control the spill. These were just *words*. Iarossi seemed not to see just how damaging this attitude was. Though he had not worked for Exxon since the year after the spill, he seemed still to personify its corporate culture.

Iarossi was the last star to appear. There were many, many other witnesses, but they were supporting players. There were more than eighty of them. It is difficult even to imagine, without sitting through it or reading the transcript, how extraordinarily repetitive the trial was. So many people testified to the same thing: a whiff of alcohol or, better yet, sharing a bottle; the shell game of the three stoppered blood vials, impossible to follow and tainted with Chalos's innuendo; the extent to which crew members did or did not rest for six hours out of twelve; the empty files of supervisors whom crew members said they had informed; so many crew members who had seen something awry, so many Exxon officials who had not. After a while, it must have overwhelmed the jury, day after day of O'Neill drilling away and the best repairmen in the world trying to put the sawdust back in the holes.

Some witnesses made a greater impression than others. A few were unforgettable. These were usually experts, who brought to the proceedings a welcome hint of colorful worlds beyond the realm of shipping. Where the plaintiffs found some of them remains a mystery.

Dr. David Smith, for example, the founder and medical director of the Haight-Ashbury Free Clinics in San Francisco, was the president-elect of the American Society of Addiction Medicine. He had helped treat thousands of cases of addiction, his patients ranging from the indigent to Jerry Garcia of the Grateful Dead. O'Neill was offering him as an expert in substance abuse testing, chain of custody documentation, and laboratory test results.

The defendants fought this tooth and nail. They said that the only expert on whether the chain of custody was intact should be the jury. There was no such thing as an expert on factual findings. The judge disagreed, and let Dr. Smith testify.

This ruling was a setback for the defense. The blood tests were the best proof that the captain had been drunk, so the defendants were arguing that the chain of custody had been broken. They wanted to get the blood test thrown out.

And now Dr. Smith was on the stand saying that the blood test was all right. "In my opinion, this chain of custody is intact . . . the most critical element is that the integrity of the specimen must be intact. There can be other issues, but the relative evaluations of the chain of custody are considered relatively minor in relationship to what we call fatal flaw."

This was exactly what the defense did not want the jury to hear. And as if that weren't bad enough, Dr. Smith then gave a second opinion—a separate expert opinion that was just as damaging to the defense.

It was about what he called retrograde extrapolation. This holds that if you know the alcohol blood content of someone several hours after an accident, you can extrapolate backward to know just what the alcohol level was at the time of the accident. (This assumes, of course, that the person drank nothing since the accident.) Captain Hazelwood's blood was drawn about eleven hours after the grounding. The blood alcohol content was found to be .061. In the transportation industry, the acceptable level is no more than .04. In many states, .08 or .10 qualifies as drunken driving. So Captain Hazelwood's test put him somewhere between an acceptable and a drunken driver. But when Dr. Smith applied the techniques of retrograde extrapolation, "my professional opinion is that his blood alcohol at the time of the grounding was .226."

A person with a blood alcohol reading of .226 is what nonexperts call pie-eyed drunk. One steps over people in the gutter who have a lower reading. It is two and a half times the drunk-driving level. No one would argue that someone with a reading of .226 should be commanding a tanker, or, for that matter, standing upright.

But the defense could and did suggest that this retroactive reading was wrong. It was absurd, they said, to say that the captain had a level of .226. He would have been slurring and reeling, obviously drunk to all the crew members who had seen him and thought he seemed sober. Even the ever vigilant Coast Guard had detected no signs of insobriety other than the smell of alcohol, which might have been the Moussy.

To this Dr. Smith had a response. There are some people whose motor functions are not visibly affected by strong drink, but the *judgment* of those persons will not be immune. The implication was that someone under the influence could cross a gangplank and speak steadily, but still be sufficiently judgment-impaired to leave the bridge at a critical moment of navigation.

Dr. Smith was an impressive and unflappable witness, but Jim Sanders did his best to discredit his testimony, through question after question deriding the chain of custody that the doctor had said was acceptable. What difference did it make what the reading was if the jurors thought the samples had not been properly handled? Smith stuck to his conclusion, and Sanders kept chipping away. When the defense lawyer talked derisively about the sample being left unrefrigerated on a windowsill, the doctor explained, "A windowsill in March on a cold Arctic March afternoon."

"What was the temperature of that cold Arctic March afternoon?"

"My assumption."

"Do you know what it was?"

"No."

"How do you know it was a cold Arctic afternoon?"

"That's my assumption."

"Right. I'm not asking you for what your assumption was now. Do you know what the temperature of that blood was from ten fifty in the morning until it went into that refrigerator?"

"No."

It would be difficult to exaggerate the degree to which this was a drunk-driving trial. There were maritime experts and such, but an extraordinary amount of testifying concerned only what Hazelwood had drunk, and when, and who had seen it, and whom they had told. Some of these accounts were more memorable than others—wine aboard ship, beer ordered over the tanker wireless—and none more so than the account of an Alamar employee in Valdez whose job it was to help out the visiting crews. He said that he had seen crew members from Exxon vessels return to their ships noticeably drunk, and had on occasion gone into the Pipeline Club where Hazelwood was drinking to pick him up and take him back to his ship. Despite loud objections by the defense, the judge allowed this witness to testify that among Alamar people, Captain Hazelwood had a reputation for being a sailor who liked to drink. This witness had been found by the ever resourceful Joe Malatesta of the Robinson office. Perhaps the jurors were thinking that if the plaintiffs had been able to discover this guy, why hadn't Exxon? Wouldn't real monitoring have come up with what so many people were saying about Hazelwood?

The subject of drink was about to be theatrically enhanced by a witness unlike any other. Dr. Garrett O'Connor did not walk like or talk like or look like the other experts in the trial, but an expert he was certified to be. He was an expert in alcohol-abuse problems and in evaluation for duty in safety-sensitive positions. Airline pilots constituted half his practice (the pilot AA group is known as Birds of a Feather). A medical doctor and psychiatrist, he himself had been a recovering alcoholic since 1977 and claimed he had attended three thousand Alcoholics Anonymous meetings.

Dr. O'Connor had been born and raised in Ireland and although he lived in Los Angeles, he had retained a lilting brogue that made listening to him talk a pleasure. This was fortunate, for his discourse continued unabated. The defense at one point objected to his seamless narrative flow, saying that he was only supposed to be answering questions. The judge, perhaps entranced, let Dr. O'Connor continue.

It is easy to imagine why the other side wanted him to shut up. He was a very charismatic witness, powerful, assured, and unstoppable, really, in his mellifluous recital of the many aspects of alcohol addiction. He smiled at the jurors when making a point, and his look to them was one of warm and sparkling inclusion. The message that this charmer was evoking for the jury was that of the need for total abstinence—at least for those in safety-sensitive positions. Once an alcoholic, always an alcoholic.

He had reviewed the facts of this case. He had retraced the famous steps in Valdez. He had formed some specific conclusions. "It is my opinion that Captain Hazelwood never really got into a state of recovery and, therefore, that he did not achieve a state of stable recovery following his discharge from South Oaks between that time and the time of the oil spill." Further, Hazelwood's alcoholism was responsible for the impairment of his judgment on the night of the grounding.

He went even further. He said that Exxon was responsible for this. Over the most persistent objections by Jim Sanders, this line of questioning was permitted:

"Based on your experience, if Captain Hazelwood had been properly evaluated before being assigned to the *Yorktown* in 1985, could Exxon have discovered the signs of his failure in recovery?"

"I believe so."

"And do you have an opinion as to whether there were sufficient signs available to Exxon to detect Captain Hazelwood's failure in recovery when Exxon reassigned the captain to the *Exxon Valdez* in 1987?"

"I believe there were."

"And had Exxon looked properly, could they have found those signs?"

"I believe they could."

"By the way, is it accepted professional conduct, in your field, to require an evaluation of someone who has gone through alcohol treatment on the basis of rumor?"

"Yes."

"Particularly when that person is in a safety-sensitive position?"

"That's correct."

And then, as if to push the hyperventilating defense counsel into spasms, a final question was allowed.

"Do you have an opinion as to whether Exxon should have allowed Captain Hazelwood to be the master on the *Exxon Valdez* as it left San Francisco in March of 1989?"

"I do."

"And what is your opinion?"

"I believe that Exxon should not have permitted him to leave San Francisco as master of the *Exxon Valdez* on that date."

The plaintiffs had no further questions. Indeed, other than the amount of punitive damages that ought to be awarded, it is hard to imagine anything that they had failed to ask.

Dr. O'Connor did not seem in the least concerned when Jim Sanders approached for his cross-examination. He looked at the lawyer as if appraising an airline pilot seeking reinstatement; he knew how to handle this sort of thing.

Or so he thought. Sanders was not there to explain a Heineken bottle found in a flight bag. He was there to draw blood. It was his duty and, in this case, his pleasure. He had been forced, despite his many objections, to listen with increasing outrage to the entrancing cadence of the tireless witness. The testimony seemed to him to consist largely of findings of fact masquerading as expert opinion. What was the *jury* there for, other than to flounder in all that blarney like otters in the spill? Sanders was angry. And he was very well prepared. Like all great cross-examiners, he took aim not at the testimony but at the expert. And his bullets were ridicule.

"Dr. O'Connor, . . . I was watching you look over, talking to the jury. You're an actor, aren't you?"

"I have been an actor in the past, yes. I'm not doing acting these days."

"Well, is there any treatment for getting over the disease of acting? Do you relapse into acting?"

"I am not familiar with acting as a disease. That's a new concept to me."

"As a matter of fact, you were an actor in certain television shows?"

"That's true."

"You were an actor on the stage?"

"That's true."

"You were an actor in the movies?"

"That's true."

"And, as a matter of fact, you're a member of the Actors Equity?"

"That's correct."

"Still a member?"

"That's correct."

Having transformed a charming doctor into an actor with a medical degree, Sanders established that O'Connor was being paid not only to testify but to consult with the plaintiffs as well. It was he who had recommended using Dr. Smith as an expert witness. Sanders made him seem a member of the opposition team. The suggestion was that he did more consulting with lawyers than with patients.

"Your medical practice, now—that's a one-man practice in Los Angeles, right?"

"Yes, it is."

"And you've been up here since, what, first of May?"

"No, I arrived here on, I think the ninth of May."

"Been up here since then?"

"Yes."

"Who's minding the store?"

For once the doctor seemed at a loss for words, and then he produced the answer that Sanders had hoped he would give.

"I have no ongoing treatment responsibilities."

Demoting the witness from Dr. Kildare to Richard Chamberlain was not sufficient for Sanders. There was still his testimony to discredit, all the lofty admonitions about monitoring and the duty to disclose.

"And in 1980, I believe, you applied for a medical license in California?"

"That's true."

"And at the time that you applied, you didn't tell them you were an alcoholic, did you?"

"Nobody asked me."

"But you didn't tell them, did you?"

"There was no way to do so."

"Just absolutely impossible for you to have communicated that fact to the authorities in California?"

"I was a recovering alcoholic with three years of sobriety at the time, and there was no particular reason to tell anybody about that."

"And I believe also in 1980 you applied for a pilot's license?"

"That's true."

"All right. Now, would you agree with me, doctor, that a physician who has the authority, the power, the privilege to prescribe medication to patients and to see patients who have trouble in their lives is a safety-sensitive job?"

"Yes, indeed."

"And I assume you would likewise agree with me that a pilot of an airplane, of whatever size, is in a safety-sensitive job, correct?"

"That's correct."

"And when you applied for your FAA license, you didn't tell them you were an alcoholic, did you?"

"There was no requirement that I should do so. I told them later on, in 1983. There was no requirement in 1980 that I should do so."

"Doctor, did you tell them? Did you tell them?"

"There was no requirement that I should do so."

"Yes or no?"

"I did not. There is no way I could have told them."

There was still the question of monitoring.

"Isn't it a fact, doctor, that the FAA never monitored you?"

"Monitoring was decided—it was decided that monitoring was not necessary because of my demonstrated five years of successful recovery in Alcoholics Anonymous."

"And isn't it a fact, doctor, that the state of California, the medical authority, never monitored you?"

"Medical authority hired me because I was a recovering alcoholic and in other areas, at least, permitted me to work voluntarily for them because I was a recovering alcoholic who did not require monitoring because of demonstrated recovery in Alcoholics Anonymous."

"They didn't monitor you, did they?"

"There was no reason for them to do so and they didn't."

Sanders' moment was at hand. "There's one piece of confusion here." He seemed genuinely puzzled. "Didn't I understand you to say that an alcoholic is never cured?"

"Once an alcoholic, always an alcoholic, yes."

Their eyes met. It took the gloating hunter's look for the rabbit to realize that it had been trapped. "No further questions," said Sanders, who walked slowly, but in triumph, back to the counsel table, eyes on the jurors as if deciding which señorita should be favored with the ears. His grin resembled that of O'Neill.

That was the standard. O'Neill had become the central player in the trial. His name was evoked all the time. When he wasn't talking in court himself, the defense was talking about him. ("Now I'll turn you over to the tender mercies of Mr. O'Neill.") He was omnipresent—and really had to be—an impudent, accusatory force who kept pointing a finger at the other side, making his case through sheer incessancy: would mere negligence merit such ceaseless condemnation? Only recklessness could deserve the withering barrage that never paused and never rested.

Many weeks before the trial began, just after O'Neill and his team had moved up to Anchorage, they all had visited their trial office for the first time. These were barren, inexpensive quarters on one floor of an office building about seven blocks from the courthouse, really no more than a long series of tiny rooms that remained unfurnished except for a few folding chairs and tables. It was a drab, spare space in which souls could be lost, but when O'Neill saw it he exclaimed, "This is the happiest day of my life." And no doubt it was, the commander's tent on the edge of the plain where soon the rival armies would clash. It was the finest moment because it could not last, but not one second of it yet had been lost. They could be fully engaged without any loss of anticipation. To have lusted all one's life for the ultimate in combat, and to be there at its outset, ready, in command, prepared, and still to have spent not yet one day, one moment even, of that perfect transitory pleasure, those days and weeks that were the fulcrum of one's life, yearned for and then later wistfully remembered, this was the last possible link between the future and one's will. The happiest day indeed was moving into the empty space, before the space was filled and the perfect time was passed.

And there was *time* to be happy, then. But once the trial had begun, there was time for nothing but its needs. The days may have seemed protracted to the jury, but not to O'Neill. There was never enough time. Each day was frenzy, each hour more like a minute. From anxious awakening to troubled sleep, the schedule was always the same. At five o'clock each morning, O'Neill met the others at the trial office, its floor now strewn with boxes, exhibits, and charts. O'Neill would be shown the cross or direct examination outlines for that day's session, forty or fifty pages for each witness, compilations of every fact and discrepancy that could be employed to trap or prod whomever was called to the stand. These had been prepared through awesome effort by one or another of many research teams. Nolting tried to review with O'Neill the questions to be asked in the upcoming session. Everyone vied at once for O'Neill's attention. There were so much data to feed into a single human memory bank, last-minute changes, corrections, admonitions, strategy, urgency, priority, entreaty. That this dissonance could be sorted out, let alone be absorbed, let alone be helpful, was simply assumed by those competing for O'Neill's attention. And then at seven thirty the trial team trudged over to the courthouse, laden with supplies and armed with weapons for the day—cardboard blowups of sixteen vodkas on the rocks, huge aerial photos of the Narrows—and got themselves seated just before the judge and the jury came in.

Then it was the trial, from eight until two, with only a fifteen-minute break every two hours, just time to gobble snacks without water in a hall off the courtroom admidst harsh whispered reminders of all the points that still needed to be made. Then back into the courtroom where there was no time, only total acuity, attention riveted on nothing in this world but each word as it was spoken in court, the response automatic, as in a squash game, no time for thought, dependent solely on the countless hours of competition and practice that had preceded it.

And then at two, when the jurors rose and left the courthouse for their homes, and perhaps a late and leisurely lunch, the litigators hauled their supplies back to the trial office, where there was always a staff meeting of less than an hour. The first thing that happened was always the same. O'Neill would stand up and wait until everyone else had quieted down, and then with stentorian tone and very dramatic timing would announce that "the lawyer of the day is . . ." and then after a pause would provide the name. This was met with cheers and clapping and laughter. It was sort of a joke—the person who had contributed the most that day—but of course it was not a joke; it meant a lot to the winner of the daily honor; it meant a lot to all of them, being part of this. Then it was time to return to work. Last-minute assignments were made and the day's damage assessed, after which the researchers went off in search of boxes of paper and then began at three in the afternoon a whole new long and aching day of preparation for the next.

O'Neill then went to his home, a rented house not far away, and at last in solitude sat with the hundreds of pages of paper that, if absorbed, would permit him to seem relaxed the following day, grinning, insouciant, able to return any ball.

At six thirty he went running, a solitary jog along the nearby shore of Cook Inlet. His workday as such was over, and the only task left was to fight off stress, to keep even the thought of his burdens at bay, to permit nothing to tighten or to tire him. After the run, cleaned up, he joined his team for dinner. They called the large house the Girls' Dorm; the women lawyers and staff lived there for the trial and the men joined them for dinner every evening. They had a full-time cook—Dave Gibson, Lori Wagner's boyfriend, a salmon fisherman who had followed her to Anchorage. They needed a cook. Sometimes there were twenty-five or even thirty of them around the big table, food and wine and jokes and groans, young tired faces flickering in the candlelight.

O'Neill would return to his own house in order to be asleep by nine. And he did fall asleep at once, the moment his head hit the pillow; the running and the camaraderie had let that happen. But too many facts had been crammed into his skull each day, and too many dangers always awaited him the next.

At about two in the morning he would come awake again, trying to remember what he might have forgotten, trying to fight anxiety, panic. He would get up then, in the middle of the soft summer Alaskan night, dress quietly, and go out for another run. That always seemed to calm him down. The running in the faint light, the silence, the clear air, the lapping water of the inlet, the occasional sight of furtive wildlife, once a moose, large against the horizon, and, unforgettably, like a vision, a school of whales, their tails gleaming silver in the auroral light. Then O'Neill would be home and able to sleep again, but briefly, for the first meeting of the morning always began at five. There was so much to do before walking over to court.

The trial itself had become as routine as the unvarying agenda outside it. Every day had new witnesses, but all the issues already had been raised and the remaining weeks were devoted to variations on familiar themes. The experts seemed increasingly specialized in precisely the arcania of this case. The last one called by the plaintiffs was expert not merely in alcohol abuse, or, as others had been, in the relationship of alcohol abuse to safety-sensitive positions, but "specifically in *monitoring* procedures for employees in safety-sensitive positions with alcohol-abuse problems."

This ultimate expert, Dr. Richard Masters, had been called to the stand by the plaintiffs only after they had questioned many other witnesses (port captains, Exxon human resources functionaries), who presumably had been involved in monitoring Captain Hazelwood. None of these witnesses could produce a paper trail of their efforts. That was the whole point of following them with Dr. Masters, who testified that in his opinion these efforts did not constitute monitoring. There simply had to be a written plan, he said, and the roles of the supervisory and medical personnel had to be clearly explained and understood.

Exxon's attempts to discredit this expert during cross-examination reveal the extraordinary degree to which each side had researched every detail of this case. Pat Lynch asked, "You did have a previous professional experience with Captain Hazelwood's father, did you not?"

Captain Hazelwood's *father!* Indeed, a connection did exist. The father of the Exxon captain had himself been a flight captain for Pan Am Airlines, some years earlier. As a member of the Airline Pilots Association, he had sought to change an FAA rule that set mandatory retirement at age sixty. He had provided information about his own good health to Dr. Masters, whom he wanted to petition the FAA for an exemption in his case. Whether or not the decision was that of Dr. Masters, the exception was not granted. A lingering familial obsession with this injustice is one of the reasons that Hazelwood had left Alaska after the spill rather than appear before the hated National Transportation Safety Board. The dispute between Hazelwood *père* and the transportation authorities was referred to by Pat Lynch as an "altercation," a characterization that the expert strongly denied.

It was a game, really. If there *had* been some bad blood between the first Hazelwood captain and a witness whose testimony was particularly damaging to his son—well, the jury could do what it wanted with that. One more seed had been planted.

The name of the game, one remembers, was Kill the Expert. Belittle his expertise. When the same Dr. Masters recited his credentials in the field of monitoring people in safety-sensitive positions, he talked about all his work for the airline industry and for NASA, and for the Atomic Energy Commission. This didn't impress Pat Lynch, who actually asked, with a straight face, "And you've never been employed to develop an alcohol policy outside the government or the airline industry, is that correct?" What Lynch was doing is what lawyers do. The original deconstructionists. By this time the jury probably would have doubted the credibility of a traffic light.

Late in the morning of May 25, the plaintiffs rested their case. Now it was the defendants' turn to call witnesses. They would summon to the stand an even larger cast than the plaintiffs had assembled: forty-four to forty-one. Of course, some of them were the same. Frank Iarossi, for example, the former head of the Exxon Shipping Company, the highest

Exxon official who had known the name Hazelwood before the grounding, the man who had sent the captain back to sea after his discharge from South Oaks, the man who had fired him as soon as the blood-test results came in, the ultimate recipient of monitoring reports, if such existed.

Earlier in the trial, during the plaintiffs' case, Iarossi first had appeared, but only on video, examined by Laddie Montague, the class action lawyer from Philadelphia. The defense then had waived the right to its own follow-up questions, saying they would call him later.

Now was later, the defendants' turn. This was no video appearance; Iarossi was present and took the stand. Beneath his high forehead was a face that showed nothing. Jim Neal questioned him, and there were many questions. Both sides recognized how critical this one witness was to their chances of prevailing. More than anyone else, his testimony could seal Exxon's fate.

Neal asked very careful questions, and Iarossi answered them with confidence. He gave his side of the story: "Our whole effort was based on self-identification of the employee. I think that weighed absolutely the most in my decision" to return Hazelwood to sea command. "If we denied him the job, we would never get anybody to self-identify.

"We didn't know what the risk was. It was undefined, so we made a choice between a risk we understood and a risk we knew we potentially had but did not know the magnitude of."

He had said the same before, but now, on the stand, something else came through, articulation of what Exxon believed that monitoring really meant. It meant monitoring only the manner in which an employee performed his or her job. "We had no business in the employee's private life. In fact, it was probably illegal, and therefore all of our activities were associated with on-the-job performance or time periods when the employee was on Exxon facilities."

The cross-examination of this witness was conducted by O'Neill. He pushed his instant-video button to great effect. He came very close to getting the witness, who no longer worked for Exxon, to say that it was reckless for the captain not to have been on the bridge.

But the most effective point he made was with regard to self-identification. Exxon claimed that its policy, its confidentiality, its lack of written reports, were all aimed at promoting the confession of alcohol and drug abusers who otherwise would never come forward.

But O'Neill, through questions that were really statements, made the point that the captain had *not* self-identified: he simply had been caught. Exxon had been investigating his drinking, and he knew it, before he entered South Oaks. An Exxon employee had suggested that he seek help. It had been a shotgun rehabilitation. If this was true, then the whole rationale for protecting an employee's privacy had no real bearing on the case of Captain Hazelwood. They could have kept him from sea duty without doing violence to their goal of self-identification.

The defense kept calling witnesses, few of whom proved riveting to the jury. There were those who had sailed with the captain and attested to his sobriety, but a witness who says that he didn't see a captain drink is less memorable than one who says he did. If there were enough of both, and there were, then it mattered less and less which sightings were the rule and which the exception. Nor did it help much to shift the blame elsewhere: if Kagan or Cousins or the Coast Guard had not performed as well as they should, the jurors never doubted that the defendant remained the man with the beard at the table. In fact, the putative scapegoats only focused more attention on the captain. When the former commandant of the United States Coast Guard said that "the primary cause or the causal effect of that grounding was a perfectly qualified third mate on a bridge of a ship that, through a period of a few minutes of inattention to duty or lack of knowledge of exactly where he was, ran the ship aground on a clear night," it was another way of saying, intentionally or not, that the primary cause of the grounding was that the captain had left the bridge.

There was another problem with many of the defense witnesses: they were not visible. Their depositions were read aloud in court. This happened time and time again. It became so boring and monotonous that one of the jurors finally complained in a note that the judge shared with the courtroom. Judge Holland reminded the jury that the subpoena powers of his court were limited, that he couldn't force many of the witnesses to appear in person. This was true, but the jurors were still stuck in their box with someone reading to them all day long. They hated it. The plaintiffs had used readers, too, of course, but perhaps not so many, and they had used them first. The cumulative effect of all these droning words was increasingly deadly. To make matters worse, for the defense, anyway, there was by way of contrast the plaintiffs' passion for visual presentation. When the reading of the commandant's testimony had finally ceased, it was followed by the plaintiffs' cross-examination of him—on video. The jurors were probably wondering why this slightly more entertaining format couldn't be used by both sides.

The endless proceedings were wearing everyone down. Some jurors seemed glassy-eyed and occasionally resentful, as if finally realizing why this interminable thing was called a trial. The lawyers, too, began to show the toll of many weeks' confinement. Tempers flared on occasion. The squabbling worsened over the truly ridiculous question of whether the meeting place in Houston where the newly recovered captain met his supervisor should be called a lobby or a bar. When Sanders, late in the plaintiff case, showed photos of a registration desk to establish the purity of the site, O'Neill stopped calling it a bar and started calling it a joint. When Sanders remonstrated, O'Neill replied, "I don't like it when people take potshots at me."

The only one who never showed a sign of strain was Judge Holland. He remained as polite and good humored as on the opening day of the trial. He ruled on objections with courtesy and dispatch. He did not let the lawyers wrangle. The case was potentially as unwieldy as a tanker, but he kept it on course. If the phrasing of a question was unacceptable, he gently coaxed the errant lawyer to simply move the words around. He didn't get excited and he didn't get angry. He didn't have to. He was in charge, and not one person in the courtroom doubted it for a second. It wasn't that he said that much; there was no need. Sometimes a smile or a quizzical look would do the job. He was never intrusive, but he was always there.

Despite his own tireless presence on the bridge, however, the craft that he commanded now appeared to be becalmed. As Phase One drew to its conclusion, the last theatricality left in the trial seemed reserved for those awesome visitors from outer space, the experts. The jurors had already been treated to the finest experts that money could buy, and Exxon's team did not retreat from this high standard.

They produced, for example, an expert who said that Captain Hazelwood was not an alcoholic. The significance of this conclusion depended on the standing of the expert. The defendants had one who seemed peerless. Even to a jury by this time inured to the luster of upper academia, Dr. Jack Mendelson had a vita to die for. A professor of psychiatry at the Harvard Medical School, he had served for twenty years as director of the Alcohol and Drug Abuse Research Center at McLean Hospital, affiliated with Harvard, and also as director of its substance-abuse treatment program.

He was the author of a widely used textbook, *The Medical Diagnosis and Treatment of Alcoholism,* and had been co-editor of the *Journal of Studies on Alcohol.* There was a lot more. And this was merely his work record.

"Have you received any honors or awards?" defense counsel happily asked before stepping back to let the floodgates open.

"I have received the major award from the American Psychiatric Society, their major research prize for studies which I and my colleagues carried out relating to the diagnosis and treatment of alcohol-related problems.

"I have also received an award from the Research Society on Alcoholism, which is the major research institutional group in the United States for investigative work, which I have carried out with my colleagues in alcohol-related areas.

"I've received the Jellinek Award, which is the major international prize given for investigators throughout the world who have conducted work in alcoholism.

"I have also served as a member of the nominating committee for the Nobel Prize in physiology or medicine."

There was no objection to his being approved as an expert witness in psychiatry and the diagnosis, treatment, and prevention of alcohol-related problems. He took the stand. What Dr. Mendelson went on to say was very similar to Michael Chalos's opening statement about his friend and client, Captain Hazelwood. The South Oaks diagnosis meant that Hazelwood was not an alcoholic, but rather someone who had abused alcohol. Further, "my opinion would be that an individual who has had dysthymia and episodic alcohol abuse could resume social drinking following completion of treatment." And if he did drink in this port or that port? So what? But this wasn't old college classmate Chalos talking, this was someone on the nominating committee for the Nobel prize.

When it came time for cross-examination, O'Neill gamely managed to give the impression that, after all, this guy hadn't *won* any Nobel Prizes. He began by telling the expert that "I took the occasion last night to read your books." Whether this was entirely the case, some research had in fact been done. Take, for example, the doctor's celebrated textbook.

"And on the front page of the text, there's an acknowledgment and the acknowledgment reads, 'Preparation of this text was made possible by a grant from the Distilled Spirits Council of the United States, Inc., Washington, D.C.' Who is the Distilled Spirits Council of the United States, Inc.?"

"They were a trade organization which provided funds to the Harvard Medical School for the preparation of the text."

"They're a trade organization, that is essentially the industry that makes hard liquor, is that correct?"

"They make wine, distilled spirits, and beer."

Another book that the doctor had authored had been facilitated by a grant from the Licensed Beverage Information Council. "You got grants from the liquor industry?" O'Neill demanded to know.

This is how opposing lawyers treat experts. It is no different from the kind of assaults that had been made on the experts whom O'Neill had brought to the stand. It makes one wonder whether there should be expert testimony at all. What is the point of purchasing the most distinguished target? There *are* experts, of course, and sometimes they are needed; not everything is a matter of common sense. The experts in the *Exxon Valdez* case were the most celebrated in their fields. But they were giving contrary testimony. One doctor says that Hazelwood should never drink again, and another says that social drinking is fine. Neither is lying, or a fake, or testifying merely for pay. Each is expressing honestly the conclusion of a lifetime of scholarly work. And their conclusions are the *opposite* of one another.

What is the jury supposed to think? None of the jurors is an expert, but every one of them knows that if one of these dazzling witnesses is right then the other one has to be wrong. But which is which? And how can we know? And at some point—certainly when both sides have limitless resources—don't these people just cancel each other out? And what if only one side can afford all the experts? Is that better, or worse?

Just as each side had its own expert on alcoholism, each side had its own expert on sleep disorders. The defendants' expert was in the finest tradition of his predecessors. "I apologize for the arcane organization of the curriculum vitae. Harvard University requires that it be organized in that way." He talked about the Multiple Sleep Latency Test, and may not have detected skeptical looks from some jurors when he proclaimed, "The longer it takes someone to fall asleep, the more alert they are."

If this was so, most jurors would have been snoring. It was becoming more difficult to feel alert. And if the trial acted on the jurors like Sominex, then how much more enervating must have been its prolonged impact on the lawyers. And of all the lawyers, surely the most exhausted must have been O'Neill. Undoubtedly there were others who managed somehow to stay awake and work as many hours each day as he. Some may have worked even more. But that was research or collation or editing. O'Neill was the lead trial lawyer. For much of the time, he was the only trial lawyer arguing his side of the case. From eight until two every day of the work week he was *on*. Actors are drained by a stage performance lasting less than half as long, and they aren't making up their own dialogue, or battling the other actors. And when the curtain comes down, they go to sleep or get drunk, they don't start a whole new day of memorizing things. And they aren't in charge of the production. And they don't have to wait for weeks or months in order to find out whether their audience of twelve is going to cheer them, or boo.

The real stars of the stage or of the courtroom know that the standing ovations go only to those who never retreat from their best. You can't just coast toward the end of the act. You have to maintain the zest of your entrance. There can be only one level; the peak must be the plain.

And nothing on earth can matter more than winning. O'Neill had reached this state. His focus on victory had been fixed since the moment he had heard on his car radio that there was a major oil spill somewhere in Alaska. Victory was his goal and his fuel. Stupendous victory, the biggest of all time. Personal victory, too, over demons and doubts and lapses. Victory on such a scale that it defined the victor, even in his own eyes, defined him not by a past inherited or bungled but in terms of nothing else than his performance in the arena where he excelled. His personal credo seemed very much like that expressed by Iarossi—all that mattered was performance on the job.

So O'Neill got out there every day and grinned at the jury, and grinned another way at his foes, and returned all their serves, and never, ever, for even an instant, turned down the full force of his own attack.

And he never stopped being on top of things, regardless of strain or exhaustion. Everything that happened he took in, and hoped that the jury could tell from his grimaced reaction just what was really going on. But it was so *hard* to remain at that level of alertness, let alone to seem cocky enough to get the defendants' goat. This thing just never ended. The witnesses were like a shooting gallery; every time you knocked one over, another popped up to take its place. They were unending: mariners, experts, naval architects, supervisors, people who said they'd spent a lot of time with the captain and never saw him drink, people who said that some of those who *had* testified to Hazelwood's drinking were not telling the truth. Four witnesses in a row rebutted what one of O'Neill's witnesses had said he'd seen. And through each of these, O'Neill had to look bemused or contemptuous or unconcerned, while all the time his mind was racing desperately to find some flaw in their accounts that could be used in cross-examination.

But the main thing was to keep attacking—keep hitting the same themes over and over, with every witness, hammer them home again and again so that even the most somnolent juror accepted argument as fact.

So, to the manager of Exxon's human relations department at the time of the grounding:

"And the company's policy with regard to taking care of this captain was such that the only thing you were going to look at was job-related performance, you weren't going to look at off-duty drinking, whether he was drinking again, that's the company's policy; isn't that right?"

"Our policy was to monitor the individual based on their job performance, as I testified, that's correct, sir."

". . . So the company policies would allow a relapsed alcoholic to be in charge of a supertanker, as long as nobody knew, so long as his relapsed nature didn't effect his job performance?"

". . . That's correct, sir, with appropriate monitoring."

"So your policies, knowing the risk to the public, of the catastrophic results of a supertanker accident, allow a relapsed alcoholic to command a supertanker?"

"Yes, sir, that's possible under our policy."

You just couldn't do too much of this kind of thing.

And then one day, unbelievably, the final witness left the stand. When Judge Holland said, "Ladies and gentlemen, this completes the taking of the evidence in this case," some jurors looked as if the parole board had finally come through. No more witnesses. Only the closing arguments remained.

12

The L Word

A s soon as the testimony had ended, the defendants tried to get a directed verdict, which is permitted by the rules when the evidence clearly has not been sufficient to establish the claim. The lawyers started arguing about this, and the defendants offered to write briefs in support of their positions.

"I don't want to write another brief," said O'Neill.

"I don't want to *read* another brief right now," said the judge.

"Point well taken, Your Honor," said Pat Lynch, who seemed to interpret the judge's remarks as victory; the evidence had been insufficient for the case to go to the jury—the judge could dismiss the case from the bench.

He was wrong. What the judge had meant was that the case now belonged neither to him nor to the lawyers; it belonged to the jury.

"I think it will be more profitable for all of us," he explained, "for you to defer writing that brief until you have some additional information that these twelve people will probably provide us. And I suggest you wait to write your briefs until we see what happens."

"Thank you, Judge," said O'Neill.

Lynch was gracious about his misconception. "Louisville slugger on my forehead, but I finally got the point, Your Honor."

This all occurred on Friday afternoon. The court would meet again on Monday morning. All that remained were the closing arguments.

The weekends were usually a little calmer than the court days, but this one was far more intense than anything else they had endured. The closing arguments! The last words the jurors would hear before retiring to reach their verdict. But which words should they be? There was no lack of suggestion of the magic phrase or argument that would do the trick. Everybody had some point that absolutely had to be included if the case was to be won.

In addition, the judge had provided both sides with copies of the instructions he would give the jurors as soon as the closing arguments were concluded. For the record, and for purposes of appeal, they could file exceptions to any instructions they didn't like. Both sides had strong exceptions. But how many should be made? This was an important tactical matter; it wasn't a good idea to be too critical of the judge who would be presiding over the other phases of the trial.

It seemed that every single member of the plaintiff team was fighting to get O'Neill's undivided attention. To protect his sanity and achieve some order, a committee of four was given exclusive access to the beleaguered litigator throughout the weekend. This quartet then itself was inundated with advice, reminders, and entreaties, which were distilled and weighed and then hurriedly shared with O'Neill, often through the intermediacy of Lori Wagner. Somehow, amidst the clamor and cramming, the speech was haltingly formed and then rehearsed and criticized and redrafted and polished and rehearsed again before the harshest critics in the land.

They were all still arguing about the details as they proceeded to the courthouse on Monday morning. Even the hall outside the courtroom was jammed. The judge and the lawyers talked about the rules for a few minutes, and after that jury was ushered in.

And then O'Neill was on. Each side had two hours for its closing argument. Because the plaintiffs had the burden of proof, O'Neill was given the right to divide his argument into two parts—before and after the defendants' closing statements—just what the jury consultant had said mattered most if you wanted to make a lasting impression.

The positioning of O'Neill's remarks seemed almost irrelevant compared to their force. He didn't build; he just started strong, and then got stronger still.

"May it please the Court, Counsel, Ladies and Gentlemen of the Jury:

When I started this trial, I vowed that I would try to keep whatever anger that I felt about the wreck of the *Exxon Valdez* in check. When Captain Hazelwood and Mr. Iarossi came in here and in a backhanded way apologized, they both said, 'I was devastated.'

"Those were the words that they used, but they weren't devastated. They didn't feel devastated and, in point, people that were devastated were over ten thousand fishermen and Natives, land owners, municipalities and Native corporations, people who make their living for the most part from the sea with their hands, purse seiners, drift-netters, set-netters, their crew, their family, the whole fabric of Alaskan life.

"And then on the last day of the trial testimony, Mr. Rouse comes in and says Exxon Corporation's policies allow a relapsed alcoholic to be the captain of a supertanker despite the known risks to society and, in this case, the known risks to over ten thousand fishermen and Natives who make their living with their hands out of the sea.

"What they did in the years leading to the wreck of the *Exxon Valdez* wasn't right. It was wrong. And what they did when they came into the courtroom and one after the other changed their stories was wrong. The oath in a courtroom, the oath in a deposition, is a serious, serious thing. When the chairman of the board of Exxon Corporation goes before the Congress of our country to testify, that is a serious, serious thing.

"In the environment of the courtroom, we try to be as polite as we can because these are long, long days that we have to put in, and to express outrage every time one of these guys changed the story would have made the environment in the courtroom unbearable for all of us."

A pause.

"But their respect for the truth doesn't exist. Their lack of respect for the truth is outrageous."

Another pause. Then, again, even more loudly:

"It's outrageous!"

The flight from the truth would be his steady theme. He left it for a moment to inform the jurors what was being asked of them. They would have to answer three questions. First, "Do you unanimously find from the preponderance of the evidence that the defendant Hazelwood was negligent as that term has been defined in the instructions and that his negligence was a legal cause of the grounding of the *Valdez,* yes or no?"

Second, "Do you unanimously find from a preponderance of the evi-

dence that the defendant Hazelwood was reckless and that his recklessness was a legal cause of the grounding of the *Exxon Valdez?*"

Third, "Then we get to the sixty-four-dollar question: Do you unanimously find from a preponderance of the evidence that the Exxon defendants were reckless and that their recklessness was a legal cause of the
grounding of the *Exxon Valdez?*"

In pursuit of three affirmative answers, O'Neill went over the definition
of recklessness in the judge's jury instructions—"you have to be subjectively conscious of a particularly grave danger or risk of harm." And he reminded them that "a corporation is responsible for the reckless acts of its
employees who are managers, and the reckless act of a corporate officer is
the reckless act of the corporation if it's done in the course and scope of
his duties." Lest this instruction be unclear, he added that "corporations
can only act through people, okay? That's what this is in English."

He then spoke about the standard of proof that was required. He
pointed out that this was not a criminal case, where the proof had to be
beyond a reasonable doubt.

"That isn't good enough in this case. In this search for truth, you are
to decide this civil case on a preponderance-of-the-evidence standard."
They can accept as fact something that they believe "is more true than not
true. Fifty-one/forty-nine. It isn't enough to say there may have been a
conspiracy to sneak into the freezer and change the blood, okay? That's
an attempt to cause some reasonable doubt. That isn't enough. It's you
who weigh the evidence, and if the plaintiffs are fifty-one percent versus
forty-nine percent for the defendants, the plaintiffs win. That's the burden of proof we're dealing with."

These niceties explained, it was time to return to the central theme: the
lack of honesty in the defendants' testimony.

"Now, let me explain to you the problem that the plaintiffs had in this
search for the truth.

"Of all of the people that we've put on the stand, over a hundred, they're
not our people. They don't purse seine. They don't set net, they don't gill
net, they don't harvest from the sea. Those were Exxon Corporation people,
some of whom told the truth—and some of whom didn't. These were the
employees of the twenty-sixth biggest corporation in America." He quickly
corrected his error. Twenty-sixth biggest institution in the *world.* And we
had to find those people at Exxon that would tell the truth before Exxon

closed ranks, which they did. So the Steve Days or the Mary Williamsons or the Jim Shaws or even the Captain Stalzers of the world, we needed to get their testimony before the party line was put into place. And you see what happens when the party line was put into place, because we got to see the president of Exxon Corporation come in here and tout the party line, and we compared that to what he told the Congress of the United States."

This was coming very close to the L word. Not a juror could have doubted that this sandy-haired dynamo was accusing Exxon of having falsified the facts. There were, of course, obvious and enormous discrepancies between what Exxon had said just after the grounding and what it now had testified to in court. O'Neill was attributing this to deliberate dishonesty.

He summarized for the jury the more salient facts of the case. "The wreck itself is proof that there must have been something seriously wrong, and let's see how we got there." He then produced a verbal panorama stretching from the Graves memorandum to the grounding. And every single incident that he related was tied by a silver cord of rhetoric to the same one precious and indispensable word: reckless.

"My question for you is: Is approving his conduct by not disciplining him safe or reckless? It's reckless.

"Senior management knew in May of '85, shortly after his discharge, that Captain Hazelwood admitted in the past he had consumed alcohol and he had returned from a ship—from port drunk several times. This is the key thing. Such conduct constituted a clear violation of Exxon Shipping Company's prohibitions against the use of alcohol and/or intoxication aboard Exxon vessels. . . . They've stipulated to this. Why wasn't he fired? Safe or reckless? Why wasn't he disciplined? Safe or reckless? Reckless."

O'Neill claimed that Hazelwood left South Oaks an alcoholic, and spoke dismissively of "that doctor who came in here, the one from the National Council on Distillers or wherever he was from."

In his trip through time he was settling every score, including the description of the meeting place in Houston—"the macaroni and cheese bar at the hotel," he called it sarcastically. "This man is coming back from alcohol rehabilitation. This isn't anything but a cocktail lounge."

Frank Iarossi became "Unfrank Frank." And then the L word was actually used. "Iarossi lies about self-I.D. He comes in here and tries to sneak by the self-I.D. thing. . . . Big Frank finds out after the fact and is shocked. Frank always finds out after the fact and he's always shocked and does nothing.

"The conclusion is, to save a thousand bucks a trip, let's put a relapsed alcoholic on the bridge of a supertanker. Safe or reckless?"

The same refrain followed each reminder of drinking episodes or corporate laxity.

"He leads a double life. At home he goes to AA and his wife goes to Al-Anon. He doesn't drink. But he resumes drinking on the road. He has an AA sponsor that he talks with; he has a bar list in his room.

"On the road he admits to drinking with St. Pierre, Dengel, Kunkel, Sturgis, Carr, Cousins, Masciarelli, Hogan, Roberson, Deckert, Kimtis, Enright and others; with Captain Enright in 1988 he has eight to ten drinks and drives. Shaw sees him drinking four times. There's the Portland Shipyard incident. Captain Stalzer testifies there were parties in the quarters. Enright saw him in the quarters, appeared he had been drinking. Carr, they drank aboard the boat. He drinks with Cousins, he drinks with Kunkel. Alamar drops him off and picks him up at bars. These are all people that are here because they drank with him. And it goes on and on and on."

He paused for a visual insertion: a video of his own question some days earlier, and the answer to it.

"So your policy of knowing the risk to the public of the catastrophic potential results of a supertanker accident allow a relapsed alcoholic to command a supertanker?"

"Yes, sir, that's possible under our policy."

Then back to the refrain: "Safe or reckless? In light of what we know, safe or reckless?"

He managed to touch on almost everything that had been introduced during the trial: the issue of fatigue, the size of the drinks at the Pipeline Club, the chain of custody rule, the six-on/six-off rule, the four-hour drinking rule, and what Exxon meant by monitoring.

"They couldn't monitor him because of confidentiality. Give me a break. The statement is stupid . . . this 'we monitor job performance in the case of safety-sensitive positions' is an interesting concept, because you know what it means? Let's wait until the airplane crashes or the boat runs aground and then we have bad job performance and then we can fire him and the public be damned. This is a company whose view is the public be damned. He's not an alcoholic? That's absolutely incredible!"

Throughout this recital the word "lie" was used with growing frequency. Exxon had lied, Hazelwood had lied, they were liars.

That word set the stage for his close, which consisted of videos of former Exxon chairman Lawrence Rawl's inconsistent statements. Embarrassing before, they seemed duplicitous now in the carefully created context of blatant dishonesty. When the tapes had finished running, O'Neill relinquished the floor.

For one hour he had owned the courtroom. Whether through anger or awe, every person in the crowded chamber had been riveted by his words. He touched every base and tied everything together, but it was more than an argument, it was a seamless display of pure energy and total will. When O'Neill finished and sat down, the void that followed seemed like a power failure.

It looked like an impossible act to follow. The jurors wondered which hapless leader of the defense would be chosen for this sacrifice. Lynch was the lead counsel, Neal the tough trial veteran, Sanders, brilliant and resourceful, the most gifted courtroom performer.

But these stalwarts of the bar remained seated. Up to the lectern came Michael Chalos. He wasn't Exxon's lawyer, of course; he was Hazelwood's. He was an unlikely person to be arguing what was essentially a drunk driving case. He was a specialist in transportation law. But the first criminal case he had ever taken part in had resulted in acquittal for his friend Captain Hazelwood up in Alaska. And now his job was once again to save his old classmate, but this time Chalos was following a speaker of such power and purpose that his own shambling passage to the lectern must have seemed to many some sort of mistake.

But who knows what lurks in the hearts of men? In the case of Chalos it was pluck. His surprising precedence in the defense lineup proved to be an inspired choice.

For he knocked one out of the ballpark. He looked around for a minute, bemused, gave the jury a wide-eyed what's-a-guy-like-me-doing-up-here look, pulled his jacket down, cleared his throat, and then he dropped the Columbo act and gave one of the great speeches of the trial.

He knew instinctively how to speak to a jury. He didn't talk down and he didn't talk up; he was one of them. He was good humored, like O'Neill, he was tough, like O'Neill, and he managed to show just as much indignation as O'Neill. Why should the plaintiffs have all the pleasure of moral disdain?

Most of all, he was simple and to the point. And basically all he was arguing was one point, with two parts: Captain Hazelwood was not an alcoholic and had not been drunk at the time of the grounding. If O'Neill wanted to turn this case into a drunken-driving trial—well, fine, okay, Chalos had already won one of those.

"Ladies and Gentlemen of the Jury: If I were a member of the jury in this case, the primary question that I would want discussed is, was Captain Hazelwood impaired by alcohol on the night of the grounding? Everyone seems to acknowledge that this is the paramount issue in this case. Because I represent Captain Hazelwood and because both he and I deeply resent the unsupported allegations that have been made that he was impaired on the night of the grounding, I've asked to go first."

This may have been the case, but his colleagues had not acquiesced through mere courtesy. If the jurors bought Chalos's main point, their client's omissions would be irrelevant. He got to this.

"I wanted the opportunity to address you on this issue and go through the evidence because, if he was not impaired on that night, it doesn't matter whether Captain Hazelwood may have had an occasional drink, social drink with his shipmates at the Yankee Whaler or whatever the place was called or at some other place at some other time. It doesn't matter whether Exxon should have returned Captain Hazelwood immediately to a ship or given him some shore leave and then returned him, and it doesn't matter whether Exxon's monitoring was good or bad, perfect or not perfect.

"I told you in my opening statement that there are two myths in this case. The first myth is that Captain Hazelwood was a recovering alcoholic. He was not. The second myth was that he was impaired on the night of the grounding. He was not."

Chalos then quoted Commander McCall, the highest-ranking Coast Guard official in Valdez at the time of the grounding, as saying that drink was not the cause of the accident. He quoted the attending physician at South Oaks as saying that Hazelwood suffered from a mild form of depression and secondarily from alcohol abuse episodic. "This is not a diagnosis of alcoholism. . . . He was not diagnosed an alcoholic and he's not an alcoholic. . . .

"He had thirteen to fifteen incidents in four years. Do you know how many days there are in four years? I figured this out. Fourteen hundred and sixty days. You know what this means? It means that he drank one time every one hundred days. That's three and a third months. One time every three and a third months. One beer, two glasses of wine.

"Ladies and gentlemen, if that isn't modest social drinking at its best, I got to tell you, we're all alcoholics.

"Folks, it's all nonsense. You've seen Captain Hazelwood. You've heard him testify on the stand. You've observed him. You've observed him here for a month. He's a good, decent, responsible man who's been unfairly trashed and unjustifiably deprived of his dignity by plaintiffs' counsel. For what? For what? So they can come in here and bolster their case, so they can give you a better argument. They should be ashamed of themselves and you shouldn't buy into it.

"I want to talk about impairment. I want to put up a chart. Ladies and gentlemen, these are twenty witnesses who saw Captain Hazelwood on the afternoon of March 23rd, the evening of March 23rd, the early morning hours of March 24th and the late morning hours of March 24th. Twenty witnesses—some Exxon employees, but a lot of people who are not Exxon employees. There isn't a single witness in these twenty who said Captain Hazelwood was impaired; not a single witness. Who said he was impaired? Nobody. Nobody came into this courtroom and said they saw Captain Hazelwood on the 23rd or 24th and found him to be impaired. The only one that says he's impaired is Mr. O'Neill, and he didn't see him."

But of course O'Neill was relying primarily on the blood test, and at this favorite red flag, Ferdinand gleefully charged. "I'm going to get to the blood test because Mr. O'Neill gave you the quick-over on that one."

Chalos preferred to take it more slowly. With the same sense of outrage that O'Neill reserved for empty bottles and meetings in bars, he retraced with relish the unique venues of the blood samples: windowsills, ensconced in an unlocked galley amidst tomatoes and lettuce, "some unattended remote warehouse here in Anchorage," an unrefrigerated Federal Express envelope, and then on to a California laboratory where the official log was later changed and no end of mischief suggested.

He had done this before, of course, but now he had something new to add: the Judge's instruction to the jury. A number of Judge Holland's instructions were helpful to the defense, and this one was treated as holy absolution. "Now, Judge Holland's going to give you this instruction and he's going to say to you, if you find that the chain of custody was breached in any way, you can disregard that test. That's what this instruction's about."

If the blood test was no good, then everyone had to go back to counting drinks on the afternoon of March 23. Chalos counted three. Three vodkas, with a fourth ordered but no clear memory by the captain or his comrades as to whether it was ever actually drunk. O'Neill's count was up to sixteen, the assumption being that each drink was a double and therefore countable as two drinks. This total relied heavily on the testimony of the two bartenders and that of Janice Delozier, the wife of the Coast Guard investigating officer, who claimed to have seen Hazelwood at the bar.

Chalos gave these accounts no credence whatsoever. "Ladies and gentlemen, what you have here is three ladies who are friends who hang around a bar together who got to talking. It's a small town and they all wanted to be part of the action. That's all there is to it. None of these ladies saw Captain Hazelwood that day." And the testimony of the proprietress of the flower shop supported the captain's story that he had spent almost an hour talking to her—not running across the street to the Pipeline Club.

There remained the violation of the four-hour rule. Once again, Judge Holland's instruction was invoked. "The Judge is going to instruct you that you can ignore that technical violation if you find that he was not impaired, and that if that violation was not a proximate cause or a legal cause of the grounding, you can ignore that violation."

Perhaps the tape recording of the captain's slurred speech might suggest to the jurors that he *was* impaired. Chalos had another interpretation. "This man just had a major calamity. He was in shock. He was under tremendous stress, he was on the verge of tears. That's what comes through, not that he was drunk. . . . I wonder how we would feel if we were on the bridge that night and that happened? I tell you what, I would be crying."

The whole point of Chalos's defense was that the captain had not been impaired. He knew full well that the greatest impediment to accepting this was the perfectly sensible view that *something* must have caused the spectacular grounding. If not a drunken captain, then what? He had an answer to this, too. He didn't blame third mate Cousins directly, but he got the point across.

"Captain Hazelwood brings the vessel and puts it right dead center in the fairway. If I could hit a golf shot like that, I'd be on the tour. Right in the middle of the fairway. And all he wants Cousins to do is a simple maneuver. Tells him, when you get abeam, and he's got it on a hundred eighty. All Cousins has to do is look out the window, look out the door. That's all he has to do when the light comes into view, start his turn. That's all he had to do. He had them lined up perfect to come down the middle of the fairway.

"Mr. O'Neill says, 'Well, he left two minutes before the turn. He should have stayed on the bridge.' Ladies and gentlemen, when Captain

Hazelwood left that bridge, in his mind his job was done. He had that ship lined up. All Cousins had to do was make a simple maneuver, well within his capabilities. Captain Hazelwood was on to the next task, which was figuring out the weather."

But if Chalos was willing to point at least a pinky at the culprit, his client was above even that.

"I want to say something about Captain Hazelwood. He didn't know why this accident happened. He doesn't know. He wasn't up on the bridge, that's true, and he doesn't know; but he has not, in five years . . . ever tried to assess blame on Mr. Cousins. As a matter of fact, the first call that he made, he got from his company, he says, 'I'm taking the responsibility; it was my fault.'

"Does that mean that he's saying, 'I was negligent'? It doesn't mean that. What it means is you've got a man of tremendous integrity and character and responsibility that's accepting it. . . .

"Now, we've spent five years in litigation trying to figure out what happened. And Mr. O'Neill suggests that the proof that we put on is a bunch of lies, everybody came in here is lying; the only people that weren't lying are the people that support his position. Everybody else is lying. Well, he hasn't suggested that the Coast Guard lied."

And with that he emphasized the fact that the Coast Guard had not found the captain to be drunk, and had, in fact, renewed his master's license after investigating the grounding.

He ended with that point. He obviously thought it should make an impact on the jury. This was a risky tactic, as he had succeeded so well in the very same speech at ridiculing the Coast Guard's handling of the blood samples, and its failure to watch and warn the tanker before the grounding. Were there two Coast Guards? One incompetent and the other sternly wise? For the purpose of Chalos's defense, yes there were, and he could only pray that the jury would accept this duality.

In the meantime, this shrewd and loyal friend had the satisfaction of having looked directly at the jurors throughout the major speech of his career and having seen in their eyes a tribute higher than mere approval: absolute, unqualified attention. He had held them; they were his. He returned to his counsel table a member of a different and much smaller club within the trial bar than he had belonged to before. Only O'Neill and Sanders were his peers.

In a sense, of course, his task was simpler than anyone else's. He was concerned with only one man. Every other lawyer in the case had to take on or defend Exxon as well.

The first closing argument for Exxon was made by Jim Sanders. He was following *two* riveting speakers, and did not retreat from the soaring standard of directness and clarity. He said that "we don't have to worry about anybody lying like Mr. O'Neill says everybody's doing." No, the real issue was beyond any testimony, truthful or not. It was the incontrovertible physical evidence of what had caused the grounding. It had nothing to do with Hazelwood. The accident had occurred simply because "in doing things that did not need to be done, Mr. Cousins simply gave the order too late for the turn of ten degrees right." Seven minutes too late. "Seven minutes past the time the captain instructed him to make the turn.

"This was an accident. Greg Cousins was trying too hard to do too many things that he did not need to do, and this is why the plaintiffs have not talked about the main event in this case. The evidence in this case shows you that the legal cause of this accident, this tragedy, was simple negligence, not reckless conduct."

The whole point of this phase of the trial was to determine whether reckless conduct had occurred. Sanders reminded the jury that O'Neill had "asked you to choose between safe or reckless. That's a lawyer's trick. He wants you to think that those are the only two choices, but you know better than that. Your common sense tells you that there's a long way between safe and reckless, and you don't have to defend on just that." He clutched the cherished straw of judicial instruction. "The Court's going to tell you, there's a long way between safe and reckless and in between there somewhere is accident, simple negligence, human error."

So why had the plaintiffs posited only two opposing poles? "They want you to concentrate on something else, ask you to go from millions, actual damages, to billions, punitive damages. Mr. O'Neill asked each and every one of you that question; can you go to a billion, can you go over a billion? That's the goal: money, money over and above actual damages."

He admitted that it was a mistake for Hazelwood to leave the bridge— and that's all it was, a mistake. His client had admitted negligence. The jury should find nothing more.

"Let me steal a page from Mr. O'Neill's book. Let me state a proposition for you. To connect alcohol to this grounding, which is the main effort that they've tried in this case, there must be proof that Captain Hazelwood went below because of alcohol. Doesn't that make sense? Of course it does." He then asserted that there was no real proof of this.

He admonished the jury not to believe that the crew had been fatigued. *They* hadn't said so; only an expert had. Sanders was hoping that the jury had had enough of experts.

His remarks took very little time. The remaining, and more extensive, portion of his client's closing argument would be made by his senior partner, Jim Neal.

All the defense lawyers had been angered by O'Neill's blunt and repeated claim that their clients had lied. Each had expressed his indignation to the jury, but none as forcefully as Neal.

"I've been in this trial lawyer business a long time, longer by far than Mr. O'Neill, and it pains me a little bit to have a lawyer stand up and say, Oh, all of these people on that side are lying. All of these people on that side are shaving the truth, except . . . except—and here's what he relies on—he relies on Dr. Montgomery, Dr. Nealy, Dr. Gould, Captain Duncan, Mr. Day, Captain Stalzer, Mr. Kunkel and a host of others who are also Exxon employees; now, those employees aren't lying. He *likes* what *they* have to say. The people at Exxon he accused of being liars are the people who say things he don't like. Well, truth of the matter is, in my business, very few people come in here and lie to you. They could be mistaken."

Mistake was the standard that he said he would apply to plaintiff witnesses whose accounts were not accurate. Take Shaw, for example, who had testified to a drinking incident that a number of eyewitnesses denied under oath had taken place. Would he call even Shaw a liar? "I don't believe he's lying; I believe he's mistaken. . . . I don't know why, but I don't think he's taking the oath in the Court of the United States and lying to you, just lying to you. People just don't do that. We don't do it and I wouldn't accuse his witnesses of doing it."

Having effectively staked out the moral high ground, he left the issue of opposing counsel and returned to his view of the case.

"Ladies and gentlemen, we didn't build a one-hundred-and-thirty-million-dollar state-of-the-art tanker, put sixteen million dollars worth of crude oil on it and recklessly and callously turn it over to a drunk. They've called us everything in the world in this case except stupid, and we ain't that stupid. We can make mistakes, but we ain't that stupid."

He defended Exxon's alcohol policy, and ridiculed the experts who had attacked it. "So apparently the only criticism Dr. Masters had of our alcohol policy is that he couldn't find the word 'monitoring'. . . . The plaintiffs bring on a Dr. O'Connor as their expert who says . . . I believe Captain Hazelwood was an alcoholic. Now, they asked him, how do you know? Well, I know because I was here a few days in court and I observed Captain Hazelwood in court.

"Well, ladies and gentlemen of the jury, you've been here thirty-some days. And *you've* observed him in court. You make *your* diagnosis!" A considerable portion of the closing defense argument seemed to be: What do experts know?

Neal defended the concept that one can monitor by looking at job performance. He said that the federal statute defining alcohol abuse as a handicap required this form of monitoring.

"So we had no motive to return Captain Hazelwood to duty except we thought it was right for Joe and we thought on balance after almost prayerful consideration, it would not increase a risk, it would *reduce* a risk because it wouldn't drive people, undeclared people with alcohol problems, into the closet."

He ended by ruefully acknowledging that under the rules, the plaintiff lawyer was about to get the last word. By this time the defendants would put nothing past O'Neill, and they knew with trepidation that if he now came up with something new and shocking, they would have no opportunity to rebut it. Neal agonized over this possibility, and did his best, which was limited by circumstance, to forewarn the jury.

"Boy, the last word is so great, but I want you to think about this: I want you to know that I don't get to talk to you again, but if he says something, I want you to know that I'll be over there fidgeting because, if I *had* another word, I could answer him."

For several hours three exceptionally resourceful lawyers with all their powers had made their case. With consummate skill they had sought to unravel the tapestry that O'Neill had labored so hard to weave. If theirs were the last words that the jury heard before retiring, surely the jurors would find in the tangled skein no pattern in which recklessness could be perceived.

But theirs were not the last words. O'Neill seemed as brash and unconcerned as ever. His first words were a rebuke to *their* rebuke of his charge that their side was lying.

"There is an old adage, and again, I don't mean to be ageist when I say this, but there is an old adage that's been around the courtroom since—as long as Mr. Neal has practiced law, which means a long, long time, which says: If you have the facts, argue the facts; if you have the law, argue the law; and if you don't have any law or any facts, argue the other lawyer."

One may be assured that over at his counsel table, Jim Neal was fidgeting to beat the band. Had he been spastic, the jurors' attention would still have remained on O'Neill, whose second riposte was to play for them one more time the audio tape of the captain's slurred speech.

Then, in grudging tribute to Chalos's efforts, he sought to rehabilitate the blood samples. He didn't try to argue that no flaws had occurred in their handling, but rather that no one had any motive to tamper with the samples. "Hey, I got a great idea; let's get Erma Lee, Janice Delozier, the Coast Guard, the Justice Department of the United States—let's all get together and let's see if we can make up a test tube that looks like that and then sneak it in. It is absolutely preposterous. It is a lawyer's argument." (It is interesting that when counsel on either side of the case wanted to really disparage something, they would call it a lawyer's argument.)

O'Neill knew that Sanders had made considerable headway with his argument—and the graphic display board accompanying it—that the grounding had been caused by Cousins's delay in following the captain's clear order. One of the jurors had seemed to be nodding! This had to be corrected. But he did not attack what Sanders had said; indeed, he embraced it.

"I totally agree with Mr. Sanders's board." He gestured toward the large chart that chronicled every moment of the dilatory seven minutes. "I think this is a very good exhibit. I think this is a *wonderful* exhibit. This is what happened, no doubt about it." He paused. "And what I find *most* interesting is the top entry: 'Hazelwood Leaves the Bridge.' And *then* this confusion or chaos reigns."

He was telling the jurors that if the grounding was Cousins's fault, well then, that only meant that it was really Hazelwood's fault. If the captain had remained on the bridge, Cousins's fatigue or indecision or whatever would not have mattered.

"And as to whether his leaving the bridge was a cause or not . . . you know, give me a break. He's supposed to be on the bridge, four eyes instead of two; remember that? And these kinds of waters, the reason we have two people on the bridge is to make sure one catches the error of the other. That's the only reason."

The job of the final speaker is in part to nullify the most damaging arguments that preceded him. He had done his best with Chalos's best, and Sanders's, too, and now it was Neal's turn. The defense lawyer's strongest line had been "we ain't that stupid," his point being that Exxon could have had no rational motive for returning a drinking captain to sea duty. O'Neill hit this one hardest of all.

"And you want a motive for all of this? You want a motive? This company doesn't give a damn.

"It isn't that they're trying to be mean. It isn't that they're trying to run a vessel on a rock. It's that they are indifferent to the rights and safety of others. That from 1985, or before, until 1989, they didn't care whether they had alcoholic captains, drinking captains, drinking on board vessels, so long as they could cover their tails with policies.

"And we see that. They don't do anything to Hazelwood, they never talk to Hazelwood. It was all in the argument and the evidence of over a hundred witnesses. Did we have somebody come in and say, 'I called Joe in, I sat down and I asked Joe, "How is your drinking, how is your recovery, how is your AA, how is your family, how is any of that?"'

"Did one person do that? Where is it?

"I mean, is that how we treat each other? They didn't do the man any favor. He is in the history books now. They didn't do him any favor. He is now in the history books as the captain who left the bridge prior to one of the great maritime accidents in the history of the world. They did this man a favor by not being decent to him? They did this man a favor by not treating him the same way that we expect to be treated? They didn't do him any favors."

He took a deep breath and waited longer than others would have dared. His tone changed. It was quieter, but portentous.

"I want to mention one more thing." He called for a visual display.

The defense counsel leaned forward. Was this the dreaded last-minute attack? It was. On all the video screens that dominated the courtroom, one single document was shown.

"This is the agreement between Exxon and Captain Hazelwood: 'The parties agree that neither shall use in any manner deposition or trial testimony or any evidence derived therefrom given by either party in the *Valdez* litigation in connection with the mediation or arbitration provided for herein.'

"That's what it says. That means that each one of them can come in here and say what they want to say and they can't use it in the fight between them.

"Now, why would anybody agree to that? So that they can come in here and tell whatever story they want to tell.

"Exxon Corporation is so big, so powerful, has had its way for over a hundred years, that it thinks it can do whatever it wants to do in and out of the courtroom, today, 1985, 1989, and ladies and gentlemen of the jury, you are the only people that can stop that. Thank you."

With that he returned to his seat. Phase One had now been fully argued. The agreement that, though he had mentioned it before, he had saved until the very final moment and then displayed again as damning proof of defense mendacity was in fact scarcely shocking to many attorneys. The captain and his former employer did indeed have ongoing disputes relating to his severance. It is not all that unusual in such situations, where a major trial precedes private negotiations, for both sides to agree that the court record is inadmissible.

There was no opportunity for rebuttal. The lawyers' role was over. Jim Neal's response to O'Neill's use of his client's document was well beyond mere fidgeting. No body language was adequate to his indignation. Marcel Marceau would have given up and shrugged. If Neal *had* been permitted to speak, it is likely that he would have pointed out to the jurors that the agreement was necessary because in the trial its signatories were under oath, and in their upcoming arbitration they were not. If the agreement was a license to lie, then the shadings of truth would take place in their private dispute, not in the courtroom. The document was necessary because they *had* to answer honestly before the jurors.

But he did not get to say this. The time for response was past. The trial, this most critical phase, anyway, was over.

It was time for the judge to instruct the jury. The lawyers had received advance copies of his instructions and had inserted into the closing arguments those most helpful to their side. They had paraphrased these instructions with considerable élan. But now Judge Holland was reading his words aloud, exactly as he had written them. There would be printed copies in the jury room.

The lawyers in the room knew from hazardous experience that those printed sheets of paper could well decide their fate. Juries take the judge's instructions very seriously. Can we consider this? Let's see what the instructions say. What does "reckless" mean? It means what the judge says it means. When the jurors would disagree on some point, or regard it with unanimous confusion, their disagreement and despair could be transcended by getting out the holy writ. The instructions were their dictionary, roadmap, and rule book—rules for what they could or could not do, regardless of how much they yearned to.

Judges have considerable leeway in the instructions they can give. If they go too far in favoring one side, of course, that gives the loser grounds for appeal. But federal trial judges, whose lifetime tenure insulates them from most rebuke save reversal, can be amazingly astute in gauging just how far the envelope of instruction may be pushed.

Many of the plaintiff lawyers suspected that Judge Holland privately favored the defendants. There were those who could never forget that once *he* had defended oil companies. There were those who remembered that in an earlier proceeding he had referred to Exxon as a "good corporate citizen . . . sensitive to its environmental obligations."

Some of these plaintiff lawyers would have been surprised to learn that the defense bar had its dark suspicions, too. There were those who still rankled at his rulings during the *voir dire*. He had overruled a number of their strongest objections to jurors suspected of bias.

When both sides doubt the Court's allegiance, they are probably blessed with a fair-minded judge. Judge Holland had recognized from the outset that this was the case of a lifetime—his or anyone else's. No matter what else he had done or would do, he was going to be remembered for presiding over *In re: The Exxon Valdez*. He did not squint at this spotlight. Let it shine. He would do his job despite the glare. He had, no doubt, a good many personal feelings about the personnel and issues of the case, but he had inwardly ruled these inadmissible. The only preconception that he brought to the bench was an abiding faith in the wisdom of the jury. That consistent faith helped explain his seeming inconsistency toward one party or another. If he was willing to let a juror serve despite the defendants' objections, perhaps he believed that that juror could excise past experience as thoroughly as he was trying to do himself. If he kept some evidence out of the trial, it was because he was in part a traffic cop who was trying to avoid gridlock. He wanted an open road to the jurors' minds. He knew that the lawyers were by this time convinced of the absolute righteousness of their cause. That always happened. Now, all the lawyers wanted was to win. What the judge wanted was to let the jurors decide.

But in devising instructions to the jury, the judge is interpreting law, not facts. No matter how dispassionately intended, it is not humanly possible to avoid entirely the residue of a lifetime's experience and philosophy. As Judge Holland calmly read his instructions, the grimmer faces in the courtroom belonged to the plaintiff team.

It was not so much that the judge was instructing the jurors, "In your decisions on the issues of fact, a corporation is entitled to the same fair trial at your hands as a private individual." That is a standard instruction, however painful to some lawyers to hear. What was more distressing to the plaintiffs was the judge's discussion of the six-hour rule and the four-hour rule, the legal requirements for rest and abstinence that they felt they had proved to have been violated. Did the judge *have* to say that "the presumption of negligence arising from violation of law is not conclusive but may be overcome or outweighed by evidence in the case which satisfies your minds that, notwithstanding any failure to comply with the provisions of the statute or regulation in question, Captain Hazelwood acted as a reasonably prudent person would have acted under all the surrounding circumstances shown by the evidence in the case"?

And even worse: "Punitive damages are not favored in the law, and are never awarded as a right, no matter how egregious a defendant's conduct, but may be imposed for conduct that manifests reckless or callous disregard for the rights of others. . . . The burden is on the plaintiffs to establish by a preponderance of the evidence in the case the essential elements of their claims for punitive damages. In this case, the essential elements are, first, that a defendant's conduct before the grounding of the *Exxon Valdez* manifested reckless or callous disregard for the rights of others; and, second, that such conduct by a defendant was a legal cause of the grounding of the *Exxon Valdez*."

And just what was "reckless or callous disregard for others"? The judge defined it.

"Four factors must be present:

"First, a defendant must be subjectively conscious of a particular grave danger or risk of harm, and the danger or risk must be a foreseeable and probable effect of the conduct;

"Second, the particular danger of risk of which the defendant was subjectively conscious must in fact have eventuated;

"Third, a defendant must have disregarded the risk in determining how to act;

"Fourth, a defendant's conduct in ignoring the danger or risk must have involved a gross deviation from the level of care which an ordinary person would use having due regard to all the circumstances.

"Reckless conduct is not the same as negligence. Negligence is the failure to use such care as a reasonable, prudent and careful person would use under similar circumstances. Reckless conduct differs from negligence in that it requires a conscious choice of action, either with knowledge of serious danger to others or with knowledge of facts which would disclose the danger to any reasonable person."

The plaintiffs by this time were parched for succor, and the judge, as if from compassion, did supply a few drops. They must have been greatly relieved to hear that "whether the United States Coast Guard does or does not have any responsibility in this matter is not an issue in this case." So much for all the time the defendants had spent on the Coast Guard failure to warn of the impending grounding.

And there was also this: "A corporation is responsible for the reckless act of those employees who are employed in a managerial capacity while acting in the scope of their employment. The reckless act or omission of a managerial officer or employee of a corporation in the course and scope of the performance of his duties is held in law to be the reckless act or omission of a corporation."

As for the defense claim that much that had occurred was in direct violation of Exxon's clearly stated rules, the judge instructed: "Merely stating or publishing instructions or policies without taking diligent measures to enforce them is not enough to excuse the employer for reckless actions of the employee that are contrary to the employer's policy or instructions."

Things were looking up for the plaintiffs. Or so it may have seemed. Toward the end of his instructions Judge Holland delivered two crushing blows to their cause.

The first had to do with the absence of monitoring by specific questions about the captain's drinking. This was a cornerstone of O'Neill's case, the fuel for repeated flights of soaring rhetorical scorn.

What the judge had to say was this: "An employee, like all citizens, has a legally and constitutionally protected right of privacy. In formulating policies for the management of its business, an employer should balance the employee's right of privacy against other equally important concerns, such as safety."

What must have gone through O'Neill's mind? *Equally* important concerns? He had argued throughout that safety was vastly *more* important than one person's right to privacy. He had argued that the captain didn't even *have* a right to privacy, since he hadn't really self-identified. Now all this seemed dismissed by one instruction.

The next instruction was even more alarming. It dealt with the blood samples. These were critical to a finding of drunkenness at the time of the grounding. The blood samples *proved* that the captain had been drunk, O'Neill fervently believed.

But the judge's instruction cast grave doubt as to whether the blood samples could even be considered.

"Plaintiffs must prove by a preponderance of the evidence that the test is reliable and that the samples remain in an unchanged condition from the time of collection until the time the samples were tested."

It got worse. "In considering whether the blood test is reliable, moreover, you may consider all the other evidence introduced, including evidence with respect to the presence or absence of observable symptoms of intoxication."

And worse still. "In order to ensure the integrity and identity of blood samples, federal regulations governing the procedures for the administering of blood tests following a marine accident require the following:

"One, a proper chain of custody must be maintained for each specimen from the time of collection through the time of testing and through the authorized disposition of the specimen;

"Two, blood specimens must be shipped to the laboratory in a cooled condition by any means adequate to ensure delivery within twenty-four hours of the receipt by the carrier";

The look on Chalos's face was beatific.

"Three, no unauthorized personnel shall be permitted in any part of a collection site when specimens are collected, nor shall unauthorized personnel be allowed access to stored specimens;

"Four, if a specimen is not immediately prepared for shipment, it shall be safeguarded during temporary storage."

That Chalos should be on the stage! He looks like he's being knighted!

"Five, every effort shall be made to minimize the number of persons handling the specimen;

"Six, chain-of-custody forms shall, at a minimum, include an entry documenting the date and the purpose each time a specimen is handled and identify each person in the chain of custody;

"Seven, . . ."

Seven! When would this torture end?

"Seven, the specimens shall be placed in containers designed to mini-mize the possibility of damage during shipment, and those containers shall be securely sealed to eliminate the possibility of undetected tampering."

That was the end of the devastating list, but the judge was not yet through with the instruction.

"If you find that these federal regulations were not complied with, you may completely disregard the blood test or you may give it such weight as you may think it deserves."

Chalos looked as if he had simultaneously won the lottery and found God.

The instructions were over. It was shortly before two in the afternoon of Monday, June 6, 1994. The judge told the jurors that if they had not agreed on a verdict by five o'clock they were to return to their homes, talk to no one about the case, and return to the jury room at nine the next morning. They could communicate with the Court only by signed note. There was already one question that the judge had to answer. A juror had complained about the temperature in the jury room. The judge smiled.

"I'll be very frank with you. I've purposefully had people keep the tem-perature down in here for two reasons. This machinery develops an awful lot of heat, and people stay awake better when it's cool. I take it from what has been said that it may be a little bit cool in the jury room. We'll try and work on that and let us know how we're doing. If you're uncomfortable in there, let us know and we'll see what we can do to accommodate you.

"Anything else before I send the jury off?"

O'Neill stood up. "No, sir, there isn't."

Neal then rose. "Not from us, Your Honor."

That left Chalos. "Nothing from us, Your Honor, except our thanks." The plaintiffs were thinking that gratitude for that last instruction was an inadequate sentiment.

The jury filed out at one fifty-five. The lawyers remained to work out

some details with the judge. One of these was how they could be contacted when the verdict came in. Phone and fax numbers were handed to
the Court. There was one designated contact party for each side.

Jim Neal suggested that O'Neill's usual location would likely be the
Alaska Bush Company, a raunchy bar of local repute. "We wouldn't want
to embarrass him by having him give you that number."

"And where does he find *you,* if he needs to?" asked the evenhanded
judge.

"At the next table," said O'Neill. His grin was back.

"I wouldn't want to say *that,*" said Neal.

"At the next table, I think," O'Neill repeated. He was still trying to return every shot.

Chalos weighed in. "I don't endorse the Alaska Bush Company, by the
way." He looked sympathetically at O'Neill. "I know your wife's in the
audience."

"Thanks, Mike," said O'Neill.

"I didn't know that," said Neal. "I take that back. I'm sorry I let you
down."

If the jurors had heard this exchange they would have been startled.
These men had been at each other's throats. Now they were joking and
friendly, like buddies.

They were not buddies. They were professionals. The ire they had
shown one another during the trial had been genuine, if exaggerated on
occasion to advance their clients' interests. They were professionals. They
had fought one another for years; hand-to-hand for the last month. But
now there was at least a temporary truce, and acknowledgment through
banter of the adversary's valor.

It was two o'clock. Only five minutes had passed. The judge was
handed a note. The lawyers were very still. A swift verdict was possible,
but not *this* swift.

The judge spoke.

"They've picked a foreman already. It's Mr. Murray. And they're going
to work from eight a.m. to two p.m." The hours they had become used to.
"Why am I not surprised?"

This minor adjustment of the work schedule was a reminder of what
every lawyer knew so well: the jury was now in charge. Completely in

charge. The world, the universe, consisted now of twelve souls, locked away in their frigid jury room.

And apparently hard at it. If they could elect a foreman in five minutes, they must mean business. They undoubtedly were anxious to return to their own lives.

They had reset their schedule to eight the next morning. They would then have six uninterrupted hours. The verdict might be right at hand.

13

The Jury

T here is no way to slow the clock like waiting for a jury to come in. The lawyers are charged with adrenalin, they can feel their hearts thumping, it takes an effort to breathe—and at this maddening peak of impatience time perversely seems to stand still.

O'Neill and his team trudged like zombies back to their trial office. The huge space was littered with exhibits and briefing books and memos and charts and displays. There were piles of discarded videos. Most of this was useless now. All the ammunition had been fired. They sat or paced amidst the casings, waiting for the smoke to clear and the result of the battle to be known.

There remained much work to do. Come what may, there would still be Phase Two, the trial over compensatory damages. And after that— well, that was why time was standing still. If the jury found in Phase One that there had been merely negligence, not recklessness, there would be no Phase Three, no trial to award punitive damages. No punitive damages. No pot of gold at the end of the rainbow. As a matter of fact, no rainbow. Instead, dark eternal night. Disaster. The quest of a lifetime unfulfilled. Failure. Shame. Recrimination.

It was best not to think about it. That not being possible, it was important to keep busy to be ready for Phase Two. They set themselves to their tasks.

That first night, Monday, with the jury just out, was all right. They could rest for once from the insane schedule of the trial. The last-minute Phase Two assignments were diligently pursued. Being busy *did* help a bit. They could joke a little about the trial, argue over which was the most harmful instruction, commiserate and pray.

Then Tuesday morning came. The hotline was monitored incessantly. The call from the Court did not come. A time warp seemed to envelop them from eight until two. The goddamn second hand never seemed to move.

The last hour was the hardest. From one o'clock on it took an agonizing effort of will not to just sit and stare at the phone.

Some thought that the verdict would come that first day. These were the optimists, who were certain they would win. The case had been powerfully made. It was so *clear.* Forget the instructions! Look at the *evidence!* There was no way to avoid finding recklessness. Come on, phone: *ring.*

Two o'clock came. Maybe the jury was just coming in. By two-fifteen that possibility was gone.

Another *day.* They were going to have to wait another *day!* It didn't seem possible that they could make it.

Dinner at the Girls' Dorm was no longer very much fun. Those who tried to be jovial were glared at. Most were far from even making the effort. There were episodes of silence, the scrape of cutlery providing the only, somehow irritating, sound.

Well before eight on Wednesday morning they started hovering around the phone once again. They came to hate that phone. It was not that it did not ring. It rang all the time. There were a number of lines, one always kept free, but all connected to the same instrument. Calls came in throughout the days—dozens of them. And at each ring everyone stopped what they were doing and looked up and listened. It was never the one call that they all lived for. Everyone else called: the other plaintiff lawyers, fishermen, journalists, Faegre & Benson partners, friends from all over. But not the Court. Another two o'clock arrived, another curtain descended on hope.

There was open testiness now at the evening meal. The optimists were less outspoken. The best they could come up with was that this *was* a big case and it took a long time to go through all the evidence.

Thursday was almost more than flesh could bear. Each ring of the phone was like a slap across the face. There were a lot of slaps. There was no call from the Court.

Phase Two was getting short shrift. It was impossible to focus one's attention on anything but the phone.

Tempers flared. Unfortunate words were spoken. Wherever they gathered together there was only a single topic: What did this all mean?

The pessimists began to be heard from. The two most horrible words in the plaintiff lexicon were actually uttered: hung jury. This did not mean that the jurors had been executed. It refers to a final lack of unanimity. To reach any verdict, the jury had to be unanimous. That was the rule. One dissenter could spell trouble. One dissenter, if unconverted, could bring down the curtain for good. If it became clear that no unanimous verdict was possible, the judge would have to declare a mistrial.

Mistrial! They would have to begin a whole new trial. There were those who honestly didn't think they had it in them. To have a new *voir dire,* to impanel a whole new jury, to get all those witnesses back on the stand— dear God! The most worldly agnostics were returning to simple piety.

There are pessimists and pessimists. Those with the darkest vision of all saw something even worse than starting over. They saw defeat. The theory was that you either thought that the captain and Exxon had been reckless, or you did not. If you did, you knew it right away. If you thought that Hazelwood had been drunk, for example, what else was there to talk about? If you didn't—well, there were a lot of things to go over, but it didn't look good.

The captain of this increasingly unruly band was not immune from the anxiety of his troops. He had endured the most for the longest, had argued single-handedly a case that would have killed or crippled many others, and knew with sharp clarity just who would be blamed if the battle were lost. Vesuvian eruptions marked his encounters with once-loyal soldiers now panicked enough to shout back. The dinners by this time were perhaps best avoided.

Friday was the last day of the week and of their hopes. The jurors would not want to go back to a deadlock after the weekend. It was surely now or never. Apparently it was never. The call from the Court did not come. Everyone *else* on earth seemed to be calling, of course, anxious to learn what could possibly be going on. The partners from the Faegre of-

fice in Minneapolis were shocked by junior colleagues telling them fero-
ciously to get off the phone. Two o'clock on Friday arrived like a ticket
to hell.

Which was just what the weekend was like. The trial itself had not been
nearly so exhausting. Everyone was either yelling or comatose.

Monday meant that the jury had been at this thing for a week. Even
some of the optimists were now praying for mistrial. Like druids wor-
shiping their oak, the shuffling band of litigants, made primitive through
dread, gathered at dawn around their only talisman, the one fading link to
their salvation.

At just after eight on Monday morning, June 13, the phone rang. It
was the Court. The jury was in. It had a verdict.

What must the Anchorage commuters have thought of that ragged
pack scurrying to the courthouse? They got there just in time. It was
slightly comforting to see the defense lawyers looking fully as haggard as
themselves. They all took their accustomed places. The word had traveled
quickly and the courtroom was hopelessly jammed. But now, with the arrival of the jury, completely silent.

The judge was looking at one of the jurors, the foreman.

"Mr. Murray, I understand you have a verdict."

Ken Murray stood. "We have a verdict, Your Honor."

"Would you pass it to the bailiff, please?"

The foreman did so, and the bailiff walked over to the bench and
handed the sheet of paper up to the judge. Judge Holland unfolded the
paper and read it carefully.

"I'm going to read the verdict," he said.

There is nothing in the theater to match this moment, no drama so arresting, no actors who decide the fate of the audience.

The judge read in a clear and even voice.

"Special verdict for Phase One of the trial, Interrogatory Number
One: Do you unanimously find on a preponderance of the evidence the
defendant Hazelwood was negligent as that term has been defined in the
instructions and that his negligence was a legal cause of the grounding of
the *Exxon Valdez* on March 24, 1989?

"Answer: Yes.

"Interrogatory Number Two: Do you unanimously find from a preponderance of the evidence that defendant Hazelwood was reckless as

that term has been defined in the instruction; that is, his recklessness was a legal cause of the grounding of the *Exxon Valdez?*

"Answer: Yes.

"Interrogatory Number Three: Do you unanimously find from a preponderance of the evidence that the Exxon defendants were reckless as that term has been defined in the instructions and that their recklessness was a legal cause of the grounding of the *Exxon Valdez?*

"Answer: Yes."

The courtroom exploded with shouts of joy of the victors. Some of the spectators cheered and whooped and hugged one another.

"Knock it off," snapped the Judge, and total silence was restored.

O'Neill had not been cheering. For once, he was not even grinning. He was wiping tears from his eyes.

Three times the judge polled the jury, for each of the Interrogatories. There must be no doubt that the verdict was unanimous, a requirement to which the parties had agreed.

"If you concur in each of the interrogatories, you should answer yes; if not, you should answer no."

He began with Ms. Smith. Was this her verdict?

"Yes."

"Ms. Hood?"

"Yes."

"Ms. Martin?"

"Yes."

"Mr. Dean, is this your verdict?"

"Yes."

"Ms. Provost?"

"Yes."

"Mr. Graham?"

"Yes."

"Ms. Moor?"

"Yes."

"Ms. Spann, is this your verdict?"

"Yes."

"Ms. Wilson?"

"Yes."

"Ms. Garrison?"

"Yes. Yes."

"Ms. Johnson?"

"Yes."

"Mr. Murray?"

"Yes."

The judge then looked at the lawyers.

"Counsel, the jury has been polled; they have all answered in the affirmative. You have a verdict. The clerk will not enter judgment at this time because of the nature of the verdict that has been returned, but the verdict will be filed at this time." There were still two more phases, but this one was over.

Judge Holland had two things to say to the jury. First, Phase Two would not begin right away, as some had expected. They would start up again the following Monday, one week from this day.

And second, "You understand, I'm sure—and I know counsel and the press understand—that it is inappropriate for any of them to contact you about this case now because you're not through.

"The general public, though, may not understand that. You may have friends, relatives, whatever, who will try and contact you to —wanting to discuss what's going on, and you just can't do that at this point. Probably for the next few days it would be a real good idea to have somebody screen your phone calls. Be especially careful for the next few days so that you don't wind up in any kind of conversations, in person or on the phone, with anybody about your deliberations, because it all has to remain confidential at this point, because you're not through. Please remember my instructions that you not read or listen to any media reports about the case because there may very well be speculation about what went on and what is to come. And you need to insulate yourself from all discussion of the case of any form until the case is finished."

With that the court was recessed. After courteous handshakes between opposing counsel, all the occupants of the courtroom swiftly left and reassembled on the plaza in front of the Federal Courthouse. Here there was no sanction against the uninhibited expression of impossible joy. There was hugging and kissing and tears and laughter. The crowd was large and grew larger still as news of the decision was broadcast throughout the city.

At the edge of the throng a tall, bearded man walked resolutely away from the building, not hurrying despite the reporters tugging at his sleeve, speaking to no one, eyes straight ahead. Captain Hazelwood betrayed no emotion as he made his departure from this place.

The plaza had become like a carnival, noisy and exuberant. In the midst of the maelstrom was Brian O'Neill, smiling now, a magnet for the well-wishers and fishermen and colleagues who pressed in from every side.

Leading the charge was the press. Microphones and cameras were thrust toward his face.

He was not unwilling to make a statement. With his one-year-old son in his arms, and squinting in the bright summer sun, he proved unmellowed by victory, announcing to the wall of scribblers and the cheering admirers behind it that "with a company as large as Exxon Corporation—that thinks it is above the law—you need to take a substantial bite out of their butt before they will change their behavior." There were still damages to be awarded.

"We want to change Exxon. We want to make the Exxons of the world aware that they are responsible the same way that you and I are responsible.

"It is really a great day. It took five years to bring it about, but we got there."

Off to one side, away from the celebrants, the defendants were giving their side of the story. Not being certain that the decision would go their way, the Exxon Public Relations Department had written several versions of the press release to be handed out after the jury came in. It was reminiscent of the scene in the great film *Citizen Kane* where the publisher's staff is watching the election returns of his gubernatorial race. When the opponent's lead becomes insurmountable, the headline proclaiming KANE ELECTED is displaced by its alternative: FRAUD AT POLLS! The press release that similarly Exxon was forced to go with quoted Exxon chairman Lee Raymond as saying, "We are disappointed with the jury's finding that Exxon's conduct was reckless and that this recklessness was a legal cause of the accidental grounding of the *Exxon Valdez*. The resulting oil spill was a tragic accident which impacted the lives of many Alaskans. For that we are truly sorry."

The defense attorneys who were present were doing their best as well. Pat Lynch told reporters that the decision had not been surprising. "I always think of Mrs. O'Leary's cow," he said. "She didn't go out to burn down the city of Chicago. But once you have something this serious happen, the emotional connection between the consequences and the conduct tends to get blurred.

"I feel that was a problem we were struggling with, particularly struggling with here in Alaska."

In a separate interview with the *New York Times,* he said, "People have an understandable tendency to equate the seriousness of the consequences with the conduct that led up to it. If a minor mistake has very serious consequences, people will see the mistake as being greater than it was."

As Mike Chalos had left the state, his colleague Tom Russo was there to tell the press, "We still believe Captain Hazelwood was not reckless in the grounding of the *Exxon Valdez.* We are hoping when all is said and done, when people look back over time and look at this objectively, Captain Hazelwood will be vindicated."

The world now knew what the jury had decided. Or did it? People knew that the verdict was that recklessness had occurred. They did not know how that verdict had been reached. Only the jurors knew that, and they were talking, for the moment, to no one. So one had to guess. It was the major topic that evening at the plaintiffs' celebration, amidst champagne toasts and camaraderie more than restored. Everyone talked about which argument had been the one to do the trick.

The press, too, speculated, though more cautiously. The following morning's *Anchorage Daily News* filled the front page with its account of the verdict, under an imposing headline whose thick type must have lain dormant since the earthquake. "The decision," the accompanying story said, "centered on Hazelwood's drinking problem and what Exxon knew about it." This was an accurate summary of the plaintiffs' *argument,* but was it the basis of the decision?

The *New York Times,* in *its* front-page account the same morning, after noting that Exxon's stock had already fallen $2.625 down to $59.50, quoted unnamed plaintiff lawyers as saying that the turning point in the trial may have been the inconsistent statements of former Exxon CEO Lawrence Rawl, concluding just after the spill that it had been a mistake for the company to send Hazelwood back to sea because of his drinking problems and then at the trial saying he had been mistaken then and now believed that Hazelwood had not been impaired by alcohol. This inconsistency had been a major plaintiff thrust, the source of repeated embarrassing video displays. For its own part, the *Times* commented that

"Mr. O'Neill's strategy was to establish a morality play pitting thousands of ordinary Alaskans whose lives and livelihoods depended on Prince William Sound's vast natural resources against a company he portrayed as an uncaring oil giant careless enough to leave its most modern super-tanker in the hands of an alcoholic." This is an excellent, indeed a perfect, summary of exactly what O'Neill was trying to do. But is it what caused the jurors to reach their particular verdict?

We now know the answer to that question, at least as much as we ever will. In a manner that will be revealed, it is known to a considerable extent what the jury did behind its impregnable doors. Among other things, it did not find that the captain had been drunk. The world's largest drunk-driving case was decided on other grounds.

The jury room was known around the courthouse as the Red Room. No other name seems possible, though the walls were painted cream. The room was dominated by a long oak conference table surrounded by twelve chairs, which were upholstered in fire-engine red. A table for cof-fee and snacks was in an alcove. Charts and exhibits littered the floor. The door to the room was kept locked at all times. The sense of isolation, if not imprisonment, was lessened very slightly for the jurors by a window from which could be sighted the smallest sliver of the world from which they had been isolated. They could see only a parking lot, the back of the nearby Nordstrom's, and the brief, glorious Alaska summer for which they all had longed throughout many dark and frozen months.

None of the women jurors had wanted to be elected foreman. That left three men. It was felt that Doug Graham, the thirty-four-year-old who cared for his mother, was too quiet. As for Bruce Dean, the fiercely moustached miner who liked to blow things up, well, he seemed a bit too radical, almost frightening. He is outspoken against such targets as Christian hypocrites, gun control, and Attorney General Janet Reno.

"I am about half scary," he has admitted. "Give me five minutes and I'll tell you everything I know. I've never been around nine women, much less locked in a room. I've never had to watch my mouth."

That left Ken Murray, the unemployed college counselor and one of the two African-Americans on the jury. He was a logical choice: the only college graduate on the jury, possessed of some business experience, ac-tive in the community.

The first day (while the lawyers were hovering around their phone) was devoted to translating the judge's instructions into simpler English. The judge had been as explicit as he could under the circumstances. He is a plain-spoken man, but questions of law must be very carefully stated, and not merely with an eye to appeal. Sophisticated issues were involved, and no jurist could fairly condense them without some nuance and a great many commas. But the jurors felt they had been assigned a law school textbook and set about rewriting it more comprehensibly for their needs.

They spent another two days trying to organize all the boxes of evidence that stood between them and freedom. This was a task that had daunted teams of the most brilliant law school graduates—lawyers who had the help of state-of-the-art computers. After a while the jurors requested a computer, too, but the judge denied their request. Hence two days of burrowing through boxes and the use of thumbs to keep one's place in a dog-eared stack of documents.

When it was finally possible to actually discuss the case, they had to deal at the outset with the subject of drink. Specifically, how much alcohol had Captain Hazelwood consumed on the afternoon before the grounding? They had endured a month of testimony directed to this query. Collectively, they remembered a great deal of what they had heard. They talked among themselves, as O'Neill had hoped they would, about the size of each drink that the captain had admitted consuming. Were those vodkas doubles or singles?

They also knew that the size of the drinks didn't matter if the blood test was valid, and if it indicated what O'Neill said it did. The key thing was whether they could rely on it. Here Michael Chalos had accomplished his persistent task. They remembered, and talked about, the window ledge and storage in a Coast Guard refrigerator, stuck among the carrots and lettuce.

There had been so *much* testimony about the amount that the captain had drunk. There was the captain's own account under oath, and that of his crewmates. There were the two bartenders. There was Janice Delozier.

These recitals had been contradictory. If someone was giving a perfectly accurate account, then someone else was not. Did anyone have it right? They went over and over the testimony, and then over it again. And they did what jurors are supposed to do when the evidence is imprecise and contradictory: they relied on their own common sense. They had to make judgments about which witnesses were most reliable and what facts they could depend on. They had to search for the needle of truth in a very

large and messy haystack, with nothing to assist their gropings but instincts honed by their own disparate lives.

They went at this for quite some time. They talked and exchanged recollections and argued and puzzled and sometimes disagreed.

And then they reached a conclusion: they were going to have to ignore
the testimony and the evidence about whether the captain had been
drunk. It wasn't possible—it wasn't fair—for them to say for sure.

Later, one of the jurors, Janette Garrison, had this to say:

"They wasted so much time with trying to prove that he was drunk,
and that he was in the bar at this time or that time. I saw that as a big mistake. They were on a different track than we were." This was said much
later, after she was permitted to read what others thought the Phase One
verdict had meant. She did not agree with most accounts.

"They were assuming that we found him drunk. I would like to tell
somebody we didn't."

"Alcohol really had no bearing," says Dean.

If they did not find him drunk, then how did they find him reckless?
With careful deliberation, apparently. They concluded that one need not
have been drunk to have been reckless. With drink, so to speak, off the
table, recklessness became for the jury a question of mistakes. Everyone
makes mistakes, they knew, but they saw it as a matter of degree. If the
captain had made enough mistakes, and they were big enough, they
would have to find him reckless.

So they started counting his mistakes. It wasn't easy. They had to re-
sort to an easel—to two easels. One listed the evidence that attested to
his alleged mistakes; the other to the rebuttals of that evidence. It was
hard to know which side was right. So they staged another trial, just for
themselves, in the jury room, with two of their number playing the
lawyers. The roles were surely cast against type. Doug Graham, whom
they had found too quiet for leadership, took the place of Brian O'Neill
and argued the plaintiff side. Opposing him was Bruce Dean, surely the
most unlikely advocate in Exxon's history.

When the two had finished going at it, each charge answered, and the
response carefully weighed, the easel on the left still proclaimed four mistakes. The jurors found these serious and numerous enough to come to a
conclusion of recklessness.

The first mistake Hazelwood made, they found, was sailing only three
hours after his last drink. The Coast Guard rules said he couldn't drink

within four hours of going on duty. This does not mean that the jurors thought he had been drunk; it means that he broke a rule and that was a mistake.

The second mistake was leaving the bridge. The captain and his attorneys had argued that this was all right under the circumstances, but the jurors didn't think so. They dismissed the excuse that he had work to do below. "He had the whole trip to do his paperwork," says Nancy Provost, the retired factory worker. "It wasn't like he had two hours to turn it in."

The third mistake, they found, was leaving the controls in the hands of an unqualified seaman.

The jurors believed that the fourth mistake was something they had found on their own. In one of the boxes of evidence they had unearthed the tanker's computerized logs. This record showed that the captain had pushed the ship's load-program-up button before leaving the bridge. The jurors believed that he did not tell the crew he had done so. The LPU button gradually increases the vessel's speed until it reaches an oceangoing rate. So the vessel was actually accelerating as it approached Bligh Reef.

Whether or not pushing the button was as serious as the jurors believed, they were not the first to discover it. The trial transcript contains a number of references to "load program up," and O'Neill in his opening statement had referred to the captain's having "pushed the pedal to the floor." It had not been a major plaintiff argument, and apparently the jurors had missed it, but it was one with which they agreed.

For a while, two of the jurors were not sure that even these four mistakes added up to recklessness. One of these was Jennifer Smith, who worked as a personnel clerk for the state court, and the other was Rita Wilson, the school secretary whose insecurities had been suggested by her answers during the *voir dire*. The captain had made a favorable impression on these jurors, as he had, indeed, on others. They didn't want to add to his woes. A finding of recklessness could ruin his life.

After reviewing the evidence yet again, Jennifer Smith came to agree with the majority. Rita Wilson did not. She didn't want to find the captain reckless.

The other jurors talked to her. They pointed to this mistake, and that. Still she did not change her opinion. They talked some more. She remained adamant.

She found the persistence of the others distressing. There were eleven of them and one of her. That made her uncomfortable. She wanted to be liked. At the outset of the case, she had brought little presents for the other jurors—pins, T-shirts, that sort of thing. She had decorated the room with stickers of butterflies and birds.

And now she was the holdout. She didn't like it at all. On two occasions, Janette Garrison recalls, "Rita Wilson would be sitting there, then all of sudden she would start screwing her face up and she would get up and go to the ladies' room. Then, three or four minutes later, she would come out and everything would be fine."

She finally said that she could support a finding of recklessness if she didn't have to agree to punitive damages later on. The other jurors told her that they would not deal with that subject until the third phase of the trial.

Perhaps reminded that the question of punitive damages had yet to be asked, Rita Wilson finally joined the others in agreeing that through a series of mistakes, Captain Hazelwood had been reckless in his conduct. The jury was now unanimous.

They had been talking about Captain Hazelwood. But what about Exxon? The jurors had bought the argument that Exxon's monitoring had been insufficient, but since drunkenness was irrelevant to their verdict, should a failure to monitor lead to a finding of corporate recklessness?

They looked once again at the jury instructions and found the one (Number Thirty-three) that said, "The reckless act or omission of a managerial officer or employee of a corporation in the course and scope of the performance of his duties is held in law to be the reckless act or omission of a corporation." Was the captain of a supertanker a managerial employee? There had been testimony that he was. He certainly commanded his crew. Yes, they concluded, he was a manager.

Which meant that Exxon Corporation was found to have been reckless, too. They voted by hand and all agreed. They sent a note to the judge, and while they waited for him to summon the lawyers and then themselves to the courtroom, they looked out their single window at the stampede of counsel, clients, and cameramen rushing to the courthouse. For only a few more minutes now, the jurors realized, they and they alone would know what all the rest of the world seemed to be rushing to hear.

14

Submerged

P hase Two need not detain the reader for long, as it did so many others. It came and it went, and while it lasted darkness fell upon the earth.

It was never intended to be fun, and it was not. People said at the time that this phase of the trial was dry as dust, but even the most arid soil may become rich loam through watering. No enhancing drop ever fell upon Phase Two.

It was a technical trial. It was a trial to award compensatory damages. The whole point of the exercise was to determine how much money the injured parties had lost as a result of the spill, and then to award them those actual damages.

Everyone had agreed that the plaintiffs should be paid something, that the fishermen and natives should be made whole for their loss of income.

It was only a question of just how much that should be. It was merely a matter of money. In this regard there was not between the parties an altogether perfect meeting of the minds. One side felt that after the most exhaustive and rational analysis, the most protracted expert study, the amount to be paid in compensatory damages should be about $100 million. The other side, though equally fastidious in its studies, calculated that the somewhat more accurate number would be $890 million. It is not necessary to say which side was which.

From such differences do lawyers pay their children's tuition. Surely the vast sums they engorged in hourly feedings were justified here as never before. Each of them, after all, had been forced to learn a whole new trade in preparation for this phase. Several new trades. The counselors, through diligence untapped since the first week of law school, had become marine biologists, fish counters, ichthyologists, coho mavens. They had immersed themselves in the polluted depths of Waterworld, to fathoms that threatened them with the bends, and when they finally surfaced they were clutching Neptune's trident honed for combat—not truly expert in the aquatic trivia so expensively disputed on land, but close enough to give the real experts a very hard time, to deflect their testimony, give them pause, force them to qualify, exempt, recant.

This is one of the things that lawyers do. They become instant experts. They quickly don the outward trappings of exotic orders whose true initiates have labored a lifetime to join. They learn an alien jargon overnight. They grow able to contend with world-class scholars, and if not to best them, then at least to confuse the jury. They ingest whole fields of specialty in about a week, albeit in a superficial and transitory way, but well enough to cause the mandarin on the stand to lose his exclusive franchise. And then, when the trial is over, the lawyers go back to their offices and soon become faux experts in some completely different discipline, with a whole new vocabulary and data bank and problems.

But this trial was not over. Nor did it seem that it would ever be. It lasted for several weeks, though it seemed far, far longer to everyone involved, possibly exempting the experts. The time was devoted to scholarly testimony on either side of the calculation that the jury was being asked to make: the losses of more than ten thousand fishermen for each year from 1989 through 1995, for six different fishing areas, for five different types of salmon, for herring and for herring roe. The jurors were supposed to count the number of fish that weren't caught the year of the spill; to decide exactly how much of the subsequent decline in some fish prices was due to the spill rather than to factors such as increased competition; to deduce the long-term effects of the spill on the size of the fish catch thereafter; and to decide just how much of the recent decline in fish-permit prices was due to the spill rather than market forces.

There was no respite from the tedium. As if the deadliness of the proceedings was contagious, even the most zestful lawyers became infected. Their efforts to enliven the proceedings were enfeebled, from O'Neill's stab at homily ("Life is like a stew.") to the mercifully rare defense foray into humor ("So during the period when the plaintiffs claim that taint was scaring people off from buying the product—taint so."). It didn't matter. Neither Wilde nor Waugh could have enlivened the proceedings. No aphorism could breathe life into a dispute over how to count salmon. From the start the enterprise was doomed to turgidity. The jurors sank like poisoned herring beneath the eddying waves of blather, their past lives swimming before their eyes. From eight until two each day, they were submerged to previously unmarked depths of total, paralyzing boredom.

Only three things really stand out from the tedium of Phase Two.

The first occurred very early in the trial. The defense counsel chastised the jurors for having found their clients reckless. Or so the jurors thought. The lawyers for Exxon and Hazelwood began their remarks in Phase Two by expressing their disappointment with the verdict in Phase One. It was tactfully done, and the strongest word used was "disappointed." But the jurors were furious. They felt that they were being criticized, being told they had made a mistake. It is difficult to imagine a motive for the defendants' remarks, but whatever their intent they were very ill received. Some of the jurors considered sending a note to the judge about it, asking not to let it happen again. They didn't do so, but some rancor remained. It was not an auspicious beginning for lawyers who had to argue two more phases to the offended jurors.

The second memorable thing about Phase Two is how long the jurors were out. The jury deliberations took longer than the trial—about a month. At first this bewildered the plaintiffs, and then it scared them to death. They were terrified that the jurors simply couldn't do what was being asked of them; they couldn't agree on how much money to award in each category. With each passing day, with each passing *week,* this seemed more likely. Failure to agree on a Phase Two verdict would mean a mistrial, starting over from scratch with a whole new jury.

This prospect had worried the plaintiffs before, when they waited in agony for the Phase One verdict. But this was a thousand times worse, because now they *had* a Phase One verdict, the verdict they had worked five years to get: reckless. They had been given the key to the vault, and now, because these jurors couldn't decide what chinook salmon prices should have been in 1990, that key might be taken away. Their *victory* might be taken away. A new jury might not find recklessness! Before, they had feared the loss of opportunity; now it was fear of losing something they already possessed. It was maddening.

They had almost lost their minds in the week that the jury was out in Phase One. This was worse. It was a *month;* and it was more than four times worse. They didn't have the distraction of getting their evidence ready for a big trial: Phase Three was not complicated, and most of the work had been done. This time there really was little else to do but stare at the phone, dumb with terror that its silence meant the reversal of all that they had already won.

There was a movie at the time that most of them had recently seen: *Groundhog Day.* It dealt with someone who falls into a time warp and is fated to live the same day over and over again, with no variation in occurrence, encountering exactly the same people at the same time each day. It now seemed that this was a movie about the plaintiff lawyers. Gerry Nolting used to joke about it—"Well, it's groundhog day, again"—at eight each morning when the same supplicants gathered near their phone. The allusion seemed less humorous when the clock struck two, for then there really would be guaranteed another day exactly like the one that they had just endured. After a month, most had stopped praying only for a good verdict; any decision would be better than none.

Which brings one to the third noteworthy thing about Phase Two. It was the most striking thing of all. It was the verdict.

For after a full month of closeted deliberation, the jury proved that it had not, in fact, been deadlocked. It had merely been very hard at work. And at the end of its labors was a verdict, shared with the hastily summoned and very apprehensive courtroom.

The verdict in Phase Two was a victory for the defendants. The award for compensatory damages was $286,700,000. This was less than a third of what O'Neill had asked. It was almost three times what the defendants had offered, but that is a multiple of a much smaller sum.

The verdict stunned the courtroom. A hung jury, a mistrial, would have been less surprising. The plaintiff case for monetary award had been significantly rejected.

It was a blow. It was a blow to O'Neill. It was a blow to his clients. It was a blow to the hope of huge punitive damages in the only phase that yet remained. It was a blow—it was a kick in the teeth—to the real goal of the entire trial, to the best years of young lives spent in ceaseless scholarly toil, to the one thing that could redeem those years, those lives. It was a painful puncture of hope.

It was *defeat*—defeat for the fishermen, defeat for the natives, defeat for the lawyers who had thought they had shown with unprecedented clarity and thoroughness exactly how much should be awarded.

It was defeat, most of all, for O'Neill. This was his baby. The case was his life, but this part of it was his baby. This was what he was *best* at— proving up actual damages. This is why he had triumphed so astoundingly in the *Glacier Bay* case. This was the proven skill for which he had been rewarded with leadership in the biggest case of all time. What about the *matrix?* What about the *magic?* This effort was supposed to be something unique, better, different in kind, than what other lawyers did, a quantum leap, through diligence and skill, beyond the ordinary claims of ordinary lawyers.

And now the star had fallen to earth. The verdict at very best was disappointing. How could this have happened? The fishermen who were in the courtroom had each calculated their individual shares of the compensation that had been asked—*demanded*—by their former savior. The money had been spent, or at least invested, in their minds. And now it wasn't there. Two-thirds of it wasn't there. They had *something*, but they had expected more. They were disappointed, confused.

Many of the plaintiff lawyers felt the same way, but with one additional emotion. They were beginning to feel resentful. Not exactly angry, but close to it. Resentful. They had placed their trust in this hotshot, they had talked big to their clients in reliance on that trust. What had gone wrong?

The defendants had not cheered at the verdict—there was no need this time for a judicial reprimand. They didn't do that sort of thing. But they did exchange looks; they couldn't help resembling kids who had just won the spelling bee and were trying to look humble, and a visitor from Mars to that Anchorage courtroom would have known right away which of these strange, tired earthlings were the winners and which the losers.

O'Neill shed no tears; those were for victory. But he left the courtroom looking like death. He thought of himself as the protector of the oppressed, but to a large extent he was what he was trained to be, a commander of troops. And now he had let his troops down, or so it seemed to him. When asked how he felt, he said "Devastated." This is the word that Exxon had used about the spill—a word he then had ridiculed. He was beyond irony now. He used the word honestly, without association. He was devastated.

He had not known that it was possible to feel so very bad. It felt like the end of everything. But even through the numbness of defeat and humiliation, the brain focused on combat was still working. And the thought that occurred was that, bad as this verdict was, what it meant for the future was even worse.

Through a consciousness slowed by shock seeped a single horrifying thought: this was a cheap jury. These twelve people didn't like to spend money—not their own, not anyone else's. They were nickel-and-dimers. They were *cheap.*

This was big-time disaster. All that remained of this trial was Phase Three: punitive damages. The absolute shame of his immediate loss was as nothing compared to his numbed but all too acute sense of what lay ahead. Worse than disaster: wipeout.

For if this jury quibbled over how much to give for *actual* damages, why would it award a dime for something beyond that, for something, as the judge had said, not-favored-in-the-law, *punitive* damages. How could there possibly be frosting on such a puny little cake?

It got worse. The Phase Two verdict made even the Phase One result now seem suspect. So *what* if the jurors had found the defendants reckless? That had only been part of what was needed. They also had to put their money where their mouth was. Exxon's money, actually. One now could suspect that perhaps no money, or a pittance, would be awarded as punitive damages. Perhaps that was why these jurors had been able to agree on recklessness—because it didn't matter, because their blank check was going to remain blank.

These dark thoughts descended like a storm cloud on O'Neill and his sullen band. They were not a sight to fuel the hopes of their clients. A general without confidence is like a second army on the other side. It can turn the tide of battle by itself.

But providence intervened, and with a most improbable angel. From the moment that the verdict came down, as the despondent trial team was straggling back to its office, a figure of dazzling energy materialized to lift their spirits. Mel Weiss had the aura of success. As the dean of the national plaintiff class action bar, he made far more money every year than any lawyer associated with the Exxon case. He had not been present for much of this matter. He was a major player on the plaintiff Settlement Committee, but the settlement offers had never come. He had flown into Anchorage as soon as it was rumored that a Phase Two verdict was at hand, and he was in the courtroom when it was read.

He immediately turned his vast persuasive powers on the dispirited trial team. He pounded away with optimism and confidence to get their hearts started again. *This* wasn't so bad. All right, so it was a little disappointing. So what? They should keep their eyes on the ball. The ball was Phase Three. They were going to *win*. He *knew* it. They were going to win *big*. So cheer up! Everything was going to be okay. He poured out anecdotes from his own rich experience, assured them that this verdict augured nothing for the coming trial.

By the time the losing team and its indefatigable cheerleader had reached the trial office, self-immolation seemed less pressing an option. After another hour of Weiss's unflagging pep talk, they actually had begun to feel all right. Not *great*, to be sure, but capable at least of sheepish grins and the renascent will to fight on to victory. Weiss had made other contributions to the case, including help in major financing at a critical moment. But if he did nothing else but raise the first team's spirits from the lowest depths, he would still have been invaluable.

Within hours of the verdict, the battered lawyers found further respite, in flight. In anticipation of the jury's return, they had planned a long weekend far away from their two worlds of courtroom and office. Float planes had been chartered, cabins rented. Even before some of the jurors had returned to their homes, the lawyers they had disappointed were already in the air. These passengers represented the heart of the original team: the trial family and their own families. O'Neill and Nolting and Peter Ehrhardt and their wives and children, Steve Schroer and his wife, Kathy McCune and Karen Hanson and Lori Wagner and Leanne Mischke. It was much of the team that had been together in and since Soldatna.

They landed on Lake Creek, which is neither a lake nor a creek but rather a river, north by northwest of Anchorage. It is one of the great fishing spots in a great fishing state. For three or four days they cast for silver salmon and lived in cabins and tents and cooked the catch of the day and sat around the fire and talked and gradually rejoined the human race. It was mid-August. All the dark rigors of the frozen months seemed now an easy price to pay for so much light and glory. The sun shone for sixteen hours a day; they walked and swam and fished always in a warm and golden glow. It was like a different planet. Had such peace and beauty been here all the time that they had been locked away? It didn't matter. They were here now, resisting sleep because the summer brightness was even more enticing.

When they did second-guess the case, and puzzle over why the jury had done what it had done, there was no end of conjecture. What had those jurors been up to? What had gone on?

Had these vacationers but known it, the jurors had been gradually bonding, too, much like themselves. They were now comrades-in-arms, close and supportive and familial. And for the same reason: enforced proximity in a common effort of giant importance and prolonged duration. A feeling of closeness challenged that of confinement.

"We were really getting along as a group," says Rita Wilson. "We started to become friends." Two of the jurors, the matronly Nancy Provost and the intimidating Bruce Dean, both lived in the Mar-Su Valley, an hour's drive from the courthouse. They shared rides every day and soon, like most of the jurors, Dean was calling her Mom. There was a lot of that kind of thing. Jewell Spann worked at a McDonald's in Kenai and had never been to Anchorage before the trial, so every Wednesday her fellow jurors took her out to a different restaurant. There was a lot of knitting and crocheting; by the end of the trial Provost had completed afghans for four of her fellow jurors. The guards outside the door didn't know what to make of the occasional outbursts of laughter from inside the locked room.

There was very little laughter at the outset, however. The jurors were furious that the defendants had expressed disappointment at their earlier verdict. And they were exasperated by the task at hand. It seemed impossible, inhuman. In the first phase there had been only three interrogatories for them to answer. Now there were twenty-six. And they weren't understandable inquiries, such as whether one man had been reckless. These involved *calculations* (forty-four separate calculations in all were required).

The lawyers may not have realized how much they were asking the jurors to do. Both sides had wanted to speed through Phase Two, and so the experts had emphasized their conclusions more than the steps they had taken to get to them. But the jurors didn't want to simply choose between one expert and another; they thought it was absurd even to try. "You got a guy with four Ph.D.'s saying, yeah, a lot of fish were hurt," says Bruce Dean. "They just kind of delete each other out."

So the jury looked in despair at the seventeen boxes of evidence preempting the floor of their cell, and then they rolled up their sleeves. Some of the jurors thought that it was beyond their ability. But "several of us got gung ho and said, 'We're going through the evidence,'" says Rita Wilson, the reluctant juror in Phase One. She had taken some accounting courses, and two other jurors, Katherine Moor and Jennifer Smith, had some bookkeeping experience. Others joined their effort. Dean and Graham resumed their roles as surrogate attorneys. Painfully, slowly, the group built dikes in the sea of data, color-coded all the fishing permits, divided up tasks on the basis of geography or type of fish. For more than a month they worked with total dedication. Toward the end they lost one of their colleagues; Rose Martin was excused from the jury for health reasons. The remaining eleven just went on as before.

The jurors used the numbers of the Alaska Department of Fish and Game to help calculate the lost harvest of fish. These had been the basis for the parties' figures, too, but had been inflated or shriveled depending on the prism through which they were viewed. Not surprisingly, a focus on the base data itself produced numbers somewhere in the middle of those advanced in court. But the Alaska state reports only went through 1992. The jurors were supposed to find damages through 1995. The parties had been willing to extrapolate for the years without official data, but the jurors were not. Their instructions said that the findings had to be supported by a preponderance of the evidence, and "there was no evidence," says Provost. So for two years, 1994 and 1995, no damages were awarded for lost harvest. The jurors threw out forty percent of the money the plaintiffs had been seeking for fish that were never caught—more than one $115 million.

But the biggest dollar claim by the plaintiffs had been for the drop in salmon prices. O'Neill said that the spill was responsible. Exxon said that many factors had together lowered prices. The jurors went with Exxon. With Exxon's experts, at least. They remembered Professor James Anderson of the University of Rhode Island talking about how salmon prices for that period had been falling all over the world, not just in the spill areas of Alaska, because the market was being flooded with farm-raised salmon. Supply and demand. The jurors bought it.

They were also impressed by all the testimony about historical market fluctuations in salmon prices. "It's a cyclic thing," says Jewell Spann, "up and down and up and down. . . . We just couldn't blame Exxon for that." So the jury only awarded damage money for depressed prices in the year of the spill, 1989: $120 million, as opposed to the $572 million the plaintiffs had asked.

This is why the plaintiffs fared so badly. "We never expected them to . . . take apart every one of the numbers and try to figure out how they were constructed, and then parse the thing themselves," says one of the plaintiff lawyers. But that is just what the jurors did.

It may be argued that no jury should be asked to decide such technical economic questions, that some other method of dispute resolution should be employed for such abstruse aspects of a case. It is far more difficult to assert that any other method would have done a better job than what was accomplished by those resolute jurors. It would be very hard indeed to deny that their conclusions were reasonable, whether one agrees with them entirely or not. It is harder still, impossible really, to doubt their sincerity, remarkable diligence, and unremitting common sense. They did what jurors are supposed to do: they were the Finders of Fact. Nothing in the backgrounds of these seemingly ordinary people would have suggested the extraordinary work that together they had achieved. But their excellence is the assumption of our judicial system, and the premise of our nation.

The young lawyers unwinding near Lake Creek knew nothing then of how the verdict had been reached. But like those mysterious far-off jurors, they had renewed and enhanced their strength merely from being together in something they felt they must do. When the float planes returned to take them back to Anchorage, they found to their surprise that they actually wanted to get back.

15

Punishment

Captain Hazelwood was back at the counsel table for Phase Three. There had been no point to his presence in the previous technical phase, and he had stayed away. The calculation of actual damages had nothing to do with him.

But Phase Three was about punishment. That was all it was about. Punishment for the captain, punishment for Exxon. The jury's job was to decide whether punishment should be meted, out, and, if so, how much that should be.

How much money. This was a civil case. It was not a question of imprisonment or flogging or exile. It was a question of money. How much money over and above the actual damages would it take to punish the wrongdoers, to teach them a lesson and to deter them, and others, from doing the same things again?

There were no teams of experts this time. There were no specialists. This was too big for that. The one question that the jurors had to answer was well beyond the reach of technical assistance. It was a very simple question with an almost impossible answer, and the only persons in the world who could give that answer were the eleven souls who now were gathered in the jury box.

There is an old joke: "In my house, I make all the big decisions. My wife just gets to make the small decisions—like what kind of car we should buy, or whether we should move. *I* make the really big decisions—like should China be admitted to the U.N." The point of this joke is that ordinary people don't have the power to make the big decisions, and so their opinions on such matters are worthless.

The joke is wrong. Sometimes decisions are so big that only ordinary people can decide them—voters, juries.

Whether even to *have* punitive damages is, of course, itself a very big question, one that has been answered and qualified through thousands of separate court decisions reaching back to the unrecorded origins of our common law. A number of states have put caps on the amount of punitive damages that can be awarded—no more than two, or three, or four times the amount of actual damages, or, as in Colorado, no higher than the actual damage amount itself. In New Hampshire, punitive damages are not allowed at all, unless specifically permitted by statute. Other states require that a substantial portion of the punitive damage award go not to the plaintiffs but rather to the state, or to some designated fund. Clearly, punitive damages are *not* favored in the law. But they are possible. They are possible if the jurisdiction permits them, and if reckless conduct is found.

The finding of recklessness in Phase One did not mean that the jury in Phase Three *had* to award punitive damages. It meant that it *could*. And if it did, it could decide how much.

The parties' positions were perfectly clear. The defendants thought that no punitive damages should be awarded. The plaintiffs reportedly had asked for as much as fifteen billion dollars. (The range they actually would give to the jury peaked at an even higher figure.)

It was to be a very short trial. Everyone had agreed to that. Just a few days, no more than a week at most, and then the decision. It was the shortest, simplest part of all the long proceedings, and it was the only thing that really mattered. It was the great moment, and all that had been endured until now was merely preamble.

O'Neill for once was well rested. There had been a full week off after he and his team had returned from the trip to Lake Creek. He was as ready as he would ever be.

In his opening statement, O'Neill said that punitive damages should be awarded against Captain Hazelwood, but only in the amount of one dol-

lar. Surely he had already been punished enough—his job gone, his income greatly reduced, his name scorned. Enough was enough.

Exxon, however, was another matter. O'Neill came directly to this
major point: "What is punishment for a poor man could be nothing for a
rich man, and in legal terms they call that the rule of proportionality."

If the wealth of the defendant was the only issue, then of course the
case was over and the plaintiffs would be very rich. But the case was not
over. There were other matters to be addressed, as O'Neill well knew.

There were no secrets in these arguments. Each side had told the other
what it was going to say. One of the pillars of Exxon's case was that it had
already been punished in the amount of billions of dollars—about three
billion paid out in cleanup costs, fines and other expenses relating to the
spill. Surely there was no point to adding to that giant figure now.

Most of O'Neill's remarks were devoted to attacking this defense before it could be made. He said that Exxon was so big and rich that the
costs it had already endured were no more than "a hiccup." To back this
up, he argued that in the year of the spill, the dividend to Exxon shareholders was actually increased from that of the previous year. He pointed
out that Exxon stock had appreciated in value by twenty billion dollars
since the spill. It did not seem to him that the company had already been
punished.

Furthermore, he argued, those billions spent by Exxon should not be
regarded as punishment. They were only the normal cost of doing business. Some of the expenses, such as fines, were legal requirements. None
of this should be considered as a penalty for recklessness. It was something they had to do anyway.

"You know that Robert Fulghum book, *All I Ever Wanted to Know I
Learned in Kindergarten?* A spiller had to clean up his mess."

His theme was that Exxon had not learned its lesson; no one, other
than Hazelwood, had been fired. The top officers had received bonuses in
the year of the spill. Clearly, only punishment could get the point across.

The opening statement for the defense was made by Jim Sanders. It
was perhaps his most effective effort.

He began by noting that in Phase One, "You found that we were reckless;
we respect your verdict, we have taken it to heart even though you disagreed
with us." These few words were very helpful to his cause, since he suspected
that his colleagues' criticism of the verdict in Phase One had greatly

annoyed the jurors. How much better it was to note that the jury had dis-agreed with the defense, rather than, as previously, the other way around.

He moved on to the main point: "Your job in Phase Three is not sim-ply to determine how much Exxon has in order for you to select how much to take away from its owners, the shareholders." The issue was "whether future punishment is necessary to deter and whether Exxon and others have gotten the message in the interest of deterrence."

Before addressing that issue, he joined with O'Neill in asking that Captain Hazelwood be assessed no more than one dollar in punitive dam-ages. And he did something else. He fired his best shot at the whole con-cept of punitive damages.

"Now, these damages are assessed against defendants, *and they are awarded to plaintiffs*. Now, Mr. O'Neill didn't mention that a while ago when he talked to you. These damages . . . cannot go to anyone else but the plaintiffs. By their very nature and under the Court's charge, they are over and above the damages actually sustained by the plaintiffs. So the money does not go into some public fund or trust; it goes to those who have already been paid their actual damages.

"In this case you have spent a lot of time, care and effort deciding how much money you should pay the fishermen plaintiffs to make them whole from the damages caused by the spill. You worked very, very hard. And you have decided their actual damages. Now these fully compensated plaintiffs and others suggest to you that you should give them more, and not hun-dreds of millions, as you decided in Phase Two, but thousands of mil-lions—*billions* . . . and at whose expense? . . . The people that own Exxon are the shareholders. . . . You have fully compensated plaintiffs . . . being enriched at the expense of a lot of innocent people. That is a good com-mon-sense reason that the law does not favor punitive damages."

Even if punitive damages could be granted in some cases, he argued, this was not one of them. Exxon had already been punished. The finding of recklessness: "That hurts, that's punishment." In addition, "the offi-cers and employees have felt the sting of public censure for over five years. . . . It's a lasting punishment."

And then there was the economic punishment. Exxon had agreed to more than a billion dollars in settlement to federal and state governments. The cost of the cleanup was about two billion dollars—Exxon dollars—and it all added up, Sanders said, to great economic punishment.

But punishment was only one of the justifications for a punitive damage award. The other was deterrence—to ensure that it would never happen again. Not to worry, said Sanders. Exxon had learned its lesson. It had already made the changes in its rules and procedures to ensure that this kind of accident could not happen again. He recited a very impressive list of changes: more mates on the ships, the installation of a special auditor who goes from ship to ship and makes sure that the crews are getting the rest that is required ("even though we didn't think the fatigue problem had anything to do with the accident"), additional training, new equipment, the designation of a Valdez port operations coordinator.

The most striking changes involved the use of alcohol. Captains and chief engineers were no longer permitted to drink on a tour of duty—not a drop during the sixty days of rotated sea assignment, regardless of how long they were ashore. And when they, or any other crew member, returned from shore to ship, they had first to pass through a security gauntlet designed to detect the slightest amount of alcohol, whether smuggled in luggage or swallowed hours before. A Breathalyzer test was mandatory. Random searches and hotlines were now in force.

Sanders outlined these changes with enthusiasm, but he knew very well that to some extent they were beside the point. He knew what the real issue was, to his opponent and possibly to the jury. The real issue was his client—its size, its character as portrayed relentlessly by O'Neill. Sanders chose to confront the issue.

"An old stand is to talk about Exxon as some evil group, suggesting to you that everyone at Exxon lies, everyone at Exxon is bad and everything done by Exxon is for some ignoble purpose. In other words, don't trust a word that they say; the only thing they understand is the lash, and the lash you have is money, so use it freely for my side." O'Neill looked serene, as if hearing God's own truth.

Sanders went on. He looked squarely at the jurors, only two of whom were white males, and, with exceptional care, managed to leave the suggestion that the plaintiffs' portrait of his client was not entirely untarnished by bigotry.

"Now, we all know from our personal experiences, from the country's experiences, what terrible unfairness and condemnations of whole groups of people it is to propagandize that way. To say or even think that all of a whole group of any human beings is bad inevitably is inaccurate; it's mean and it's downright stupid. It's an insult to everybody."

He then expressed with some passion the reasonable belief that his side had been too reluctant throughout the trial to defend the integrity of its client. And then he sat down.

Next to appear was Michael Chalos. He expressed gratitude that no one was asking more than one dollar from his client, Captain Hazelwood. He spent a little time bolstering the assertion that his client had been punished enough. It wasn't hard to make the case. "There was one year when he made about $8,000. There was another year he made zero. He now—if this isn't enough punishment—he works for lawyers. He works for our law firm. Imagine having to spend the whole day working with lawyers after being in charge of a vessel." The jurors were looking at the captain, and the captain was grinning back, but no person thought it was a truly happy grin.

After Chalos was through, the judge read a number of stipulations into the record. One of them dealt with "Defendant Hazelwood and his annual income." It had been agreed between the parties, the judge said, that, "in 1987 Defendant Hazelwood had taxable income of $70,901; that in 1988 Defendant Hazelwood had taxable income of $117,374; that in 1989 Defendant Hazelwood had gross wages of $37,489 and taxable income of $167,298. That last item is footnoted to show that in 1989 Defendant Hazelwood was required to cash out of a profit-sharing plan upon termination by Exxon. In 1990 Defendant Hazelwood had no gross wages, and taxable income of $43,918; in 1991 Defendant Hazelwood had no taxable income. In 1992 Defendant Hazelwood had taxable income of $32,396; in 1993 Defendant Hazelwood had taxable income of $44,177."

The plaintiffs then brought their witnesses to the stand. They began with an accountant who reviewed the information in Exxon's annual reports and proxy statements. The point, of course, was to show that this was an immensely successful company. No other conclusion could have been possible. In 1993, for example, Exxon's revenues were $111 billion, expenses were $103 billion, and taxes were $2.77 billion. That left an after-tax net income for the company of $5.28 billion.

This was critical. The plaintiffs were zeroing in on the net profit at the end of each year. Pat Lynch was sustained by the Court in his objection to the items being referred to by the plaintiffs as "clear gravy at the end of the year," but the numbers themselves, of course, were admitted. In 1988 the net was $5.26 billion; in 1989, $3.52 billion; in 1990, $5.01 billion; in 1993, $5.28 billion.

There was considerable anxiety on the part of the defense team over the focus on annual net return. Was this the suggested punitive damage award? At the very least, it showed that the company had not been crippled by the spill. Even the one year—the spill year—in which net profits had been down, it was argued, was due to Exxon's purchase of a Canadian company for more than four billion dollars.

That ended the day's proceedings. The following day, there were no proceedings. The judge and the jury took off a day to personally inspect the damage to the beaches of Prince William Sound.

It was like a royal progress. It certainly seemed that way to the jurors as they boarded the waiting helicopters at dawn with guards and guides attendant. There was even a Bear Guide, whose sole function, it seemed, was to protect the jurors from ursine attack.

The flight from Anchorage to the sound was not long, and it was a passage of great beauty. The physical grandeur of Alaska is astonishing even in the winter; in the summer the vistas are achingly lovely, and awesome when seen from the air. The helicopters whisked like dragonflies past peaks crowned by ancient ice, darted through a pass whose walls were glaciers, and hovered over shoreless pools of almost painful glitter in the bright white sun.

One of the helicopters was large enough to hold all the jurors as well as the judge, some federal marshals, and a medic. Everyone was clad in bright orange gear, which had flotation capacity, and hip boots. There was grave concern that a chopper might crash, or that errant tides could trap the visitors on one of their island stops. The jurors had been required to view a film on hypothermia, for if they were indeed trapped overnight they would find that the day's warmth vanished promptly at dusk.

Another, smaller helicopter held two lawyers, Lori Wagner for the plaintiffs and Doug Serdahely for the defense. They had to be segregated from the jurors, of course, so there they were, flying up high in the sky with the Bear Guard and his rifle.

Each side had prepared a little written statement that would be read to the jurors upon arrival. These were as divergent as the sums being sought. The plaintiffs warned that beneath the rocky beaches could be found vast pools of stubborn oil from the spill; the defendants emphasized all the pink salmon, which perhaps could be glimpsed cavorting offshore, happily returning to a cleansed habitat.

The point, of course, was for the jurors to look around for themselves. They wanted to see firsthand how effective the cleanup had been. Their impressions in this regard could greatly affect the size of the Phase Three award, and both parties had negotiated furiously over nuance and detail in the statements that the jurors would hear. The level of concern was very high. Both sides had made trial runs to visit the designated sites. The sites for the juror visit (known as the Jury View) were themselves a matter of tough compromise—three selected by each side. At five in the morning on the date of the visit, a frantic call from the defendants warned the judge that one of their sites had been polluted overnight: someone had poured oil on the beach. The judge was asked to cancel the visit, but he said that he would look at the site before the jurors did; he thought he could tell fresh oil from that which had adhered to the rocks for the last five years. (Upon inspection, he judged the oil not to be of recent application. The jurors were permitted to see it.)

As it turned out, there wasn't time to see all six sites. Only three were actually inspected: two chosen by the defendants and one by the plaintiffs. The jurors, though somewhat stunned by the protocol and equipage of their journey, took their inspection duties very seriously. Having discarded much of their bulky uniforms in the heat of the day, they resolutely walked the rocky shore and dug with shovels to see if oil lingered beneath the surface.

It was hard to know how effective the cleanup had been, what a desolate beach was *supposed* to look like in terms of oil traces. But the jurors were not all strangers to the splendors of Prince William Sound. A number of them had vacationed there in the past. What struck some of these jurors was the absence of wildlife. "The entire day I never saw one bird flying around or anything else," says Janette Garrison. "No otters. I mean, we spend a lot of time in Homer, and I am used to seeing otters." And hearing the call of birds overhead. Those birds previously had been so abundant. Now the skies were clear, but the only sound was that of the surf and of their own boots on the gravel. It is estimated that more than three hundred thousand murres, a local bird, had perished in the spill. This lawsuit was not about the loss of wildlife as such; it dealt only with economic loss. And yet it was hard not to be affected by the silence and all the living things that, despite the passage of years, still could not be seen.

The next day everyone was back in the courtroom. The plaintiffs had almost no more witnesses. Former chairman Lawrence Rawl appeared on video to verify that few had been fired over the spill and that Exxon had been one of only fourteen domestic companies to merit a triple A credit rating from Standard & Poor's. A few other Exxon spokesmen, also on brief videos, confirmed the company's size and credit worthiness.

And then it was the defendants' turn to call witnesses to the stand. Those whom they called to testify proved to be something of a surprise. The tables had been turned. No more executives and admirals. These were ordinary working people, who looked and sounded much like the jurors themselves. They were Exxon employees, called to the stand to recite the role they had played in cleaning up the spill.

This was, of course, the mirror image of O'Neill's most basic tactic, highlighting the common man in juxtaposition to vast impersonal forces. Now it was the plucky little Exxon people fighting tirelessly to roll back the vast spill. The defendants apparently felt that imitation is the sincerest form of victory. It is a wonder that it took them so long to get it. Their donning of the populist mantle marked the final O'Neillization of the trial, the triumph of a tactic made ubiquitous whether through Darwin's law or Gresham's.

It was very effective. The first defense witness was Constance Buhl, an Exxon engineer who was also the only woman to be licensed by the Coast Guard as chief engineer of steam and motor. Of imposing stature and projecting self-worth without arrogance, she was a very impressive witness. She had been on temporary shore assignment in the Exxon Shipping Company office in Houston when the spill occurred. Though Good Friday was a holiday, she had gone to the office very early to catch up on some work. She arrived at six thirty in the morning, and thus became one of the first Exxon employees to learn of the spill. Since she was herself a highly trained mariner and engineer, she soon found herself on the Exxon spill response team. She and a co-worker found the company manuals that dealt with oil spill responses, and started making the calls that were prescribed. As more and more people arrived, she found herself in the middle of a global effort to locate equipment and have it brought as soon as possible to Valdez.

She worked twenty-four hours that first day, and sixteen hours on each of many days that followed. Her efforts and dedication at first were hard to believe.

She was being questioned by Jim Sanders, who was trying to establish that such an exhausting schedule had not been required by the company.

"Now, were you required to work sixteen hours a day?"

"No, sir."

"Why did you work like that?"

Her voice suddenly was very strained. "It was our ship." On the last word of that sentence she broke down, and tried desperately to hide her tears. "Excuse me," she sobbed.

"That's all right," said Sanders gently. "Do you want some water?"

"Yeah," she replied, and then, "I'm an *engineer.*" Whether that was meant as explanation or self-reproach, she was obviously struggling with all her will to regain self-control.

"Pardon me," she said, "it was very emotional, and it is now. It was our ship and we were going to do whatever it took to clean up what we did." She had to stop again. "Excuse me."

"That's all right," said Sanders, who must have been in heaven. "I have no further questions, Your Honor."

Which meant that it was time for cross-examination. O'Neill was required to get up and walk over and adversely question the most sympathetic figure in the trial. This was not one bit like attacking CEOs.

But he was highly professional and quickly adaptive. He would no more harangue this brave and tearful lady than he would slaughter a seal. He could not possibly have been more solicitous.

"Do you want to take a break for a second?" he asked softly.

"I think I'm going to be okay," she sniffed, and then, smiling, "but thank you for offering. Go ahead."

Go *ahead!* O'Neill was no doubt thinking. Does this woman think I'm crazy?

"Thank you for your work on the spill," he said instead. After a pause, and tentatively, he added, "And I have a few questions."

"You bet," she said pluckily.

The questions quickly shrank in number. In a few minutes, Constance Buhl was excused, and O'Neill, though smiling his concern, was probably wondering why the hell *he* never had a witness like this.

All the witnesses whom Sanders then called were also very good. They told tales of heroism; of lightering (extracting cargo), at great risk, almost a million barrels of oil from the stricken *Valdez*, thereby preventing the spill from being even worse; of rushing from voluntary teaching at a church camp in Australia back across the world to Alaska to help out; of cleanup hiring priorities that favored Alaskans and women; of hiring eleven thousand cleanup workers at seventeen dollars an hour; of putting into place tough new rules and monitoring procedures. O'Neill did his best to undercut this testimony by vigorous cross-examination, hammering away at the points that much of the cleanup had been required and that almost none of those accountable for the spill had lost their jobs. But the story told by the defense witnesses survived despite these taints. The picture of ordinary people working hard and long and clearly dedicated to cleaning up the spill was effective and affecting, if very late in the game. It was a game that had been defined at the outset by O'Neill, from the opening moments months before when he introduced his fishermen clients to the courtroom. It was good guys versus bad guys, and the bigger the guys the badder. Exxon could do nothing about its size, but it had finally learned the language of its adversaries and put some good guys of its own on the stand.

The question was whether very big guys could ever be seen as good guys too. The test came. Lee Raymond, the current chairman of the board and CEO of Exxon, was called to the stand and questioned by Jim Neal.

Many in the courtroom were surprised to see him there. He certainly didn't have to be. He lived far beyond the jurisdiction of the court and so could not be subpoenaed. He was there voluntarily; he was a defense witness. Which meant that later he would have to face cross-examination. For this reason, some defense lawyers had been opposed to his appearance. But there were other forces at Exxon who thought that he could save the day. These forces had prevailed. The thought was that no one could better state the Exxon case than the Exxon chairman.

He was in fact a remarkably good witness. He was a courteous and strong man of obviously high intelligence who was in complete control of his facts and himself. His lack of pretension could not have been feigned. It was obvious that the witness was a human being and not a stereotype of thoughtless greed.

There were a good many questions about his early life. He had been born and raised in a small town in South Dakota, where his father was a railroad engineer. He wanted to be a chemical engineer and ended up getting a Ph.D. from the University of Minnesota, which has the best chemical engineering department in the nation. Upon graduation, intending to spend his life in industrial research, he went to work for Exxon. His considerable talents were spotted, and he moved steadily upward in the corporate ranks; he had become president of the company by the time of the spill.

The jury seemed to be hanging on his words. But Neal still had a lot of corrective work to do. A CEO in a punitive damages trial is a natural target, and Raymond already had been riddled in absentia with the buckshot of invective. O'Neill had begun Phase Three by zeroing in on Raymond's salary (about a million dollars) and holdings in Exxon, including options (about ten million dollars).

This always happens. Success is a blessing, but not on the stand. Or so it is assumed by trial lawyers on both sides. They may well be wrong. Most people, and therefore most jurors, probably respect those of proven achievement. They *want* hard work and ability to be well rewarded. But it's difficult to convince the trial counsel of this. Their usual response is, tell it to the jury. So one side spotlights the personal wealth of its opponent, and the other side tries to minimize the amount.

This was the effort that Jim Neal now made. He spent some time establishing that many CEOs of comparable institutions were paid much more than Raymond. This was quite true, but somewhat beside the point. To those who resented executive pay, one million dollars was as bad as five. And it wasn't very helpful to say that the heads of Mobile, Chevron, and Texaco all had higher salaries even though Exxon was as large as all three of them together. Why aggrandize Exxon's size in a punitive damages suit? It was better to move on to something else.

They did, and it was obvious why some had wanted Raymond to be there. He was one of the best spokesman that his company had had in the trial. He talked about how horrified he had been by the spill, and what an impact it had made on all of them. "Maybe the most telling comment would be the one my wife made to me. She's been with me on this Exxon odyssey from back in graduate school, and her comment to me was that it's the first time she had ever been embarrassed that we worked for Exxon."

He also spoke about Exxon's new alcohol policy (which Sanders had enumerated earlier). No longer could a graduate of a drug or alcohol re-habilitation program return to a safety-sensitive position, ever again. Random testing and detailed monitoring were now the rule. The point clearly was that further deterrence was uncalled for.

Raymond concluded by saying, "I can't think of a single event that really shook . . . the bedrock of our employees' view of themselves and the corporation as did this event. . . . This has had a very, very serious impact on them, and their whole focus is . . . they worry about whether or not we'll ever be able to regain the position we had in the communities around the world."

Lee Raymond's testimony had clearly helped to rehabilitate his company in the jurors' eyes. It is unlikely that anyone else could have made so convincing a case for Exxon's accountability and contrition. He should have been proud.

And he should never have taken the stand. Those who cautioned against it had been right. For now it was time for cross-examination. And the pleasant man who sat there calmly waiting, like a tethered goat in tiger country, had not a clue as to what was coming.

O'Neill, who could scarcely believe his good fortune, sauntered up to the witness stand and promptly did to Raymond what dogs do to trees. It was not a pretty sight. Even for him, this attack was relentless. There was nothing that Raymond had said that did not provoke withering scorn. His unfamiliarity with AA's twelve-step rehabilitation program was seen as shameful ignorance. Every word of Raymond's testimony had become a brick to be thrown. He had said that the spill had left him "devastated to a degree."

"What does it mean," O'Neill asked, "to be devastated to a *degree?*"

"Well, I think the point, Mr. O'Neill, is if I had been totally devastated personally, because the question was a personal question, if I had been totally devastated, I wouldn't have been able to get up and go to work, and I concluded that wasn't the right answer, that somebody in the company had to say, 'Come on, guys, let's get going; we've got some serious problems to deal with and I want to be there to deal with them.'"

These were people from two different galaxies. There was no basis whatsoever for communication. It was words versus action, it was symbol versus explanation, it was generational, it was the most radically opposed life views possible, it was two men of great ability not having a clue as to what the other was about.

This became even more apparent when O'Neill, anxious to destroy this effective witness, used the strongest weapon in his arsenal, the Litany of Omission:

"Do you know any fishermen from Prince William Sound?"

"No, I do not."

"Do you know any fishermen from Upper Cook Inlet?"

"No, I do not."

"Do you know any fishermen from Kodiak?"

"No."

"Do you know any Chignik fishermen?"

"No, I do not."

"Do you know any people that live in the Native villages in Alaska?"

"No, I do not "

"Do you know the names of any of them?"

"You mean the Native villages?"

"No, the people. Do you know the names of any fishermen?"

"No."

"Natives?"

"I wouldn't want to make a comment on that."

"Do you think it might be appropriate as a matter of contrition to at least learn the names of some of the victims of the spill?"

"Mr. O'Neill, I've read the whole list of claims, and my interpretation of your question was do I personally know any of them. I could go back and memorize a whole list of names that came out that I looked at as to who got payment and that type of thing, but that wasn't particularly responsive."

"No it isn't, and I wasn't concerned about the payment of money, I was concerned whether you knew the names of these victims to come up and say, Fred, John, Mary, Susan, I'm sorry about what my company did to you?"

"Well, I am sorry about what happened."

"Well, they don't know that because you haven't told them that, have you?"

"We've said that publicly—I won't say an infinite number of times because that's an overstatement, but it's a very large number of times."

"Including in the advertisement, is that right?"

This was the letter of apology from Exxon that had appeared nationwide.

"I believe I already commented the only way you could get a letter like that in a paper was to pay the advertising rate. Newspapers don't—I mean, I know it shocks all of us, but they don't publish things for free."

"Yes. And it was important to make sure we got all the Kodiak fishermen that lived in Detroit and Boston and New York and Washington, D.C."

Jim Neal leapt to his feet. "This is grossly unfair," he yelled. "Objection!"

"The question was a bit sarcastic," the judge said mildly. "If you want to ask it again, rephrase it."

There was no need to ask it again. The point, that the apology had been merely part of a national public-relations campaign, had been made.

There were still some trees standing, and O'Neill's was a scorched-earth policy. Raymond had spoken of paying out $300 million early on, and O'Neill's questions produced the fact that much of that money went to seven or eight major food processors, rather than to his clients.

"So you decided to duke it out with the fishermen in the court system?"

"That is not a fair characterization. . . . The purpose in the law is to come to a reasonable decision as to what the right level of compensation was, which I think is the issue,"—there was a twinkle in his eye as he evoked the Phase Two verdict—"one of the issues that this jury has already dealt with."

To his credit, Raymond was unflappable under attack, and often returned the serve of the younger player. He kept his sense of humor. When O'Neill joked that another plaintiff lawyer was "smarter than me, although not as handsome," Raymond said, "I assume that wasn't a question." But the litany had mesmerized the courtroom, and presumably had had some impact on the jury. On redirect examination, Neal worked hard on a cleanup operation of his own. He got into the record the names of many small-town Alaska newspapers where the ad of apology had been published. He tried to minimize the increase in Exxon's dividends by factoring in inflation. When he had finished his list, he turned to the judge and said, "May it please the Court, the defendants rest."

The trial was almost over. There would be no more testimony; Lee Raymond had been the final witness. All that remained were the closing arguments.

As always, these would be an O'Neill sandwich: he was permitted to speak both first and last, with the defendants' closing argument inserted in between.

If there was one speech that mattered most, this was it. In the other phases, part of the summation had been to remind the jurors of telling facts. This phase was not about facts. It was about punishment, and in an amount that everyone agreed could not really be quantified. It was a time for rhetoric, not calculation. It was the last chance to alter the mood of the jurors. It was the best opportunity to reach their hearts.

"What amount of money is necessary to punish Exxon Corporation for its reckless acts, reckless acts that caused the worst environmental disaster in United States history?" O'Neill began. "And that's the question before us. . . .

"Jury Instruction Twenty-four says that the amount of punitive damages that is necessary to punish a defendant is the penalty that is necessary to express society's disapproval of conduct that society condemns, and that's what I'm talking about. You are here to express society's disapproval of conduct that society condemns. . . .

"The world is looking at you. The directors in mahogany polished boardrooms in Houston, New York, Brussels, Paris, Hong Kong, are going to know exactly what you did. And what you do in this Phase Three is an expression of what our society's values are. That's how it's going to be interpreted and everybody is going to know about it."

He told the jurors about the standard for punitive damages they would encounter in the jury instructions: the degree of reprehensibility of the conduct, the magnitude of the likely and actual damage caused, and the financial condition of the defendant. At this last point, he pushed his favorite button:

"What is punishment for a poor man can be nothing for a rich man."

But capacity to pay was not his only point. He also had to show that the defendant was deserving of punishment.

"The conduct wasn't a result of paper policies. The conduct was a result of a sickness in the organization, and that sickness had to do with the way we treat each other as decent human beings. . . . If somebody has a problem, you say how are you doing on your problem, how is your treatment, how is your family, are you happy, unhappy, is there something I can do for you, is there something the company can do for you?

"What happened here was the result of a lack of basic human decency. And what happened as a result of that lack of basic human decency at Exxon Corporation? A lot of people were hurt."

He was not through trying to discredit Raymond.

"I'm going to suggest to you that Exxon Corporation lives in a different world, and the corporation executives live in a different world. . . . Now, Mr. Raymond has fourteen million dollars in stock options that he has yet to exercise. He makes a couple million dollars a year, he lives in a different world than we do. . . . [The salary and options figures used by the two parties were somewhat divergent.]

"He didn't know what a twelve-step program was. Now, in the world that most of us live in, we know about Alcoholics Anonymous and the twelve-step program. . . . If I was a chairman of the board of one of the biggest companies in the world and my company caused the biggest environmental disaster in the history of America and there was alcohol involved, I'd learn a little bit about the problem. . . .

"Now, what happens in Japan if in fact something like this happens? The chairman of the board of a Japanese company steps down. But I guess in the United States, in one of the biggest companies in the world, if you create a disaster, you give people bonuses. . . . I would suggest to you that most of the people who brought you the wreck of the *Exxon Valdez,* if they haven't been given bonuses they have been promoted. And that isn't right, either."

He jabbed again his favorite punching bag, the dispute resolution agreement between Exxon and Hazelwood, calling it "a contract to lie by both parties. Does this signify remorse?"

He was contemptuous of the argument that punitive damages would come out of the pockets of the shareholders. "The stockholders are not without complicity, because the stockholders have had five years to express their disapproval of Mr. Rawl and Mr. Raymond and their management team and their board of directors, and haven't. The stockholders haven't gotten the message. Like the board, the stockholders haven't gotten any message."

And just how much money did he think it would take to deliver that message?

"Exxon thrives, and money is the language of corporations. You and I have souls to damn and bodies to kick, we do. Exxon Corporation has no soul and has no body, and its language and the language of the people in boards of directors rooms throughout the world is this . . . Five billion is the average yearly net profit . . . this five billion—Exxon, because of its size and wealth, can sustain a five-billion-dollar award and shrug their shoulders, just shrug their shoulders. One year's average cash flow is ten billion. Exxon spent sixteen billion of its cash in buying its own stock back. . . . The poor Exxon shareholders get the benefit of a twenty-billion-dollar appreciation in stock."

So how much was he talking about? It was hard to tell, though the defendants could not possibly have been listening more closely. They wanted to hear exactly how much money he realistically expected to get. For a while they just had to keep listening, for O'Neill had plunged once again into the populist pool.

"If the headline in the newspapers (and in this case it will be *Barrons* or *Fortune* or *Money*) is that Exxon Walks Away, Exxon Gets Off, Exxon Goes Scott-Free, what does that say to the rest of the oil industry, what does that say to the big fifteen or sixteen powers of the world—that we can mount a defense in a courtroom that gets us off the hook?

"You know, it's interesting who they fired. They didn't fire anybody who wears a white shirt. As the kids would say, there is an attitude there."

His time was almost up. How *much*, the defendants, and no doubt some jurors, were wondering.

"What amount of punitive damages do you find to be necessary?" O'Neill finally asked the latter group. Everyone leaned forward, attentively.

"We know it's more than five and we know it's less than twenty." He let this sink in, and then repeated it. "We know it's more than five and less than twenty. And I could give you a number that I think, and that is bringing my life experience to bear on a very difficult question, and I think that's a waste of time because each of you are going to go back in there and bring your life experience to bear on a very difficult question.

"But it's more than five, and it's less than twenty."

And that was it, the end of his speech. The jurors may have found this imprecise, but to the lawyers on both sides, it was artful enough. O'Neill's words had been very carefully planned.

For one thing, he had raised the floor of the range. He had raised it from nothing to five billion dollars (though "billion" and "dollars" had been absent from his declaration). This was the sum, he was suggesting, beneath which no jury could possibly sink. It was worth a try.

More important, he had signaled that five billion dollars was *accept-*

able to his side. This reduction was not casually achieved. Much internal debate had preceded it. The plaintiffs wanted to win big, but not so big as to risk the award being reduced by the Court of Appeals. There was no question that Exxon would immediately appeal to a higher court any punitive damage award at all. If that award were twenty billion dollars, they could well succeed in having the appellate court whittle—indeed, chop—away at it. Greed had its risks, and the plaintiffs knew them.

Five billion dollars, however, seemed in this context an award that could withstand attack. It was an average year's net profit for Exxon. This wasn't an automatic linkage, but if punishment were the goal, it was an understandable sum.

A number of those in the plaintiff camp were praying for an even larger award. *Let* the jury give us ten, fifteen, twenty billion dollars, they argued, and *then* worry about the Court of Appeals. Others weren't so sure. The appellate courts had been cutting back a lot of jury verdicts as excessive. Don't tempt fate.

The consensus was not to tempt fate, but not to preclude it, either. The jury was given a floor, admittedly on stilts, and a very lofty ceiling, and then, well, que será, será.

The defense then gave its last speech to the jury. Jim Neal began by saying, "I waited for an hour and a half while Mr. O'Neill was up here to simply admit to you that this massive amount of money that he's asking for doesn't go to charity, it doesn't go for something else. It goes solely to their side, who have already been awarded all their actual damages. Not once did he mention that."

He was starting with his strongest shot. This was his last chance at the jury, and he made the most of it, delivering with power and emotion his client's best side of the case.

And this time there was certainly no criticism of the jury. Far from it. Whether the low damages in Phase Two had strengthened his colleagues' faith in the jury system or whether he was a skilled trial lawyer who understood where the decision would be made, he enveloped the pleasantly surprised jurors in a honeyed haze of southern charm.

"Let me tell you from the bottom of my heart, and I know this to be a fact, every man and woman at Exxon, whether they agree with your verdict or not, appreciate your methodology. We appreciate the way you went about resolving Phase One and Phase Two. We appreciate the obvious care you took to decide the case on the facts as presented in this courtroom and under the law as given you by His Honor. . . .

"Your reward is simply your knowledge that you've done the best you can do under the circumstances. And, by golly, let me tell you, you keep doing that and that's good enough for me."

And speaking of following the law as given by the judge, he wanted to call everyone's attention to some of the instructions. He particularly liked the one that said, "You should assume that all plaintiffs have been or will fully be compensated for all damages they may have suffered as a result of the spill." Then there was, "You may not make an award of punitive damages for the purpose of compensating any plaintiff." And of course he could not help but refer to that sacred line, "Punitive damages are not favored in the law."

Then he went over all the money—"two billion seven hundred and ninety-eight million dollars after taxes"—in cleanup, fines, and other expenses. He strongly denied that much of this expenditure had been required. And he talked again about the changes Exxon had made. "This is getting the message, this is acting responsibly, this is acceptance of responsibility, this is punishment, and it is deterrence."

He described the bind that his witnesses were in. "This is the kind of Catch-22 you get into sometimes with a clever lawyer like Mr. O'Neill. If Mr. Raymond had said, oh, we were reckless, you would have been hearing from Mr. O'Neill saying that we were lying in Phase One when we thought we were not reckless. If we say we are not reckless, then you'd hear Mr. O'Neill say we are in denial and therefore we didn't get the message. Mr. Raymond said it best when he said, look, what I think is not important, what I thought isn't important. The jury decided we were reckless, now let's move on, and that is the perfect answer to that question."

He expressed shock at the kind of award money that O'Neill had suggested to the jury. "Because we've dealt with such numbers, it's hard for me to comprehend them. Fifteen billion dollars is five hundred million more than Exxon's entire investment—entire investment, not income, but entire investment in the oil and gas business. . . .

"I want to close by picking up another theme that Mr. O'Neill has said time and time again: 'Send the message.' Now, I'm not going to be as flowery as he was talking about the world watching. But how the world is watching you has nothing to do with your duty. Do justice. Forget the world watching business, as he said.

"But he does keep saying, 'send the message, send the message.' Members of the jury, whatever you do, you're going to send the message—whatever you do. . . .

"Now, if you say now that enough is enough, the message you will send to companies is if you accept responsibility and you act responsibly, when it comes to punitive damages, we will give that great weight.

"On the other hand, if you hit us now, the message you may send to other companies is: don't do anything. Drag your feet. If you got any responsibility, make them take you to court because you'll be hit anyway."

Mike Chalos had been allocated only a few minutes for his summation. He used it largely to combat the notion that the agreement between his client, Hazelwood, and Exxon was a "contract to lie," and of course to plead that no more than one dollar be asked from a man who had already suffered so much.

And then it was the bottom slice of the sandwich, O'Neill's second closing argument, the very last speech of the trial. Those who felt that he had already reached the limits of unrestrained rhetoric now saw him turn the dial even further.

"Accept responsibility? They didn't have any choice but to accept responsibility. It's on a reef, the state authorities are coming out; what are they going to do, paint the smoke stack and put Sea River on it? . . . Give me a break! It's *their boat!* I mean, Exxon has no place to hide. So they say, having no place to hide, we accepted responsibility. That is a stupid, stupid, misleading thing to say, and what it means is they are making up arguments so they won't be punished. . . ."

Of all the money spent to date by Exxon on spill cleanup and fines, "Show me a dollar of that that is attributable to reckless behavior. It is not fair and it is an improper, chronic message to send to society that innocent spillers and reckless spillers are going to be treated the same, and you don't need to be a genius to figure that out. . . .

"And if you want to talk about them learning their lesson—you know, I have a boy and a girl. Boy is older than the girl. And, you know, we've all heard it: but I didn't hit my sister. If I hit her, she made me do it. I didn't hurt her anyway. And that's what we've heard. And when your kid comes in and says—goes through the litany, you say: hold it there, cowboy, we're going to have to have a serious discussion about accountability."

The defense had hammered away again and again that punitive damages would benefit not society, but rather O'Neill's clients. This was a very effective argument, one that had seemed too risky to try to rebut. O'Neill now charged it head-on:

"Mr. Neal starts off by saying, what about this money to the plaintiffs, and why didn't Mr. O'Neill mention that? Do you recall when he said that at the beginning, why didn't I mention it, like I was trying to hide it? Do you want me to show you why I didn't mention it? Because I was told not to—because it's irrelevant to the purpose of punishment, because it's irrelevant to the purpose of punishment. The fact that the punitive damages would go to Alaska fishermen, Native corporations, every community in Southcentral Alaska and benefit this economy is irrelevant to the purpose of punishment. And the jury instruction tells you that. . . ."

He returned to his major theme.

"You know more about what happened in their company than they do, and they are here to tell you that they fixed the problem. . . .

"Corporations can have sick cultures. And in a corporation, because everybody has got a specialized role, medical department, 'that's not my responsibility,' that kind of thing, people avoid responsibility. . . .

"How do we police against that attitude? We're not policing against paper policies, we're policing against attitudes. How do we police against attitudes? We police against attitudes, against institutions that are as big as this one, through the jury system, and the message from the jury has to go not to Connie Buhl, but it has to go to the board of directors and it has to go to Mr. Raymond so that five years after the grounding of the *Exxon Valdez*, boards of directors have an interest in finding out what happened, and the chairman of the board of Exxon Corporation has an interest in finding out what happened, and so that the boards of directors and the chairman of the board have enough concern about the people that they have to at least know the names of a few of them. . . .

"We need tough love. . . .

"Saying that you're sorry when you hurt somebody, and coming to grips with the full scope of what you did and not hiding it from the public, are the first meaningful steps to changing attitudes and moving forward. . . .

"Now my part is over. You know, five years of work and all these depositions and looking at these documents, it's over, and now you can go and do your work. And we wish you all Godspeed and thank you for your time—and we'll hang around and wait until you come back.

"Thanks."

The role of a lifetime was over, and no ovation could ever equal merely having been on that stage.

But the stage was not yet empty. Judge Holland had to read his instructions to the jury. A number of them had been previewed by the lawyers in their previous remarks. But these had been snippets, paraphrases, summations. As the final instructions were read, the power of the judge seemed awesome indeed. In the previous phases there had been so much evidence for the jurors to weigh. Here there was only their gut feelings, their instincts, their general sense of right and wrong. It was no longer a matter of counting drinks or fish. This was so general: did the defendants deserve to be punished, and how much money would that take? There were no guideposts in this strange and empty landscape. But there was one road map, the judge's instructions, and it soon became clear that his map required a route through formidable terrain. The road to punitive damages was strewn with the boulders of qualification and the potholes of mitigating factors. As the judge droned on, the road seemed nearly impassable, and the horizon receded farther into the distance.

The tollgate was easy enough to pass: you could award punitive damages to punish or to deter.

But after that the rocks and gullies were abundant.

With each new intonation from the pleasant judge, the plaintiffs winced. Not favored in the law was one thing, but qualified incessantly by this judge was another. It seemed to some that they would be lucky to receive twelve dollars and forty cents.

The judge's admonitions were not without legal backing, but there were so *many* of them:

"The fact that you have determined that the conduct of Joseph Hazelwood and of the Exxon defendants was reckless does not mean that you are required to make an award of punitive damages against either one or both of them. . . .

"If you find that punitive damages are appropriate, the amount of punitive damages may not be determined arbitrarily. You must use reason in setting the amount. When I say you must use reason, I mean that any punitive damages award must have a rational basis in the evidence of the case. A punitive damages award may not be larger than an amount that bears a reasonable relationship to the harm caused to members of the plaintiff class by a defendant's misconduct, including any harm to any persons set forth in the stipulation that was read to you. Also, the award may not be larger than what is reasonably necessary to achieve society's goals of punishment and deterrence. Punitive damages, if any, should not reflect dislike for, bias, prejudice or sympathy toward any party. An award of punitive damages may not be made for the purpose of taking revenge on a defendant. . . .

"In determining whether to make an award of punitive damages, you should assume that all plaintiffs have been or will be fully compensated for all damages they may have suffered as a result of the oil spill. . . .

"You may consider as mitigating factors (a) the existence of prior criminal sanctions or civil awards against the defendants for the same conduct and (b) the extent to which a defendant has taken steps to remedy the consequences of his or its conduct or prevent repetition of that conduct. . . .

"In considering whether an award of punitive damages is appropriate against a corporation, you may consider not just the fact that a corporation may have legal liability for the acts of its employees, but also whether corporate policymakers actually participated in or ratified the conduct that was wrongful and whether the conduct that was wrongful was carried out by lower-level employees and was contrary to corporate policies.

"If you find that corporate policymakers did not actually participate in or ratify the wrongful conduct, this is a factor that you may consider in mitigation of any award of punitive damages that you might otherwise find proper. Similarly, if you find that wrongful conduct was contrary to company policies, you may take this factor into account in mitigation of any award of punitive damages that you might otherwise find proper. . . .

"Evidence of changes in policies, practices and procedures by the Exxon defendants has been put before you so that you can consider this issue. The fact that changes have been made after an event does not tend to show that such changes should have been made before the event or that the policies, practices or procedures in place before the event were negligent or otherwise improper. Accordingly, if you find that changes were made that have reduced the likelihood of an oil spill in the future, you may consider the making of such changes as a factor tending to mitigate any punitive damages award that you might otherwise find proper. . . .

"You may also consider the extent to which a defendant has been subjected to condemnation or reproval by society as a result of other means, such as loss of standing in the community, public vilification, loss of reputation and similar matters."

By the time the judge was finished, the plaintiffs were filled with dread. You mean installing that damned Breathalyzer is going to get them off the *hook?* they despaired. Oh, God!

At twenty minutes after one o'clock on Monday, August 29, 1994, the jurors left the courtroom for the unhappily remembered confines of the Red Room just behind it.

The lawyers had started to pack up their briefcases, but the judge still had something to say.

"One final housekeeping matter. I wish that counsel and whoever amongst you has the duty for the physical facilities here, would coordinate with our Clerk of Court on undoing the courtroom."

Undoing the courtroom! Taking out all the equipment, the control panels, the giant screens, everything. Yankees at Tara! How could they?

"Kind of a sad thing, Judge," said O'Neill, and not one word that he had spoken in this trial had been more heartfelt.

"Well," said the judge, "I'd *like* to leave it this way. The fact is, we have a criminal jury trial involving a number of defendants coming up in about a week, and we need to replace the arrangement with . . ."

It was over. Now it really was over. They were striking the set. It was over.

Except for the verdict. And here it is necessary to enter the Red Room.

16

Behind Closed Doors

How can one know what went on within the locked and guarded jury room? The judge repeatedly had ordered the jurors to speak to no one. But after the trial was over, after the very last verdict had been reached, he could no longer order the jurors to do anything, other than to refrain from talking, ever, to the lawyers in the case. Beyond that, he could not prevent them from speaking about their deliberations with anyone who wanted to listen. He could not prevent, but he could implore, and this he did. He recommended to the jurors that they keep silent about what had gone on.

There were good reasons for his words of caution. If jurors think that everything they say is someday going to make it into print, they may throughout their deliberations refrain from candor, and their job is to speak to one another freely. Further, there are twelve jurors (by Phase Three, eleven). If some of them say what went on, and others do not, the report may be misleading. It may leave things out. And even if all the jurors spoke together, much would be omitted. If the trial itself had been in secret, with no transcript, even the lawyers, working together, would have a hard time accurately re-creating exactly what went on. Many judges feel that no information about the jurors' deliberations is far preferable to a partial picture.

These points are well taken. Jurors perhaps should refrain from speaking to the press. But sometimes, in a celebrated case, public interest is so high and requests for debriefing so intense, that some jurors succumb.

That is what happened in the *Exxon Valdez* case. Not long after the trial had concluded, Natalie Phillips, a reporter for the *Anchorage Daily News,* contacted the jurors and found six who were willing to be interviewed.

Ms. Phillips was no stranger to the case. She had been in the courtroom every day of the trial, and her published accounts each morning of the prior day's proceedings were the best continuous coverage that most Alaskans had. The plaintiff team thought that her articles were too favorably inclined toward the defense and were trepidant lest the jurors disobey the judge and start each morning with her version. (There is no indication that they did so, nor indeed that the articles were less than objective.)

After talking with some jurors, Ms. Phillips produced a very long article on what had gone on in the jury room. It filled most of the front page of her paper, and many full pages thereafter. Whether or not reporters ought to do this sort of thing, she did it very, very well. With a keen eye for detail, anecdote, and character, she brought to life the tribulations of the trial, what the jurors said and did in reaching their decisions in all three phases.

Slightly earlier, Emily Barker had done an article for the *American Lawyer* that was also based on juror interviews. Hers is also a fine piece of journalism, rich in incident and re-creative of the entire deliberative process. These two lengthy accounts provide the quotations from the jurors, and the information about their proceedings, that are used in this narrative.

Are they accurate? The quotations presumably are. As for the facts themselves, half the jurors would not speak to the press. Was the other half enough? Is this the full story? Is it fair?

We shall never know. Even weeks after the trial, memories perhaps were cloudy, and with the passage of years now are certainly so. The jurors, even in those early interviews, had had time to read the press accounts and their honest efforts to recall the truth may have been affected by what they had read or heard.

Still, this is all that exists of what one can know of the jury deliberations in the *Exxon Valdez* case. Though limited by their numbers and their memories, six jurors, sometimes in group interviews, did strive to recall the extraordinary experience that recently they had shared. The two articles are the Dead Sea Scrolls of the trial, incomplete and priceless.

It is certain, for example, what happened when the door was closed and locked behind them and they first began their work in the last phase of the trial. They filled out ballots to see where they were on the amount of punitive damages. The results did not suggest that they would be out of there soon. They were all over the map. The awards ranged from zero to twenty billion dollars, with many votes in between: eight billion, thirteen billion, five billion, one billion. Of those who thought that some punitive damages should be paid, the lowest initial figure was $861 million—three times the actual damages. The author of this conclusion was Bruce Dean. He surely didn't *look* like a cautious spender, nor did he harbor much reverence for large institutions. The defendants could be forgiven if they had imagined him to be the biggest spender of all when using their money. But he was in fact quite conservative on the amount of punitive damages. Perhaps this was because he had consistently played the role of defense counsel in all the mock trials that the jurors had staged for themselves. It is common for trial lawyers to become progressively convinced of the merits of the case they are arguing; this is part of human nature. Even, apparently, when one is only pretending to be a lawyer. Dean's adversary in those jury-room debates had been Doug Graham, playing the role of plaintiff counsel. Now Graham, a quiet and unassuming man, was near the high end in terms of dollars sought from Exxon—more than ten billion dollars. We do become the roles we play.

It soon became apparent that what was really dividing the jurors was not the dollar amount but whether punitive damages should be awarded at all. There were two votes for zero payment. These came from Jewell Spann, the McDonald's employee from Kenai, and Rita Wilson, who had expressed reservations about the finding of recklessness in Phase One because that could lead to punitive damages. Both questioned the concept of awarding punitive damages, though in the *voir dire* each had answered in the affirmative O'Neill's question about whether they could award them. Rita Wilson had answered it twice.

The jurors' secret ballots were not so very secret at all. As they talked things over and more ballots were cast, it became clear where most people were. Or were not. There was no sense discussing amount if two jurors were unwilling to award any punitive damages at all.

Though perhaps not in their *voir dire*, the two holdouts were perfectly ingenuous now. They didn't *like* punitive damages. They didn't think the concept was fair. This is of course a perfectly reasonable view, shared by a great many laymen and students of the law, and it is why prospective jurors are carefully questioned on the point. But some do slip through the net, and two jurors were now philosophically opposed to the intention of the other nine.

Throughout all their deliberations, when the jurors reached an impasse, they looked for inspiration to their temporary bible—the judge's instructions. This soon would work for Jewell Spann. In the jury instructions, one of the definitions of punitive damages had been "the penalty that is necessary to express society's disapproval of conduct that society condemns." O'Neill had emphasized these words in his speech to the jurors (there weren't that many other instructions he cared to bring to their attention). Spann now reflected on what this one meant. Speaking for society, rather than merely herself, changed things a little. She thought some more. She dropped her objection to punitive damages.

That left Rita Wilson. And she wasn't about to change. She felt very strongly about it: no punitive damages. Perhaps a dollar, as a token, but no more. Exxon *had* worked hard to clean up the spill. Wasn't that enough? Besides, conceptually, "This was a civil case, not a criminal case. I had a feeling that was important, but I couldn't verbalize it," she says. The point seems to be that she found punishment an inappropriate remedy outside a criminal context.

Whatever her reasons, she stuck to her guns. She soon found that there were ten other guns in the room. The other jurors tried to win her over. They claim they did so with reasoned debate. She insists that she was browbeaten and ostracized. What is truth? There never will be a unanimous jury on this question.

What is clear, however—and had an astonishing impact on what was going to occur—was the effect of the debate on Rita Wilson. She broke down repeatedly in tears. She would flee sobbing to the bathroom. She had a very difficult time dealing with pressure, and regardless of how respectful her colleagues tried to be, a holdout juror is in an uncomfortable position. For Rita Wilson it was more than uncomfortable, it was torture. She was able to remain adamant but not to avoid the pain of being opposed. When other jurors tried to reason with her, she began crying. They did everything to win her over. It was thought that the most helpful tool would be analogy. O'Neill had used one most effectively in making the case for punitive damages, and the jurors tried their version of it on Rita Wilson. "You've got a kid that throws a rock and breaks a window," said Nancy Provost. "You compensate the person for their broken window. But what do you do for the child? You punish the child for throwing the rock in the first place."

Not if they were *her* children, Wilson said. Having to pay for a new window would be punishment enough.

And so it went. Other analogies were tried, and then rejected. Arguments both subtle and direct were assayed, all to no avail. Straw votes were taken, sometimes at the end of the day and sometimes at the beginning, as if either rest or exhaustion might alter the holdout's resolve. Neither did. Days passed. The other jurors begged, entreated, wheedled, insisted. Rita Wilson just sat there with her crocheting and cried.

The combination of strong will and extreme sensitivity can be deadly. Something has to break. At about noon on the fourth day of deliberation, Tom Murtiashaw, the Deputy Clerk of Court, discovered Rita Wilson in the small vestibule off the jury room. She was weeping, and another juror, Linda Hood, a former flight attendant, was trying to comfort her. Murtiashaw quickly went to get Judge Holland, who came over and spoke with the two women. He told both jurors that they were not to reveal to him anything at all about the state of the deliberations. He then had what he later reported as "some diffuse conversation with both of them about what the problem was, and frankly learned little or nothing about what the problem was." After consulting with the attorneys, the judge then contacted the jury foreman and "solicited a note from him, which in substance said we want to take the rest of the day off." The judge of course assented. It was the Friday of Labor Day weekend, and now the jurors would have an extra long holiday, not returning until Tuesday. Perhaps that would help.

In the meantime, the judge had to talk to the hastily summoned lawyers. He told them what had happened and said that when the jurors returned on Tuesday he was going to give them a new instruction. It would be something of an augmentation of his previous instructions. Its purpose was to get them to behave better toward one another. This was more than fine with the defense counsel, who didn't want what they presumed to be a holdout being browbeaten into unanimity. In fact, they wanted an additional instruction: that each juror had equal standing. They believed that the holdout juror thought the jury foreman, Ken Murray, had greater powers than the rest—that only he, for example, could communicate to the Court by note.

O'Neill's strongly stated view was that no further instructions were appropriate. Let the jurors work it out themselves. He did not prevail.

Just after eight on Tuesday morning, the jurors were brought back into the courtroom to hear the new instruction. It was called Supplemental Instruction A, and it did in fact repeat much of what had been said before.

"In the course of your deliberations, do not hesitate to reexamine your own views and change your opinion if convinced it is erroneous, but do not surrender your honest conviction as to the weight or effect of evidence solely because of the opinion of your fellow jurors or for the mere purpose of returning a verdict."

He got to the new heart of the matter. "Due to the duration of these proceedings, it is especially important that in your deliberations you observe some of the niceties that are required of attorneys and witnesses in the courtroom. We do not interrupt one another, we do not raise our voices—at least not very often. We often disagree, but we do not disparage the views of others. Courtesy and consideration of the views of others will surely facilitate your deliberations."

While the judge did not proclaim, as the defense had asked, that each juror was the equal of the other, he did make it clear that any juror could send a note to the Court.

The jurors returned to the Red Room, perfectly aware that they had just been asked to be nicer to each other, and that "each other" meant Rita Wilson. It wasn't going to be easy. In fact, it wasn't going to happen. Be nice to *her*, some jurors were thinking; why can't she be nicer to *us?*

It just wasn't working. At twelve fifty-five the jurors sent a note to the judge saying that they had reached an impasse and needed help. The judge immediately called the lawyers back and read them the note. The defense reaction was very swift: the judge should declare a mistrial. O'Neill was adamant that he should not.

The lawyers had been civil, even friendly, to one another throughout the trial, but now jaws were clenched and tempers short. This was it: the cutting edge, the bottom line, the moment of truth, the end of the road. Years and billions and careers, everything that was at stake seemed focused now on a single note, a single juror.

This was why the defense had so vigilantly asked in the *voir dire* whether a prospective juror had the strength to hold out against group pressure. They *wanted* a mistrial; it was clear to O'Neill that they sensed this jury was against them, they wanted to pull the plug. They were willing to *start over.* It was important to breathe deeply and not think about that. Mistrial! The lawyers argued back and forth about it, and finally the judge said that they had better meet the next morning, Wednesday, in the courtroom and get everything on the record. In the meantime, he'd think about it.

Most assuredly everyone was there at eight. The first lawyer to speak was Pat Lynch, and he didn't waste any time.

"On behalf of the Exxon defendants, we move the Court to declare a mistrial. We believe this note indicates that this jury has reached an impasse . . . the deliberation process has taken an emotional toll on the jurors and there is a risk that they will surrender their individual judgment solely for the purpose of reaching a verdict, which you have instructed them repeatedly that they should not do. . . .

"Instructing the jury to continue deliberating would be a coercive event."

O'Neill spoke in opposition to the motion. "The jury, in comparison to Phases One and Two, has deliberated a short period of time. The jury has asked the Court for an additional instruction. We believe that the defendants, in fact, have created the issue in requesting Supplemental Jury Instruction A." He cited some case law, then sat down.

"Couple of thoughts here," said the judge. It is safe to say he had the lawyers' undivided attention. And what he then had to say was not a matter of case law, but of common sense. The judge acted like a judge, and what he shared with the lawyers was wisdom, beginning with the fact that he blamed himself for much of the problem.

"While I think it was appropriate to give the Instruction A that we gave, I do have a little concern in retrospect that that instruction might have almost invited the response that we got at twelve fifty-five yesterday. It may be that, and probably is, that the jury is into some tough duty . . . and an instruction telling them to be nice to one another, which is in substance what that instruction said, may, and out of frustration, have caused a juror to say, 'Well, if we have to be nice to one another, to heck, you can have this job back.'

"For that reason I think it's important that at this time we give a very soft response to the note that we have received—that we not overreact to the note.

"At this time I decline to treat that note as a real statement that we are at an impasse, and I choose to focus on the second sentence of the note, which really says, give us some help. Hopefully that's what our supplemental instruction will be, will do. . . .

"The prudent thing to do at this point is to ignore the suggestion that there might be an impasse. . . . If a soft instruction quickly leads to some other declaration that they are having problems, obviously we'll revisit the situation. But this jury has demonstrated over, I think it was something like twenty-three days as to Phase Two, that they are quite able to work hard, quite willing to work hard, quite able to deal with very complex problems, and I want to see if we can't breach what I think is a frustration problem."

With that, the jurors were brought back to the courtroom—but not for long. The judge told them that he had received their note and was not surprised that at this state their views were still divergent. He told them to review his instructions and to take as much time as they needed in their deliberations. That was all. Seven minutes after they had left it, they were back in the jury room.

The judge had bluntly told the jurors to get on with it, and at first they surely seemed to be trying. Before nine, the jurors sent a note to the Court requesting the data on Captain Hazelwood's past salary figures. This, of course, alarmed the defendants. Not only did the jurors seem to be working together, which would kill their motion for mistrial, but they seemed to be working on *damages,* on actual amounts, not whether to award them at all. And not only damages—damages for Captain Hazelwood! For whom both sides had agreed that one dollar was sufficient punishment! Now they wanted his *salary* figures! What was this jury up to?

Not much, it soon developed. Changing the subject in the jury room to Hazelwood had helped restore civility, but that was only temporary. As soon as they returned to their major dispute, the impasse returned as well, and tears and tantrums with it. Before the end of the deliberations, Rita Wilson had stormed out of the jury room and gone home.

The jurors then decided to send another note to the judge. They didn't want to be tactless or cruel. The note they ended up sending said that they had reviewed the jury instructions as requested.

And: "We have one juror that we feel is emotionally unable to deliberate within the jury instructions the court has provided. We have reached a crucial stage in our deliberation that has left us concerned about her emotional and physical health." The note was signed by the foreman.

It was received at the end of the day. The judge contacted the lawyers, and first thing the following morning, Thursday, there was a remarkable meeting held in his chambers.

The only persons present were Judge Holland and the absolute minimum of lawyers: O'Neill for the plaintiffs, Lynch for Exxon, and, for Captain Hazelwood, whose usual counsel had left Alaska, Martin Casey, a young lawyer in the Chalos firm. A court reporter was present, too, creating a transcript that was ordered sealed until after the trial was over.

Pat Lynch the day before had asked the judge to consider interviewing all the jurors on this now-critical matter. He raised that possibility again, but the judge cut him off.

"It is my intention to talk only to the juror that is the subject of this note," he said.

A few moments later, the door to the judge's chambers was opened and through it came Rita Wilson. She had been summoned by the judge. She appeared to be slightly nervous, but not particularly distraught. Some of the lawyers looked worse.

"Mrs. Wilson," said the judge. "We got a note from the jury foreman yesterday. I want to read it to you."

"Okay."

"I take it you had not seen it?"

"No. I had already left."

The judge then read to her the note proclaiming her emotional inability to serve on the jury. Whatever her reaction to this statement, her face remained impassive. It remained so during the judge's next pronouncement, which was even more surprising than his first.

"Your husband came to see me yesterday, and I don't know whether you know this or not. Do you know he came to see me yesterday?"

"No."

"He was concerned about you. He was concerned about you and he was concerned about your emotional reaction to the case. He was very calm, cool and collected about it, and we had a nice conversation about it. I told him that we were all concerned, also. I hadn't seen this note at that point. We then got the note that expressed some concern about your health, so that's why we're here this morning.

"What I would like to know at this point is—" he looked around at the lawyers—"other than how the jury stands on anything, are you okay?"

She shrugged. "I'm just stressed out."

"Is there any concern from outside of this case or is there . . ."

"No. It's just—it's just what happens in the jury room. I've never been in this kind of position, and it's—and I'm learning something every day on how to deal with it, but I tend—my health does go to pot when I get stressed out, and people that I haven't been around me don't realize that."

The judge's voice was gentle, but he was looking her right in the eye. "Our concern is whether you are going to be okay continuing these deliberations."

She returned his gaze. "I feel really strongly that if I wasn't there I'd feel worse."

"That if you weren't there you'd be worse?"

"Yeah."

"Okay." He then asked the question that was keeping the lawyers from breathing. "Is it—and I don't want to put words in your mouth now—but is it fair to say that you feel up to going on with the deliberations?"

"I feel like it's my duty to. I feel like I have to stick it out."

"Would you let us know if there should come a point where you are having some kind of a health problem?"

"Yeah."

"The last thing we want is for there to be—you know, this process must not physically or emotionally damage you; we don't want that to happen."

She spoke very clearly. "In some ways that's too late. I feel really strong, and I have to be there. I feel that I make a difference."

"I'm satisfied," said the judge, who then turned to the still ashen lawyers. "Unless you all have some other thoughts?" They did not.

"Okay," said the judge. "That's all there is to it." Rita Wilson turned and left.

When she came back into the jury room, ready to work if not to compromise, her fellow jurors were dumbfounded. They thought that they had seen the last of her. They had sent the judge that *note*. The judge had sent for Rita Wilson. She had gone. But she wasn't gone. Here she was, back again. It was as if nothing had happened. It meant to some that the jury now was doomed to deadlock, and they didn't *want* it to be deadlocked. They didn't want their work of the past four months to be nullified, the tedium and calculations and confinement all for nothing, nothing but waste. The shock they felt at the return of Rita Wilson soon turned to resentment, and then worse.

One hour after she had left the judge's chambers, Rita Wilson sent him a note. She said that she wanted to speak to him.

The judge did not answer her note. Instead, he walked over to the jury room and met her at the doorway. He told her that there was nothing more that he could do. He had given her a choice and she had made her decision. That was it.

So Rita Wilson found herself irretrievably locked up in a small room with ten people whom she regarded as her tormentors. The other jurors, for their part, feared that their chance of resolving this case had finally run aground. They had now been deliberating for more than a week. The *trial* of Phase Three had lasted only four days. This was like a nightmare.

It got worse. Another week passed. Now that there seemed no way out, each ballot that was taken seemed only to sharpen the acrimony. Unfortunate things were said. Indeed, shouted. On one occasion, Wilson just threw her ballot on the table and said, "There! It's what you want. It's what you're going to get." Nancy Provost, a widow in her sixties, exploded.

"I don't want the damn thing and you're not going to vote like that," she snapped.

The foreman, Ken Murray, tried to calm them down and found himself in the line of fire.

"God damn it," Provost told him, "I've sat here for . . . weeks and been screamed and yelled at. It's my turn. Don't tell me to shut up!"

Provost had a history of heart disease, and that afternoon on the way home, she had Bruce Dean take her to see her doctor. She had started having angina pain. Her doctor offered to write a note that would take her off the jury.

"Okay," said Provost. "You write it, and I'll put it in my purse." That is just what happened. She now had what Wilson had coveted: a letter of transit out of there. She told the foreman about it, and Wilson soon learned of it, too. She was very upset. What were they doing to each other? Was death the only alternative to compromise? She became moody and withdrawn. She didn't eat the food that was brought in for their meal. The other jurors had stopped sharing rides with her. She was isolated.

But she was there. She had to be there. They all did. And gradually the judge's hope was justified. They began to come together. Most dramatically, Rita Wilson became willing to talk about damages.

Equally important, the other jurors became more willing to examine their own fixed positions, to seek a number on which all could agree.

In part this occurred because of the judge's abjuration to read and reread the jury instructions. That road map helped some to descend from their solitary peaks. One instruction, for example, stated, "You should not consider any damage to natural resources or to the environment generally." Some of them *had* been considering such things; the death of wildlife had prodded their punishment number higher. When they saw that they weren't supposed to do that, they followed the instruction. The highest numbers were reduced.

And the lowest slowly were raised. After dozens of ballots, the eleven jurors were very close together, and the number they were close to was five billion dollars. This was about the size of Exxon's annual net profit, but many jurors insist that that wasn't the attraction of the number. Rather, they say, it was something of a compromise figure, with people moving up and down in search of a consensus. They got to the point where eight of the eleven jurors agreed on the five-billion-dollar figure. Then they were joined by a ninth. It was Rita Wilson.

The two holdouts were Bruce Dean and Nancy Provost. Both wanted the number to be three billion five hundred twenty million dollars— Exxon's net profit for the year of the spill. After a while, not wishing to block consensus, Dean voted for five billion, too.

That left only Nancy Provost. She felt strongly about the lower figure. She didn't want to change. And then, one evening, it occurred to her that Exxon's profits in the year of the spill would have been much higher if not for the clean-up costs. They would have been about five billion dollars. Nancy Provost joined the others; the verdict was unanimous. Though they did not know it, they had just awarded the highest punitive damage amount in legal history. (A case against Penzoil had resulted in a higher total verdict but that was subsequently settled for a figure lower than the Exxon award.)

They had reached another verdict, too. They had decided how much to punish Captain Hazelwood. From the start, they had scoffed at the one dollar figure that was being endorsed by both sides. It wasn't that they disliked Hazelwood. Quite the contrary. They thought he was a decent man, and obviously very intelligent. Many of the jurors liked him a lot, and some wished that they could get to know him better.

But liking him had nothing to do with their job. Their job was to assess punishment. They had previously found that Hazelwood was reckless. Only that had made it possible to find Exxon reckless, too. They had found that the captain was responsible for the grounding. How could they consider punishing Exxon and not Hazelwood as well?

There was considerable debate over how much money he should have to pay in punitive damages. Some wanted to go as high as a quarter of a million dollars. The jurors studied his income figures. They wanted a sum that was more than a slap on the wrist though short of lethal. They wanted a sum that he could pay, but not casually.

The number they reached was five thousand dollars. Actually, for some time, the number was four thousand nine hundred eighty-nine dollars. The figure 4989 supposedly represented the fact the that Alaska was the forty-ninth state and the spill had occurred in 1989. At the very end, by adding eleven dollars, they rounded out the number to an even five thousand. (There were eleven jurors.)

They had reached their verdicts. It had taken them more than fifty ballots, but they had done their job. It was almost noon on September 16. It was autumn. They had missed the summer. But they were done.

Or were they? They had sent a note to the judge saying that they had a verdict. Now they had to stay in their littered room for just a little bit longer, waiting for the lawyers and the press to fill the courtroom. But did they really have a verdict? Many harbored the same fear. They shot quick looks at Rita Wilson. She *looked* all right. But you never know. It wasn't enough to announce the verdict. The judge was going to poll the jury, too. He was going to ask each of them if they agreed. If a single vote dissented, then what? There were dark suspicions, doubts, and fears even while they were filing into the courtroom.

Someone had changed the courtroom. It looked different from before. But the same people as always were gathered now. The room was very crowded.

"Mr. Murray," said the judge. "I have your note saying you have a verdict. Would you hand it to the bailiff, please."

"Glad to, sir," said Ken Murray.

He handed it to the bailiff, who handed it to the judge, who unfolded the note and looked at it forever. Then, aloud, he read the verdict into the record.

"Interrogatory Number One: Do you unanimously find from a preponderance of the evidence that award of punitive damages against defendant Hazelwood is necessary in this case to achieve punishment and deterrence?

"The answer is yes.

"Interrogatory Number Two: If your answer to Interrogatory Number One is yes, what amount of punitive damages do you find necessary to be for those purposes?

"Answer: Five thousand dollars.

"Interrogatory Number Three: Do you unanimously find from a preponderance of the evidence that award of punitive damages against Exxon defendants is necessary in this case to achieve punishment and deterrence?

"Answer: Yes.

"Interrogatory Number Four: If your answer to interrogatory number three is yes, what amount of punitive damages do you find to be necessary for those purposes?

"Answer: Five billion dollars.

"Signed 16 September 1994 by Ken S. Murray, presiding juror.

"I will poll the jury at this time.

"Mrs. Smith, is the verdict which I have just read in its entirety your true and correct verdict?"

"Yes, it is."

"Mrs. Hood."

"Yes."

"Is the entire verdict which I have just read your true and correct verdict?"

"It is."

"Mr. Dean, is the verdict which I have read your true and correct verdict?"

"Yes."

"Mrs. Provost, is the verdict which I have read your true and correct verdict?"

"Yes, sir."

"Mr. Graham, is the verdict which I have read your true and correct verdict?"

"Yes, sir."

"Mrs. Moor, is the verdict which I have read your true and correct verdict?"

"Yes, it is."

"Mrs. Spann, is the verdict which I have read your true and correct verdict?"

"Yes, sir."

You could tell which juror was next; the other jurors were looking at her.

"Mrs. Wilson, is the verdict which I have read your true and correct verdict?"

"Yes, sir."

"Mrs. Garrison, is the verdict which I have read your true and correct verdict?"

"Yes."

"Mrs. Johnson, is the verdict which I have read your true and correct verdict?"

"Yes, sir."

"Mr. Murray, is the verdict which I have read your true and correct verdict?"

"Yes, sir."

"Ladies and gentlemen, the jurors have all answered in the affirmative. The verdict shall be filed with the Court at this time."

There were no cheers and there were no tears. The plaintiff lawyers clasped each other's hands beneath the table. O'Neill just sat there. He felt partly in shock, but what he was beginning to feel as well was relief, not having to feel responsible for everything anymore, and beyond the relief, a void.

He looked around the courtroom, which was already emptying. The great adventure of his life was emptying, too. The players were beginning to disperse. His new family was already back in Minnesota. Hazelwood and his lawyers were long gone. Those now heading out were like parts of his life departing: Leanne Mischke and Page Reeves, and Kathy McCune, who had been with him long ago in Soldatna, dazzling the fishermen at the claims processing center, working so hard and so long; Lori Wagner, strong beyond belief; Ken Duffus, one of the first drift-netters to sign up, now laughing; Gerry Nolting, who had never looked so happy; Dave Oesting, whose smile was like a blessing; this lawyer and that one; Pat Lynch, gracious in defeat; reporters—more reporters than he'd ever seen—jostling one another to get to the hall and the phones first.

It was hard to stand up from the table. But he did, and he even managed a grin before heading quickly to the door. He really did not want to be the last one to leave that room.

17

Epilogue

Just outside the courthouse, the trial pool of journalists had recoalesced into a number of small puddles, perhaps seven in all, scattered across the plaza. O'Neill immersed a toe in each and gave the same ebullient quotes to every group, and then he and Gerry Nolting walked back to the trial office. It was nearly barren, sadly waiting for some other use. Most of the materials had been shipped back to Minnesota. Only a few tables and chairs remained, and the no-longer ominous telephone. Now they were the ones to do the calling. They talked to their friends in Soldatna, and then they dialed their own office, back in Minneapolis, knowing that it was three hours later there, hoping that people would still be around. Especially the naysayers, who had claimed this could never be done. Those dubious partners were about to get quite a surprise.

As it turned out, they already knew everything. The news of the victory had gone out over the wire. A celebration was going on at Faegre & Benson. The trial team heard laughter and hearty congratulations and toasts in absentia of what must have been champagne. They talked to partner after partner, shouting over the din, and then hung up and realized that they were standing in a bleak and empty room. There was no party. There was nothing but the empty ache of memory. Soon, Dave Oesting would send over champagne and the trial lawyers would have their own celebra-

tion in Anchorage, but it seemed strange somehow that the first big party
had gone on down there, not up here.

It was not strange at all to the Minneapolis celebrants. They were
going to be *rich,* or so it seemed. In the first euphoria, the calculations
erred on the side of excess. Most of the Faegre partners knew little or
nothing about their firm's share of the profits. Both supporters and de-
tractors of the contingent fee arrangement tended to be equally ignorant
about the details of the deal.

This made conjecture all the more thrilling. The one certain number
was five billion dollars. They got a percentage of that. As they thought
about it, the air became dangerously thin and the adrenalin kicked in:
they got a percentage of five billion dollars! In the first giddy moments, it
may have seemed that their share would be in the billions, too. Corporate
lawyers, paper shufflers, will drafters, and contractual nitpickers who
knew about contingent fees only that they were how the lower orders
earned their bread, now seemed to recall that the usual percentage of the
odious arrangement was one-third. One-*third!* One-third of the take—
that is to say, the judgment. Working out the math was almost erotic.
One-third of five billion, now let me see, that would be—well, it would be
one billion six hundred sixty million dollars. There was no need for more
champagne. They were going to be *rich.*

The few who actually were familiar with the financial arrangements
urged their colleagues to lower their sights. For one thing, the percentage
was certainly going to be less than one-third. *Some* of the class action
firms were asking for the full third share, of course, but cooler heads recognized that the legal fees would have to be approved by the presumably
frugal judge, so this was one of those times when Mies was right and less
is more. The final figure would be slightly more than twenty-two percent.
Of course, to that would be added reimbursement of some costs—costs
being the millions of dollars they had so resentfully wired to Alaska during the last five years.

More than twenty-two percent of five billion was more than one billion
one hundred million dollars, still no small change.

But it had to be divided among the lawyers—all the lawyers, not merely
those at Faegre & Benson. There were, after all, more than eighty plaintiff
law firms, every single one of them at the moment drinking champagne
and scratching out calculations. These figures, if added together, would

probably have totaled more than twenty billion dollars. The slices far exceeded the pie. Each firm, no matter how remotely connected, if at all, to the actual trial, now saw its role as indispensable, and perhaps unique.

This excess of conjecture could not last. It had been anticipated years before by the wisest leaders of the case. A tentative Plan of Allocation had been agreed upon and signed by the plaintiff law firms, though it had yet to be submitted to the Court.

The firms that would receive the most money were those that had the most plaintiffs, or whose plaintiffs would receive the largest awards. Faegre ranked very high in both regards, and a commensurate reward would be in order. It could be as much as a fifth of all legal fees.

Two hundred twenty million dollars wasn't so bad. But then some killjoy in the know pointed out that Faegre & Benson was contractually obligated to split the fee with the Robinson firm in Soldatna. The split, originally sixty percent for Faegre and forty percent for Robinson, had been subsequently amended to seventy-thirty, subject to some side agreements. Which meant that if these numbers held, the three partners in the Robinson firm would split a fee of more than sixty million dollars.

There are those who resent the good fortune of others. It is an all too common failing. And among those who share it, doing well oneself does not seem to mitigate the resentment that others are doing even better. For some, the prospect of personal enrichment was almost spoiled by the thought of vaster riches headed north. To these arid souls, it seemed not to have occurred that the Robinson firm might have earned its share. It had had the clients: fishermen plaintiffs, and many of them. If the three Soldatna lawyers had signed up with anyone other than the two Faegre lawyers who came knocking at their door—and many others were knocking—then stale coffee, not champagne, would have been the drink of choice at Faegre on the night of September 16, 1994, coffee grimly drunk to spur the completion of one more billable hour.

All right, all right, it was reasoned, let the Robinson law firm have its share. It was, after all, a matter of *contract,* a word as holy for lawyers as "market" is for businessmen, and if ever supply and demand had met to form a market price, it was the fee arrangement between the big firm with the means and the small one with the clients.

So the pencils and paper came out once again, and newer calculations were made. Even after the Robinson amputation, Faegre's fees could still be over $150 million—perhaps even higher. That was about a million dollars per partner.

Putting it just that way caused some of the partners to think. What they were thinking was that not all partners had the same share. Some received more than others. This was, it will be recalled, the only law firm in the land in which the discrepancies in partners' incomes were not precisely known. But that there were discrepancies was quite certain. Would the normal partner shares apply to this extraordinary distribution? Those who guessed themselves to be in the higher ranks of compensation saw merit to such consistency. Younger partners saw some virtue in equal shares for all.

There was no end of speculation over how the money would be handed out. And the more one thought about it, the clearer it became that the central problem was not the most equitable distribution among the single category of partners. It was the existence of another category. It began to be clear that the trial team expected to be paid for its efforts—paid over and above the regular partners' shares.

It is difficult to exaggerate the horror evoked by such a prospect. Obscenity from the pulpit would not have been as shocking. In the long and rigid history of Faegre & Benson, partners had been paid on merit as defined by the Management Committee. They had not been given a percentage of their billings. The very idea was alien—the sort of thing that other kinds of firms were forced to do. There was even a name for it, a wry joke among the bar; it was called "Eat what you kill." This was a crude but accurate description: some firms paid their lawyers largely on the basis of hustle—if you brought in a big case, you were paid big money.

This had never been the Faegre way. And there were those who saw no reason to change. So *what* if this award was unusually large?! The fundamental things apply, as time goes by. Don't change the rules—ever.

The trial team was of the view that circumstances can alter procedures. This was not only the largest fee in the firm's history, it could be a hundred times larger than whatever puny sum was in second place. They had spent five years of their lives at this—five years away from home and hearth and comfort, five years of uncertainty over whether there would be any money at all. If the Anchorage jury had found Exxon negligent rather than reckless, their careers would have been ruined. They had risked everything on this case. Profit is the reward for risk.

Exactly, was the rejoinder. And the monetary risk had been borne by Faegre & Benson. The firm had put up all the money. The members of the trial team had been paid regularly each and every month.

The printable part of the trial team's response to this was that the case had not been argued by a checkbook. There had been *people* involved. And if money talked, then their side of the fee dispute should be shouting; if the Robinson firm had found the plaintiffs, then the Faegre trial team had found the Robinson firm. The economic argument was the same in both cases.

Aha, replied the other side. The Robinson firm had a *contract* with Faegre & Benson. And so, for that matter, did O'Neill and Nolting and the rest of the trial team: it was called the Partnership Agreement. It defined what each partner's share would be each year. Period. That was it. There could be no further compensation.

The rebuttal to this was that over the years there always *had* been extra compensation. It was called a bonus, paid at the end of the year. Many factors went into it, but bringing in a large fee was surely one of those factors. The fee from the *Exxon Valdez* case could be hundreds of times greater than previous receipts that had led to significant bonuses. It was perfectly consistent with past practice to reward these litigators now.

Even for those who grudgingly saw some merit to this point of view, the size of the special compensation was a completely different matter. Maybe those who had won the Alaska victory should get *some* special reward, but the real question was how much.

The rumor spread throughout the firm that O'Neill and his colleagues wanted an enormous sum for themselves. There is no evidence that such a demand had been formally made, yet it was clear that the trial team felt it deserved compensation significantly above the other partners' shares.

For a while, no one in the firm seemed to be talking about anything else. It is a wonder that the clients' calls got through. The keenest of legal minds were now focused as never before, and in opposition to one another.

A relative truce was finally achieved by the Management Committee, which forcefully reminded the partnership that no money at all was actually at hand. Exxon was going to appeal the decision. An appeal could take years. And at the end of that time, the judgment could be significantly lowered, or even completely reversed. The lawyers were advised not to spend any money until they received it, which at best was a long way off. They were urged to waste no time on calculations or assumptions. The time for distribution schemes was not at hand. In the meantime, get back to work. Pretend that this huge award had never happened.

This worked, but not perfectly. The burner was turned down, but not off. Acrimony was replaced by whisper, but the basic divisions remained and continued to simmer.

It didn't help that O'Neill had suddenly become famous. He had enjoyed a certain local renown before, but now there was an explosion of coverage in the press. Some of his partners felt they couldn't pass a newsstand without seeing his face grinning back from the front pages.

Even before the huge verdict, while the Phase Three jury was still out, O'Neill had been featured in a major profile in the *New York Times*. Under the full-page headline, TENACIOUS LAWYER TURNS EXXON SPILL INTO POLLUTION CASE FOR THE AGES, and a subhead stating, "A Flamboyant Minnesotan Becomes the Star of a Trial," the article noted that

"Like Alaska itself, everything about the *Exxon Valdez* disaster and its legal aftermath was oversized. . . .

"But what really transformed an already sensational pollution case into a transcendent political event was the emergence of Brian O'Neill, a rumpled, stubborn, mouthy 47-year-old Minneapolis lawyer, as the leader of the plaintiff's trial team." The article went on to recount what was becoming the Legend—the road from West Point to environmental law to admission into the biggest case of all through the back door of *Glacier Bay*. It was the portait of a firebrand, fighting against authority. "Until recently he wore his hair to his shoulders and favored shorts, T-shirts and sandals at the office, even in winter. Some colleagues at Faegre & Benson grimaced at his name, hating his clients and loathing his style." The flamboyance was noted, the ferocious attacks on Exxon, the attempt to transform the trial into a referendum on corporate excess. A large picture of O'Neill accompanied the story.

This was *before* the Phase Three result. After that, O'Neill was the Five-Billion-Dollar man. His name was everywhere, as was the five-billion-dollar verdict, a new record high, commanding headlines, inspiring editorials.

The reviews of the verdict were mixed. In a lead editorial, the *New York*

Times supported the verdict. "Despite its size, the penalty is appropriate to the scale of the ecological havoc wrought by the spill and the reckless behavior that caused it . . . Exxon will surely appeal. But this one deserves to stand . . . These were not runaway jurors. They were keenly attentive through 20 weeks of trial and they did not automatically reject Exxon's contention that shortfalls in salmon and herring may not have been entirely related to the spill."

Forbes had a very different view. In a story titled "We're Partying Hearty!" a line directly quoted from one of the ebullient plaintiff lawyers, the magazine attacked the verdict as outrageous, wildly disproportionate to the actual damage done. The subheadline of the article said it all: "Exxon's Alaska oil spill was a lucky break for a lot of Alaskans, a bonanza for lawyers and a kick in the teeth to countless pensioners and stock owners." Experts were quoted to the effect that the spill had been much less destructive than supposed. "The truth is pretty clear, though no one is telling it: This is one giant deep-pockets lawsuit. It is an opportunity to gouge money out of someone so rich and so unpopular that no one will sympathize with the victim."

The *Dallas Morning News* commented that "the award is a harsh slap at a company that already has invested more than $3 billion in efforts to correct the environmental woes caused by the tanker disaster . . . That leads us to conclude jurors hit Exxon with a $5 billion punitive damage assessment because they were convinced the company could afford to pay it. They based their decision on Exxon's financial ledgers rather than its reaction to the Valdez crisis . . .

"But when a major oil company responds affirmatively and appropriately and still is hit with the largest punitive damage award in history, the message jurors said they were trying to deliver becomes unfair."

Another argument against the five-billion-dollar award was made by Griffin Bell, the former U.S. Attorney General in the Carter administration. In a widely distributed article, he was quick to identify himself as counsel to the outside directors of Exxon. "But my concern here is not with the merits of Exxon's case; it is with the $5 billion verdict. The amount of that award shows that the time has come for Congress to reform punitive damages.

"The ostensible purpose of punitive damages is to punish wrongdoers, but I am very troubled by the use of the civil justice system to administer punishment . . . I question whether punishment ever can be fairly imposed in the civil justice system, because the procedural safeguards are insufficient to avoid unjust verdict."

Is this right? Some of those who denounced a high punitive damage award in the *Exxon Valdez* case cheered it in the civil trial of O. J. Simpson. But of course such inconsistency proves nothing. The argument against punitive damages must stand or fall on its own merits. So, is Griffin Bell right? If he is, that is no reflection on the eleven jurors in Anchorage. They were following the law and the instructions of the judge. The evidence suggests that they did so reasonably.

If one year's net profit is an unreasonable penalty, then the law should say that. Indeed, as has been noted, many states do restrict punitive damages, through placing caps on the award, or directing that only part of the payment can go to plantiffs, or, in at least one state, prohibiting punitive damages altogether.

The argument against reducing punitive damages is that it destroys the incentive of plaintiff lawyers to stay with a case until the end. Shrink the pot of gold and they're not always chasing rainbows. This brings one to the crux of the matter. Do we want all this litigation? Of course not. But is it sometimes desirable, or, to be more precise, does the pot of gold sometimes serve the cause of justice?

It often serves the cause of justice of the plaintiffs. It may have done so in the *Exxon Valdez* case. For the point of monetary incentive is not to get lawyers to sue, anymore than the point of a field of wheat is to attract locusts. The point of some kind of incentive is *to serve the injured plaintiff.* There is no other justification. But no other is needed.

All thoughtful people are repelled by the horror stories of greedy lawyers filing suits that are, in fact, nothing other than legalized blackmail: to avoid the risks of bankruptcy and the costs of trial, businesses agree to settle claims that they really believe to be false. They settle cheaply. Not cheaply for the businessess; many millions are still involved. Not cheaply for the class action lawyers who have brought the action; one third of even a fractional settlement is still a lot of money for them, particularly if not much time has been spent on the case. But the settlement can be cheap for the plaintiffs; if their cause was just, then they are being cheated.

The most significant fact about the *Exxon Valdez* case is that it was never settled. It was tried all the way through. It was tried after five years of backbreaking work and horrendous expense.

It was tried the way a plaintiff case is supposed to be—and almost never is anymore. It was tried with victory, not settlement, as the goal. It was tried primarily by some lawyers who were representing specific individuals, each of whose claims had to be specifically proved. This effort took time and brains and money. It took years. It took the leadership of two large, highly ethical and usually business-oriented law firms. They were not in it for quick money or easy money, but they would not have undertaken in a million years such a gargantuan effort were there not the prospect of enrichment should the verdict be in their favor.

Was justice done? This must be debated. But, we do know that justice would not have been done for the plaintiffs had their lawyers not stayed with the case to the end. Absent the punitive award, would the plaintiff side have been willing to hold out until even the compensatory judgment was made?

To be sure, some of the plaintiff lawyers will become rich. But not disproportionately to what they were able to win for their clients. This is true for more than the handful of those who actually tried the case. The lawyers in the Robinson firm in Soldatna are probably going to be *very* rich, but that is because they did not steer their fishermen friends toward a settlement that would have much sooner enriched themselves. They assigned the case to a firm that would pursue it to the end. In doing so they traded the certainty of a quick killing for the prospect of a long haul. Profit is the reward for risk. The Robinson firm should be well rewarded because its early seminal choice was probably more helpful to the fishermen's just recovery than any other decision in the case.

Of course, what works to achieve justice for the fishermen may not be fair to Exxon. Isn't one year's net profit an extraordinarily high punishment? Wasn't paying out voluntarily billions of dollars for the cleanup enough? Wasn't the publicity, the infamy, the national howl of outrage, punishment enough for the corporation? There's not an Exxon executive who hasn't received frowns or smirks from those who learn just where he or she works. Isn't that enough? It is surely true that these things do not even out. Justice can be achieved by one side despite—or even through—its partial denial to the other.

In one of his speeches about the case to a large audience, O'Neill said that the *Exxon Valdez* trial was "a great moral play, with bad and good." This is wrong. At least it is wrong to say that one side is all good and the other all bad. Exxon is not the evil empire, nor are all the plaintiff lawyers shining knights. Both sides were motivated at least in part by money, ego, and psychological need. It is also true each side honestly believed that it was right and had behaved honorably.

Does everything have to be a moral drama? Good people can do bad things, often through neglect, and it is reasonable for society to apportion cost to error. But it's impossible to set up a mechanism that does so with perfect fairness. And fairness isn't the test. The test is whether a verdict is reasonable. If it is unreasonable to demand that Exxon pay five billion dollars in addition to the billions that it had already spent, then Congress must pass a federal law that covers that. Unless the jury has acted arbitrarily, only voters should change what jurors have done—and not retroactively.

But headlines are not subtle. Distinctions do not fit the page. Good versus evil is easier to understand. In reporting the Phase Three verdict, the tone was often jubilant: David versus Goliath.

And landing the role of David, in laudatory articles with photographs now in full color, was not surprisingly Brian O'Neill. The apogee of his new and mythic status was achieved by a local alternative newspaper, the *Twin Cities Reader,* which devoted its cover to a photo of a tough-looking, arms-folded O'Neill, what looks like a gun sticking out from his vest, under a huge red headline, GIANT KILLER.

O'Neill was accused by his foes of courting the press, but the reverse was equally true. Reporters loved to call him. The stories wrote themselves. The quotes were unbelievable. The war stories were too good to be true. There was, for example, the oft-told tale of O'Neill arriving late one evening in New York from a vacation in Ireland, and finding no flights left to Anchorage. He had to be there the next morning for a hearing. So he found a China Air flight that was going to refuel in Anchorage. Before he landed there, he pretended to be sick and insisted on getting off at the next stop. The airline complied, and he made it to the hearing, but his luggage went on to disappear in China.

The Faegre lawyers on the twenty-second floor of the Norwest Bank Building became accustomed to the sight of cameras and lighting equipment being dragged down the hall to O'Neill's corner office. And journalists were not his only audience. He was out on the lecture circuit. Sometimes the audiences came to him. Faegre & Benson sponsored a major seminar in the ballroom of a local hotel just so he could share with its corporate clients the lessons gained from his adventure. The attendees were numerous, prosperous, and rapt. Officers and counsel of very major companies and banks listened most attentively while O'Neill described how Exxon might have acted differently in order to avoid its costly fate. He expressed the view that if the Exxon CEO had flown immediately to Valdez and apologized profusely and on site, the plaintiffs might never have prevailed in court. (This is one of those things, of course, that one can never know. Perhaps it is true. A lesson of greater certainty would seem to be that companies faced with disasters of great magnitude should coordinate their public-relations efforts with their legal needs—what works in the short run may ensure legal liability down the road. Putting the blame on Hazelwood's drinking proved disastrous to Exxon because if that were true, the liability would be theirs as well, either through agency law or proof of inadequate monitoring. Taking all blame unto itself at the outset might have risked a finding of recklessness, but blaming a drunken captain and then switching the story in court probably made such a finding inevitable.)

O'Neill usually wowed the groups he spoke to. He was, of course, a riveting public speaker; he could mesmerize a jury, let alone a group that *wanted* to be there. And people did want to hear him—to hear of all the futuristic equipment he had installed to transform the courtroom into a theater, to gasp and laugh at tales of perfidy and triumph, to learn the path to salvation through contrition.

The celebrity status now enjoyed by O'Neill was less favorably received by many of his partners. To them, this did not auger well for the final payout within the firm. People everywhere were calling it *O'Neill's* great victory, not Faegre & Benson's. All their talk would only strengthen his hand when decision time arrived. It struck them as downright unfair.

Even some of those who had shared the Alaskan sojourn with O'Neill were not altogether thrilled by his new media stardom. It was not that they minimized his role—he was the leader of their crusade. And it was the crusaders, not those who had stayed at home, who deserved the credit. These veterans had for years endured in bewilderment the taunts and frowns of their home-office colleagues. They couldn't understand why their diligence had earned such scorn. Hadn't they brought back the Holy Grail? They resented being thought of as an economic drain. They knew that the *Glacier Bay* fees alone would almost pay for all the costs of trying the Exxon case. They saw their own team's efforts as indispensable to the enrichment of the firm.

That was the thing, though: they thought of it as a *team* effort. Not one person connected to that effort has failed to name O'Neill as their leader, the indisputable commander in chief. They had bonded with him over the years; they were family now. No one else could have kept the team—and perhaps the case—together. No one on earth could have argued it as he had. His team speaks of him with reverence and affection. They find him larger than life.

It was just that *they* were there, too. But not so much in the stories and the articles and the speeches that had proliferated since the verdict. O'Neill was getting all the publicity, and they had played a role as well.

Theirs was an understandable reaction. None of them takes personal credit for his or her own achievements, but many point to the contribution that other team members made. Everyone speaks of Gerry Nolting, except Nolting himself. The critical role of his tireless labors is always described with awe. It is almost as difficult to imagine the success of the effort without him as it is without O'Neill. The others, too, worked longer and better than ever before in their lives. They gave it everything they had, and now, in victory, they felt vaguely, somehow, left out.

It is no one's fault. It is surely not a question of O'Neill hogging the spotlight. It followed him, and no one else. Such is life. The story of Patton is more appealing than a history of the Third Army, which presumably helped him cross France. The troops who slogged through the fields know this, and accept it, and even joke about it, but they know in their hearts that history's truth is not always their own.

Soon enough the interviews subsided, and the musings about them as well. There were too many other things to do. The case had not ended with the verdict. It kept on coming, apparently too big to really finish off. It seemed sometimes that there was more work on the case than ever.

As soon as the verdict was in, for example, Exxon had filed motions for a new trial. They were challenging some of Judge Holland's rulings and instructions, and of course the monetary award itself. The parties filed briefs and argued them and waited for the judge to rule. The plaintiffs didn't know what to make of this. They had often found the judge's rulings and instructions to favor Exxon, but now, for example, Exxon was arguing that instead of making "reckless disregard for the rights of others" a test for punitive damages, he should have required an even stricter test: malicious conduct. The judge now disagreed. He upheld all the rulings and instructions. Since they were his own, this result was far from surprising.

But there was some anxiety over the size of the award. The judge could reduce it if he chose. Perhaps he would choose. There was surely no pride of authorship: it was the jury's award, not his own. No one knew for sure what he would do.

What he did was to uphold the award. It had not been excessive, he said, and should not be reduced. This was very significant. On appeal, it would be one thing for Exxon to argue that the jury didn't know what it was doing, but now the award had been endorsed by a federal judge, the same judge who had sat through the case, the chief judge of his district, a member of the Petroleum Club who formerly had represented oil companies.

And the judge's language was even less comforting to Exxon. He dismissed the comparisons to other cases with lower awards, saying that the *Exxon Valdez* spill was "the greatest environmental disaster in United States history and disrupted the lives of tens of thousands of people." The jury had made a "qualitative assessment based on a host of facts and circumstances unique to this particular case . . . and their verdict should not be overturned simply because of its record size."

And then, stunningly, Judge Holland went on to say, "The evidence established that, with relatively small expense, Exxon could have ensured that its supertanker crew were rested and not captained by relapsed alcohol abusers."

The effect of these words was electric. Perhaps even more than the jury, the judge had bought the plaintiffs' case. His comments now would be part of the record on appeal.

But Exxon had not given up its efforts to alter the verdict even without appeal. It had struck out with the judge, and now it went after the jury.

The jury was not, perhaps, beloved by the defense. The respectful tones of the cordial days following the low Phase Two award had been displaced by scorn. On learning of the massive punitive damage verdict, Pay Lynch had told reporters that "I think it's a case of the jury not appreciating what five billion dollars means." To which one of the jurors, the always quotable Bruce Dean, replied, "Well, he can kiss my ass. It *is* a chunk of change. But eleven million gallons is a chunk of oil." This exchange may serve as metaphor: the relationship between the jurors and Exxon was not marked by mutual respect.

When Natalie Phillips's long article debriefing the jury appeared in the *Anchorage Daily News,* the defense lawyers saw one last chance to ask for a mistrial. The article contained several anecdotes that they found disturbing. One concerned what they considered intimidation of a juror: When Margaret Johnson had returned to her Anchorage home after the Phase Two verdict, a decision that was, of course, bitterly disappointing to the fishermen, she found that someone had placed three dead salmon on her lawn. To Exxon, "it is clear that the dead fish were left to convey a threatening message." This "grotesque gesture" was "reminiscent of *The Godfather,*" these defendants said in a motion calling for the jurors to be questioned.

Judge Holland, who was probably tempted to say "I told you so" to those jurors who had disregarded his advice and had spoken to the press, called ten of the jurors into his chambers, one at a time, for half-hour sessions, where he questioned them about possible threats and any other contacts they had had during the trial with anyone who wanted to discuss the case. One lawyer from each side was present.

The sessions were closed, but at their conclusion the judge released a transcript of the conversations. In terms of the accusations, there seemed to be less there than meets the eye. Margaret Johnson confirmed that she had found dead fish in her yard, but she had thought little of it. She had told the other jurors about it, and those who remembered her mentioning it said it hadn't bothered them, either.

The *Daily News* story also suggested that some jurors had occasionally listened to broadcasts or read newspaper stories about the case. When asked about this by the judge, they said that had not really been so. They certainly hadn't read any newspaper articles about the trial until after it was over. They admitted to having glanced at headlines or walked into a room when the television report was on. Basically, they claimed, they had followed the judge's instructions to avoid the news and to talk to no one about the case.

Of course, some people had tried to talk to *them*: a taxi driver giving one juror a hard time over having found Captain Hazelwood reckless, a friend worried about driving the oil industry out of the state. But fundamentally, the only remarkable thing about their conduct was how conscientiously they had followed the judge's admonitions. The trial had been spread out over more than four months. They had been in court almost every weekday from eight until two, but the rest of the time they had been free—at home, out doing errands, seeing friends. There had been every opportunity to discuss the case with others, but there was no evidence that anyone had deliberately done so. Of course, the jurors could have been lying, though it is unlikely that every one of them would have done so face to face with the impressive and resourceful judge, and with the lawyers being permitted follow-up questions.

Perhaps the most significant part of the Natalie Phillips article on the jurors, so far as Exxon was concerned, was its account of the ordeal of Rita Wilson. Her husband had been quoted in the article as saying that she had agreed to the verdict only because she was worn down by the other jurors. Although this had been heatedly denied in the same article by other jurors, it certainly caught the attention of the defendants.

But the judge could not ask Rita Wilson whether her acquiescence had been coerced. The Federal Rules of Evidence prohibited such inquiry, or any question about actual jury deliberations.

There was another reason Rita Wilson could not be questioned. She was not there. Her fate had been the bombshell of the Natalie Phillips article:

"Three weeks after the verdict, Wilson's husband called police to report her missing. Police bulletins were issued. Twenty-four hours later, Wilson called from a hotel to turn herself in. Distraught over what she had been through, she had tried to commit suicide by taking pills and slitting her wrists, Jerry Wilson said."

Now Jerry Wilson had come to the judge's chambers to answer questions in place of his wife, who was receiving therapy. He couldn't be asked about the browbeating he had alleged, but in response to other questions that were permitted by the rules, he said that the Wilsons, too, had found dead fish on their lawn. He said he hadn't thought much about it, and his wife had not mentioned it to the other jurors.

At the end of all the questioning, the judge said that the next step was up to Exxon. If the defense thought that these interviews justified a mistrial, they should file a motion for one. (Months later, they did.) O'Neill's comment to the press was that the whole inquiry was "totally a wild-goose chase."

There were a number of posttrial sessions with the court, but the really big job after the verdict came in was working out a plan to distribute the money to the fishermen and Natives. O'Neill and his colleagues, who had labored so long to build up the database, were essential to this effort. The five and a half hour flight from Minneapolis to Anchorage became a regular and frequent posttrial commute.

There were fourteen thousand plaintiffs, and figuring out how much each should receive from the punitive damage award was a formidable task. Basically, each share was related to the amount of damage each plaintiff had suffered, though the correlation was neither automatic nor perfect, and the punitive award was not meant to be compensatory. The money *could* have been split up in equal shares for each plaintiff—about $300,000. Tying the distribution to actual loss meant that some plaintiffs would receive millions of dollars and some a few thousand.

There was a great deal of resentment among some fishermen that others would receive more money than they. It was startling to tell a setnetter that he was going to be a millionaire and to see his face darken at the proffered number because the drift-netter in the adjacent cove would be made slightly richer still. A number of those on the Faegre posttrial team saw in the fishermen's response the mirror image of what they had been confronting back home. Human nature seems to be much the same for Yale Law graduates as for Alaskan fishermen. There are those in every place and station of life who are less concerned with their own fate than its comparison with someone else's. There are those who would willingly take less if it meant having more than others were receiving. The salmon swimming upstream seem a more advanced species, since their own survival seems to be an exclusive concern, and the comparative fate of their peers irrelevant.

For about two years the lawyers talked to fishermen, and argued with other lawyers, and checked and rechecked the database, and created charts and graphs and numerous other aids to the proper distribution of the massive unpaid sum. Finally, when egos and equity had been massaged about as well as possible, it came time to ask the Court's approval of the formidable, final, Plan of Allocation. Not all the parties were pleased with the proposal, and the Court received a number of objections to the plan. All of these were taken under advisement.

Some of these objections were relatively minor, and could be dealt with fairly easily by the Court. But one of them most assuredly was not. It was a time bomb. It had been sitting there out of sight for many years. No one had even heard it ticking. But in June of 1996 in Judge Holland's Order Number 317 approving the plaintiff's Plan of Allocation, the bomb was uncovered, moved to another site, and very loudly detonated.

The bomb was an agreement. A settlement agreement. A settlement agreement between Exxon and a group of major seafood processors known as the Seattle Seven. This group had sued Exxon soon after the spill, seeking both actual and punitive damages. They certainly had some kind of case: if there were fewer fish, there was less canning.

Early in 1991, years before the trial, the Seattle Seven reached an agreement with Exxon to settle the case. In exchange for surrendering all its claims—actual and punitive both—the Seattle Seven were paid seventy million dollars by Exxon.

The fact of the settlement was known, but little else about it. The settlement agreement was very strictly confidential. The other plaintiffs had been curious about it at the time, and somewhat exasperated, too. Why didn't Exxon make *them* a settlement offer as well? Why just these canners? Indeed, perhaps the most puzzling aspect of this whole gargantuan case is why, in fact, it never settled. Had Exxon offered a billion dollars, or even less than that, to the plaintiffs early in the game, before they had incurred many costs, the pressure from fishermen and some of the class action lawyers to accept the settlement would have been intense. The plaintiffs had a Settlement Committee, ready and willing to negotiate an Exxon offer. But no offer ever came. This made the Seattle Seven settlement seem a little curious, but after a while everyone pretty much forgot about it.

Until it came time to approve the Plan of Allocation, when the Seattle Seven were heard from again. They filed an exception to the plan. They had not been included in that plan, and now they came forward to ask for some money. A great deal of money. They were asking for $745 million. The theory of their claim was that since they had received by settlement nearly fifteen percent of the money later paid out in actual damages, they were entitled to the same percentage of the punitive damage award—a share of nearly three-quarters of a billion dollars.

To support this claim, it was necessary for the Seattle Seven to produce for the first time a copy of the settlement agreement, and of a subsequent clarifying agreement reached in 1996.

And that is when the substance hit the fan. It was immediately apparent why the Seattle Seven had not previously revealed the contents of the agreement. It was an absolutely astonishing document. In exchange for the seventy million dollars, the Seattle Seven had secretly agreed that later, if there was an award for punitive damages, they would, if requested by Exxon, apply for that award, and then, also secretly, hand the money back to Exxon.

Those who had wondered throughout the long and exhausting trial what it would take to make Judge Holland lose his temper now had their answer. In his written opinion denying the Seattle Seven claim for part of the punitive damage award, the equable jurist was transformed into Krakatoa.

"The court finds that the Seattle Seven specifically and unequivocally settled their punitive damages claims in their Agreements with Exxon; no additional punitive damages may be awarded . . .

"In any event, the terms of the 1991 and 1996 Agreements themselves are such pernicious and flagrant violations of public policy as to render unenforceable their requirements that the Seattle Seven seek punitive damages on behalf of Exxon. As the court will describe, the provision in the 1991 Agreement that its terms would be kept strictly confidential is a startling affront to the jury system."

The use of phrases such as "pernicious and flagrant violations of public policy" and "startling affront to the jury system" in an opinion that would be part of the record on appeal, must have been alarming to Exxon. But the judge was not yet through. He had barely gotten started. He expressed outrage not only that the jurors were kept ignorant of the fact that their award would be reduced by a kickback scheme, but over what the jurors *had* been told by Exxon. The chairman of the board, Lee Raymond, had said on the stand that Exxon had paid off the canners "because it isn't good not to pay people" and that it had not even bothered to get a release from future lawsuits.

"In fact," wrote the judge, "Exxon asked for much more than a receipt; Exxon asked that nearly fifteen percent of any punitive damages be returned to Exxon. As the result of a secret agreement, neither the Court, nor the jury, nor plaintiffs knew that Exxon intended to share in the very punitive damages award which the jury deemed necessary to fulfill society's goal of punishment and deterrence.

"The jury was instructed to determine the amount of money which would punish and deter Exxon. Upon considering the payment to the seafood processors, and numerous other factors, the jury decided that Exxon should pay five billion dollars in punitive damages. Had the jury been told the whole story, and learned that Exxon had arranged a secret deal to capture nearly fifteen percent of the punitive damages, the jury may very well have increased the punitive damages by fifteen percent. The jury determined that five billion dollars, and not a penny less, was the amount reasonably necessary to punish and deter Exxon, and must pay the amount of punitive damages that the jury determined. Public policy will not allow Exxon to use a secret deal to undercut the jury system, the court's numerous orders upholding the punitive verdict, and society's goal in punishing Exxon's recklessness.

"What is really pernicious about the Seattle Seven issue is that Exxon sought to reduce its exposure to punitive damages twice: once by informing the jury of its voluntary payments to the seafood processors, and a second time through its secret agreement with the Seattle Seven. The court will not countenance Exxon's astonishing ruse and allow it to manipulate the jury and negate its verdict."

And just in case someone had missed the point, he added this:

"Since the outset of *Exxon Valdez* litigation, the court has been singularly impressed with the apparently fair, professional, and responsible manner in which Exxon has managed its legal proceedings. Yet in this instance, Exxon has acted as Jekyll and Hyde, behaving laudably in public, and deplorably in private. The court is shocked and disappointed that Exxon entered into such a repugnant agreement with the Seattle Seven. Although the court does not so find, it is probable that more than one of the many attorneys who represent Exxon and the Seattle Seven violated Rule 3.3 of the Alaska Rules of Professional Conduct requiring candor toward the tribunal."

This scorching language was reminiscent of O'Neill at the peak of fiery passion. The amazing thing was not merely that Exxon was somehow able to pick itself up from the smoldering landscape but that it actually stumbled forward to ask for more. It filed a motion asking the Court to reconsider its opinion on the Seattle Seven matter. In support of that motion was a document signed by Griffin Bell, who had written so forcefully of the problem regarding punitive damages, and supportive opinions by other leaders of the bench and bar.

"We are disturbed," Exxon said in its motion, "not so much by the ultimate result stated in Order No. 317 (although we think the Court's conclusion is erroneous) as by the Court's observations that the Settlement Agreement was against public policy, and/or that improper or unethical conduct took place. We think these suggestions are unwarranted;

given the publicity the Court's remarks have received, we believe that simple fairness suggests that the Court should look at the matter again."

So the judge gave it a second try. He did not change his mind, but his rhetoric was different; the tone of his second opinion was one of patience, of trying to make someone understand. What he seemed to be saying was that Exxon doesn't get it: the parties to the secret agreement "have not grasped what it is about Exxon's agreements with the Seattle Seven which precipitated the court's strong reaction . . ." So he tried to state it very simply. It was not the plan to rebate punitive damages that he had found so offensive. It was the manner in which Exxon had used those agreements. The substance of the agreements had been misrepresented, and not only to the judge and jury. "It is the court's belief that (Exxon) trial counsel were deliberately left in the dark" as well. What had bothered the judge, and continued to bother him, was "the strong public policy that courts and juries must not be deceived." The heart of that deception was not that the settlement agreement was kept secret, but rather that part of it—the settlement amount—had been made public as grounds for future payment, while the rest remained concealed.

"Exxon disclosed part of the agreement; and in making that disclosure, Exxon misrepresented the part of the agreement which was crucial to the punitive damages issue."

So now the defense was stuck with *two* exceptionally unhelpful opinions in the pipeline to the Ninth Circuit Court of Appeals. The Seattle Seven agreement was perhaps the most damaging mistake that had been made and could turn out to be the most significant event in the case. It prompted two judicial opinions so vituperative that the Ninth Circuit might well see the appeal as being not only from a jury decision but from that of the judge as well.

At least as significantly, it affected one's perception of the moral stance of the parties. Punishment is for bad guys, and Exxon in this instance, even more than with regard to the spill, allowed itself to be characterized as ignoble. The Legal Affairs editor of *Business Week,* which is scarcely a bleeding-heart rag, devoted a whole page of commentary to excoriating the Seattle Seven deal. "Of course, many of the complaints that large corporations have against America's legal system are valid," *Business Week* intoned. "But the recent trial tactics of Exxon . . . are inexcusable. No one—and no one company—should hold itself above the law. And their obtuseness may yet backfire. By refusing to play by the rules, these companies have undercut their moral authority to criticize the U.S. tort system. If these companies and others expect popular support in their legitimate battle for legal reform, they are going to have to start behaving better than the plaintiffs' lawyers they so frequently criticize."

It is puzzling that such an outraged reaction to such a devious scheme could not have been foreseen by Exxon. In any event, there was nothing they could do about it now.

There is very little that anyone on either side of the case can do now, except wait. The appeal will eventually be heard, and considered, and an opinion issued in due course. Until then, though there is plenty of busywork, everyone must sit and wait. The fishermen must wait, and the Natives, and the defendants, and the lawyers, and Judge Holland. It could take years. No one knows how long the wait will be.

Most of the partners at Faegre & Benson do what they always have done: they practice law, for long hours every day, and some evenings. They often come in on weekends. The firm continues to prosper, and they along with it. Their friends in other firms, and sometimes clients, too, joke with them about all the money that the papers say is coming their way. "Bet you'll be trading in that Honda for a Jag, ha-ha-ha." They have their answers down pat. They smile and say, "*If* we get the money," or some such thing, and shake their heads ruefully as if the whole thing is just too nebulous even to talk about.

But in the few moments of leisure allotted to them, they *do* think about the money. Driving home from work in the dark, or waiting for a child's soccer practice to be through, it is hard not to think about what would happen if they had money, a *lot* of money, not income, which they have now, but *capital,* which most do not.

"It's a good thing that it isn't even more money," says a member of the Management Committee. "If it was five million apiece or more, the day after the payoff, there'd be no one left in the office." The thought is that if they had enough wealth to be truly independent, they would be in Jackson Hole or New Zealand or Umbria or on a farm in southern Minnesota, writing that novel, perfecting that serve, or just sitting in the sun and reading. But the economics of even the largest victory are different in a large law firm than in a three-lawyer office. Most know that while a few of the partners with the larger shares may receive close to two million dollars, most will get something less than that—perhaps only one million, perhaps, for the youngest partners, three or four hundred thousand dollars. A lot of money, but not enough to walk out of the office and ride the marble-walled elevator down to the lobby for the last time. So they daydream not about escape, but rather about more attainable things, a week at the Cipriani in Venice, a Porsche 944 and never mind that you have to store it in the winter, a gift to one's college in honor of that one professor who made such a difference. And occasionally, just every so often, they do the calculations of what it would take, added to the pension and investments that they already have, to buy the most precious thing of all, their freedom.

Not every one of them is sitting and waiting and hoping. Some actually have left the firm. To do so, of course, is to abandon all claim to the money that will later come in. So who would leave?

One who left is Tony Leung. Born in Hong Kong to refugees from mainland China, he came with his family to Minnesota when he was seven. He attended public schools in an inner-city neighborhood. His father worked first as a cook and later started his own small restaurant. The Leungs had very little money, but considerable pride. Tony's mother reminded her children of her own family's mandarin heritage dating back to the Han Dynasty. Perhaps her children could obtain in this new land the eminence and security that the family had once known in China.

Tony was a brilliant student. He graduated with honors from Yale and then NYU Law School. He returned home to Minnesota, and to Faegre & Benson. He put in the requisite long hours and long years as an associate, and at the beginning of 1994—together with Lori Wagner, who was off in Alaska—became a full partner.

Not long after that, Tony Leung was offered a judgeship. If he accepted he would become the first Asian-American judge in Minnesota history. The deadline for responding to the governor's offer was October 1.

On September 16, the five-billion-dollar verdict came in. Even without the Exxon money, a Faegre partner made far more money than a judge, but the Alaska verdict made the sacrifice even more difficult. Tony wasn't sure what to do. Everyone around him was talking of millions of dollars. His mother advised him to stay where he was. There were only two weeks in which to get back to the governor.

"Every morning, I would stand in the shower, and that was all I could think about," he says. At the end of the two weeks, extremely clean but still anguished, he could delay his decision no longer.

He accepted the judgeship. He says that the deciding factors were the desire to be the first Asian-American so elevated, and, though he blushes when he says it, to do good. "When I am seventy, do I want to say that I made a lot of money—or that I did what was helpful, what I most wanted to do?" Perhaps by this decision, and despite his mother's objections, he did indeed renew his family's golden past of public service. In any event, by declining the prospect of sudden wealth, he was able to achieve what his colleagues seem to need that wealth to be able to do—he was free to choose his own destiny.

Another partner who has left is Steve Schroer, who had been part of the very first group that opened the Claims Office in Soldatna. He was as much a veteran of the long ordeal as O'Neill. When the case was over, he returned to his practice in Minneapolis but soon accepted an attractive offer from a Chicago law firm, where he now practices. He was married while working in the case, and he and his wife are expecting their first child in late summer 1997.

His departure shocked the firm. It seemed to mean that he was voluntarily *giving up money,* certainly his regular partner's share. But since he was an important member of the Alaska trial team, if special compensation is singled out for that group, he may receive his reward.

His departure highlighted the issue of eligibility for sharing the prize. Specifically, what was going to happen to those who left the firm during the years between the jury verdict and the actual receipt of cash? For many, this was a subject of some urgency. There were those who were nearing retirement age. Must they stay in harness in order to retain their share? There were those who were ill. There were those who were thinking of other careers. Depending on the length of the appeal process, one could imagine a law firm of the aged and infirm, rickety barristers shuffling painfully toward their desks, seeing death or retirement as equal threats to the long-prayed-for share.

Fortunately for everyone, it wasn't going to be like that. In order to resolve the uncertainties stemming from the appeal, the firm has revised its Partnership Agreement. No event since the building burned down has so captured the partners' attention. The new agreement has provided a much higher level of certainty. It says that partners who retire at the usual age for doing so, or who leave for reasons of health, will still be entitled to the Exxon share. Voluntary departees will not. And the new agreement says that each partner's share of the once-in-a-lifetime award will approximate the same percentage as that of the person's annual partner share in the year of the revised agreement. This provision was passed by a vote of all the partners, presumably with enthusiasm somewhat ascendent by age.

There is still one matter to be resolved. It is the special compensation for O'Neill and his team. There are those in the partnership who say that the matter has been resolved, that no one will get one nickel beyond the regular partner share. They believe that the Partnership Agreement precludes special compensation, and it *is* very precise on how the partner's pie must be divided. There are others who point to the same Partnership Agreement and form a very different conclusion. They see that only eighty percent of the firm's profits in any year must be distributed to the partners, in the designated way. The other twenty percent can be spent at the discretion of the Management Committee. If special compensation is paid out, that is how it will be done.

The Management Committee is no longer self-propagating. Its members are now elected by the entire partnership. It was thought by many that a little democracy was finally in order, though in this regard the firm has not succumbed to anarchy. The compensation figures are still kept secret.

Not many months after his victory in Phase Three, Brian O'Neill ran for a spot on the Management Committee. His candidacy did not go unnoticed by his peers. In fact, it became something of a rallying point for the substantial number of his partners who strongly opposed any compensation beyond the normal partner share. They feared that O'Neill's presence on the Management Committee would undermine this objective.

There were some who supported O'Neill's candidacy on the grounds that inclusion in the leadership's deliberations would moderate his demands and lessen the chance of his opposing the decisions after they were made. This sort of approach was best described by the earthy President Lyndon Johnson, who once said he wanted to place a particular foe in his administration because "I'd rather have him inside the tent pissing out than outside the tent pissing in." Some of the Faegre electorate, however, may have seen the possibility of someone inside the tent pissing in. O'Neill was not elected to the Management Committee.

The head of that committee until very recently was Tom Crosby. It was a fortunate placement in this difficult time. His own inherited wealth, far greater than any partner's projected share, and his strong reputation for fairness, removed any suspicions of self-interest as he went about trying to keep the lid on the kettle. It is hoped that his own dispassion may prove contagious, though no one can say what will happen or who will prevail on that fateful day when the money finally comes in.

So everybody waits.

Kathy McCune and Leanne Mischke have been waiting in the Claims Office, but that office is no longer in Alaska. It is on the twenty-second floor of the Norwest Tower in downtown Minneapolis, down the hall from O'Neill's office. The two young women have continued the same work they had been doing for seven years. They have worked on the fishermen's claims, and the names they encountered are not just names to them. They are faces and stories and memories of a far-off land and of a time that went by too fast. The names are friends, friends who took them fishing, friends who took them dancing, friends for life whose hopes they continue to share. Kathy McCune has just moved to Chicago, but she does not need to be close to all the files in order to remember

Sarah Armstrong, the first one to volunteer when O'Neill asked, "Who wants to go to Alaska?" now lives in Alaska. She lives in Clam Gulch, a small town on the inlet, and she no longer practices law. She lives with Dean Osmar, the Iditarod champion, one of Alaska's great sports heroes. They both are fishermen. She has her own permit now. She is a set-netter. She is waiting, too, for the final payment to be made. Dean Osmar is one of the plaintiffs. Together they are waiting to see how it will all turn out.

Lori Wagner is waiting at Faegre & Benson, where she is a very busy partner. She is no longer together with Dave Gibson, the fisherman who became the trial team's cook, and who now lives in Oregon. She is busy working on posttrial matters, and other, newer, work, but sometimes she thinks back to when she was really busy, when she was the ultimate door-keeper, blocking the hordes of lawyers besieging O'Neill in the precious moments before eight each morning of the trial. She smiles at the memory, and then she goes back to work.

Gerry Nolting is in his old office, the map of Alaska still dominating one wall. He travels frequently to Alaska, where he works with the fishermen on the allocation of their claims. Almost uniquely, he has the same family as before the Alaska adventure. His wife and children are the cen-

ter of his life. His role in the victory was spectacular, but he remains as
low-key as ever. He doesn't seem to be an adventurer, but he is, though
the journey of his life is not so much a question of travel. In Robert Service's poem, "The Men Who Don't Fit In," there are lines for him as well:

> And each forgets, as he strips and runs
> With a brilliant, fitful pace,
> It's the steady, quiet plodding ones
> Who win in the lifelong race.

He is the man who does fit in.

In Alaska the fishermen are waiting. Some may be rich if the verdict is
maintained, but they try not to count on that. Unlike most of the lawyers,
many have suffered great economic loss, and their waiting is not softened
by regular income. Some drive cabs while they wait, and some take odd
jobs if they can find them, and of course some continue to fish for salmon.
The fishing isn't the same as it was, and people still argue about why that is.

In the Robinson firm in Soldatna, the practice of law seems much like
it was in the old days before O'Neill and Nolting showed up. Chuck
Robinson and Pete Ehrhardt and Al Beiswenger are still partners and still
busy representing their neighbors on a wide variety of matters. With or
without the money that will come, they have found a good life. They can
go home for lunch. Chuck Robinson is still a set-netter during the annual
salmon season. His grown sons come up from the Lower Forty-eight to
help him out. His wife helps run the office.

Pete Ehrhardt's beard has grown back. He looks like Captain Hazelwood again.

Captain Joe Hazelwood still lives on Long Island and commutes to
work at the law office of his friend Mike Chalos. He has an office of his
own there, from which he works on investigating maritime matters.
Down the hall on one long wall hangs a huge aerial photograph of the
stricken *Exxon Valdez*.

Captain Hazelwood still has one last criminal charge pending from the
spill, and he hopes that soon it will be resolved. He, as well as Exxon, is appealing the civil verdict. He had a job teaching young sailors, and he loved
it, but there was an uproar when this work became known, and he left the
job voluntarily rather than embarrass his employer. He doesn't complain
about that. He seems good humored and resolved. The firestorm of pub-

licity has died down, but there are still reminders—the film *Waterworld*, for example, had a scene with his tanker, with villains carousing beneath his portrait. In comic strips or one-liners, he is still a subject of ridicule and attack. So he is waiting, too, perhaps most of all for the time when that will pass.

Exxon is waiting to argue its appeal. The briefs have been written. Oral arguments before the Ninth Circuit Court of Appeals are scheduled for early in 1998.

The company does not want to talk about the case until after the appellate proceedings are over. That may be quite a while. If the Ninth Circuit sustains the findings of the trial court, it is thought that Exxon may well attempt to appeal the matter to the U.S. Supreme Court.

It is probable that Exxon sees itself as a victim guilty only of size, not malfeasance. The officers of the company must view sardonically some of the reactions to its effort to respond constructively to the spill. The cleanup itself, which cost Exxon about two billion dollars, is now attacked in some quarters as counterproductive; the near-boiling water that was sprayed on the rocks at firehose velocity is said to have destroyed vegetation. One study claims that the beaches that *weren't* cleaned up in this fashion recovered more quickly. The Exxon decision to not permit confessed drinkers to return to sea duty has resulted in more than one hundred employment discrimination claims being filed against Exxon. No doubt some within the company feel that nothing it does, however well intentioned, will ever be good enough. They are putting their hopes on the appeal.

Brian O'Neill is waiting, with a grin. He has, of course, continued to be involved in every aspect of his big case that still needs any attention. He will argue the *Exxon Valdez* case before the appellate court. He has received numerous awards and honors from his profession and from environmental groups. He is still on the lecture circuit. Last year he gave between sixty and seventy speeches.

He has programmed his computer to show how much interest the Exxon award is earning while the matter is on appeal. It is more than $800,000 a day. He presses a button on the computer and visitors can see the interest dollars whirl by just as they are earned. The screen reminds one of the meter on a gas pump, but the numbers shooting past in a blur represent thousands of dollars, not pennies.

What O'Neill wants more than anything is to try another big case. "My firm is a defense firm," he says, "and now I am known as a plaintiff's attorney." It is a problem.

Recently he won new fame in the environmental area by stepping into the Boundary Water Canoe Area dispute as a mediator. It was not thought possible that anyone could win accord between such disparate and warring sides, but he may have done it. There were plaudits for this effort, and considerable publicity, too.

But that's not what he's after. He's after the kind of case that he's already won. He may never get it. Such an event is said to happen just once in a lifetime. But not all lifetimes seem subject to the same laws of chance. Perhaps even now, late at night somewhere, some great and awful and wholly unexpected disaster is about to happen. If it is really big, and controversial, and difficult, if the road to success is strewn with traps and pitfalls, he will surely be on the next plane.

In the meantime, he is waiting, too. That is all that anyone can do.